0/80

THE BOOK
OF
THE ROSE

THE BOOK OF THE ROSE

MICHAEL GIBSON

illustrated by
DONALD MYALL

consultant editor Dr R.C. Allen

additional line drawings by
Roz Pickless and David Ashby

M&J

MACDONALD GENERAL BOOKS
Macdonald and Jane's · London and Sydney

To Dee

First published in Great Britain in 1980 by
Macdonald General Books,
Macdonald and Jane's Publishing Group Limited,
Paulton House, 8 Shepherdess Walk,
London N1 7LW

ISBN: 0 354 04470 2

This book was edited,
designed and produced by
New Leaf Books Limited,
38 Camden Lock,
Chalk Farm Road,
London NW1 8AF

Edited by Michael Wright and Sue Minter
Designed by Michael McGuinness and Sue Rawkins
Picture research by Jackum Brown
Admin and indexing by Sue Wright and Sue Minter

Filmset in Bembo by Parker Typesetting Service, Leicester
Display photosetting by TJB Photosetting, Grantham
Printed and bound in Great Britain by W. S. Cowell Limited,
Butter Market, Ipswich

CONTENTS

PLATES BY DONALD MYALL

All the flowers are shown approximately three-quarters life-size.

PHOTOGRAPHS AND
OTHER COLOUR ILLUSTRATIONS

INTRODUCTION

TOWARDS THE END of the last century the poet and dramatist Stephen Phillips wrote in his *Marpessa:*

> As rich and purposeless as is the rose,
> Thy simple doom is to be beautiful.

This book is a celebration of, and a tribute to, that simple doom.

It will be evident, however, without reading very far, that simplicity all too soon flies out of the window, for the world of the rose is one of infinite and bewildering variety. Another quotation, this time from Edward FitzGerald, was certainly not meant in its original context to illustrate the exact point I am making, but it does so nevertheless:

> Each morn a thousand roses brings you say;
> Yes, but where leaves the rose of yesterday?

At times it really does seem that a thousand new roses are displayed to tempt the baffled rose grower, if not each morn at least each season. Many are good, but many – though proclaimed by the town crier far and wide, and their blue touch-paper lit by their promoters – will never, however much the spark is fanned, rise very far to take their place among the stars. But together with the fine new roses that do come along, there are still the wonderful and half-forgotten varieties of yesterday waiting in the wings to be discovered – or re-discovered – and add scarcely dreamed-of beauty to any garden. This book, with descriptions in word and picture, gives more than a glimpse of what is in store for the uninitiated, but it goes much farther even than that.

Rose history, closely linked as it is at every turn with the history of mankind across the world, has a fascination only to be fully appreciated by those who have started to delve into it. The roses we grow today evolved only slowly over many thousands of years, and the story of how this came about, full as it is of doubts and apparent contradictions, is told in the following pages. So delving can begin from the first few paragraphs and then, gathering momentum, weave a corkscrew way through the facts and myths, right up to the present day. By-ways divert the path from time to time and bring with them, as by-ways in nature always do, sudden and unexpected delights to charm the reader.

Those who may be devotees of the rose already will need no further tempting, but others who may pick up this book perhaps realize that, through lack of any real enthusiasm, the gardens they own and the roses in them would better grace the grounds of Castle Dracula (pruned by the sabres of Attila's hordes), or perhaps more tactfully may be compared to Tennyson's 'careless ordered garden'. For them, there is the beauty of Donald Myall's paintings, reward enough, which are the answer to the impossible task of trying to describe in words the true loveliness and subtle tones of a particular rose. Even Chaucer did, I think, stumble a little when trying to convey the delicacy of (presumably) the dog rose:

> Next the foule nettle, rough and thikke,
> The rose waxeth swote and smothe and softe.

The inspiration the paintings must surely give should bring about a change of heart in the most reluctant tiller of the soil. A driving urge will be felt to have roses just like or even surpassing those which are shown, so look further and you will find out just how this can be done. Where words (once more) might have proved inadequate, pictures and diagrams have been allowed to take over. Among many other things, from these it can be learned that pruning is not to be carried out by an exuberant sweep of a mechanical hedge-trimmer across a bed or, more seriously, that roses can be made to grow in almost any soil and almost any climate with little difficulty.

Of course, there are a few people whom neither my words nor Donald Myall's images will ever convert. As H. L. V. Fletcher recounts in *The Rose Anthology*,

> Anne of Austria, wife of Louis XIII of France, although otherwise very fond of perfumes, had such an antipathy to the rose, that she could not bear the sight of one even in a painting. The Duke of Guise had a still stronger dislike, for he always made his escape at the sight of a rose. Dr Ladelius mentions a man who was obliged to become a recluse, and dared not leave his home, during the season of roses; because if he happened to imbibe their fragrance, he was immediately seized with a violent cold in the head.

History shows, however, that the rest of the world has always felt, like myself, that the more roses there are, the more beauty there is around us. Few would not want to play their part in spreading it in the future.

M.G.

ACKNOWLEDGEMENTS

The author and publishers would like to thank the following for permission to quote: The Hamlyn Publishing Group Ltd for the quotation from *The Rose Anthology* by H. L. V. Fletcher (above); The Loeb Classical Library (Harvard University Press–William Heinemann) for extracts from Sir Arthur Hort's translations of Theophrastus's *Enquiry to Plants* and Pliny's *Natural History* (pages 20–21 and 22–23); The Royal National Rose Society for an extract from 'A Garland of Wild Roses' by Tess Allen in *The Rose Annual 1976* (page 42); Humphrey Brooke for the extract from a letter (page 63); John Murray (Publishers) Ltd and Jonathan Clowes Ltd for the extract from *The Naval Treaty* by Sir Arthur Conan Doyle (page 75); and A. P. Watt Ltd for the poem by Rudyard Kipling (page 159).

Thanks are also due to the following officials of national rose societies for the helpful advice and information they have provided: Heather MacDonell, secretary of the National Rose Society of New Zealand; J. L. Priestly, secretary of the National Rose Society of Australia; Marianne v. Rosenthal, of the Verein Deutscher Rosenfreunde; A. Souzy, president of the Société Française des Roses; and Mary Wise, president of the Rose Society of South Africa.

The artist is extremely grateful for the generosity of many rose growers, nurserymen and garden owners for allowing their gardens and the roses in them to be freely used (and in many cases cut blooms taken) for the painting of the plates. In a number of instances, too, much time, help and advice was given. Most notable among these helpers were Len Turner (secretary) and Donald Maginnis (garden superintendant) and his staff at The Royal National Rose Society, St Albans; Dick Balfour of Little Waltham, Essex; Humphrey Brooke of Claydon, Suffolk; Margaret Lang of Danbury, Essex; and Helen Robinson of Rettendon, Essex. Grateful thanks are also due to Dr R. C. Allen; Mrs S. Bowers; H. Cohen; J. H. G. Deamer of Warley Rose Gardens; Mrs I. Feesey; J. F. Harkness; Mrs M. W. Hindmarch; Brian Hutchinson of Castle Howard Estate; Mrs Jo Juett; Gwen Key of Cramphorns; George Longley & Sons; Clifford Pawsey of Cants; Mrs D. E. Pertwee; Rex Pertwee; Mrs C. Reed; David Stone, of Mottisfont Abbey, and The National Trust; and H. D'O. Vigne.

CHAPTER ONE

THE HISTORY
OF THE ROSE

SINCE THE STORY of the rose covers millions of years, it is hardly surprising that by far the largest part of it is made up of a snippet of information here, a snippet there. Even in comparatively recent times – recent that is in the time-scale we are thinking of – nobody sat down each day to record what happened. They did not even do it every hundred years or so, and there was no diarist for the rose world. One can only draw on the few writers from the past who have commented from time to time on a particular aspect of the rose as they knew or, more often than not, imagined it.

Such accounts come from many periods and many countries, are often contradictory, and there are large gaps when no information at all is available. Assembling the bits and pieces so that they make something approaching a connected story is like making up a necklace from unmatched beads into a presentable whole. Archaeological finds and research are of some help in confirming or dispelling certain beliefs that have been passed down as truths from one writer to another, but all the time the romance of the rose keeps rearing its head and getting, often in the most delightful fashion, in the way of the facts.

The rose itself is, of course, to blame for this. Its beauty and fragrance have always inspired people, especially poets and other writers, to the most picturesque flights of fancy, and sometimes these fancies have been assumed at a later date to be a true account of what things were really like or what really happened. Legends abound, and all one can do in trying to put it all down is to sound a warning that some of it may or may not be true, and to keep the words 'maybe', 'possibly' and 'perhaps' to a minimum. Otherwise they would appear on almost every line.

The rose in the arts
The rose is identifiable in the floral background of portraits, tapestries and miniatures from numerous cultures and over many centuries. Here, a dwarf rose hedge encloses the characters in 'Le Goût', one of a series of 16th-century French tapestries known as The Lady and the Unicorn that are now in the Musée de Cluny, Paris.

THE ROSES OF THE
ANCIENT WORLD

Having safely covered myself against any possible charge of error, and before plunging headlong into the story, it would be as well to say a little about what the roses were like in far-off times, because they were certainly not like those which most people grow in their gardens today. Of this there is no doubt, for a number of them do still exist and can be bought from specialist nurseries by those who love roses and want something both very lovely and very different. There were no Hybrid Teas and no Floribundas, all in the very beginning being species or wild roses.

A list of suppliers will be found on page 267.

A true species rose has flowers with only five petals, with the exception of *Rosa sericea pteracantha* and its close relative *omeiensis*, which have four. All of them, again with an isolated exception or two, have one flowering period, generally during early summer, though some start in spring and others, coming into bloom rather later, carry over into late summer. They are for the most part large, prickly shrubs, which ramble happily and haphazardly if left to themselves.

There is no firm agreement as to how many species survive today – the figure is usually put at around 120 but may be as high as 150 – so it is not surprising that nobody can even guess at how many there may have been in the past which, for one reason or another, died off and became extinct. The problem in deciding about those that are left is that so many of the species, if not all of them, interbred among themselves in the wild. In some cases they produced hybrids which had single flowers and looked like species, though they differed in some way from both parents. But it was quite usual, when two species with single flowers were crossed together, for the resulting rose to have semi-double or even fully double flowers. Further crosses might increase the number of petals yet again, so that many of the roses growing wild in early times were not true species and were multi-petalled.

Again, it used to be thought that only a species rose would reproduce itself exactly from seed if pollinated by another of the same species. On the other hand, a cross between two hybrid roses might result in anything short of a geranium. To produce a second hybrid like the first, it was necessary either to take cuttings or to graft a bud of the hybrid onto the roots of another rose, which it would then use as its own. This process was known from very early times and is still the only way to get quick results, as cuttings take several years to produce a full-sized bush. But roses are not solely dependent on insects or the wind for carrying pollen from one to another so that the seeds are fertilized; they can, in fact, fertilize themselves from their own pollen. It seems as a result that some of the toughest surviving hybrids have continued to do this over perhaps thousands of years, to a point where new plants will come true from seed, just as in a species. Some of the oldest Alba roses come into this category, though their general characteristics indicate a mixed ancestry in which the dog rose (*R. canina*) played its part.

So the roses of the ancient world, up to and well beyond the time of recorded history, were first of all the species and then hybrids from them – such as the Gallicas, Damasks, Albas and so on – though these group names only appeared when the first attempts were made to sort out the multitude of roses into more or less recognizable categories. Even when this happened, however, it was not realized that these three main groups, and others rather less old like the Centifolias, were not species; they were given Latin names to which, botanically, they were by no means entitled, and which I cannot imagine that they welcomed.

Despite their love of changing names, the botanists have left these old roses alone, or almost so. They still carry their original Latin tags of *R. gallica, R. damascena, R. alba* and *R. centifolia*, but the one concession one now has to make to authority is to insert an × before the 'species' name, which indicates that it is of hybrid origin. An exception is *R. gallica*, as in this case there almost certainly was a species; but for the rest, one of the best-known Albas, for instance, becomes *R. × alba maxima* because the dog rose, as mentioned above, and an early Damask would appear to have been the parents. If there was an original species Gallica – and nobody can positively swear to this – it is not in cultivation today. All that is known with reasonable certainty is that the Gallica, in its early forms, was the earliest rose to be cultivated by Western man.

For this breakdown of the early rose groups applies to the Western world, excluding North America and Canada, and extending as far east as Iran, or Persia as it used to be called. The North American continent had separate species which jogged along on their own quite happily without anything very much of note happening until imported hybrids of the Western and the Near and Middle Eastern species rushed in amongst them, stamens vibrating at the idea of new fields to conquer.

No native wild roses have ever been found south of the Equator, but in China, Burma, Japan, Korea and other countries of the Far East different hybrids were developing through the same natural processes but from completely different species. Many of these hybrids had a quality practically unknown in the West but which was, in due course, to be of major importance there. They were either more or less continuous in their flowering right through the summer, or at least had two main flushes of bloom, one early and one late, with some casual sprays of bloom in between. The only Western rose to put on any sort of show late in the year as well as at the beginning was the 'Autumn Damask' or four-seasons rose, though it was hardly an eye-catcher in the autumn. Its late-flowering tendency did, nevertheless, play a vital part in the development of our modern roses, as will be seen later.

China and its neighbouring countries were either so primitive or so remote and politically isolated that the story of the early development of roses in them must be largely guesswork, based on the types which eventually emerged. Though specific information is far from plentiful there as well, one can pick up far more clues to the Western rose story, though the very early writers tend simply to mention a particular rose or roses and do not attempt to commit themselves further. From Greek and Roman times a few apparently useful descriptions do emerge, but these can be misleading. Where petals are meant, for instance, they are sometimes referred to as leaves. The word *folia* is the plural of *folium*, meaning leaf, so the name of *R. × centifolia* actually means that it is a rose of a hundred leaves, not petals. Or again, where a rose is described as red, it may well have been what we would call deep pink, as is found in the oldest Gallica we know, *officinalis* or the apothecary's rose. There were no deep red or crimson roses until the arrival of crimson varieties from China in the 18th century, which is a long way removed from the time we are talking about. So these and other discrepancies, some of which will never be sorted out, make identification difficult and in many cases impossible.

THE FIRST ROSE –
MYTH AND LEGEND

There are countless accounts, many of them highly romantic, of how the rose came into being in the first place. The old-time writers really gave their imaginations full play. But I have news for them. Fossils of roses, or bits of them, at least 35 million years old, have been found in Oligocene rock deposits in places of which the writers could hardly have heard: Oregon, Colorado, Alaska and Japan, for instance. And there are examples from rather later periods from France, central Europe and Bulgaria. It is true that in only three cases out of twenty-five is the identification of the leaves, bits of stem and thorns as belonging to the rose family definite, according to the Swiss authority Robert Keller, but the three can be said with reasonable certainty to be from rose bushes. The fact that no actual flowers have been discovered does not help, and for the unscientifically-minded the legends make much better and, if one chooses to believe them, a more glamorous and attractive story of the whole matter.

Considering the number of mortal and immortal hybrids produced indiscriminately by the Olympian gods, one can understand the empathy they must have had with the promiscuous rose, and why a number of the stories of its origin should appear in the Greek myths. Adonis (himself of some horticultural interest as he sprang into the world as a baby from a myrtle shrub) was, so they say, being wooed simultaneously by Aphrodite and Persephone, the Queen of the Underworld. It had been decreed that each should have him to herself for six months of the year, but when Aphrodite began to keep Adonis from going back to Hades at the end of his spells with her, Persephone called on her uncle Ares, the Greek God of War, to help. The latter agreed, and when Adonis was hunting one day in Thrace in the far north, over which the war god ruled, Ares turned himself into a wild boar and gored the young man to death. Thus Adonis's return to Hades and the arms of Persephone was assured, and where his blood fell on the Thracian soil, the first red rose sprang up.

Another version has Ares killing Adonis, as he was in love with Aphrodite himself. She, trying to save her lover, rushed headlong over the sharp, stony ground towards him where he lay dying, and where blood flowed from her torn feet red roses bloomed.

A further story with a Greek setting comes from a 17th-century poem and concerns Rhodanthe, Queen of Corinth. Fleeing from persistent but unwelcome admirers, she took refuge in the temple of Artemis, Goddess of the Hunt and twin sister of Apollo. There she cried out to her subjects for help, and they, seeing her beauty, decided to worship her instead of the goddess to whom the temple was dedicated. No mortal who wanted to live a long and happy life tried that sort of thing on in those days, and Apollo took swift revenge on behalf of his sister – rather unfairly it would seem – on Rhodanthe rather than her followers. However, he did show a certain delicacy of feeling, in that he turned her into a bush with the most beautiful flowers to be found anywhere on earth – the rose.

The idea was obviously catching. Roselia was a priestess of Artemis, and as such was forbidden to any man. Foolishly her mother took the innocent girl away from the temple, intending to marry her to a suitor, one Cymedor, but this time Artemis took a hand and stabbed Roselia to the heart. Cymedor embraced his dying love, but found clasped in his arms a thorny bush bearing blooms of a perfection none had seen before – the rose. An emotional experience it must have been for him, and a very uncomfortable one as well.

The following account of the birth of the rose comes from the 17th-century *Sylva Flora* in almost Jamesian prose:

> Flora, having found the corpse of a favourite nymph, whose beauty of person was only surpassed by the purity of her heart and chastity of her mind, resolved to raise a plant from the remains of this daughter of the Dryads, for which purpose she begged the assistance of Venus and the Graces, as well as all the deities that preside over gardens, to assist in the transformation of the nymph into a flower that was to be by them proclaimed queen of all the vegetable beauties. The ceremony was attended by all the zephyrs, who cleared the atmosphere, in order that Apollo might bless the new-created progeny by his beams. Bacchus supplied the rivers of nectar to nourish it; and Vetumnus poured his choicest perfumes over the plant. When the metamorphosis was complete, Pomona strewed her fruit over the young branches, which were then crowned by Flora with a diadem that had been purposely prepared by the celestial to distinguish this queen of flowers.

The phrase 'vegetable beauties' might be differently received today.

In a poem, possibly written by Sappho over 1,500 years before the birth of Christ, Zeus, King of the Gods and father of Artemis, Apollo and Persephone (though in the case of the first two it is regrettable to say that Hera, Zeus's wife, was not their mother), wills it that the rose should rule as the Queen of Flowers. When the goddess Athene first sprang into the world from the top of Zeus's head with, it is said, the assistance of the Smith-God Hephaestus, who wielded an axe to make the hole large enough, the Earth was jealous of such beauty which it had not itself created, and fashioned the rose to outshine the fair looks of Athene. Even Zeus had then to acknowledge that the rose had won.

And once the rose had been created, during one of the Olympian feasts, Cupid 'in the midst of a light and lively dance, overthrew, with a stroke of his wing, a cup of nectar; which precious liquor, falling on a rose, embalmed it with that delightful fragrance which it still retains'.

The Mahommedans held that the rose originated from the sweat of the Prophet and one must assume, to put it at its simplest, that a considerable olfactory metamorphosis must have taken place since then. Fallen roses in the Middle East were gathered up and put in a place of safety so that no one should walk on them and spoil their beauty.

Moving on in time, a medieval legend tells how a maiden in Bethlehem was to be burned at the stake. She called on God, protesting her innocence, and the brushwood, which was already alight, turned into rose bushes covered with red flowers; the wood which the flames had not yet reached bore white blooms. But there are much older accounts of how roses came by their various colours. Opinion seems to have been divided as to whether the white or the red rose came first. A poem by Catullus gives a slightly differing version of the story of Adonis. According to him the white rose was already in existence at the time, but:

> While the enamoured queen of joy
> Flies to protect her lovely boy,
> On whom the jealous war-god rushes;
> She treads upon a thorned rose,
> And, while the wound with crimson flows,
> The snowy floweret feels her blood, and blushes.

Another account tells how Aphrodite (alias Venus) hid Adonis in a rose bush, on which she pricked her finger so that the red blood dropped onto the flowers, and yet another writer says that it was the wine of Dionysus which stained the petals red, and that a scent bottle dropped in the gardens of Olympus gave the rose its scent.

Much later, the red was attributed to the blood of Jesus, but from Germany comes a contradiction. It was the tears of Mary Magdalene which bleached the red rose white. Thorns came to the rose only after the expulsion of Adam and Eve from the garden of Eden.

EARLY HISTORY
OF THE ROSE

And so, one way or another, we now have the rose. What next? Almost since man crept tentatively out of his cave, sniffed the air and began his long progress towards the present day, the rose has played a part in his life. Apart simply from being an object of his admiration, it has found a place in his history, religion, art, literature, diet and social life. It has even been unwise enough to dabble on the fringes of his politics, and has been of scientific interest to him, not solely in the botanical sense, but because the rose was long thought to be a source of cures for many physical and even mental ills.

The extraction of health-giving vitamin C from the hips of roses is merely the most modern (and soundly based) in a long line of such beliefs, and it may be that it was because of the rose's alleged medicinal powers, rather than for the beauty of its flowers, that many roses from the Near and Middle East were first brought to Greece and Crete, and from there moved on westwards. Preparations from the scented oil which can be extracted from roses have made them an important economic factor in man's story for many centuries, and to this the mass, world-wide sale of new varieties in modern times has been added. Rose production and that of aids to keep the plants growing healthily is a very substantial industry.

See the section on attar of roses (pp26–29).

Babylon and Assyria
However, getting down to what is known of the early years, it is necessary first of all to go back in our imagination perhaps 5,000 years to take note of a discovery by the archaeologist Sir Leonard Woolley, during his excavations of Ur in Chaldea (Babylon), that Sargon, a Sumerian king, returned to his country from one of his campaigns bearing vines, figs and roses. The mention

of these appears on clay tablets, which describe sweet-smelling flowers from which oil was extracted and which are almost certainly roses. On the other hand, accounts elsewhere of roses carved or painted as decoration on both Babylonian and Assyrian buildings must be treated with some caution.

Delaporte describes the largest court of Nebuchadnezzar II's palace as having decorations of 'white roses with yellow centres', and he also mentions a model from Nineveh in which there is a carving to represent a carpet, strewn with what appear to be roses, even though they have six petals. This model is now in the Louvre in Paris, but looking at these various representations, are they really roses? A child, asked to draw a flower – any flower – would produce something very similar; a boss of stamens with petals around it, a purely geometric pattern that makes a pleasing design. In any case, when these ancient decorations were created, if a real flower had been chosen as a model, it was much more likely to have been a chrysanthemum.

In general, modern archaeological research has tended to discount some of the long-accepted evidence of man's earliest involvement with roses. However, as one who has had some practical experience of archaeology, and who has listened to eminent members of the profession sniping at each other's interpretation of evidence with the malicious enthusiasm and subtlety of schoolboys (or rose historians), perhaps it would be best not to be dogmatic and to say that much of what we have thought of as fact should be looked at with an open mind and not accepted without question. The archaeologist may even be right.

Ancient Egypt

So, proceeding with the caution of one who does not wish to fall over his own trip-wire, it seems practically certain that there were no roses growing in the Egypt of the early Pharaohs. Their scribes and artists recorded in such detail the life that went on there that, had roses been part of the everyday scene, they would hardly have been omitted from the meticulous inventories of their tablets or from their writings and drawings in temples and tombs. The Egyptians' flower was the lotus, and it was not until much later that the first rose plants, or more likely seeds, came laboriously by camel train from countries farther east, such as Persia and Mesopotamia, or even from the Ethiopian plateau in the south. The earliest record of roses in the Nile valley dates from about 400 to 200 BC, the time of Alexander the Great. A wreath embossed with roses was found by Sir Flinders Petrie in an Upper Egyptian tomb in 1888, and has been dated as coming from Alexander's time or possibly a little later. The roses themselves were identified as being close relatives of the Gallica, and may have been what the Romans later called the holy rose or *R. sancta*, which had pale pink single flowers and was grown extensively at one time around religious institutions and churches in Ethiopia.

Certainly by the time of Cleopatra roses were being cultivated in the Nile Delta on a massive scale, both for the Egyptians' own use and for the Roman market. However, not everyone outside Egypt agreed with the wisdom of the latter, as the following quotation from the Roman writer of epigrams, Martial, testifies:

> The land of the Nile in her conceit has sent thee, Caesar, winter roses as a rare offering. But the sailor from Memphis, when entering the outskirts of Rome, thought scorn of Egyptian gardens, such was the vernal beauty, and fragrant

Flora's grace, and the glory of our Paestum country; so sweet did all the road blush with woven garlands, whereon, as he wandered, he turned step and eye. Bid Egypt henceforward to yield the palm to the Roman winter; send us, O Nile, *thy* grain, and take *our* roses.

The 'winter' rose trade with Egypt flourished largely because the plants flowered two months earlier than those in Rome, though the Romans, with typical ingenuity, managed largely to overcome this handicap, as will be seen later. Perhaps, as Martial remarks elsewhere that 'roses in winter command a high price', this may have had something to do with his lack of enthusiasm for the imported ones, which presumably would have been even more expensive.

Just how the roses were transported across the miles of sea from Egypt to Rome has been the subject of much speculation, as strangely there is no mention anywhere as to how it was done. The Egyptians were, of course, past-masters at preserving things from decay (not least themselves), and may have had some long-forgotten way of keeping roses fresh – refrigeration perhaps – or the bushes may have been grown in pots and taken across the sea as living plants, just coming into flower. The Greeks are said to have preserved roses by enclosing a number of them when in bud in a split reed, bound with papyrus, but it would seem unlikely that such a method would keep them fresh on a long voyage.

However, there is evidence from what is known of the planting of the gardens that lined the approach to the palace of Queen Hatshepsut, in the arid land and burning heat of the west bank of the Nile not far from Luxor, that the Egyptians were no strangers to container-grown plants and to their transport from place to place. Paintings on the walls of the palace show all the plants that were collected on the famous expedition the queen organized to the land of Punt in the south (possibly Somalia) and, while most are recognizable, there are in this case no roses. However, the plants were carried in clay containers and the idea might have been passed on.

By Cleopatra's time roses abounded, and it is more than possible that the idea of the extravagant use of roses at banquets and other ceremonial occasions came to Rome from Egypt. 'The roses of the Sinian Nile, or garden of the Nile, are unequalled; and from their leaves mattresses are made for the people of rank to recline on,' runs a quotation from *Flowers and Flower Lore*, obviously by a writer who had not got together with Martial. For leaves, by the way, read petals.

Ancient Persia and Palestine

Roses form a motif in many of the early Persian paintings and illuminated manuscripts. The Avasta, their holy script, uses the rose as a religious symbol, but despite this and all Omar Khayyam has to say, very little is really known, except that there certainly were roses in Persia and that they probably spread from there to the West. We do know that the Persians extracted rose oil, but as in the case of Babylon, a great many examples, which have been frequently described, of the use of what has been described as the symbolic rose in architectural decoration, could equally well be made up of other flowers. As often as not they have six or more petals, which do not overlap as those of a semi-double or double rose would do. They are what are known as rosettes, certainly, but not necessarily roses.

Persian tradition linked the rose with the nightingale or bulbul, which was

The rose in Roman times
The Roses of Heliogabalus, painted in 1888 by the then fashionable painter of classical scenes, Sir Lawrence Alma-Tadema, captures the luxury and voluptuousness of a Roman orgy, the guests literally smothered with rose petals. This use of roses may have been Egyptian in origin.

said to utter a protesting cry whenever a rose was plucked. The birds would hover among the blooms until overcome by the sweetness of their scent, when they would fall senseless to the ground – all a bit like San Francisco in the 1960s. Oscar Wilde used the nightingale and the rose theme in one of his sad little stories for children, though he does not specify the setting as being Eastern, and of course it comes into Edward FitzGerald's translation of *The Rubaiyat*.

There is some evidence that roses were grown in Palestine before the birth of Christ, but the Bible references to them are uncertain. What could have been roses are mentioned in the Apocrypha and also in the Authorized Version, the best-known quotation being: 'The wilderness and the solitary place shall be glad for them; and the desert shall rejoice and bloom as the rose,' from Isaiah. Nowadays it is thought that this is a mistranslation and that the rose of Sharon, a British common name for the St John's Wort, a member of the hypericum family, may have been meant. Others, according to Norman Young, think that some form of bulbous plant, possibly a narcissus or an autumn crocus, is more likely. There are a number of other Bible references, but all are equally doubtful, which is a pity.

Ancient Greece

The Ancient Greeks did not make nearly as much practical use of the rose as did the later Romans, confining it mainly to religious symbolism. Whether there were native Greek species or not and, if not, when the rose arrived in Greece is far from certain, though the historian Herodotus in the 5th century BC gave it as his opinion that when King Midas went into exile in Macedonia from Asia Minor in about 700 BC, he brought the rose with him. Herodotus does not give the source of his information, however.

This idea does make some sort of sense in the light of what is now known, but at the same time it does not tie up with Homer's *Iliad* (written some 200 years before all this was supposed to have happened), in which it is said that Achilles' shield during the Trojan War was decorated with roses, and which goes on to describe how Aphrodite (whose money was misguidedly on the Trojans) anointed the dead Hector with perfumed rose oil after Achilles had slain him before the walls of the city. As the Greek Goddess of Love, the rose was Aphrodite's flower, and Anachreon, a later writer than Homer, recounted how the first rose sprang from the pillar of foam from which Aphrodite first emerged from the sea into the world above.

I am leaping onto firmer ground in saying that the Greeks placed rose garlands on the graves of their loved ones, a custom which spread to many other countries and which is still practised today by people of widely differing faiths. And I am really on dry land when I come to the Greek philosopher Theophrastus (382–287 BC), a pupil of Plato and Aristotle. He wrote the first systematic descriptions of a number of flowers in his *Enquiry to Plants*, and had this to say about roses:

> Among roses there are many differences, in the number of petals, in roughness, in beauty of colour, and in sweetness of scent. Most have twelve petals, but some have twelve or twenty, and some a great many more than these; for there are some they say, which are even called 'hundred-petalled'. Many of such roses grow near Philippi, for the people of that place get them on Mount Pangaeus, where they are abundant, and plant them. However, the inner petals are very

small (the way in which they are produced being such that some are outside, some inside). Some kinds are not fragrant nor of large size. Among those which have large flowers those in which the part below the flower is rough are the more fragrant. In general, as has been said, good colour and scent depend on locality; for even bushes which are growing in the same soil show some variation in the presence or absence of a sweet scent. Sweetest-scented of all are the roses of Cyrene, wherefore the perfume made from them is the sweetest.

Theophrastus also observed that: 'A rose-bush lives five years, after which its prime is past, unless it is pruned by burning. With this plant also the flower becomes inferior as it ages.'

One or two comments on the above might be useful. Philippi was in Macedonia in north-eastern Greece (to which Midas fled), and Cyrene was not in Greece at all, but on the north African coast. The mention of sweet-smelling roses with the parts below the flower rough tempts one to wonder if this was an early form of Moss rose. After all, that group sprang spontaneously from the Centifolias much later on, and there is no reason why there could not have been a Greek version which has long since vanished. And, talking of Centifolias, Herodotus also mentions many-petalled roses, and for a long time it was thought that what they were referring to was what we now know as the cabbage rose or R. × centifolia. However, modern research has indicated that this is not of quite such antiquity. It is more likely that these two writers were talking about one of the many hybrid Gallicas, and in any case neither of them actually admits to having counted the petals.

Theophrastus, as can be seen, went further than vaguely botanical description, and covered cultivation as well in considerable detail. With him, the perennial bogey of pruning first raises its head. Elaborating on the comment above, he goes on: 'If the rose is burnt, or cut over, it bears better flowers; for then, they say, the roses are improved.'

This has caused considerable debate over the years and it still goes on, though nobody will ever know for certain what was meant. I suppose it is not impossible that the thickets of the short-growing Gallicas with their dense, twiggy growth and rampantly suckering roots might be renewed in vigour by a not too frequent conflagration, springing up once more like gorse does after a heath fire, but I would prefer someone else to prove it on their roses rather than mine, remembering that Theophrastus would be difficult to sue. On the other hand, some people hold that what may be meant by 'burning' is the singeing of the ends of the pruned canes to prevent the entry of disease. Again this is possible, but could it simply be that it was the prunings which were burned, just as we do it today? One theory is, I suppose, as valid as the other, since all of them can only be guesses, but in the first alternative may lie the salvation for those rose-growers who face pruning with the same enthusiasm they would show if asked to carry out a daffodil census in spring.

Ancient Rome

Although there would almost certainly be some native species in most European countries – for those like R. canina have a wide natural range – it seems likely that the Greek traders and colonizing armies brought varieties of which only they had knowledge to southern Italy, Sicily and many of the other Mediterranean islands, and possibly even to Spain and France. The rose had certainly reached Rome before the time of Christ, and was well established when Pliny the Elder wrote extensively about it around AD 50. As there are striking similarities in their information, Pliny may have drawn to some extent on the writings of Theophrastus, but there is no doubt that there were roses all around for him to see for himself.

It was in the height of Roman power and in the years of its decline that the rose was cultivated there, particularly in areas to the south of Rome itself, on a scale that has scarcely been equalled since. If he knew the right people, at certain banquets Pliny might quite literally have been up to his neck in them (see below), but in-between times he occupied himself with producing some thirty-seven volumes of his *Natural History*. Here he is on roses:

> The rose grows on what is not so much a shrub as a thorn, appearing also on a bramble; there too it has a pleasant though faint perfume. Every bud appears at first enclosed in a shell full of grains, which presently swell and, after sloping itself into a green cone like a perfume box, gradually reddens, splitting and spreading out into a cup, which encloses the yellow points that stand out of the centre.
>
> The most famous kinds of roses recognized by our countrymen are those of Praeneste and those of Campania. Some have added the Milesian rose, because of its brilliant fiery colour, though it never has more than twelve petals. Next after it is esteemed the Trachinian, of a less brilliant red, and then the Alban-danian, less highly prized, with whitish petals; the least prized, having very many, but very small petals, is called the Prickly rose. For roses differ in the number of their petals, in the smooth or rough nature of the stem, in colour and in perfume. Those with the fewest petals have five, but in other roses they are more numerous, since there is one kind called the hundred-petalled rose. In Italy this grows in Campania, but in Greece around Philippi, which however is not its native soil. Mount Pangaeus in the neighbourhood grows a rose with many but small petals. The natives transplant it, improving the variety by mere change of place. This kind, however, has not a very strong perfume, nor has any rose whose petal is very broad or large, in brief, an indication of the degree of perfume is the roughness of the bark.
>
> In other districts too the genuine rose also depends to a very great extent upon the soil for its main characteristics. The rose of Cyrene has the finest perfume, for which reason the finest perfume is to be obtained from there. At Carthage in Spain [*sic*] there is an early rose which blooms throughout the winter. Weather too makes a difference; for in certain years the rose grows with less perfume, and furthermore all roses have more perfume on dry soils than on moist. It likes to be grown on soils that are neither rich nor clayey nor irrigated, being content with a rubbly soil, and found in particular ground on which rubble has been spread. The Campanian rose is early, the Milesian late, but the one which continues to flower the latest is the Praenestine. The ground is dug deeper for roses than for crops, but shallower than for vines.
>
> They are very slow in growing from seed, which is in the shell itself, right under the flower, and covered with down. For this reason it is preferred to graft shoots into an incision in the stem. And into the eyelets of the root, as with the seed, there is grafted one kind of rose that is pale, prickly, with very long twigs and five petals, the second among the Greek roses. Every rose, however, improves with pruning and burning; by transplanting also, as with vines, there is the quickest and best success if slips of the length of four fingers or more are planted after the setting of the Pleiades [ie, in autumn] and then transplanted at intervals of one foot while the west wind is blowing, the earth being frequently turned over around them. Those who try to get their roses early dig a trench a foot deep about the root, pouring in warm water as the cup is beginning to bud.

Parts of this are a little strange to us, and we would not nowadays advocate transplanting roses to improve their performance, but most of the advice could appear in any gardening journal today with little change. I doubt, however, if Pliny could persuade the editor of a medical journal to accept the following:

The rose is both astringent and cooling. There are separate uses for its petals, flowers and heads. The parts of the petals which are white are called nails. In the flower, seed and filament are distinct, as are shell and calyx in the head. The petals are dried, or the juice extracted from them by one of three methods. They may be treated by themselves, when the nails, in which is most moisture, are not removed; or when what is left after removing the nails is steeped in oil or wine in glass vessels in the sunshine. Some add salt also, and a few alkanet or alpalathus or fragrant rush, because so prepared the essence is very beneficial for complaints of the uterus and for dysentery. With the nails removed the petals may also have their juice extracted by being pounded, and then strained through a thick linen cloth into a bronze vessel; the juice is then heated on a slow fire until it becomes thick as honey. For this process only the most fragrant petals must be selected.

Rose juice is used for the ears, sores in the mouth, the gums, as a gargle for the tonsils, for the stomach, uterus, rectal trouble, headache – when due to fever either by itself or with vinegar – to induce sleep or to dispel nausea. The petals are burned to make an ingredient of cosmetics for the eyebrows, and dried rose leaves are sprinkled on chafed thighs. Fluxes of the eyebrows are also soothed by the dried leaves. The flower induces sleep, checks menstrual discharges if taken in vinegar and water, as well as the spitting of blood. A cyathus of it in three cyathi of wine relieves stomach-ache.

As to the seed, the finest is of saffron colour, not more than a year old, and should be dried in the shade; the dark seed is harmful. It is used as a liniment for toothache, is diuretic, and may be applied to the stomach or in cases of erysipelas that is not of long standing. Inhaled by the nostrils it clears the head. Rose heads taken in drink check diarrhoea and haemorrhage. The nails of rose petals are healing fluxes for the eyes, for eye-sore discharge if the whole rose is applied, unless it is at the beginning of the flux, and then the rose must be dry and mixed with bread. The petals indeed taken internally are very good for gnawings of the stomach and for complaints of the belly or the intestines, good also for hypochondria, and they may be applied externally. They are also preserved for food, in the same way as sorrel. Care must be taken with rose petals, as mould quickly settles on them. Some use can be made of dried petals, or those from which the juice has been extracted. Powders, for example, are made from them to check perspiration. These are sprinkled on the body after a bath and left to dry, being afterwards washed off with cold water. The little balls of the wild rose mixed with bears' grease are a remedy for mange.

See the illustration of the uses of roses in a Roman orgy on page 19.

Roses by the hundreds of thousands were used for garlands and the decoration of the triumphal chariots when victorious Roman armies returned from war. They decorated public games and banquets, where guests would walk on a carpet of scented petals and drink wine from goblets in which more scented petals floated. Not all approved of this, however, for the Roman statesman, writer and orator Cicero took Verres (whoever he was) to task for going on a tour of the island of Sicily in a waggon made up into a bower of roses. And I do not suppose that there was general approval, at least from his guests, when Nero is said to have suffocated a number of these under an avalanche of roses which descended on them from the ceiling of his banqueting hall. This charming if misguided gesture, carried out surely with the best of intentions, has also been attributed to other hosts, but it fits the popular picture of Nero better than most, so he may as well be allowed the distinction.

The number of roses used by the Romans staggers the imagination, and though there were huge rose fields in Italy, quantities had to be brought in from abroad – from Egypt, as has been seen, and also from the island of Rhodes, the very name of which is said to be derived from the Greek word *eruthos*, meaning red, because of the red roses that grew there. Almost inevitably there is a conflicting version of the name's derivation: the alternative explanation being that it comes from *rhodon*, the Greek word for rose. Both involve roses anyway, and either one may be right. Either may also be wrong; or both.

Coins from Rhodes and also some Roman ones have on them representations of roses (if they are not, as some authorities hold, pomegranate flowers), and if they are roses they are probably the earliest coins to feature them. Sometimes earlier dates and different places of origin are given, but according to Dr Krussmann, late director of the German National Rosarium, who has investigated the matter very thoroughly, these claims cannot be substantiated. In fact, in some cases the dates given are actually from a period before the first coins were minted in about 500 BC.

A reference in the writings of the poet Virgil has led to the belief that the roses of Paestum, the town on which the main Roman rose-growing district of Campania was centred, flowered more than once in the season. This seems most unlikely because there is no mention of this quality in later writers like Pliny. What has caused something that is probably a semantic rather than an horticultural problem is Virgil's use of the phrase *bifera rosaria Paesti*, the word *bifera* indicating that the roses were twice-flowering. A little reflection and a little checking up, and one realizes that he did not say that the same bushes flowered twice, and this being so, there is really quite a simple explanation. There were two flowerings of the roses at Paestum, but this was not because of any special quality they possessed or peculiarity of the Italian climate. It was because the Romans knew all about forcing flowers out of season and had greenhouses heated by hot water pipes.

They had, in fact, vast rose beds under glass to cope with the insatiable demand for them that did not slacken off in the winter months. Martial triumphs could not be put off to suit the season, and even if the greenhouses must have been rather murky places by modern standards – for the Romans would hardly use their best-quality glass on such a scale, and their second-best was murky – they did produce what was wanted, helped no doubt by the strong southern sun. All of which must have put the handsome noses of the Egyptian suppliers of early blooms very much out of joint. The Romans were also skilled at propagating roses by budding their selected varieties onto wild rose stocks.

There are pretty firm grounds for saying that the expression *sub rosa* (under the rose) is of Roman origin. At meetings, a rose would be hung over the table in the council chamber as a sign that anything said there must not be revealed to others. This was supposed to have been done at banquets, too, but it is difficult to believe that, rose or no rose, discretion was a major ingredient in the make-up of Roman revellers. On the other hand, according to legend, the whole idea had its beginnings in an indiscretion. Venus (whom, in her Greek personification, has already been encountered as Aphrodite) had a loyal son in Cupid, and he made Harpocrates, the God of Silence, a gift of a rose in return for keeping his mouth shut about something (which remains unspecified) that Venus had been up to.

At any rate, despite its possibly rather frivolous beginnings, the linking of the symbol of the rose with silence caught the popular imagination and has survived over the centuries, so that it still keeps the same meaning today in many countries. Thomas Miller, in his *Poetical Language of Flowers*, published in the last century, comments pithily of the idea:

> What faith, and what confidences there must have been between man and man in the olden time, when only the presence of a flower was needed to prevent the maligning whisper – to freeze up slander's hateful slime – and destroy that venom, which, when once circulated, proves so fatal to human happiness! Beyond the circle to which the expressive text was assigned that wound about the Rose, not a whisper wandered. The pleasure only was remembered; the painful word forgotten ere it had gathered utterance; or, if remembered at all, it was only as having existed for a moment 'under the Rose'. Truest test of friendship! inviable bond of brotherhood! sacred altar, on which heart was sworn to heart! thou didst need no golden chains to bind thee to thy trust; no solemn vow sworn but to be broken. Nothing but a simple White Rose, to bind these men of true hearts and strong faith together.

There is reference here to the white rose, and though colour is not usually considered important in this connection, it is possible that Miller may have had in mind the rose of the Jacobites (probably an Alba) which they adopted as their emblem. This was certainly white, and the wearing of it proclaimed where their loyalties lay without a word having to be spoken. An old 17th-century Dutch *Book of Inscriptions* contains the following:

> All that is done here, under the Rose,
> Leave it here and do not divulge it.

The Alba rose has another and closer Roman connection, and one that we can certainly thank them for. They are said to have taken it with them on their conquests of the West and to Britain with their invading armies, establishing it there. One can, on the other hand, read that Britain was given its Roman name of Albion because of the white roses growing there when they arrived, though there is no record of Albas before the Roman occupation. The most common true white rose native in the British Isles is *R. arvensis*, the field rose (though there are some others that fade from blush-pink almost to white), but, though a lovely decoration for the hedgerows, it is not usually by any means showy enough, one would have thought, to have a country named after it. So it does seem more likely that Albion came from the White Cliffs of Dover, and that it was the Romans who brought the Albas. Another point is that there are actually more pink or blush-pink Albas than there are white, though the oldest ones did have snow-white petals.

I have digressed a little from the question of roses and secrecy and must come back briefly to it. The belief, as we know, survived the period when the rose was moving from its early pagan connections to Christian respectability. Roses were hung over confessionals in churches and one can still be seen in Worms cathedral in West Germany. If one keeps one's eyes open they can be found everywhere and it is not, I think, stretching the imagination too far to suggest that modern ceiling 'roses' for electric lights take their name from this ancient source.

With the decline of Rome, the fortunes of the rose changed, too. Its unfortunate association with the wild orgies and the extravagances of the later Roman period made the pious draw their skirts aside. Its beauty availed it nothing, and there is a time gap in its story in the West about which virtually nothing is known; so perhaps this is a good place to leave it and to move on to the Far East, though the visit must needs be brief for lack of information about this region as well.

China

We owe an enormous debt to China and her neighbouring countries for their species and their cultivated roses, for very many from that part of the world have passed on to us much beauty and also their remontant (repeat-flowering) habit. However, there is one attribute, to which we attach great importance, that most of the Chinese roses lacked. With the exception of the Tea roses, the Rugosas, a number of climbers and a few others, few have any fragrance, and it seems surprising that, in a country where scented shrubs were so valued, the rose should have been given a place of honour, if not quite the highest accolade. Nevertheless, it was, and may have first come to Chinese gardens from northern Burma at some time long before the start of the Christian era. Whether the repeat-flowering qualities the varieties possessed came from the original species, or whether a spontaneous genetic change took place some time over the centuries during which the rose was undoubtedly cultivated in Chinese gardens, is not known.

The Chinese seem likely to have been the first to use the rose as a garden plant for its decorative properties alone, and roses do appear in their early paintings, though it is fairly clear that the paeony and the chrysanthemum were the favourites. Just the same, the philosopher Confucius, writing about 500 BC, mentions that there were some 600 books on roses in the library of the Chinese Emperor. Where are they now, one wonders? And what fascinating things could they tell us?

The roses from China first came to the West late in the 18th century, and most of them were beyond doubt cultivated hybrids, but whether the Chinese had mastered the theory and acquired the skills of deliberate hybridization is not known. If not, they must at least have practised rigid selection of the best of the natural crosses, and have cultivated them with great love and care, propagating them by cuttings or by budding. To take for the moment just one example, the lovely and early-flowering Banksian rose is not a species, though no one knows what its ancestry may be. It is an example of the point I am making, but on reflection was perhaps not the best of choices to cite, as it is once-flowering only and so does not represent the most important aspect of the China roses. However, more detail about how these eastern varieties crossed the world will be given later in this story, with a full appreciation of their unique qualities.

Attar of roses

The Chinese, like most others of the ancient peoples, knew about the extraction and distillation of fragrant oils from rose petals, though rose oil was a possession only of the privileged few. (The lesser breeds could and did carry the petals, which were thought to ward off evil spirits.) The art or science of such extraction spans all periods of history, right up to the present day. And if, as seems certain, it was carried out in China, at least some of their varieties must have been sweetly scented; if there were not many of them, this might explain the restriction of rose oil to the noble families. Perhaps things have not

Pot-pourri

This is a little less daunting to prepare than attar of roses. You need the petals of about 40 strongly scented roses, such as 'Zéphirine Drouhin', 'Mme Isaac Pereire' or the Centifolias, plus a handful each of scented leaves and flowers to taste – for example, rose-scented geranium leaves; borage, rosemary and lavender flowers; philadelphus and honeysuckle flowers; or the flowers and leaves of lemon-scented verbena and mint. For colour, add larkspur, calendula (pot marigold) and delphinium flowers. You also need 15g (0.5oz) oil of geranium, 15g (0.5oz) oil of lavender, two or three cinnamon sticks, 30g (1oz) whole cloves, 30g (1oz) ground nutmeg, 30g (1oz) coriander seed, 125g (4oz) table salt and 125g (4oz) orris root powder. Optional extras: orange and lemon peel, or one whole orange stuck with cloves, dried and crushed (in this case omit the whole cloves).

Gather the roses in a dry condition. Spread in a cool, airy place out of direct sunshine, and turn them to dry them as quickly as possible. When as dry as paper, layer them in the salt in an airtight jar. Cover and leave, stirring twice a day, for five days.

Gather the scented leaves and flowers and dry these on sieves. Do not dry more than the volume of the rose petals. Add these to the roses and salt on the fifth day of preparation.

Put some of the orris powder in a container and add the oils, stirring until the mixture is powdery. Add the spices and the flower mixture. Stir well, cover and leave for three or four weeks, stirring occasionally. If the result is too dry add more salt; if too moist add more orris powder. Place in bowls or net sachets.

changed much over the centuries and the oft-repeated and to a large extent false statement that 'roses have lost the scent they used to have' is of ancient Chinese origin. Certainly it is not new and comes up time and again in rose literature. It has been seen in Theophrastus and, to take only one more example, Richard Jeffries (who was not of course a Greek or an oriental gentleman), writing in the late 19th century, said: 'There are no Damask roses now, like there used to be in Coombe Oaks. I have never seen one since I gathered one from that very bush. There are many grand roses, but no fragrance – the fragrance has gone out of life.' The truth is, of course, that there have always been some roses with scent and some without.

However, back to the oil. Since the word for it in its distilled form, attar of roses, comes from the Persian word *atir*, meaning a fragrant essential oil, one must believe the legend of its first discovery in that country, though its use was so widespread across the northern half of the globe that its secret was probably unravelled in other places too at various times, rather than passed on from one single country to others. But as far as Persia is concerned, one must go back to the time of the mogul Emperor Jehan Ghir and his marriage to Princess Nur-jehan. As they walked together by an artificial pool which Jehan Ghir had caused to be strewn with rose petals to perfume the air, the princess noticed an oily substance on the placid surface of the water. She bent and scooped some into her hand, and its fragrance was such as she had never dreamed of. It was named *Atar-jehanghiri*, and though this could not have been pure attar, as only very primitive distillation by the heat of the sun had taken place, it must have been the next thing to it.

In many countries, particularly around the eastern end of the Mediterranean Sea and in the Balkans, production of attar (or otto) of roses has been a considerable industry for many hundreds of years. Bulgaria is one of the main producers, and a number of different roses have been tried out there. Early on, the Albas were the main source of rose oils, and the sweet-smelling Rugosas and Centifolias have been tested as well. However, experiment showed that a Damask rose, *R. damascena trigintipetala*, though its soft pink flowers are not particularly large, gives something like double the yield of the Albas and is much better in every way than any other. It was probably brought to Bulgaria from Persia early in the 17th century, and was first cultivated round the town of Kazanlik (or Kazanluk), and as a result became known as the Kazanlik rose.

The Bulgarian rose fields are in valleys sheltered from the cold north winds by mountains; humidity is reasonably stable and clouds frequently ward off the excessive heat of the summer sun. The roses are picked early in the morning when, with the dew still on them, their scent and oil content is at its highest. For a long time rather primitive small local stills were used to get the attar from the petals, but as world demand increased what was practically a cottage industry became big business, the state took over, and such words as quality control and technology began to pass from uncomprehending and possibly resentful peasant lip to peasant lip. It takes thirty roses to produce one minute drop of attar, or three tons (which is well over a million blooms) to make just over two pounds – figures which I will leave to others to cross-check for accuracy – so the hundreds of acres under cultivation can be imagined and the high price of the resulting product is not surprising.

France has always been a major producer of rose oils, too, particularly in the south, and there was even an industry in the south of England at one time, in

the county of Surrey. Less known generally in this connection is India, which is a producer of attar on a considerable scale. The district of Ghazepoor has for a number of centuries been a noted centre, with rose fields occupying many hundreds of acres. An account of the process as practised there appeared in *The Royal Dispensatory* of 1842:

> To procure Attar, the roses are put into the still, and water passes over gradually, as in the Rose-water process. After the whole has come over, the Rose-water is placed in a large metal basin, which is covered with wetted muslin, tied over to prevent insects or dust getting into it: this vessel is let into the ground about two feet, which has been previously wetted with water, and it is allowed to remain quiet during the whole night. The Attar is always made at the beginning of the season, while the nights are cool; in the morning, early, the little film of Attar, which is formed on the surface of the Rose-water during the night, is removed by means of a feather, and is then carefully placed in a small phial; and day after day, as the collection is made, it is placed for a short period in the sun; and after a sufficient quantity has been procured, it is poured off clear, and of the colour of amber, into small phials. Pure Attar, when it has been removed only three or four days, has a pale greenish hue; by keeping, it soon loses this, and in a few weeks becomes a pale yellow.

The patience demanded of anyone wishing to emulate those Bulgarian peasants, and distil the essence of their garden roses, is obvious.

THE ROSE IN
THE CHRISTIAN ERA

Never was there a truer illustration of the saying, if you cannot beat them, you should join them; than that shown in the story of the rose after the decline and final ending of Roman dominance of Europe and the coming of the Dark Ages. The Catholic Church grew in power and frowned mightily on the pagan flower and its symbolism. But in vain. Love of and veneration for the rose was too deeply implanted in people's minds for them to abandon it, and they continued to offer up rose wreaths to their dead and to scatter roses on the graves of their loved ones as they had done down the centuries, however much Christian writers and priests condemned them. And what you cannot deny, it is better sometimes to accept. That at least was the Church's thinking, and a complete if gradual change of mind took place. The red rose became a symbol of Christ's blood, and more respectable than that you cannot get. White roses were a sign of chastity and became the flower of the Virgin Mary. They have been found, emblems of sanctity, in the tombs of saints.

The Order of the Golden Rose was an early manifestation of the changed status of the rose. The Golden Rose is consecrated by the Pope on the fourth Sunday in Lent, and in the beginning it was bestowed to honour the Pope's envoys and also conferred on virtuous women. Later it was used to show esteem for Catholic sovereigns, heads of state, and high dignatories of the Church. The first rose was presented by Pope Urban II to the Comte d'Anjou in 1096. Both Henry VI and Henry VIII of England later received this mark of distinction, though I have not discovered whether Henry VIII was ever asked to give it back. The rose was 'emblematic of the frailty of the body and the

The 'rose' in Christian architecture
One of the finest examples of a 13th-century rose window, the North Rose in the cathedral of Notre Dame, Paris; but, to be honest, the link with the living rose seems a little tenuous. Like many, this one does not even have five-fold symmetry.

short duration of life; while the precious and unalterable metal in which it was modelled alluded to the immortality of the soul'.

Almost every account I have read gives a different date for the founding of this custom and names a different Pope as the originator of the order, but I believe that the version I have given is the correct one. There are even more versions of the origin of the rosary, one being that it was first a wreath or chaplet of roses, later and more conveniently to become beads, though the latter may well go back to much earlier times to India and Tibet, before its practicality recommended it to the Christians.

In the 13th century, rose garlands were so popular in France that a special guild was formed, *Les Chapeliers de Fleurs*, which was given a dispensation by the Church to work on Sundays during the flowering season so that they could keep up with the demand. Rose windows appeared in Gothic churches, some of the most outstanding examples being in the cathedrals at Rheims, Chartres, Amiens and Lincoln, and in York Minster – so-called rose windows, at any rate, for I tend to agree with Miss Aldous, writing in the Royal National Rose Society *Annual* after seeing the churches of Verona: 'Most of the twenty-three churches have Rose Windows (so-called) and yet not even at St Anastasia, covered with paintings from floor to roof, could I say "That is a rose".' She does, however, find an undoubted rose in Florence in the Bargello, the National Museum, in the wonderful painting of the 'Madonna of the Rosebush' by della Robbia, showing a small white single rose with seven leaflets.

See the photograph of a rose window on page 28.

And so the comeback of the rose continued. Rose water was used in church fingerbowls and there were rose festivals once more, some of which are carried on today. Monastery gardens were places where roses grew, and as the monastries spread their religious teaching across Europe, so the cultivated rose followed in their wake, from the south into the Netherlands and Scandinavia some time during the 12th century, taking in northern France and branching off to the British Isles on the way. During the 13th century the Crusaders were in full cry, but the rigours of their bloody campaigns against the infidel did not entirely blunt their finer feelings. They spared time to collect rose varieties and to bring them back to Europe, and it was thus, they say (though nobody quite knows who 'they' are), that in 1270 the Damask rose, originating in the region around Damascus, came to Europe.

The rose in medicine

Herik Harpestrong's *Herbal*, which was published early in the 13th century and so preceded the much more famous Gerard by nearly 300 years, contains the first mention of roses in Danish literature, and it appears from what he says that they were well established in Europe by then. There is other evidence that they reached western Germany considerably earlier, but a reminder should, perhaps, be given that we are talking not about native species, but about cultivated varieties.

These were not at that time primarily plants to be admired in gardens for the beauty of their blooms. Rather they were for medicinal uses, as were so many plants in their early history. Pliny has told how they were used in Rome, and the ladies of his time had no doubts at all that a skin treatment consisting of rose petals would banish the wrinkles of age. This kind of belief survived for hundreds of years all over Europe, and in France the town of Provins, east of Paris, became the centre of commercial rose growing on a tremendous scale, but they were rarely used for decoration. One reasonably frivolous usage, however, is recounted by Thomas Rivers, who tells us how, 'When Marie-Antoinette came to France in 1770 to espouse Louis XVI, she passed through Nancy, a city about 160 miles to the south-east of Provins, the inhabitants of which presented her with a bed strewn with the leaves of the Provins roses. Alas! her bed was twenty years afterwards more abundantly strewn with thorns by the inhabitants of Paris.'

Otherwise their use was much more utilitarian, and the rose mainly grown became known as the Provins rose (the Gallica or French rose), which should not be confused with the rose of Provence which is the Centifolia. From it – the Provins rose, that is – French apothecaries produced rose oil and rose water, and they used the flowers for rose honey, rose vinegar and rose conserves. For the last, the petals were pounded in sugar or honey, and were considered a great delicacy as well as being excellent remedies for lung and liver complaints. Rose vinegar helped with all sorts of ills and rose sugar countered the ravages of consumption. Patients were advised to consult an apothecary 'properly trained in the art' on the colour of the rose to be used which was best suited to cure his particular ailment. This must have been very skilled work, for rose colours in those days were limited to various shades of pink, lavender-pink and white.

As I am now dealing with the rose in medicine for the second time, it might be as well to complete the subject. The most famous *Herball,* which goes into considerable detail, is Gerard's, published in 1599. He has been accused of taking a lot of his material from earlier herbals, but he was for many years superintendent of Lord Burleigh's gardens in the Strand, in London, and at Theobald's in Hertfordshire, and he grew more than a thousand plants in his own London garden, so he cannot have been a complete ignoramus. However, if he did use the work of others, William Turner's *Herball* of 1568 might well have been a good and readily available source, and in it Turner says of rose water: 'It is good for ye head ache, the ache of the eyes, of the right gutte, and of the mother, if it be layed to with a feather or poured on.'

Gerard himself recommends: 'In fluxes at sea, it shall avail the Surgion greatly to carry a store [of rose water] with him, which does there prevaile much more than at the land.' Or again: 'The leaves of the flowers [of the Musk Rose] eaten in the morning, in the manner of a salad, with oyle, vinegar and pepper, or any other according to the appetite and pleasure of them that shall eat it, purge very notably the belly of waterish and cholericke humours, and that mightily, yet without peril or paine at all.'

Nicolas Culpepper was a 17th-century doctor who combined medical knowledge with astrology – to good purpose, as his *English Physician Enlarged,* first published in 1652, went through five editions. Of the rose, he had the following to say:

> What quarter have Authors made with Roses, what a racket they have kept? I shal ad, Red Roses are under Jupiter, Damask under Venus, and White under the Moon, and Province under the King of France. The White and the Red Roses are cooling and drying, yet the White is taken to exceed the Red in both the Properties, but is seldom used inwardly in any medicine.... Of the Red Roses are usually made many Compositions; viz. Electuarry of Roses, Sugar of Roses, Syrup of dried Roses and Honey of Roses; the Cordial Pouder; Distilled Water of Roses, Vinegar of Roses, Oyntment and Oyl of Roses. To unite at large of every one of these would make my book swell too big.

31

Just the same, he does not stop there, and credits the rose with healing powers for practically everything. One more extract:

> The Bryar Bal [gall] is often used being made into Pouder, and drunk to break the stone... In the midst of these Bals are often found certain white Worms, which being dried and made into Pouder, and some of it drunk, is found by experience of many, to kil and drive forth Worms of the Belly.

The rose was the universal panacea. Three cheers for vitamin C!

THE
SYMBOLIC ROSE

Going back once more in time to the point where I diverged into medical byways, and moving on to a more esoteric plane, as a love potion the rose also had its followers. Removing first, one hopes, Tennyson's 'little wilful thorns', a girl would wear a red, pink or white rose on her breast for three days and then place it in a goblet of wine for a further three. Whoever could be persuaded to drink the result became hers for ever more.

The rose has, of course, always been linked with romance and at times considered a sensitive soul, if not downright prudish, at least where others were concerned. The stories of how it blushed with shame on seeing something that offended its delicate sensibilities, and so became red instead of white, are legion. One of them recounts how white roses were planted in the Garden of Eden (though no flowers are mentioned in Biblical descriptions of it), and blushed for shame when Eve offered the apple to Adam – or, more precisely I suppose, at what followed. Ancient Rome must have been pretty grim for it, unless it was of a tougher breed by then.

Though there were a few yellow rose species growing wild in the West – *R. spinosissima*, the Scotch or burnet rose of the sand dunes round the coasts of northern Europe is an example – yellow roses in the early days are associated more with the Near, Middle and Far East, and the few stories about them come mainly from there. One concerns a wife who fell in love with a Persian nobleman in her husband's absence. Suspecting something was afoot, the husband consulted a wise man, who said he should tell her to dip some object in the palace well; if his suspicions proved to be true, the object would change in colour. Shortly afterwards, seeing his wife near the well with a spray of what must have been pink or white roses, the husband asked her to dip them in the water. As she did so they turned the brightest yellow.

The rose in heraldry

The rose as a symbol of one kind or another has been mentioned a number of times, but not so far when used as a family badge or as part of a coat of arms. But they have been made use of countless times in this way, possibly deriving from the Roman custom of allowing victorious generals to attach a rose to their shields, though they were not the only ones to do something of this sort. An interesting custom commemorates the Battle of Minden in 1759, when the French were defeated by the British and Hanoverian armies. One of the

The symbolic rose: the Rose Queen
Roses played a graphic part in the history of the Tudors, especially in the imagery surrounding Elizabeth I, the 'Rose Queen'. In this portrait, painted about 1574 in the manner of Nicholas Hilliard, she is wearing a blouse with the rose motif in black point embroidery.
The Tudor rose is shown top left.
She was also known, flatteringly, as the 'Rose without a Thorn'. This symbolism was important in a national and a religious sense. The thornless rose symbolized the Virgin Mary, and Elizabeth, the Virgin Queen, was seen to be married to England in the same way that Mary was married to the Church.

British units was the Twentieth Regiment (to become known as the Lancashire Fusiliers) and, passing through gardens as they advanced, the men plucked roses and wore them in their caps during the battle. To mark the occasion, on Minden Day, all ranks of the regiment still place a red rose and a yellow one in their caps, and a wreath of red roses is hung on the portrait of their commanding general at the battle. The dinner table that night is likewise decorated, but, strangest of all, visiting officers are required to stand on their chairs and actually eat a rose, served with champagne.

There are nowadays some 4,000 German families with roses in their coats of arms, and in France one of the earliest records of a rose used as a personal emblem goes back to the Breton crusader De Bruce, who used a six-petalled one. In the English royal line, the use of a rose as a badge started with Edward I's golden rose. Edward III had small roses incorporated in the design of his great seal, but it was not until the conclusion of the Wars of the Roses in the late 15th century that the Tudor rose became the badge of England. One of the varieties that go to make it up was almost certainly the old French Gallica rose. Edmund Crouchback, second son of Henry III, was the first Earl of Lancaster and had a French wife and large estates in northern France, from which the rose probably came. The white rose of York may or may not have been an Alba, *R. alba semi-plena*, though once again, as with the question of its possible introduction by the Romans, there are those who say that it was the field rose (*R. arvensis*).

At any rate, on the marriage of Henry VII (Henry Tudor) to Elizabeth of York, the eldest daughter of Edward IV, the white rose and the red were combined in one badge and the Tudor rose, with a crown above it, has remained a royal badge of England to this day. One of the finest examples of it to be seen is in Westminster Abbey in the Henry VII chapel. It has been adapted by subsequent monarchs, sometimes with odd results, none more so than in the badge of James I and Queen Anne, who had a rose and a thistle growing from a single stalk. This may have made sense in the mysterious world of the herald, but would have raised eyebrows if it had appeared in a nursery catalogue. Among others of the royal line who used roses, Henry IV had a red rose and Edward IV a white one. Henry VIII as well as Henry VII used the Tudor rose, and three of the former's queens used various combinations of them. Queen Elizabeth I had as her motto *Rosa sine spina* (a rose without a thorn) and the Tudor rose as a badge.

See the illustration of Queen Elizabeth I, the 'Rose Queen' on page 33.

Shakespeare and the rose

There is a Damask rose known as the York and Lancaster rose (*R. damascena versicolor*). This has some red and some white flowers, and some with both red and white petals, and is supposed to be the one from which the Somerset and Warwick factions picked their respective flowers in the Temple Garden in Shakespeare's *Henry VI, Part 1*. Unfortunately, although first described by Monardes in 1551, it was not, as far as can be found out, known in England until the 17th century, and in any case I am not really sure whether Shakespeare's text states that there was only one bush in the garden. There might have been a white and a red, and as the story is so often quoted without supporting details, the passage is included here, almost in its entirety, so that individual judgements can be formed concerning the origins of these emblems of the Wars of the Roses.

ACT II, SCENE IV. London. *The Temple Garden.*
Enter the EARLS OF SOMERSET, SUFFOLK *and* WARWICK;
RICHARD PLANTAGENET, VERNON, *and another* Lawyer.

Plan. Great lords and gentlemen, what means this silence?
Dare no man answer in the case of truth?
Suff. Within the Temple-hall we were too loud;
The garden here is more convenient.
Plan. Then say at once if I maintained the truth;
Or else was wrangling Somerset in error?

. . . .

Plan. Since you are tongue-tied and so loth to speak,
In dumb significants proclaim your thoughts:
Let him that is a true-born gentleman,
And stands upon the honour of his birth,
If he suppose that I have pleaded truth,
From off this brier pluck a white rose with me.
Som. Let him that is no coward nor no flatterer,
But dare maintain the party of the truth,
Pluck a red rose from off this thorn with me.
War. I love no colours, and, without all colour
Of base insinuating flattery,
I pluck this white rose with Plantagenet.
Suff. I pluck this red rose with young Somerset;
And say withal I think he held the right.
Ver. Stay, lords and gentlemen, and pluck no more,
Till you conclude that he, upon whose side
The fewest roses are cropp'd from the tree,
Shall yield the other in the right opinion.
Som. Good Master Vernon, it is well objected:
If I have fewest I subscribe in silence.
Plan. And I.
Ver. Then, for the truth and plainness of the case,
I pluck this pale and maiden blossom here,
Giving my verdict on the white rose side.
Som. Prick not your finger as you pluck it off,
Lest, bleeding, you do paint the white rose red,
And fall on my side so, against your will.
Ver. If I, my lord, for my opinion bleed,
Opinion shall be surgeon to my hurt,
And keep me on the side where still I am.
Som. Well, well, come on; who else?
Law. Unless my study and my books be false,
The argument you held was wrong in you;
                              [*To* SOMERSET.
In sign whereof I pluck a white rose too.
Plan. Now, Somerset, where is your argument?
Som. Here in my scabbard; meditating that
Shall dye your white rose in a bloody red.
Plan. Meantime your cheeks do counterfeit our roses;
For pale they look with fear, as witnessing
The truth on our side.
Som. No, Plantagenet,
'Tis not for fear, but anger that thy cheeks
Blush for pure shame to counterfeit our roses,
And yet thy tongue will not confess thy error.
Plan. Hath not thy rose a canker, Somerset?
Som. Hath not thy rose a thorn, Plantagenet?

Plan. Ay, sharp and piercing, to maintain his truth;
Whiles thy consuming canker eats his falsehood.
Som. Well, I'll find friends to wear my bleeding roses,
That shall maintain what I have said is true,
Where false Plantagenet dare not be seen.
Plan. Now, by this maiden blossom in my hand,
I scorn thee and thy faction, peevish boy.
Suff. Turn not thy scorns this way, Plantagenet.
. . . .

War. This blot, that they object against your house,
Shall be wip'd out in the next Parliament,
Call'd for the truce of Winchester and Gloster;
And if thou be not then created York,
I will not live to be accounted Warwick.
Meantime, in signal of my love to thee,
Against proud Somerset and William Pole,
Will I upon thy party wear this rose.
And here I prophesy: this brawl to-day,
Grown to this faction, in the Temple garden,
Shall send, between the red rose and the white,
A thousand souls to death and deadly night.
Plan. Good Master Vernon, I am bound to you,
That you on my behalf would pluck a flower.
Ver. In your behalf still would I wear the same.
Law. And so will I.
Plan. Thanks, gentle sir.
Come, let us four to dinner: I dare say
This quarrel will drink blood another day.

[*Exeunt.*

Shakespeare had, of course, a good deal else to say about roses, mostly of the wild kind, and someone more industrious than I am – or perhaps with a different sense of priorities – has estimated that there are about sixty references to them in his works. Nor is he concerned only with using their beauty for his imagery. He clearly had considerable practical knowledge, for in *The Winter's Tale* we read:

> We marry
> A gentle scion to the wildest stock,
> And make conceive a bark of baser kind
> By bud of a nobler race;

And he has a comment, too, on the lasting qualities of the roses of his time in *Othello*, unless he was back once more with his beloved but short-lived wild eglantine.

> When I have plucked this rose,
> I cannot give it vital growth again,
> It needs must wither: I'll smell it on the tree.

Poems about the largely unidentified roses of olden times are legion, but one anonymous one should not be omitted, whatever else is. It is possibly from the 12th century, and is believed to be the first one in the English language to honour the rose.

Of a Rose is al Myn Song

Of a rose, a lovely rose,
Of a rose is al myn song.

Lestenyt, lordynges, both elde and yinge,
How is this rose began to sprynge;
Swych a rose to myn lykynge
In al this world ne knowe I non.

The aungel came from Hevene tour
To grete Marye with gret honour,
And seyde sche schuld bere the flour
That schulde breke the fyndes bond.

The flour sprong in heye Bedlem,
That is bothe bright and schen:
The rose is Mary, hevene qwen,
Out of her bosum the blosme sprong.

The ferste brauche is ful of myght,
That spronge on Cyrstemesse nyght,
The sterre schon over Bedlem bryght
That is both brod and long.

The secunde brauche sprong to helle,
The fendys power doun to felle:
Therein myght non sowle dwelle;
Blyssid be the time the rose sprong!

The thredde brauche is good and swote,
It sprang to hevene, crop and rote,
Therein to dwellyn and ben our bote;
Every day it schewit in prystes hond.

Prey we to here with gret honour,
She that bar the blyssid flour,
She be our helpe and our socour
And schyld us fro the fyndes bond.

THE

SPECIES OF ROSES

Having now taken a look at early rose history in a very general sort of way, it is time to become more specific in dealing with the various groups, examples of which we know and grow today. It will still be necessary to move backwards and forwards in time every so often, particularly with the older groups like the Gallicas, Damasks and Albas; but what I will try to do is to follow the main lines of development from the very earliest of roses until we reach the modern Hybrid Teas, Floribundas, Climbers and so on – the story, in short, of the cultivated or garden rose.

See also the listing of species roses on page 96; the section on using species roses on page 196; and plates I, II, XV and XXXIV (pp40, 46, 94 and 197). The first move backwards must come right at the beginning, as so far the wild species from which the garden roses are all descended have only been touched upon. How to use these to advantage nowadays will be dealt with in a later chapter, but historically there should certainly be some more detailed reference to a number of the more important ones, giving their country of origin, the dates of their discovery or introduction where it is known and the use to which some of them have been put in breeding lines, and bringing out other points of general interest about them. The dates given must not, of course, be confused with the true age of the various species. Nobody knows how old they are. All one can do is to say when they were first discovered and recorded by botanists or horticulturists.

It will soon become clear that, even among the species described, there is considerable variation in flower form and size, in the leaves, the hips, the canes, the thorns and the size and habit of growth of the plants. This is in part – but only in part – because for convenience and clarity it seems sensible to include here those roses that are closely allied to true species and that, in general terms, resemble them. Some will be hybrids of which the species parents are known, while others will be of unknown origin. Hybridizing in the wild will have had its effect on their looks and character, but even the true species vary enormously, as will be seen. Not included are the species climbers and ramblers, as these will be dealt with when we come to the story of climbing roses. The only exception to this is where hybrids of some of the species discussed have produced climbers, and when this has happened it will be mentioned. In addition, in the right climate such as that found in New Zealand, for instance, or in parts of America, where Hybrid Teas will top 2.5 m (8 ft) with ease, some species are counted as climbers in their own right which would be big shrubs elsewhere.

Rose species of the Far East

As I propose to take the roses country by country or, where they are more widely distributed, continent by continent, it seems appropriate to start with China, which has provided us with so many of the best. And with the first of all, *R. bracteata*, the Macartney rose (named after Lord Macartney, who introduced it to England about 1793 from eastern China at a time when plants from that area were a great rarity), there occurs the sort of classification problem I have been talking about. It is sometimes listed as a climber and has the distinction, in combination with a Tea rose, of being one of the parents of the pale-yellow-flowered climber 'Mermaid'. It will itself go up to 4.5 m (15 ft) on a sheltered wall, or else make a dense shrub of 2 m (6 ft) or so. Like its offspring, it is continuously in bloom, its 8–10 cm (3–4 in), white, scented, single flowers with their golden stamens being surrounded by leaf-like bracts (from which the name *bracteata* derives). It is almost evergreen in a cool climate, and even more so in a warm one, and has particularly fine, glossy and very healthy foliage. It cannot be said to be completely hardy, so wall protection is advisable in climates on a par with those of the British Isles. In the southern states of America, on the other hand, it is a rampant grower, has become naturalized over the years and has been planted quite extensively to combat soil erosion. The orange-red hips are covered in pubescence, making them appear woolly, but it does not seem to set seed very freely, so hybrids from this fine rose are few.

No date appears to be recorded for the discovery of *R. davidii* by the French missionary and naturalist Armand David, but it was brought to the West by E. H. Wilson in 1908. A large, open-growing shrub, it has small, bright pink flowers in corymbs, appearing in the second half of the summer when many species are over. Bunches of bright scarlet hips come later. Of *R. farreri* the best-known form is *R. farreri persetosa*, which will make a twiggy, mounding bush 2 m (6 ft) high and quite a bit more across, and which was selected by A. E. Bowles from seedlings introduced from north-west China by Farrer in

For illustrations of Far Eastern species roses, see plates I, II, XV and XXXIV (pp40, 46, 94 and 197); see also the section on Asian species on page 48.

1914. The tiny, pale pink flowers have white eyes, and their size has earned it the name of the threepenny-bit rose, which may cause furrowed brows in the younger generation and a leafing through history books. The blooms are well matched by the small, fern-like foliage, each leaf having seven to nine leaflets, which colour attractively in the autumn. *R. forrestiana*, from western China, is a stronger pink, again with a white eye, the scented flowers coming in clusters and being surrounded by green bracts which persist into the autumn to frame the brightest of scarlet hips. I have found it slow to establish, but well worth while waiting for.

R. hugonis, upright and reaching 2 m (6 ft), is one of the best known of the spring-flowering yellow species – a soft, primrose-yellow in this case – and came to us in 1899, sent to Kew Gardens as a seedling by Pater Hugo, a missionary. A very fragrant seedling from it, 'Headleyensis', was raised in England by Sir Oscar Warburg in the early 1920s and is a good deal better than the original, which has a reputation for die-back and whose flowers do not always open as well as they might. The flowers of 'Headleyensis' are larger and the growth more arching. Another seedling of *R. hugonis*, 'Cantabrigiensis', is also an improvement.

The Cherokee rose, *R. laevigata*, was for long considered to be a native of the United States, and there can be no doubt as to where it gained its popular name. It is certainly naturalized in the southern states, and grows almost like a weed right down into Texas, though it is not completely hardy in the north and needs some shelter. Its true country of origin is now known to be China, and it makes a large, semi-evergreen shrub or, with its long canes, it can be used as a rambler. It is not an easy rose to breed from but, crossed with *R. wichuraiana*, it produced Van Fleet's lovely white-flowered rambler 'Silver Moon' in 1910 and, even better, 'Anemonoides' and its richer pink sport 'Ramona', which will festoon a (warm) wall like a large-flowered clematis. The white fragrant flowers of *R. laevigata* itself are 8–10 cm (3–4 in) across, come singly from each leaf axil, and appear early in the year.

One of the stars of the species roses from China is *R. moyesii*. It was introduced first in 1890, and William Robinson in his book *The English Flower Garden* had this to say about it:

> The most startlingly beautiful rose that has come to us for many years. It is splendid in colour and vigour, with its red, bottle-shaped fruits. In Sussex it grows as freely as any Brier. The colour is not easy to describe. Excellent for trellis or as a single bush, or for any purpose for which a wild Rose can be used. Native of W. China, it was found by Mr A. E. Pratt on the Tibetan frontier at an elevation of 9,000 ft. Men talk of getting fine things by crossing this, but you will never get anything so good.

No one nowadays would quarrel with any of that, but on first reading the quotation I was puzzled. Robinson's book was published in 1883, so could it be that the term 'sneak preview' was older than I had supposed? The answer is that *The English Flower Garden* went through sixteen editions, so do not look in the first one for a reference to *R. moyesii*.

Despite Robinson's praise, the rose did not really attract general attention until E. H. Wilson reintroduced it in 1903. The type makes a very tall-growing, rather open and upright shrub, the canes having few thorns. Being bolder than Robinson, I would say that the single and disappointingly scent-less blooms are of the most intense scarlet-crimson, offset by cream stamens,

and in the late summer and autumn these are replaced by spectacularly large hips, which look like the decorations on a Christmas tree. There are many modern hybrids with generally similar characteristics, including 'Geranium' (not quite so big), *R. holondonta* (*R. moyesii rosea*), with the biggest and brightest hips of all the group, 'Fred Streeter' and 'Sealing Wax', the last three with pink flowers. The cerise-crimson hybrid, *R. × highdownensis*, was raised by Sir Frederick Stern in Sussex, England, in about 1925, and in this one the velvety flowers are 6 cm (2½ in) across and the hips orange-scarlet. The justly famous, repeat-flowering, creamy-white shrub rose 'Nevada' is a Moyesii hybrid, though probably not, according to Mr E. F. Allen, an authority on species roses, a first-generation offspring of *R. moyesii* itself.

R. multibracteata makes a big prickly shrub, with massed small pink flowers in late summer. It is another Wilson introduction, from which the lovely modern shrub rose 'Cerise Bouquet' was bred. Also large and with small fragrant flowers, this time pale yellow fading to white, and about the size of a buttercup, is *R. primula*. It comes from northern China, and was also found in Turkestan by the American botanist F. N. Meyer. Its leaves, which have from seven to thirteen leaflets, will, on damp, humid days, have a fragrance of incense, which becomes even more noticeable if they are crushed between the fingers. Not surprisingly, it is also known as the incense rose. It was introduced around 1910.

R. roxburghii (also known as *R. microphylla*) is something very different, and comes from both China and Japan. There are two forms, *normalis* with single pink flowers, and *plena* with very double ones, opening flat. The double form came West first, some time before 1814; the single not until 1908. The leaves are noteworthy, very long and made up of up to fifteen pairs of leaflets, and these and the rough, greyish-brown, peeling bark of the stems give the rose an almost mahonia-like appearance when it is not in bloom. And that is not the only remarkable thing about it, for the tomato-shaped hips are covered with stiff prickles, so that *R. roxburghii* has also come to be known as the chestnut rose or the burr rose. It came to the West via India, where it was grown by Dr Roxburgh, who had obtained it in turn from Canton, and was first taken to the American continent in 1820.

The wild form of *R. rugosa*, the ancient ramanus rose of Japan, has been surpassed by numerous hybrids which will be discussed in some detail when we come to garden usage. The type's original habitat was the sandy coastal areas of both China and Japan and it thrives and has become naturalized in similar situations in north-eastern America and in the British Isles. Strangely, the very knowledgeable German hybridist Wilhelm Kordes says in his book that it does not thrive in dry situations, but this is certainly not the experience of myself and others. Constantly in flower, its blooms are large, purplish-pink, and followed by red, tomato-like hips, which on the hybrids appear only on those with single or semi-double flowers. The healthiest of roses, it has particularly striking, deeply veined (rugose) leaves, which take on yellow tints in the autumn. It is widely used for understocks, particularly for standard or tree roses, for which it gives a stout hardy stem, only offset by a tendency to sucker freely. All stems and branches are armoured with multitudes of needle-sharp thorns and prickles. (Strictly speaking, they are all prickles, but I will stick to the term thorn because of its popularity, even though it is botanically incorrect.)

Plate I: Species roses (1)
There is just one rose, R. sericea pteracantha (top left) from the Far East that has the distinction of having four petals instead of the usual five of the other true species, but it is of greater garden interest because of its remarkable and decorative thorns. R. farreri persetosa (top right) from China makes a large bush, though with very small leaves and flowers, each of a size that gained it the name threepenny-bit rose.
Both R. californica semiplena (bottom left), and R. × harisonii, otherwise known as 'Harison's Yellow' (bottom right) come from the United States. The latter is probably a hybrid between two species, and became widely naturalized after spreading westward with the wagon train pioneers.
See also plates II, XV and XXXIV (pp46, 94 and 197).

I am indebted to the article by Mrs Tess Allen in the Royal National Rose Society's *Annual* for getting me out of the state of bewilderment I had reached in trying to reconcile the various accounts of *R. rugosa*'s introduction to Europe. She says:

Modern Roses 6 records that it was introduced in 1845 and was known by Lawrance as *Rosa ferox*. Under this name it is figured in Mary Lawrance's book *A Collection of Roses From Nature* published in 1799, and also in H. C. Andrews' book printed in 1828. In his book on the *History of the Rose*, André Leroy records that *R. rugosa* was collected by Joseph Banks and it was subsequently reintroduced at a later date into Europe. This solves one problem. However, *R. rugosa* could only, in fact, have been collected on James Cook's third voyage, and Joseph Banks sailed with Captain Cook on his first, but not his subsequent expeditions. The third voyage was undertaken primarily to find the North-West Passage. The ships *Discovery* and *Resolution* surveyed the west American coast to the Bering Straits and beyond, where their passage was barred by ice. They then turned southwards to winter in Hawaii where James Cook was killed in February 1779. The expedition then sailed for Kamchatka and the eastern countries of Asia, where *R. rugosa* occurs, and it was probably Joseph Banks's protégé, David Nelson, who collected *R. rugosa* (*R. ferox*).

From western China and also from the Himalayas comes the early-flowering, four-petalled *R. sericea* and *R. omeiensis*, which some say are close relatives and some say are the same rose. As to all intents and purposes they are identical, the argument can wash over us and we can concentrate on the best form, *R. sericea pteracantha*. Apart from the unique cruciform petallage, this has strong and rather rigid canes, armed when young with huge, flat, translucent red thorns, like the scaly crest along the back of a prehistoric monster. They do not vanish with age, of course, but they do lose their glow and become extremely hard and formidable. There are two yellow forms of this rose, 'Hidcote Gold' and *R. omeiensis lutea*.

R. soulieana, its introduction dating from 1896 in France and 1899 in England, is a great rumbustious shrub with strikingly grey-tinted leaves, which will in summer be almost smothered out of sight by the starry white flowers. It is not quite hardy in the less temperate countries, but another Chinese species, *R. willmottiae*, is tougher. Where *R. soulieana* rampages, the latter is much more restrained and elegant, as befits a rose named after that great rose-lover Miss Ellen Willmott. E. H. Wilson (and how much we owe to him) brought it from that part of China which borders on Tibet in 1904. Wide-spreading and with delicate, ferny foliage, the 2.5 cm (1 in) flowers are a mauvish-pink and have creamy stamens, always an attractive combination.

We have now reached the last few of the riches from China that I am going to discuss – those, that is, that can be classed as shrubs and not climbers. *R. xanthina* cannot be left out, for it is lovely in its own right, but it has achieved fame mainly as a probable parent of the rather similar 'Canary Bird', the most deservedly popular of the spring-flowering yellows. *R. chinensis* itself was not discovered in its wild habitat (in central China) until about 1900, though many garden forms had reached Europe since the latter part of the 18th century. The two most important of these were 'Old Blush China', introduced in 1752 and later known as 'Parsons's Pink China', and 'Slater's Crimson China' in 1792. However, since the development of the China roses forms an integrated story within that of the cultivated roses it will be better to include it in the appropriate place later.

For the introduction of China roses, see page 60.

For illustrations of American species, see plates I, II and XV (pp40, 46 and 94).

Rose species of the Americas

Moving eastwards across the Pacific Ocean, the first three species from the New World, *R. acicularis* (found in north-east Asia and Japan as well), *R. arkansana* (the Arkansas rose) and *R. blanda* (the smooth rose or meadow rose) are all on the small side and, except for *R. blanda*, rarely top 1 m (3 ft). The flowers are pink in each case and all are hip-bearing, those of *R. acicularis* (also known as the Arctic rose) being particularly large, pear-shaped and pink. It dates from 1805, while *R. arkansana*, which comes from the mid-west, was first classified in 1917. Its double form, *plena*, is found farther north and in Canada. *R. blanda*, also from the northern states, was a much earlier discovery, going back to 1773. It is known both as the Hudson's Bay rose and as the Labrador rose, and can grow taller than the other two if conditions suit it. Some strains are thornless.

The next two roses are much better known outside their country of origin. *R. californica*, a native of the west coast as its name might imply and which is found wild as far north as Oregon, is a graceful, pink-flowered species, more usually seen in cultivation in its semi-double form *R. californica plena*. Though quite easily obtainable in Europe, surprisingly true stock of the latter is not always easy to obtain in America, and it is thought that the rose sometimes supplied instead is 'Banshee', a rather similar, very sweetly-scented pink variety of unknown origin that is common in western Canada. The autumn colouring of the leaves suggests *R. virginiana* as a possible parent, but it is not *R. californica*. The true *californica* will reach 1.8–2.4 m (6–8 ft) at its best, its long canes bowed down by the weight of the clustered blooms.

R. carolina and the double form *R. carolina plena*, of 1826, hail from the east, and make small, 60 cm (2 ft) but dense-growing thickets, bearing rose-pink flowers 5 cm (2 in) across. Though tough enough in its native habitat, it does not seem to appreciate extremes of climate either way. Another low-growing, suckering shrub is *R. foliolosa*, from the mid-south, useful in that its bright pink, fragrant flowers appear in late summer and continue into early autumn. They are followed by red hips and some attractive colouring of the narrow, rather willow-like leaves.

R. × harisonii should not, from the purist's point of view, be among the species, as it is almost certainly a comparatively recent hybrid of a rose of the Spinosissima group and *R. foetida persiana*, both of which will be mentioned shortly. However, it has almost assumed the status of a species and is so much a part of the American scene that it really fits in here as well as anywhere. It was raised in New York by George Harison in 1830, caught on quickly, and spread across the country as the pioneers moved west. The old trails, it is said, can be followed by spotting the 'Harison's Yellow' roses naturalized along them. A vigorous, medium-sized shrub, it can at times grow rather leggy, but all criticism vanishes at the sight of the very freely borne semi-double, cupped, brilliant yellow flowers which come very early in the year.

While still in the east, in the north-east and Canada, from Newfoundland to Massachusetts, is found the dwarf (45 cm, 18 in), suckering, prickly *R. nitida* of 1807. In this the flowers are again pink, and the glossy leaves give a brilliant show of red in the autumn. 1876 saw the introduction of *R. nutkana*, again pink-flowered and whose range extends up to Alaska, and 1726 the rather sparse-growing *R. palustris*, which however prefers swampy, moist ground, anywhere from Nova Scotia in the north to Florida and west to Mississippi. In

1738 Bartram's nursery received a request from a Peter Collinson in England for plants of *R. palustris* and also *R. lucida*. They were listed in the *Gentleman's Magazine* of 1751, but though both Mary Lawrance and Ellen Willmott enthused about them, they never really caught on as garden shrubs on either side of the Atlantic.

Much better known is the prairie rose, *R. setigera*, of the mid-western states, a sprawling grower with its long, rambling canes with their deep green leaves spreading all over the place and rooting from the tips of the shoots as they go. This habit and the fact that each leaf has only three leaflets, has led to the use of another common name, the bramble-leaf rose. The mallow-pink flowers are 5 cm (2 in) across and appear towards the end of the summer; it is one of the last into bloom. A tough and persistent rose, this, which is said to withstand temperatures as low as −29°C (−20°F). Another tough one is *R. stellata*, which hails from the mountains of southern New Mexico. The form *stellata mirifica*, the Sacramento rose, dates from 1916, and comes from the Sacramento Mountains in central New Mexico. It has striking, ivory-coloured prickles rather than true thorns, and rose-purple flowers, but is becoming scarce and has reached the status of an endangered species.

The last two American roses I will discuss are natives of, respectively, the north-east and Canada, and the central and western states. *R. virginiana* (formerly called *R. lucida* and mentioned above) is a fine, almost thornless, low-growing and spreading suckering shrub. It gives a spectacular display of autumn colouring, at which time the leaves first turn to purple, then orange-red, crimson, and finally to yellow. Vivid, cerise-pink flowers, borne perhaps not quite as plentifully as on some roses, come in mid to late summer. Rose d'amour or the St Mark's rose (*R. virginiana plena*) has much more profuse and more double flowers of singular beauty, and possibly has the blood of *R. carolina* in it. This form dates from 1768, and *R. virginiana* itself was the first American species to be cultivated in Europe. It is mentioned in Parkinson's *Theatre of Plants*, published in England in 1640, under the name of the Virginian briar rose, though not in his earlier *Paradisus In Sole* of 1629, which gives an idea of when it must have arrived. The second and last rose is *R. woodsii*, the type dating from 1880 and the most usually seen form, *R. woodsii fendleri*, from 1888. The latter has a more southerly range, right down to Texas. Both make medium-sized, dense-growing shrubs with clusters of bright, lilac-pink, scented flowers and fine, round red hips later.

European rose species

And so over another ocean, the Atlantic this time, to Europe. One rose that is widely distributed is *R. arvensis*, which, as mentioned earlier, is also known as the field rose and was almost certainly Shakespeare's musk rose, though it is not all that strongly scented. Let the Rev Joseph Pemberton, writing in 1908, take over the description:

For illustrations of European species, see plates II, XV and XXXIV (pp46, 94 and 197).

> Next to *canina*, *R. arvensis* is the most abundant of all the British species; in Essex particularly so. Coming into bloom about a week or ten days later than the dog-rose, it continues in flower some time after the petals of the last dog-rose have fallen. I have seen it in bloom in September, but this is abnormal. It is most free in flowering, and quite distinct both in bloom, habit and foliage. The branches are long and slender, trailing over last year's growth or anything else handy. The wood is a dull purple, with scattered prickles, sometimes hooked,

but generally straight. Those on the old wood are white, but on the young growth are red and smaller. The leaves are glabrous and shiny above, rarely downy, something like the foliage of the tea-scented class. At midsummer *R. arvensis* needs no seeking, it forces itself into notice, being one mass of flowers, pure white, with a yellowish base, golden stamens, and having a sweet scent peculiar to itself. The disc is elevated and fleshy, the calyx purple, like the wood.

Actually the flowers, like those of the dog rose, are too fleeting for garden use, but *R. arvensis*'s habit of growth made it a good parent of the climbing Ayrshire roses such as 'Dundee Rambler' and 'Bennett's Seedling', which were very popular at the end of the 19th century and used extensively by Gertrude Jekyll in her planting schemes. Its distribution is not, of course, confined to the British Isles.

To northern Europeans, the dog rose (*R. canina*) needs no introduction, and it is also a native of western Asia as well as having been naturalized for many years in America. It was mentioned by Jocelyn as growing in Plymouth Plantation there as long ago as 1636. There are countless forms, with flowers ranging from the palest blush to quite a strong pink, and attempts have been made by those botanists known colloquially as the 'splitters' (who would like to classify separately anything which varies in the slightest degree from the norm) to establish them all as separate and distinct species. The splitters *par excellence* of the moment are the Russians, who claim no less than 249 species all their own – though in the last century over 6,000 were claimed for the West. All one can say is that, thank heavens, the arch rivals of the splitters, the 'lumpers', have prevailed, as they like lumping everything together as much as possible. Nevertheless, one or two variations of *R. canina* are still worth mentioning.

Some time before 1800 a prize of £50 was offered in Dublin for the discovery of a new and truly Irish plant, and it was won by a Mr Templeton, who found a rose that seemed to be new growing in the countryside near Belfast. It was given the name of *R. hibernica*, but it is almost certainly a form of *R. canina* or possibly a hybrid. According to Pemberton it has since been found in England and also in France, but it is by no means common anywhere. *R. canina andersonii* is another fairly distinct rose derived from *canina*, having considerably larger pink flowers, but in general most variations are more noted for their use as understocks for garden roses, particularly on heavy ground, on which they thrive.

Certainly the Romans knew the dog rose, and it is said that it gained its popular name because they believed that a distillation from its roots was a cure for hydrophobia. Pliny mentions such a cure carried out on a soldier of Nero's army and described by the physician and herbalist Dioscorides, but as is always the way with these stories of early beliefs, there are those who say that this is nonsense; the thorns simply resemble the teeth of a dog. So take your pick, but as I said, from the utilitarian point of view, the roots of *R. canina* have been more useful than the top-growth, except in one thing. It was probably one of the parents of the first of the Alba roses.

There is an interesting account of a very remarkable bush of *R. canina* in Thomas Rivers's *The Rose Amateurs' Guide* of 1861. This was, so the story goes, planted by order of Charlemagne, who was something of a gardening enthusiast. On the spot where it was planted Charlemagne ordered the build-

ing of Hildesheim Cathedral, and the rose is still there today in the cloisters and some 10 m (32 ft) high. According to attested historical evidence it is at least 500 years old, and though the cathedral was destroyed in an air raid in 1945 and the old bush reduced to about 2 m (6 ft), it sprang up again with seemingly inexhaustible vigour. This is the famous Hildesheim rose, and one might add here that it was during Charlemagne's reign that the first gardening book written by an amateur – *The Little Garden* by a monk called Walafrid Strabo – appeared, and in it he gives the rose his top accolade.

R. pomifera (*R. villosa*) of central and southern Europe is usually grown in its double form, *R. pomifera duplex* or Wolley-Dod's rose, named after the clergyman in whose garden it was raised or at least found, and is probably a hybrid. The original goes back to 1771 and is also known as the apple rose because of its very large, roundish, rather bristly crimson hips, which are actually more like dark red gooseberries than apples. It has pale pink flowers, not as profuse as they might be, and grey-green rather downy foliage.

R. rubiginosa (*R. eglanteria*) is the sweet-briar and Shakespeare's eglantine. It has some of the most beautiful single, pink, fragrant flowers of any wild rose, and glittering, orange-scarlet hips follow them. A hedge of it, 18 m (60 ft) long, planted in the garden of the Roman villa of Fishbourne, near Chichester in southern England, is truly a sight to see, both at midsummer and in the autumn; it might well be what the Romans themselves would have had there, though in nature the rose would ramble through other shrubs in hedges and thickets. Richard Jefferies records an old English country superstition that a child, passed under the flowering sprays of a hedgerow brier at sunrise, would be cured of whooping-cough and other ills, though I suppose he could have been thinking of the dog rose just as much as of the sweet-brier.

There have been many notable hybrids from *R. rubiginosa*, particularly those raised at the turn of the century when Lord Penzance crossed this rose with *R. foetida* and its hybrids, the so-called Austrian briers, and with a number of Hybrid Teas. His new group of roses became known as the Penzance Briers, and includes the varieties 'Lord Penzance' (fawn-yellow), 'Lady Penzance' (coppery-yellow) and many named after female characters in Sir Walter Scott's novels. 'Julia Mannering' (light pink), 'Meg Merrilees' (crimson) and 'Amy Robsart' (mid-pink) are some of these, and are all tall, vigorous growers, rather fleeting in bloom, but with a good display of hips and with the aromatic foliage of the common parent, which is one of their main attractions. This 'perfumes the breeze on a dewy morn' or, as Dryden put it:

> And the fresh eglantine exhaled a breath,
> Whose odours were of power to raise from death.

The lovely modern German blush-pink rose 'Fritz Nobis' is another offspring and a much better garden plant than the others unless you have room and to spare. *R. rubiginosa* has become naturalized on the west coast of America and, like the dog rose, is described as being at Plymouth in 1636. And George Washington bought it for his garden from a nursery in Pennsylvania.

R. rubrifolia, from the mountain regions of central and southern Europe, is one of the few roses not grown primarily for its flowers, which, though attractive enough when seen close-to, are not showy, being very small, pink and fleeting. It is above all a foliage plant, and the leaves on the almost

Plate II: Species roses (2)
All the cultivated varieties we grow are descended from species or wild roses. *R. canina* (top left) is one of the most widely distributed in Europe and has been naturalized in North America. *R. moschata* (top right) is the historic, sweetly scented musk rose of western Asia, and 'Canary Bird' (bottom left) probably the best of the early-flowering yellow 'species' for the garden; it is probably very closely related to the Far Eastern species *R. xanthina*.
The fourth rose (bottom right) is *R. foetida bicolor* from Persia, perhaps the most startling colour of any wild rose and one of the group from which all bright yellow and orange modern hybrid roses are descended. See also plates I, XV and XXXIV (pp40, 94 and 197).

thornless laterals (which are plum-red when young) are a soft grey-green with a distinct mauve sheen, the intensity of which is increased in light shade. There is a good show of scarlet hips, which hang in clusters and are of a size far bigger than one would expect from such insignificant flowers. The bush will reach 2 m (6 ft) or so and is of fairly open habit. Its hardiness is emphasized by the fact that self-sown seedlings germinate and prosper even in a relatively harsh climate. There is a white-flowered form, but it is not very often seen. *R. sherardii*, or the northern downy rose, is another with attractive leaves, greyish-green, but this one also has lovely clear pink single blooms of about the same size as the dog rose.

The Spinosissima group, the Scotch or Burnet roses – also known as the Pimpinellifolias – make up a big group with many offshoots, both from the wild and man-made. *R. spinosissima* (or *R. pimpinellifolia* if you are a pimpinellifoliaphile) itself has a wide range and can be found in north Africa as well as Europe – and elsewhere as well, but outside these two areas it is probably naturalized. In its original form it is a low-growing, thicket-forming rose of the coastal sand dunes, and it suckers in a most undisciplined way. Its recognition as a species dates from some time after AD 1600. The flowers are small and single, creamy-white or pink, and are followed by black or dark maroon-black hips. The leaves are small, too, and fern-like, with five to nine leaflets. Varieties of the same stature include 'Bicolor' (semi-double, pink with lighter reverse), 'Double White' (globular blooms), 'Double Yellow' and 'William III', which is crimson-purple.

Much taller at about 2 m (6 ft) is one of the loveliest of all spring-flowering shrub roses, *R. spinosissima altaica*, brought out of hiding some time before 1820 from the Altai Mountains of Siberia and obviously one of the Russian 249. The beauty of its large, creamy-white flowers attracted the German hybridist Wilhelm Kordes, who crossed it with the Hybrid Tea 'Joanna Hill' to produce 'Frühlingsduft' and 'Frühlingsanfang', and it is also in the breeding of that pearl among moderns, 'Frühlingsmorgen'. Another cross, with the ivory-white *R. spinosissima hispida*, resulted in 'Frühlingsgold', produced in 1937 and probably the best-known and loved of the 'Frühlings' series. Then, in 1956, Roy Shepherd in the United States crossed *R. spinosissima altaica* with 'Soeur Thérèse' to produce 'Golden Wings', a fine medium-sized recurrent shrub with 8 cm (5 in) sulphur-yellow flowers.

Much earlier, in 1838, a possibly accidental cross in a Stanwell, London, garden between a Scotch rose and another (from the flowers probably a Damask) gave us the non-stop-flowering 'Stanwell Perpetual'. Large, pale pink quartered blooms, which fade almost to white, smother this sprawling, lax and very thorny shrub early in the year and appear intermittently right through the summer, well set off by greyish-green leaves. All the Spinosissimas have the sharpest of spines, from which came their name. A very limited selection survives today, and I have touched on only a few of these, but at one time there were no less than 174 forms or hybrids listed.

Rose species of Asia

With one or two of the European roses discussed so far I have strayed over the border into Asia and back again. Now we move on there once more, first to the south-west, to find a species that revolutionized the colours of garden roses. This is *R. foetida* (also known as *R. lutea* and the capucine rose), which

For illustrations of Asian species, see plates II and XXXVI (pp46 and 203); see also the section on Far Eastern species on page 38.

gave yellow and orange and flame to the petals of the varieties we cultivate today. The story of how this happened will be described later, in correct historical sequence, but for the moment it can be said that *R. foetida* is an open-growing shrub, not too tall as a rule, with bright, sulphur-yellow flowers about 5 cm (2 in) across and single. Its sport *R. foetida bicolor* is similar in all respects, except that its petals are a brilliant coppery-red with a yellow reverse. Both have been known and cultivated since 1590 at least, and in the course of time have become naturalized in parts of Europe. They seem to thrive there despite the cooler climate, though they are a rather doubtful proposition farther north than about the middle of the British Isles. It was through being found in Austria after their migration from the east that they gained the quite misleading names of Austrian yellow and Austrian copper.

Another form, *R. foetida persiana* – alias the Persian yellow – has very double globular flowers and, crossed with Hybrid Perpetuals and perhaps some early Hybrid Teas late in the 19th century, gave rise to the Pernetiana race, of which more later. *R. foetida* has been blamed for the introduction to the West of the black spot fungus disease on roses, and certainly if you read books on rose gardening published prior to about 1900, when *R. foetida* was brought into European breeding lines, there is only a rare mention of the disease. Mildew, yes, again and again, together with some pretty fancy remedies for it, but not black spot. However, it certainly was known earlier, and I think the truth must be that *R. foetida*, a rose which is extremely prone to it, was responsible only for a dramatic increase in the disease as a result of mass hybridization because of the exciting new colours it produced. There are few modern varieties that do not have a trace of this Persian rose in their veins. A loaf of bread and a jug of fungicide would have been a better bet in the particular Asian wilderness from which it came.

Still more or less in south-west Asia (Afghanistan, actually) is found *R. ecae*, upright-growing and early-flowering, its small bright, buttercup-like blooms set against the ferny foliage and chestnut-brown canes, being as dazzling as anything in the spring garden. The name *ecae*, we are told, comes from the initials E.C.A. of the wife of Dr Aitchison, who introduced it in 1880, and it is difficult to think of any other good reason for such an odd name for a rose, for which I have heard more hesitant attempts at pronunciation than there are blooms on 'Nevada'. For some reason early writers (right up to Gertrude Jekyll) claimed that it came from Abyssinia, and certainly it is only completely hardy in reasonably warm climates. Good drainage is essential if it is to thrive.

Turkestan produced *R. fedtschenkoana*, which makes a 2.5 m (8 ft) arching shrub with markedly bristly stems. Discovered in the late 1860s, it is one of the few species which can be said to be really perpetual-flowering, newly formed shoots bearing its single white blooms right through to the autumn. Grey-green leaves are an unusual and added attraction. *R. primula*, whose range extends into the same area, has already been described, but mention should certainly be made of *R. hemispherica* (*R. sulphurea*), in cultivation where conditions suit it (and often, optimistically, where they do not) since before 1625. It is a very warm wall or conservatory rose in northern latitudes, and before the Persian yellow form of *R. foetida* was introduced was the only yellow rose with double flowers of a reasonable size. Unlike the latter, it is sweetly fragrant, for the name *foetida* is an indication that the scent of that group is a strange one, though I would by no means classify it as foetid. Still, it

Plate III: Gallica roses (overleaf)
'Officinalis' (left hand page, top left) is the apothecary's rose, so called because it was grown, from at least the 16th century onwards, largely as a medicinal plant. It may well also be the red rose of Lancaster, and from it sported the striped 'Rosa Mundi' (left hand page, top right) – named, it is said, after Fair Rosamund, mistress of Henry II. These two, together with 'Charles de Mills' (right hand page, bottom left), make quite small, bushy, upright shrubs, the latter's flat, quartered, crimson-cerise flowers being quite unique. 'Tuscany' (left hand page, bottom left), 'Cardinal de Richelieu' (left hand page, bottom right) and 'Camaieux' (right hand page, bottom right) are a good deal more lax and spreading, with 'Camaieux' making the smallest bush of the three and the other two giving us some of the darkest colourings among the old roses. 'Scarlet Fire' (right hand page, top left) and 'Complicata' (right hand page, top right) are two hybrids by no means typical of the Gallica family, being very large and spreading and more nearly resembling species. Both can be used as semi-climbers or for rambling through other shrubs.

will open its flowers in the northern airs, which *R. hemispherica* will rarely do, making one wonder how the old Dutch painters managed to contend with it, for they featured it, along with Centifolia and Alba roses, in many of their masterpieces of the 17th century.

Not so very long ago I would have had some hesitation about including the musk rose, *R. moschata*, here. The English name has been given to so many roses, from *R. arvensis* (probably) to, at the other extreme, a number of small-flowered climbers from the Far East. In fact, at one time it seemed to be given to almost any rose with a sweet smell, but a lot of work has been done, notably by Graham Thomas, in trying to sort things out. It does now seem that the true musk rose is a western Asian, strong-growing if rather lax shrub with branching heads of creamy-white single flowers that come into bloom exceptionally late. The scent is, not surprisingly, outstanding and has been passed on over the years to many fine garden hybrids, both shrubs and climbers, though the link between it and the so-called Hybrid Musk group would appear to be tenuous to say the least if the sketchy material available as to their origin is true.

The following description of the musk rose, written in 1844 by Robert Tyas (Fellow of the Royal Botanical Society) under the heading *Capricious Beauty*, is of interest even if there must be, I suppose, at least an element of doubt as to just which rose he was talking about. He says: 'This species lacks freshness. Its mean flowers would be entirely without effect if they did not grow in panicles, containing from twenty to one hundred or more. They please by their fine musky odour, exhaled from their white blossoms in the autumnal months. It is said to be a native of Barbary, and is found wild in the hedges and thickets of the Kingdom of Tunis. This plant seems full of caprice. It languishes suddenly in situations which at first appeared most favourable to its growth – one year it displays innumerable bouquets, the next it may not flower at all.' It should be remembered that this was written at a time when the big and sumptuous blooms of the Bourbon roses were beginning to be considered the only kind worthy of growing.

A most attractive but not very well known, almost thornless, 2 m (6 ft) species of fine arching growth comes from the Himalayas. This is *R. webbiana*, discovered in 1879, which bears on its purplish-red canes some of the most enchanting lilac-pink 5 cm (2 in) flowers, which appear almost to be luminous on a dull day. It should be much more widely planted and is perfectly hardy. *R. macrophylla*, from the same region, comes into my selection mainly by virtue of the fine wild form 'Master Hugh', which has an upright habit, few thorns, pink flowers, and perhaps the largest orange-red hips of any wild rose. The variant *R. macrophylla coryana* appears in the McGredy breeding line of the series of 'hand-painted' Floribundas that started with 'Picasso'.

Having now encircled the globe we come finally in this round-up of representative species to a final three which are of uncertain origin and which may even be garden hybrids. *R. × dupontii*, possibly a musk rose crossed with a Gallica or a Damask, was named after M Dupont, Director of the Luxembourg Gardens in Paris and one-time head gardener to the Empress Josephine at Malmaison. It may actually have been raised there, and makes a big, loose-growing shrub, 2 m (6 ft) tall and as much across, with 8 cm (3 in) flowers, fragrant and paling from blush-pink on opening to creamy white. They are borne in clusters in the second half of the summer. *R. × macrantha*, or simply 'Macrantha', as it is sometimes known, makes a spreading, mounding bush with flowers even larger than those of R. × dupontii – up to 10 cm (4 in), fragrant and again pink, fading to creamy-white. Two good forms are 'Lady Curzon' and 'Daisy Hill', to which should be added the rather different 'Raubritter'. This has the same spreading habit as the others, but has pink, cupped, rather globular blooms, reminiscent of the Bourbon 'La Reine Victoria' but smaller.

And so we come to the last in my list, R. × paulii (white) and its pink and slightly less vigorous form R. × paulii rosea, which for sheer wealth of bloom at their peak are hard to match. Flower form and leaves are undoubtedly Rugosa, and the other parent is thought to be R. arvensis. Spreading and mounding like 'Macrantha', it will rarely exceed 1.2 m (4 ft) in height, but will cover some 4.5 m (15 ft) of ground all round. It has truly formidable thorns.

THE
CULTIVATED ROSES

For some modern roses it is possible to trace a 'family tree' fairly accurately from generation to generation back over many years, but as we progress along the various and more and more diverging lines, guesswork begins to take over. Eventually, all one can say is that such and such a rose is, because of botanical characteristics, probably or certainly an Alba, say, or a Damask, without having any idea of which specific roses were its parents. This is not simply because no records of it were kept, but because in the early days nobody knew how to create a rose by deliberate planning.

For the technique of hybridizing, see page 263. Nowadays new introductions are produced by transferring by hand the pollen of one chosen rose to another under carefully controlled conditions. The process takes place under glass, and temperature and humidity are carefully regulated to achieve the maximum ripening of the seed and to prevent disease, but the practical application of these ideas only began early in the 19th century. Even then, knowledge of what was involved spread slowly. Nurserymen did not rush to find out all about it. They were doing all right as they were, though most of their new varieties were the result of natural crosses that took place quite haphazardly in the open in the nursery fields. Later, varieties chosen as parents might be planted close together in the hope that nature would do what was wanted, and undoubtedly this must have worked at times. Just the same, nobody could be certain that another rose altogether, planted perhaps at a considerable distance, was not involved instead of the planned one, or that one of the chosen variety had not fertilized itself. A large number of the roses raised in this way were marketed, though customers were not always too happy with the results, particularly when virtually identical varieties were sold by different firms (and even sometimes by the same firm) under different names. There was no such thing then as the registration of new roses, which came along much later to prevent this kind of thing happening.

Even with modern methods, rose breeding is a very unpredictable business, and the odds against producing something really new and worthwhile are enormous. I have seen them quoted as 20,000:1, though how this was worked out and by whom is wrapped in mystery. Probably it was just an intelligent guess, and it cannot be too far out, for with the rose we are dealing, as has been seen, with something whose ancestry has ingredients resembling a gipsy's stewpot. Anything may have gone into it, and anything might come out.

Although rose varieties were eventually grouped according to their botanical characteristics, this does not always simplify matters to the untrained eye. The habit and/or appearance of a particular group from the past can suddenly emerge in whole or in part in a variety belonging to another group generations later. Or two roses which seem on the surface to be completely different may well be hybrids of the same group, a situation that can best be illustrated by an example.

'Complicata' is a great romping, arching rose, which will scramble up through surrounding shrubs if you let it, and on its own will grow fully 2 m (6 ft) high and more across. All along its branches it has saucer-sized, single pink flowers which pale almost to white in the centre and have an eye of golden stamens. A marvellous species, or something very close to it, one would say; it has all the qualities. But it is in fact a Gallica hybrid, listed sometimes as *R. gallica* 'Complicata', and typical Gallicas, if there can be said to be such a thing, are short-growing, upright, rather twiggy shrubs, displaying their semi-double or double flowers well above the foliage – as instanced by *R. gallica officinalis* or its striped sport 'Rosa Mundi'. Burgundy-red 'Charles de Mills', another Gallica, has the habit of growth of the last two, but the flower formation is entirely different – very double, opening flat, with the multitude of petals infolded. And so it goes on.

Hopefully I have by now established something. It will appear at times in what follows that I am contradicting myself or even, I hope on rare occasions only, talking complete nonsense, but this will not necessarily be so, as should be clear from the above. The odd statement or two may possibly cause the botanical Mafia (under Godfather Linnaeus) to clench its teeth and stomp around a bit, but in case any of its members should feel inclined to give me a real drumming about any point I make, I can only say (to bring all gardeners to my side) that it was not I who changed *Iris stylosa* to *Iris unguicularis* or made cosy old japonica (as generations of British gardeners have called the flowering quince) first into *Cydonia* and then into *Chaenomeles*. My aim is to try to make an incredibly involved subject as clear as possible without confusing either the reader or myself any more than can be helped.

Probably the best plan will be, first of all, to follow the main line of development from the Gallicas to the Hybrid Teas of today. On the way, this will bring in the China roses. Then we will link up with the Albas, Centifolias and Moss roses, which followed a different path, and say something more about the Rugosa family and about the Climbers, Ramblers and Floribundas, and last of all about the enchanting Miniatures.

The Gallicas

It all starts, then, with the Gallicas, about which I have said a good deal already, though a brief recap may be useful. It is almost certain that there was a species Gallica, though it no longer survives. Where there is a species, from which the first botanical description was made, this is also known as the type plant. Where there is no definite species, the description may be taken from the earliest known member of the family, which becomes the type plant, and this

Plate IV: Damask roses
The 'Autumn Damask' ('Quatre Saisons'; top), though not in the forefront as a garden shrub because the flowers are rather formless, played an important role in rose history. Almost all repeat-flowering roses have its blood in their veins. 'Mme Hardy' of 1832 (below left) is a much later hybrid, and one of the most lovely white roses ever raised, though matched in the pink colour range by 'Celsiana' (centre right) of at least 100 years earlier. The unique, crimson-flecked petals of 'Leda' (bottom right) led to it being given the common name painted Damask.

For a listing of Gallica varieties, see page 99; for illustrations, see plate III (pp50–51).

is so with the Gallicas. In this case it is a low-growing and rather sprawling shrub with single, bright pink flowers, but it is not of much garden interest. However, there have been countless hybrids, and the oldest one we know which has really made its mark is *R. gallica officinalis*, with glowing, deep pink semi-double flowers, the petals surrounding golden stamens. This is the apothecary's rose, and was very likely the red rose of Lancaster.

It and its closely related forms were the roses most widely distributed throughout the ancient world in the West, and probably varied somewhat from place to place according to local conditions. It is thought that the rose depicted in the frescoes in the Minoan palace of Knossos in Crete is a Gallica, and the Romans, Greeks and later Egyptians knew it as *R. sancta*. Perhaps they chose it for cultivation not solely because of the attractions of its flowers, but because of its handy size and habit of growth. Also it could be propagated easily from suckers and was not too fussy about the kind of soil in which it grew. It would fit happily into the courtyard of a Greek or Roman villa, and having bristles on the stems and only a very few thorns, would be unlikely to grab out at wind-blown togas.

·*R. gallica officinalis* has appeared in the past under a number of names in addition to those already given, and this has led to some confusion. *R. rubra* was one; *R. provincialis* another, and the red Damask yet a third, under which name it was known in England for something like 300 years. The closely related Gallicas and Damasks often became muddled, and as recently as 1936, in Bunyard's *Old Garden Roses*, there is still a rose described as *R. gallica damascena*, so the confusion lasted a long time. To be fair to him, Bunyard does point out in the text that the rose he is describing probably had a Damask origin. However, under whichever name takes your fancy (except, of course, Damask) you can take it that *officinalis* does represent a typical early Gallica, rarely topping 1–1.2 m (3–4 ft) in height, with many quite slender and twiggy canes coming freely from the base of the plant. The buds, carried upright on stiff, wiry stems, have the characteristic Gallica roundness and short calyx. The leaves are rather rough, and do not have the refinement of most of the old groups of roses.

Most of the Gallicas we grow now are much later introductions, in a number of which the darker tones of maroon and purple have appeared (as in the variety 'Tuscany') together with a much more lax habit in some cases. It is generally said that, alone among the old rose groups, there is no white Gallica, but I have found a reference to one in *Cultivated Roses*, published in 1899 and edited by T. W. Sanders, who was then editor of *Amateur Gardening*. It was called 'White York' and there must be a suspicion that the classification is not correct. One of the earliest and best-known Albas, *R. × alba semi-plena*, is known as the white rose of York and it should be, but is not, in the list of varieties given by Sanders. On the other hand, 'White York' is described as dwarf, which *R. × alba semi-plena* certainly is not. It is a bit of a puzzle, but one's doubts increase on finding in the same list *R. alba* (without qualification as to variety) classified as a China rose and, under the Gallicas, *rose des peintres*, which is the popular French name for one of the Centifolias.

R. gallica officinalis has a famous sport called 'Rosa Mundi' (*R. gallica versicolor*), which is identical in habit but has the gayest flowers with deep pink stripes and splashes on the palest of blush-pink petals. Legend has it that this rose was named after Fair Rosamond, who was mistress of Henry II, but as he dates from the 12th century and the first written record of 'Rosa Mundi' is from the 16th, we must let our sense of romance overcome any scepticism if we are to accept this as being so. Sometimes 'Rosa Mundi' carries the odd branch or two with the deep pink flowers of the parent, and occasionally it will revert completely.

From the 18th century onwards, intensive breeding of Gallica hybrids took place in the Netherlands and Germany, and in the 19th century enthusiasm for them spread to England, Italy and France. The Empress Josephine is believed to have had no less than 107 varieties in her garden at Malmaison, where Redouté painted many of them. Only a comparatively small number of those he depicted have survived, and among the most fascinating-sounding losses must be the group with blue-tinted leaves, such as his *gallica caerulea* (for which name there is no botanical authority).

To allow for a breather, I have deliberately kept yet further names for *officinalis* to the end of this account of the Gallicas. In the state of Virginia in America in the old days it was known as the tulip rose, and in Mrs Keays' book on the old roses she tells the story of one plant of it being 'rescued' from the advancing British armies during the War of Independence; it was transplanted to a Richmond garden, after which it was renamed the Offley rose. And 'Rosa Mundi' was sometimes called, both in America and elsewhere, 'Village Maid'.

The Damasks

For a listing of Damask varieties, see page 100; for illustrations, see plate IV (p55).

The Damask roses have, like the Gallicas, already appeared from time to time in our snipe-like progress through history. They, too, are of great antiquity, but botanical analysis has shown them to be offspring of the Gallicas, so they do not go back quite so far. There have been two distinct lines of Damask development, resulting from different crosses. The Summer (early-flowering) Damasks were the result of a cross between a Gallica and the species *R. phoenicia*, the Phoenician rose, a climber of the *R. multiflora* type with large corymbs of small white flowers. The 'Autumn Damask' (we only know of one) came from a Gallica and *R. moschata*, the late-flowering musk rose, and is more or less perpetual in its blooming – as has been seen, it is the only Western rose, apart from its sports, to be so. Botanically it is *R. damascena semperflorens* or *R. × bifera*, and in more popular parlance the four-seasons rose. Probably it is pre-Roman in date, and it is thought to have grown at Pompeii, which may prompt the question: Could it not be the twice-flowering rose to which Virgil referred as flowering at Paestum? It could be, of course, but it does seem rather unlikely as the pink flowers are of very poor quality and would hardly have been an attraction for the kind of mass production of blooms that went on there. Nowadays it is a curiosity rather than a good garden plant, and it occasionally throws sports of the equally undistinguished 'Quatre Saisons Blanc Mousseux' or 'Perpetual White Damask Moss'. The moss on this is brown and rather harsh and bristly, very unlike that on the more numerous Moss roses descended from the Centifolias. The flowers are small, pink-flushed early and then white, and always poorly shaped. I know this to my cost as it was once supplied to me as 'Shailer's White Moss', which is a very different cup of tea.

This may be thought of, so far, as a very unenthusiastic introduction to the Damasks, but the picture will change when we come to the summer-flowering kinds. The 'Autumn Damask' obviously survived through the

centuries because of its unique recurrent habit, and it was lucky in the long run that it did so, for very shortly will be seen the part it was to play in the story of the present-day roses. The word damask usually conjures up a vision of richness of texture, which is often associated with deep, dusky reds and purples. The texture is there in the petals of the Summer Damasks, together with a sumptuous fragrance, but not the dark colourings such as one finds in some of the later Gallicas. The majority are in shades of pink, so the association in this case is purely in the mind, derived from the colourings sometimes found in Damask cloth and tapestries which bear the same name.

According to Graham Thomas, the oldest Damask rose known is probably the kind grown in the fields of Bulgaria, discussed some pages back, and the 'York and Lancaster' rose, which has been known since 1629 and so is almost as old as the Bulgarian variety and may be a sport from it. However, if we do take these as the originals, it is very difficult from looking at them to trace any close resemblance to many others in the group. Damasks vary more than any other group, and some that are usually classed as such have, because of obviously mixed ancestry, characteristics that appear on the surface to move them far from any direct line of descent. However, in general it can be said that they are considerably taller and more lax growers than the Gallicas, with their flowers tending to nod rather than be held upright as in the latter family. They are certainly more thorny, and the leaves downy and less rough. The hips are long and narrow, compared to the rounded ones of the Gallicas, and there is not the same tendency to sucker. Probably the Gallicas are among the hardiest of the old roses, which is worth noting if you live where a real winter freeze-up occurs. There will be little damage in temperatures as low as −15°C (5°F), but the Damasks would suffer. This is especially so with the 'Autumn Damask', which may have problems in surviving at −12°C (10°F).

Omar Khayyam knew the Damask rose and asked that 'My tomb shall be in the spot where the North wind may scatter roses over it', and a rose tree was planted on his grave at Naishapur. A hip of this rose was brought to England in due course and sent to Kew Gardens. There the seeds were germinated and the rose was shown to be a Damask, now available under the variety name 'Omar Khayyam'. A bush of this was later planted on the Suffolk grave of Edward FitzGerald, the translator of the Rubaiyat. Shakespeare, too, knew the Damask, as evidenced by this couplet from *Twelfth Night*:

> Concealment, like a worm i' the bud,
> Fed on her damask cheek.

Plate V: China roses
'Old Blush' (top left) is also known as 'Parsons's Pink China' and the monthly rose, the latter because of its perpetual-flowering habit. It is one of the oldest Chinas, brought to the West in the 18th century. 'Fellemburg' (top right) and 'Hermosa' (bottom right) are hybrids of about a century later, but still have the typical, light, airy growth of the group. The fourth rose, 'Mutabilis' ('Tipo Ideale'; bottom left), is a China of unknown age and origin, with flowers remarkable in that they open flame-coloured and pass through buff-yellow and then pink to crimson.

But despite its undoubted qualities and appeal to the poets, this group of roses never seems to have become a popular favourite, at least in modern times. Early on it spread quite widely, and the first one to reach the American continent may have been brought to California by the Spaniards. Its popular name, rose of Castile, suggests a Spanish origin, though *Modern Roses 7* simply says of it: 'A name applied to the Damask rose.'

By 1841 William Paul's catalogue listed 23 varieties, but this had fallen to five in 1864. In *Cultivated Roses*, out of a list of 2,128 roses altogether, there are only seven Damasks. These include five that we still grow today – 'La Ville de Bruxelles', 'Leda', 'Mme Hardy', 'Mme Zoetmans' and 'York and Lancaster' – together with 'Panachée de Lyon', which is now considered to be one of the closely related Portland rose group but which was early on called a Perpetual

Damask. The seventh rose in the list is 'Mme Stolz', which seems to have vanished, but the 'Autumn Damask', the most important of all, for some reason appears only in its white Moss rose form, while 'Hebe's Lip' appears as a Brier. Strangely there is no mention of such beauties as 'Ispahan', 'Marie Louise' or even 'Blush Damask', unless I have failed to find them under other names. A modern gardener would certainly do better than this meagre seven, for discerning individuals have kept others going from which they are now propagated once more.

There is one Damask, however, that would not appear in any early list, for it was found as a chance seedling in 1950 in a Yorkshire garden. This is 'St Nicholas', with the most beautiful semi-double flowers in clear pink, followed by a good display of red hips. Otherwise there have been no new Damasks for many, many years and no one tries to breed them now.

The first roses from China

It is at this point, with the old Damasks established and growing well, that the cultivated roses from China really enter the story, though they will do so in two stages, the Tea or Tea-Scented roses coming rather later than the others. The first to arrive in Europe were sent to Sweden in 1752 by Peter Osbeck, a friend of Linnaeus. The roses were 'Old Blush China', also known as 'The Monthly Rose' and many other names indicating its ever-blooming habit, and R. × odorata, which will figure later when I come to the story of the Tea roses. Both of these were purchased from a nursery in Canton, and specimens were sent to England shortly afterwards, but though they were noted as novelties and established at Kew Gardens in 1769, nothing very much resulted. It was not until some time later that people began to sit up and take notice of what they had got and realize what it might lead to.

In those days the journey from China to Europe was a long one, taking months rather than weeks, and it was common practice for specimen plants to be rested during the journey in India, at the Botanical Gardens in Calcutta. When they continued on their way and finally arrived in the West, this led to some confusion among those whom one would have thought should know better, and the China roses ended up under the classification R. indica rather than R. chinensis. At a more popular level they were known as Bengal Roses or, in France, as roses de Bengale, under which name they are featured in Redouté's plates and in other works of the period. Thus it was that a rose called R. indica semperflorens came to England from Bengal in 1792, introduced by G. Slater, a director of the East India Company. It became known as 'Slater's Crimson China' and, in 1793, 'Old Blush China' was reintroduced by Parsons and became 'Parsons's Pink China'. Here is an 1844 description of 'Slater's Crimson China' from The Language of Flowers. Notice the reference, even at this considerably later date, to Indian skies and the fact that the year given for its introduction does not tally exactly with what is now known. Clearly, however, the rose was enjoying considerable popularity. The heading for the extract is Beauty Ever New:

> This is an ever-blooming evergreen shrub, attaining the height of ten feet; bearing beautiful crimson flowers from January to December. Leaves are ovate-lanceolate. This plant, so frequently seen clustering round the cottage porch, as well as in the immediate outskirts of busy smoky towns as in the remotest vales, was originally brought to England in 1789. It was then thought so delicate as to

For a listing of China varieties, see page 100; for illustrations, see plate V (p58).

Plate VI: Hybrid Perpetuals
The immediate forerunners of the Hybrid Teas, this is a group that only gradually evolved from the Bourbons through an extra infusion of China rose blood. They vary widely both in growth and flower form, some – like that fine white rose 'Frau Karl Druschki' (top right) – being rather tall and leggy. It much resembles a Hybrid Tea and is sometimes listed as such, but that cannot be said of 'Reine des Violettes' (bottom right), which is bushy and has flowers like a Gallica. The fine pink 'Mrs John Laing' (bottom left) is shorter in stature than some, while 'Général Jacqueminot' (top left) was much used for breeding and appears in the lineage of many of the red roses we grow today.

require the constant heat of the stove, and small cuttings were sold for several guineas each. This was soon found not to be necessary; and in a short time, almost every country casement was ornamented by this Chinese beauty; until our cottagers, wanting means to purchase flower pots, planted them in the open ground; where persevering in the habits of the warmer climate, they quickly surpassed, in strength and beauty, all the inmates of the gardens in which art supplies the fervour and the force of Indian skies.

This is the earliest flowering rose; and in mild seasons, when planted against a wall, will sometimes flower at the beginning of April; and, being protected by glass in autumn, or aided by artificial heat, may be continued in bloom until Christmas.

On their reintroduction, the possibilities of these two roses as breeding material to be introduced into the once-flowering European groups was quickly realized. Their habit of growth was much less robust than the roses already grown, but the fact that they flowered early and then kept on and on, together with the novel colour of 'Slater's Crimson China', were revolutionary features and led to their rapid spread into the rest of Europe and to America not long after 1800. Nevertheless, the most important step towards perpetual-flowering Western roses took place neither in Europe itself nor in the United States, but on the French Ile du Bourbon, right in the middle of the Indian Ocean, which you will find on maps nowadays under the name Réunion.

The Bourbons and Portlands

It was here that some China roses had been planted in a hedge, in all likelihood with the 'Autumn Damask', which itself would stagger fitfully into autumn with a few blooms. Chance hybrids resulted, and the seedlings were seen by a French botanist called Bréon, who sent seeds of them back to France in 1819. Thus was created a new race of roses which combined the vigour of growth and toughness of the Damasks with the novel properties of the Chinas – and had bigger and more sumptuous blooms than either. The first of the Bourbon roses had arrived, then known incorrectly as *R. borboniana*.

For listings of Bourbon and Portland varieties, see pages 102 and 103; for illustrations, see plates XVI and XVII (pp98 and 101).

At much the same time, late in the 18th or at the very beginning of the 19th century, another chance cross came about, possibly between the 'Autumn Damask' once more and *R. gallica officinalis*. This time it occurred in Italy, and resulted in another race of repeat-flowering hybrids. Samples taken to England were named after the then Duchess of Portland and became the Portland Roses, which, you will recall, also went under the name Perpetual Damasks. They were a fine group, not always as tall-growing as the Bourbons, but no more than a dozen of them have survived. It was the Bourbons that took over, probably because of the size and energy of the French nursery trade at the time, which concentrated on them to the exclusion of everything else. Of their immediate forebears, 'Parsons's Pink China' (or 'Old Blush China', if you prefer) has remained in cultivation in a small way for those who know a good rose when they see it, but 'Slater's Crimson China' was thought to have vanished until it was rediscovered growing in Bermuda in 1957.

Many hundreds, if not thousands, of Bourbon rose varieties were raised and put on the market, the majority in France as their names testify. Their appeal was not only in their robust growth – most of them did make big shrubs – and not only in their remontant habit, but also in the huge, many-petalled, rather globular flowers, opening in many cases cupped, and usually breathing the fragrance that had come to them from the Damasks. Their colour ranged from the crimson-purple of 'Prince Charles' through the glowing cerise-pink of 'Mme Isaac Pereire' to the pure pink of 'La Reine Victoria' and the shell-like, blush-pink petals of its sport 'Mme Pierre Oger'. 'Boule de Neige' of 1867 was white, and there were others with flowers splashed and striped a deeper pink or maroon on a pale pink or white ground, such as 'Commandant Beaurepaire'. The last, incidentally, was one of a number that betrayed their ancestry by being once-flowering only. Some others did have a rather unreliable second flush, while some (and 'Mme Isaac Pereire' was an example) bore their best flowers in the autumn. On the whole, however, this wonderful new race of roses behaved well and flooded into gardens everywhere.

Their popularity lasted well into the late 19th century and a reasonable selection of the best has survived. In 1921 'Ferdinand Pichard', perhaps the last of the race, was raised in France. It has enchanting white flowers, striped crimson, reminiscent of 'Honorine de Brabant', and blooms well into the autumn. Rather strangely it appears in G. A. Stevens's book *Climbing Roses*, listed as a Wichuraiana Rambler, and of it he remarks, 'Interesting to a collector of freaks'. All I can say is that I do not agree! Had he actually seen it, I wonder? As a matter of fact, while it is certainly not a rambler, there is some doubt about its classification. It is one of the in-between roses, sometimes listed as a Bourbon and sometimes as a Hybrid Perpetual.

The Hybrid Perpetuals

For a listing of Hybrid Perpetual varieties, see page 103; for illustrations, see plate VI (p61).

The Hybrid Perpetual roses followed the Bourbons and the Portlands, and in the story of their origin it seems that confusion reigns. On first investigation it seemed to be quite straightforward, but I have been taken to task in the friendliest way by Mr Humphrey Brooke, who has researched the subject very extensively, for (deliberately) simplifying things in my book *Shrub Roses for Every Garden*. There I provided a chart that showed the parents of the Hybrid Perpetuals as being Bourbon × Portland and rashly appended the date of 1837 to the Portlands. In a letter to me, Mr Brooke points out:

> The Portland Rose was certainly in Dupont's garden by 1809, and the varieties whose seed was used by the French nurserymen such as Laffay (to raise Hybrid Perpetuals) were much later ones, eg, 'Brennus' (1830). The date 1837 is especially misleading in this context since that is the year when the first of Laffay's *Rosiers Hybrides Remontantes*, 'La Princesse Hélène' was produced. In addition to the Portlands and Bourbons, Hybrid Chinas (as summer-flowering crosses between the Bourbons and Gallicas were then called) are important ancestors of Hybrid Perpetuals. Probably other groups were also used. William Paul in *The Rose Garden*, 1848, described how Laffay alone raised 200,000 seedlings in a year to produce his HPs, and it is hardly credible that only the Portland and Bourbon contributed. The point is even more complicated than you suggest, since Dr C. C. Hurst in Graham Thomas's *The Old Shrub Roses* describes 'Rose du Roi' (an important Portland, variously stated as being introduced in 1812, 1816 and 1819) as the first Hybrid Perpetual. He has been followed by other authorities . . . but it is worth noting that this presumed Hybrid Perpetual appeared several years before the Bourbon. I have written the above to stress that the origin of the Hybrid Perpetual is not a simple matter.

It looks as if this is where the knives come out, but the truth of the matter is that in the early 19th century, after the coming of the Bourbon and the Portland roses, nurserymen, particularly in France, were crossing everything in sight with everything else (including the Chinas) and in most cases only had the sketchiest idea of which rose had resulted from which cross. It is as certain as anything can be that Laffay's 200,000 seedlings were not the result of careful and planned hand pollination, any more than those of his competitors, and that, at this distance in time, nobody can put his hand on his heart and say that this rose or that one was the very first of this new family. There are almost as many theories as there were varieties of Hybrid Perpetuals.

Nevertheless, despite this haphazard approach to things, a number of good roses did result. 1824 saw 'Lilacé' from Vetillard and 1827 the pale pink 'Félicité Boitard' from Noisette (whose brother was to give his name in due course to a race of climbers). It was followed in 1828 by Menard's deep pink 'Olivier de Serres'. Others working in the field were Prévost and Vibert, who went on to market many fine roses, but these early Hybrid Perpetuals (before about 1837) had flowers lacking the substance of the later ones and their remontancy was poor. 1843 saw the introduction of Laffay's rosy-pink 'Rose de la Reine' (later shortened to 'La Reine'), which was a great step forward, and also Desprez's 'Baronne Prévost' in a paler colouring; its qualities were such that it has survived to the present day. These later introductions flowered well into the autumn and were followed by others as good or better, such as 'Géant des Batailles' in crimson-purple and the velvety-red 'Général Jacqueminot' of 1846. All these gave rise to good seedlings, especially the latter, to which can be traced directly a large number of the red roses we grow today.

Despite their name, the Hybrid Perpetuals – even the best of them – were not perpetual in their flowering by modern standards. They bloomed in summer and then in most cases there was a long gap before the autumn flush – and sometimes, as with their Bourbon ancestors, this was not as good as it should have been. However, when the flowers did come they were large by the standards of the time and tended to be globular or 'cabbagey' before they became full-blown. With the deep pink 'Paul Neyron' of 1869 they reached a size bigger than most Hybrid Teas of modern times. In their growth, many of them had a tendency to send up very long canes in late summer, and these bore flowers in small clusters only at their tips the following year. The answer was to peg these canes down; to bend them over and to tie the tips to pegs driven into the ground all round the plant, or to a wire frame, so that the side buds would break. These formed flowering shoots all along the canes in much the same way as will happen on a climber that is trained horizontally to make flowering growth low down.

The results of this practice, carried out in many a Victorian and Edwardian garden, helped the Hybrid Perpetuals to achieve enormous popularity on both sides of the Atlantic, and they were also used extensively for exhibition when rose shows first became popular in the latter half of the 19th century. Probably something of the order of 2,500 varieties altogether were put on the market until they gradually merged with and were ousted by the Hybrid Teas. But even as late as the turn of the century there were 826 varieties given in a list in my possession.

The colours of the Hybrid Perpetuals ranged from white, through pale and deep pink to red, violet, maroon and purple. Two varieties, 'Baron Girod de l'Ain' (1897) and 'Roger Lambelin' (1890), were a deep, dusky crimson with petals flecked white along the edges, something that has not been achieved in a rose since. Of the whites, Robert's 'Hélène Marette' of 1850 was probably the

Plate VII: Pernetiana roses
These were the first bright yellow cultivated roses. They were named after the French nurseryman Joseph Pernet, who originated them by crossing Hybrid Perpetuals and others with the Persian yellow, R. foetida persiana. 'Soleil d'Or' (bottom) was the first to be put on the market in 1900, to be followed by 'Rayon d'Or' in 1910. These early ones were not, however, very robust, and it was not until Dickson introduced 'Mrs Wemyss Quinn' (centre left) in 1914 that any of the Hybrid Teas among them could be called strong growers. 'Lawrence Johnston' (top) is a climbing member of the family, and 'Réveil Dijonnais' (centre right) a comparatively modern shrub rose or semi-climber.

first to achieve complete purity without shadings of pink or lavender. The well-known pure white, scentless 'Frau Karl Druschki' ('Snow Queen') did not come along until much later, in 1901, and some people maintain that it is a Hybrid Tea anyway. All in all, quite a wide range of colours, but there were no yellows until . . .

The coming of the yellow garden rose

The longing for yellow garden roses was nothing new. Parkinson, who goes back to 1629, had this to say: 'Some again doe advise . . . to make Roses bee yellow, that you should graft a white Rose (some say a Damaske) upon a Broome stalk, and the flower will be yellow. Some affirm the like, if a Rose be grafted on a Barberry is yellow.' He seems to have taken the information from Gerard, and goodness knows where Gerard got it from, but this strange belief in grafting to produce unlikely qualities in plants was strongly held in the early days, despite what must have been the evidence of their eyes if anyone actually tried it. Grafting a rose on to a holly by 'putting a rose-bud into a slit of the bark and so put clay and mosse, and bind him featly therein' would, it was said, make an evergreen rose.

However, one man at least held no such beliefs: Joseph Pernet of the nursery trading as Pernet-Ducher at Lyon in France. He was one of the few in the 1870s to be carrying out a systematic breeding programme and, following suggestions made by Jean Sisley in the *Journal des Roses* of 1877, he started work with the double yellow form of the species *R. foetida*, *R. foetida persiana* or the 'Persian Yellow'. Neither the species nor its sports are easy to breed from, as they are largely infertile, though Pernet's patience and persistence proved that they are not entirely so. After years of work, he first achieved results in 1891, using as a seed parent the purplish-red Hybrid Perpetual 'Antoine Ducher'. This produced a rose that was pink on the inside of the petals and yellow on the outside, but it was a chance find a year later among his other seedlings that was to be the real breakthrough. This was 'Soleil d'Or', orange-yellow with sometimes the odd splash of red inside and a yellow reverse; it had the flower form of a typical Hybrid Perpetual, and went on the market in 1900.

In the case of 'Soleil d'Or', 'Antoine Ducher' is likely to have been the parent at one remove, for the new rose was repeat-flowering. A first-time cross between a once-flowering rose like the 'Persian Yellow' and a repeat-flowering Hybrid Perpetual would only produce a once-blooming hybrid, as had been the case with Pernet's earlier rose. This may have provided a self-sown seedling (that is, a second-generation one) which resulted in the remontant 'Soleil d'Or', the first of a race to become known as the Pernetiana roses, though as we have seen it was not the first pure yellow garden rose. This was to be 'Rayon d'Or', of which 'Soleil d'Or' was one parent, and which was put out by Pernet-Ducher in 1910.

As the late Norman Young has pointed out in *The Complete Rosarian*, it has often been said that *R. foetida bicolor* (red, with a yellow reverse) was a parent of our modern bicolor roses, but there is no evidence to support this. In fact the first of these was 'Juliet', which resulted from a cross between the Hybrid Perpetual 'Captain Hayward' and 'Soleil d'Or' itself, which was carried out in England at William Paul's nursery. However, as *R. foetida bicolor* was a sport from the pure yellow *R. foetida*, as was the 'Persian Yellow', obviously the bicolor potential was lurking not far below the surface.

The Pernetianas are not listed separately in chapter 2; for a listing of some of the varieties, see pages 142 and 146; for illustrations, see plate VII (overleaf).

An American grower, the late Roy Hennessey, has written that Pernet's greatest contribution was not in producing the first of the Pernetianas but in his work to improve the breed afterwards. For his early yellow roses were far from being robust and healthy plants, and in all but the mildest climates the soft, sappy wood would as often as not die back to almost nothing each winter. Also they were by no means colour-fast, the yellow tending to fade to a creamy-white in the sun – a habit still to be found in many modern yellows that have descended from them. Hennessey's book *Hennessey on Roses* is great fun to read as well as being informative, for he is no respecter of other authorities where he does not agree with them. One wishes that his imaginary roses such as 'Golden Globule', 'Exploding Star' and 'Climbing High' really were on the market.

Up to 1914, the Pernet-Ducher nursery was the only one to offer yellow roses for sale, and they showed a steady improvement, even if the yellow still lost its first brightness. Apart from 'Rayon d'Or', varieties like 'Le Progress' (which brought him into the Hybrid Tea era), 'Mrs Aaron Ward' (1907), 'Souvenir de Claudius Pernet' (1920), 'Le Rêve' of 1923 (which was a climber and sister seedling to the rose now known as 'Lawrence Johnston') and 'Julien Potin' ('Golden Pernet') followed. 'Souvenir de Claudius Pernet' was named in memory of one of Joseph Pernet's sons, killed in the First World War. It proved a failure in the English climate, where the blooms often failed to open, but elsewhere, notably in parts of North America, it produced 108 worthwhile seedlings and is regarded as a very important parent in the story of the modern Hybrid Tea.

One among many who entered the fast-growing competition for the yellow rose market after 1914 was Alex Dickson in Ireland. He put out in that year the canary-yellow 'Mrs Wemyss Quin', the first yellow rose in which real hardiness and strong growth were achieved. Encouraged by the progress being made, the public welcomed the new colours, and breeders everywhere crossed the Pernetianas with a multitude of other varieties of every colour combination then known. As a result, roses with orange- and flame-coloured petals emerged for the first time, as well as further bicolors, all of them going back in their ancestry to that one French nursery and one rose. However, the mixing of the Pernetianas with other strains, especially the rapidly rising Hybrid Teas, caused their features to become so diffused that they vanished as a separate race. Only occasionally is the term now used.

However, Pernet himself continued to thrive and, except in 1918, his roses were awarded the Bagatelle Gold Medal, the premier French award, each year from 1916 to 1926. His 'Mme Edouard Herriot', or the 'Daily Mail Rose' (still grown nowadays, though mainly in its climbing form), was the first rose to achieve a colour break to a most attractive pale orange-terracotta. I still have it as a bush, and it probably produces more flowers per flush than any of my other Hybrid Teas, though they are not of a good shape by modern standards. It also has more and bigger thorns than any other.

With the 'Daily Mail Rose' we are actually going back quite a few years from the most recent date I have mentioned, for it arrived in 1912. This is deliberate, as we have in one sense got somewhat ahead of ourselves. It is time to talk about the Tea roses, and their story covers much the same period as that of the Hybrid Perpetuals. The development of the Hybrid Teas which followed them also parallelled the Hybrid Perpetuals' later period.

Roses from China – the second stage

The Tea roses were the second of the very important introductions from China to which I referred earlier, and once again we have a case of 'Wake up at the back there, Sweden!', for they arrived in that country as early as the middle of the 18th century. But that was that. It was not until 1810 that things began to move after Sir Abraham Hume of Wormley Bury in Hertfordshire received a pale pink, ever-blooming semi-double rose from an agent of the British East India Company in Canton. He called it 'Hume's Blush Tea-scented China' in honour of his wife, who was a botanist in her own right, and it was given the specific name of *R. odorata* because of its scent. This, and that of the other Teas, was supposed to resemble the aroma of freshly packed tea, which was also being imported from the East, and has variously been described as emanating from the leaves and from the petals of the flowers. I must confess that, having smelled both, I find this description quite baffling, but Tea roses they became and Tea roses they have remained.

The second Tea to arrive in England was brought by John Dampier Parks, who was collecting plants, mainly chrysanthemums, in China for the Royal Horticultural Society in 1824. This became known as 'Parks's Yellow Tea-scented China', for it had pale yellow double flowers. It turned out to be a much more prolific breeder than 'Hume's Blush' and was actually introduced as the first Tea rose. Certainly it was the first to found a dynasty, and though other Chinese roses followed, such as the not-very-vigorous climber *R. odorata major* and the salmon-yellow *R. odorata indica*, 'Hume's Blush' and 'Parks's Yellow' were the two most important.

The Teas had long pointed buds, large leaves for a China rose, and a delicate refinement in their flowers and colourings that was new. However, they were nothing like as hardy as the earlier 'Parsons's Pink' and 'Slater's Crimson' Chinas and needed considerable protection in their new northern European homes. This was, however, not a bar to their popularity, for those were the days when roses were grown mainly by people in large country houses who had no need to count their small change, and who could afford the building of large conservatories and greenhouses. And an added attraction of the Teas was that they were remarkably healthy, in common with others from the same part of the world.

The breeding of new Teas of European origin was soon under way, and in France (almost inevitably) the lilac-pink 'Adam' appeared; this is usually described as the first Western Tea. A good many earlier ones have, however, been recorded from as far back as 1821, but 'Adam' was the first to have at least part of its pedigree known. It came from 'Hume's Blush' and (it is said) the original Bourbon rose, but the first Tea to have been hand-pollinated – from 'Parks's Yellow' and the lilac-pink Bourbon 'Mme Desprez' – was Beauregard's deep saffron 'Safrano' of 1839. 'Hume's Blush' is still in cultivation as a collector's piece, but 'Parks's Yellow China' has unfortunately vanished, though its beauty can still be appreciated in the lovely plate of it in Redouté's *Les Roses* under the name *R. indica sulphura*. In 1841 'Devoniensis', the first Tea of English origin, appeared; it was also the first one to produce a climbing sport in 1885.

Teas were extensively grown for the cut-flower trade, though one imagines that they must have been wired to be successful in this, because if they do have a fault it is that their flower stalks are weak so that they tend to hang their

For a listing of Tea roses, see page 105; for illustrations, see plate XVIII (p104).

Plate VIII: Early Hybrid Teas
'La France' (top), appearing in 1876, is generally considered to have been the first Hybrid Tea, though Hybrid Perpetuals continued to be the most popular roses for quite a long time after this. It was only on looking back that it was realized that a new race had emerged almost unnoticed, with 'La France' as its tardily recognized herald. 'Mme Edouard Herriot' ('The Daily Mail Rose'; bottom right) shows well the rather thin and formless flowers of many of the Hybrid Teas of the early part of this century, but was a prizewinner in its day and the first rose in shades of terracotta and pink. It is still popular as a Climber, as is 'Crimson Glory' (centre left), which for many, many years held pride of place as a dark, dusky-red bedding rose.
See also plates IX, XIX, XX, XXI and XXX (pp73, 108, 112, 113 and 145).

heads. As pot plants they were the rage on both sides of the Atlantic, and they could, of course, be grown out of doors in the southern United States; on occasion they reached a stature there quite unknown anywhere else, where they could hardly be described as vigorous.

An attribute often credited to the Teas as a class is the classic high-centred shape of their flowers, which came to perfection in the later Hybrid Teas. The Bourbons and most of the Hybrid Perpetuals had short centre petals, which caused the flowers to open cupped or to retain a globular outline if they were so double that they did not open right out. In fact the majority of Teas were exactly the same and only a comparatively small number achieved what we now consider the ideal, before which exhibitors go down on their knees. Notable among these were 'Souvenir d'Elise Varden' and the beautiful pink 'Catherine Mermet' of 1869, which was a great favourite in the United States.

The Hybrid Teas

The Teas reached their peak of popularity about the end of the 1800s, but meanwhile other things had been happening. In 1859 Lacharme, a nurseryman of Lyon, brought out a pink rose called 'Victor Verdier'. If the parentage recorded is correct it was the Hybrid Perpetual 'Jules Margottin' crossed with the Tea rose 'Safrano', which would make 'Victor Verdier' the first known Hybrid Tea. However, this classification had not been thought of at the time, and the new rose was thought to be simply another Hybrid Perpetual. We are, as may be guessed, once again entering an area of considerable uncertainty due to the lack of proper records, and there were probably roses that should have been called Hybrid Teas even before 1859. Many the argument there has been about this, and the Hybrid Teas were not the only case where varieties came into existence which were eventually looked back on as the forerunners of a new race, but were not recognized as such at the time. It happened later with the Floribundas, as will be seen.

It was not, in fact, until 1867 that a rose came into existence, a rose of very high quality, that has come to be regarded by most people as the first Hybrid Tea. This was 'La France', which had beautiful soft-pink flowers, which were globular in shape and far removed from present standards, but which did have the reflexing outer petals which we now accept as normal in the class. It was raised by Guillot in France – though not, it would seem, from a deliberate cross, even though the Hybrid Perpetual 'Mme Victor Verdier' and the Tea rose 'Mme Bravy' are often quoted as its parents. Even the raiser did not agree that this was certain, and the first Hybrid Teas to emerge from a properly controlled breeding programme came from Henry Bennett in England. One of these, 'William Francis Bennett', crossed the Atlantic to great acclaim, and must have been the first fully testified Hybrid Tea to reach the American continent from Europe. 'Lady Mary Fitzwilliam', for long considered the finest Hybrid Tea of all, was another of Bennett's introductions.

From that time the Hybrid Tea, reliably recurrent, elegant of bloom and aided by the colours introduced from the Pernetianas after 1900, swept all before it; the Bourbons and Hybrid Perpetuals vanished like a light snowfall on a sunny morning. A new colour came in the early 1950s with Kordes's 'Independence' (also known as 'Sondermeldung' and 'Renia Elisenda') which, though it turned out a poor variety for the garden in cooler climates, led to the brilliant vermilion of 'Super Star' ('Tropicana') and others. Development goes

For a listing of Hybrid Tea varieties, see page 106; for illustrations, see plates VIII, IX, XIX, XX, XXI and XXX (pp69, 73, 108, 112, 113 and 145).

on, mainly concentrated now on new colour breaks and healthier plants. Other targets are a robust, unfading yellow without the pink flush to the petals' edges, which may well go right back to 'Soleil d'Or', and rain- and mildew-proof whites and deep, dusky reds that do not 'blue' as they age.

The story of 'Peace'

For the listing of this rose and its offspring, see pages 106 to 119; for illustrations, see plate XIX (p108).

But there is one Hybrid Tea that has for over thirty years stood out above all others and as recently as 1976 was voted in an international poll to be The World's Favourite Rose. Its story, the story of 'Peace', has been told many times, but in any history of the rose it cannot be ignored. It would be like recording the history of England and omitting Queen Elizabeth I. It all began with a pale yellow seedling under the code number 3-35-40 in the Meilland nursery at Antibes in the south of France in 1935. This, when grown on and budded onto an understock, was attracting considerable interest among potential distributors by 1939. Distributors, particularly if they come from other countries, do not take whole plants from a raiser of a new variety. They take what is known as budwood – that is, strong canes from which buds can be cut for use in propagation. Budwood of 'Peace' (though it was not yet known as this) was sent to Germany and Italy, though not to England because Meilland had no regular distributor there at that time.

As far as the United States was concerned, the story is that the American ambassador was visiting Meilland's when the German invasion of France had already begun, and asked if he could buy this startling new rose – bigger by far than any other Hybrid Tea of that time – in his own country. He was told that this would only be possible if some way could be found for budwood to reach America despite the disruption of communications that the invasion had brought in its wake. Things happened rapidly, and it left in the diplomatic bag of the American consul in Lyon.

Not wanting a French name for the rose, the German and Italian distributors chose 'Gloria Dei' and 'Gioia' respectively. In France, now isolated from outside contact, it went out as 'Mme A. Meilland' in memory of the raiser's wife. It was in America that the name 'Peace' was chosen, for the Conard Pyle Company began to build up stocks from the budwood they had received of what they could see would be a really great rose. In 1945 they launched it, and not long afterwards at a meeting of the newly-created United Nations in San Francisco, each delegate had placed in his hotel room by the American Rose Society a single bloom of 'Peace' with an inscription which read: 'This is the Peace rose which was christened at the Pacific Rose Society exhibition in Pasadena on the day Berlin fell. We hope that the Peace rose will influence men's thoughts for everlasting world peace.' A truly great rose it undoubtedly was (and is), but a good part of its immense commercial success must be credited to the timing of its release and the happy choice of name. It was 1947 before it could be sold in Britain, but when it was it carried proudly with it the Gold Medal of the Royal National Rose Society – only one in a long line of awards from every country in the world that loves and grows this wonderful rose. Its qualities have been passed on to numerous offspring.

The quest for the blue rose

For listings of some blue varieties, see pages 107, 111, 114, 118 and 132; for illustrations, see plate IX (p73).

There is one aspect of Hybrid Tea breeding that I have deliberately left to the last, separating it out as it does not concern them alone. Floribundas figure in it just as prominently, so that it would fit under either heading equally well. I am talking about the search for the blue rose.

I have never yet met anyone who has said that they would welcome one in their garden, but just the same if a real blue rose were to be put on the market there can be little doubt that the novelty appeal alone would make the raiser rich beyond the dreams of avarice. From this point of view (but no other) I would like to raise one myself, but the chances of success for me – or for anyone else for that matter – are pretty slim. The make-up of the rose lacks an essential chemical ingredient, delphinidin, which gives traditional delphiniums their marvellous colours (though perversely delphinium breeders appear to be intent on breeding in other colours). So it looks as if the blue rose can only arrive through a freak of nature, which is not of course impossible. If it happens in my garden, you will hear about it.

The 'blue' roses raised so far are actually nothing of the sort. The nearest any of them get is a lavender-mauve, and the odd thing is that to achieve this the ancestry of most of them is made up of yellow, fawn, coppery-red and red roses. The majority can trace their family tree right back to the red and yellow species *R. foetida bicolor*, and the orange-red Hybrid Tea 'Charles P. Kilham', which was raised in 1926 of unknown pedigree, figures prominently.

Though there had been the more pink than mauve 'Lilette Mallerin' from France in 1937, the first of what we now know as 'blue' roses to attract serious attention was 'Grey Pearl', which came from McGredy in 1945. It was such a dingy greyish colour that it was known in the nursery as The Mouse, but rose breeders saw it as a colour break towards the goal they were aiming for. They worked with it, and 'Lavender Pinocchio' (with 'Grey Pearl' as one parent) appeared in 1948. Many others followed, successful in varying degrees, until the Hybrid Tea 'Sterling Silver' caught the public imagination in 1957. However, though the flowers were attractive and fine under glass, it turned out to be a poor grower and an unsatisfactory garden plant in many areas.

The same year produced 'Simone' in France, and since that time there has been a string of so-called blues, among them 'Heure Mauve' and 'Lilac Charm' in 1962, 'Intermezzo' and 'Blue Diamond' in 1963, 'Blue Moon' ('Mainzer Fastnacht' or 'Sissi') in 1964 and 'Lady X' in 1966. Others have been introduced since, but 'Blue Moon' – sweetly scented and with fine, high-centred blooms and reasonably strong growth – and 'Lady X' have still to be bettered. But even they are not blue. Maybe everyone should go back to the Moors who, as William Paul reported, were said to have had blue roses which 'were obtained by watering the plants with indigo water. . . . A French writer, Marquis d'Orbessan, states that he saw them.'

The Albas

Having reached the present day with the Hybrid Teas, there are still some subsidiary but nonetheless important early lines to be followed. Most of them have been touched on already from time to time, but they must be amplified if a true picture of the rose in history is to be given. As a matter of fact, in the case of the Albas, what we know about their early history has been covered, but as the facts are scattered about a marshalling of the main ones may help.

They are certainly of great antiquity and were in cultivation in Greek and Roman times. Their botanical characteristics, and those which the layman can see in the form of leaves, hips and habit of growth, indicate a Damask rose and

Plate IX: Blue roses
Not blue, of course, nor anything really near it, the roses in this plate represent the efforts made by hybridizers to reach a most unlikely goal. In 1945 the strange colouring of 'Grey Pearl' (top left) gave some encouragement that success might be on the way (though to the layman it is difficult to see why) and work continued using it as a parent, together with many other roses.
In 1964 'Cologne Carnival' (bottom right) appeared, and also what is probably the best 'blue' rose so far – the sweetly-scented Hybrid Tea 'Blue Moon' (top right). Two years before this the red stamens and single flowers of the low-growing and bushy 'Lilac Charm' (bottom left) gained it considerable acclaim among the Floribundas, though it needs partial shade to keep its colour.

For a listing of Alba varieties, see page 119; for illustrations, see plate XXII (p117); see also plate XV (p94).

For a listing of Alba varieties, see page 119; for illustrations, see plate XXII (p117); see also plate XV (p94).

R. canina (the dog rose) as parents of the first Alba, so only the Gallicas and Damasks are of greater age in the list of cultivated varieties. Of the oldest Albas, the 'Great Double White' (*R.* × *alba maxima*) is also known as the Jacobite rose, as it was the badge of Bonnie Prince Charlie and his followers. The very similar semi-double form, *R.* × *alba semi-plena*, is thought to be the white rose of York, and was one of the varieties used at one time for the extraction of attar of roses. Parkinson described the Albas as the 'most ancient and knowne Rose . . . King of all the others'. They may have originated in the Crimea, where they have been reported growing wild.

Despite their name, there are more Albas nowadays in blush-pink like 'Maiden's Blush' and pink like 'Königin von Dänemark' than in the pure white of the first two mentioned. The flowers are generally double, on fine upstanding bushes that will reach 2 m (6 ft), though one or two, such as the hybrid 'Félicité Parmentier', raised in 1836, will keep to about 1.2 m (4 ft). The leaves, of a soft grey-green, are in all the Albas an outstanding attribute and an asset to any general shrub planting. They are, too, singularly disease-free.

The Centifolias

For a listing of Centifolia varieties, see page 121; for illustrations, see plate XXIII (p 120).

Botanical analysis has shown that the Centifolia roses originated in a cross between the 'Autumn Damask' and an Alba rose. Thus they have in them a mixture of two species, the dog rose and *R. phoenicia*, and both Gallica and Damask strains, which confusion is reflected when one looks at early attempts to classify them. Even discounting the much earlier belief that they were a species in their own right and were the 'hundred-leaved' roses of Theophrastus and Pliny, they were variously described by 17th- and 18th-century botanists and writers as a form of Gallica or Damask. Additional complications still arise because, while the Gallica is the rose of Provins, the Centifolia is known as the rose of Provence, though I have not been able to discover why.

Probably the first Centifolias appeared at the end of the 16th century and were developed, largely in Holland, over the next hundred years or so, explaining why they figured so largely in the paintings of the Dutch masters. However, their progress must have been carried out by careful selection rather than by cross-breeding, for the Centifolias are almost sterile as a race. On the other hand, they throw out bud-sports with considerable freedom, and it was on these that the Dutch concentrated until the great Holland rose became a popular name. It has not stuck, but one which has is the cabbage rose, which is much less appropriate. The typical, sweet-smelling Centifolia bloom is, at least in its early stages, globular or goblet-shaped, with an open centre of short petals. Unless cabbages have changed over the years, the Hybrid Perpetual flower, with its closed centre, is much more like a cabbage at the same stage of development.

Though they vary and there are some quite small Centifolias – reasonably compact and almost rockery plants – and some much larger, in the main they make 1.2–1.5 m (4–5 ft) rangy shrubs with long, thorny canes of lax growth which need support if they are not to be borne down by the weight of the flowers. These nod and must be seen from underneath for their full beauty to be appreciated, and the big and rather coarse leaves droop as well. Altogether, they behave rather like the characters in an Ibsen play, except that they have not, as far as is known, a frustrated desire to reach St Petersburg! Quite a lot of skill is needed in the garden to display many at their best, though others (such as the lovely blush-pink 'Fantin Latour') are much more upright and need little attention. All of them, despite the drawbacks of some, have had their devoted followers over the years on both sides of the Atlantic.

The Moss roses

For a listing of Moss varieties, see page 121; for illustrations, see plate XXIV (p123).

As you read the following, try to guess the speaker:

> He walked past the couch to the open window, and held up the drooping stalk of a moss rose, looking down at the dainty blend of crimson and green. It was a new phase in his character to me, for I had never before seen him show any keen interest in natural objects . . .
>
> 'Our highest assurance of the goodness of Providence seems to me to rest in the flowers. All other things, our powers, our desires, our food, are really necessary for our existence in the first instance. But this rose is an extra. Its smell and its colour are an embellishment of life, not a condition of it. It is only goodness which gives extras, and so I say again that we have much to hope for from the flowers.'

Believe it or not, this is Sherlock Holmes giving, in *The Naval Treaty*, the one indication I know of in any of the stories that he was even aware that nature existed. He was speaking, of course, at the time when the Moss rose was at the height of its popularity, for these roses will long be associated in people's minds with the coloured cards and valentines – and the gardens – of the Victorians, even though the first mention of a Moss rose goes back to France in the late 17th century. They had reached Holland by 1727 and were in England not long after that. Varieties from Europe reached America in colonial times.

The first Moss roses, kinds like R. × *centifolia muscosa* and R. × *centifolia muscosa alba* (variously known also as 'Shailer's White Moss', 'Clifton Moss' and 'White Bath') were direct sports from the Centifolias, while the later varieties were sports from the early Mosses themselves. In general terms, their characteristics are the same as the Centifolias, except for the mossy, glandular growth on the flower stalks and sepals. This is usually green, but on some varieties brown, and it gives off a distinctive scent, particularly when crushed gently between the fingers. The colour range of the petals is from white, through pink and what could be described as the nearest to scarlet-pink among the old roses (in the variety 'Henry Martin' of 1863), to dusky purples. Possibly as an inheritance from the white Moss sport of the 'Autumn Damask', a few such as 'Salet', 'Mousseline' and 'Mme Delaroche Lambert' have a sporadic autumn flowering, but they could not be said to be truly remontant.

The Rugosas

For the origins and introduction of Rugosas, see pages 41 and 42; for a listing of Rugosa varieties, see page 122; for illustrations, see plate XXXIII (p185); see also the section on roses for hedges (p183).

The early history of the Rugosas has already been told in the section on species, but when R. *rugosa* did arrive in Europe its purplish-red rather loosely-formed flowers, which did not last when cut, were not popular. Despite its other fine qualities of vigour, dense bushy growth, handsome disease-resistant leaves, a sweet scent, a spectacular display of hips in late summer and autumn, and the fact that throughout the summer it was seldom out of flower, it was almost a hundred years before much notice was taken of it. Then breeders in France and America began to experiment and found that it was an easy rose to hybridize with others, even though many of the resulting varieties were sterile so that no further progress with them could be made.

During this century, work has been done with Rugosas in Germany, where the parent rejoices in the somewhat peculiar name of potato rose but where its hardiness in the cold winters was seen as a great asset – as was also the case in Canada and the northern states of the United States.

Two distinct groups of hybrids have been produced, one closely resembling the species in flower form, leaves and habit of growth. Examples are the white 'Blanc Double de Coubert', the single pink 'Frau Dagmar Hastrup' (or Hartopp), the wine-red 'Roseraie de l'Hay' and the deep crimson-purple 'Hansa', which was raised by Schaum in Holland in 1905. In the second group the influence of other roses seems to be the stronger – sometimes, for instance, there are smoother leaves and much more substantial flowers. These may even rival those of a Hybrid Tea, as in that lovely but gaunt-growing, back-of-the-border hybrid 'Conrad Ferdinand Meyer' and its sport 'Nova Zembla'. Almost alone among roses, Rugosas have produced (in the Grootendorst range) varieties with clusters of small flowers with the petal edges pinked like a carnation. These are quite well known, but there is another, by far the most attractive, with a blush-pink delicacy which 'F. J. Grootendorst' and 'Pink Grootendorst' lack. This is 'Fimbriata', also known rather charmingly as 'Phoebe's Frilled Pink' or as 'Dianthiflora'. It is, surprisingly, a cross between *R. rugosa* and the white-flowered Noisette Climber, 'Mme Alfred Carrière'. For some reason it is rarely listed by growers.

The Polyanthas and Floribundas

The group of roses known nowadays as Floribundas took a good many years to catch the imagination of the rose-buying public. It was in 1924 that a Danish breeder named Svend Poulsen put on the market the first rose to resemble the Floribunda as we know it. The variety was called 'Else Poulsen' and it was followed by 'Kirsten Poulsen' later in the same year. At that time these roses were known as Hybrid Polyanthas.

Most of the early Hybrid Polyanthas had single flowers. There were some that were semi-double, but not more than one or two had the full complement of petals of a double bloom, and though they flowered in great profusion and repeated much more quickly than the Hybrid Teas, single flowers in a rose have never for some reason been really popular. So the Hybrid Polyanthas made comparatively slow progress, and it was not until after the Second World War, when Eugene Boerner of the United States introduced his new semi-double and double varieties like 'Masquerade' and 'Fashion' that they began to sweep the board and, in some countries, outsell the Hybrid Teas. In the meantime, they had gone through two name changes, often being called (incorrectly, as you will see) Polyantha roses before the American-inspired term Floribunda – more commercially attractive than Hybrid Polyantha – was universally adopted.

So many of the landmarks in rose breeding took place in France that it is not surprising to find that the story of the Floribunda starts there. The French breeder Guillot (who raised the first Hybrid Tea, 'La France', in 1867) crossed a Japanese species rambler, *R. polyantha* (known now as *R. multiflora*), probably with one of the China roses. *R. polyantha* carries large clusters of small white flowers, which attribute was passed on to the new type of rose that he produced. The first of these, a small bush and not a rambler, was 'Ma Paquerette' of 1875. He called it a Polyantha rose and the group was developed rapidly – or at least rapidly in rose-breeding terms – until the pink 'Orleans

Plate X: Polyantha roses
These had a considerable vogue between the two World Wars as small, cluster-flowering bedding roses, but the coming of Floribundas – with their larger flowers in a wider colour range, more healthy foliage and stronger growth – led to the almost complete eclipse of the Polyanthas. Two roses of the type, 'The Fairy' (bottom left) and 'Cécile Brunner' (top left), are still popular, though neither of them is a true Polyantha, unlike 'Eugenie Lamesch' (bottom right), which came very early on and is one of the few yellows. The later 'Orleans Rose' (top right) perhaps had more influence on their development than any other. 'Baby Faurax' (centre left), having largely run its course in the garden, has taken on new lift in being used in the breeding of a number of modern roses, including the lovely 'Yesterday'.

For listings of Polyantha, Floribunda and Grandiflora varieties, see pages 124 to 139; for illustrations, see plates IX, X, XI, XXV, XXVII, XXVIII, XXIX and XXXV (pp73, 77, 80, 126, 135, 138, 141 and 200).

Rose' of 1909 really put them on the map. Short and bushy growers with sprays of small and often globular flowers – which gave them the additional name of Poly-Pompons – the Polyanthas were enormously popular in the early part of this century, though a tendency to mildew was a serious draw-back with many of them. A few survive today, of which 'The Fairy' (1932) is probably the best and is still well worth growing – though in fact a sport of the Rambler 'Lady Godiva' rather than being a direct descendant of *R. polyantha*.

Inevitably the Polyanthas underwent experimentation, and Joseph Pernet was one of the first to try to combine their features with those of larger-flowered roses such as the Hybrid Perpetuals. An early result was 'Mlle Bertha Ludi', and this was possibly the first of what would have been called Flori-bundas if the name had been invented then. Others came from Germany, and one of them, 'Annchen Muller' of 1906, is still around if you look hard enough. Another, from three years later, is easier to find, and is in fact becoming quite popular as its fine qualities as a bedding rose are recognized once again. This is the beautiful low-growing cluster rose called 'Grüss an Aachen', which has large very double flowers of the old-fashioned kind in flesh-pink, fading almost to white. It is usually included in the category we are talking about and is certainly more Floribunda than anything else in habit, but its immediate parents were actually a Hybrid Tea and 'Frau Karl Druschki'.

Svend Poulsen, the Danish breeder mentioned earlier, realized the potential of these little roses and worked for a long time in crossing various Polyanthas with Hybrid Teas in an effort to increase the size of both the bush and the flower while at the same time retaining the cluster-flowering habit and cold tolerance. In 1912 came his first real success with 'Red Riding Hood' ('Rödhatte'), though it took until 1924, as already seen, to achieve commercial acclaim with 'Else Poulsen'. Many other varieties followed and for a time practically every Hybrid Polyantha on the market was of his raising – so much so that they were sometimes known as Poulsen roses. Notable names of the period were 'Anne Poulsen' and 'Karen Poulsen', together with two non-Poulsen varieties, 'Donald Prior' and 'Betty Prior', raised in England.

There were also notable Polyantha sports from a rose called 'Echo', itself a remontant dwarf sport from the climber 'Tausendschön'. 'Echo' was intro-duced in 1914 by Lambert, and from this sported 'Greta Kluis' in 1916, beginning a series of roses sporting from each other and culminating in 'Anneke Koster' in 1927, pink 'Dick Koster' in 1929, and finally the orange-salmon 'Margo Koster' in 1931. The last two especially are still popular in the United States, both for the garden and as pot plants, though not so well known now in Europe.

'Echo' also played its part in the first rose actually to be called a Floribunda. This was 'Rochester', a fragrant buff variety with an orange-carmine reverse, raised by the late Dr J. H. Nicolas of Jackson and Perkins in 1934. It was a cross between 'Echo' and the Hybrid Tea 'Rev F. Page-Roberts', and the blooms were so unlike the usual Hybrid Polyantha of the time, being high-centred like those of a Hybrid Tea, that it was decided that it was really a new type. The name Floribunda was chosen, though it had no botanical validity, and it was not until several years later that it was officially recognized by the American Rose Society and the late 1940s before it was used in England.

From the 1940s onwards, another important series of these roses, mostly with large semi-double flowers, was produced by Le Grice of Norfolk, in

England. They included 'Dainty Maid', 'Bonnie Maid', 'Dairy Maid' and 'Dusky Maiden', and they played a big part in increasing the popularity of this type of rose. In the late 1940s came the revolutionary new double and semi-double Floribundas from Boerner of America, 'Goldilocks', 'Masquerade', 'Fashion' and 'Spartan', the last three also bringing new colours to the rose scene on top of their other virtues.

Through the crossing of Floribundas with an ever-widening range of Hybrid Tea varieties, the flower size was increased, though there was a tendency for fewer flowers on the truss. In many of the new roses each individual flower took the form of a Hybrid Tea in miniature (as can be found in such varieties as 'Sea Pearl') and since some Hybrid Teas do bear a number of flowers per stem, it has gradually become more and more difficult to separate the two. In Germany, their country of origin, 'Fragrant Cloud' ('Duftwolke') and 'Stella' are, for example, classified as Floribundas, though they are considered Hybrid Teas elsewhere.

In Britain, the large-flowered Floribundas have been given the rather clumsy name of Floribunda Hybrid-Tea-Type, and in the United States the taller-growing varieties became Grandifloras. 1954 saw the start of this with the large-flowered and spectacularly tall china-pink 'Queen Elizabeth', which has proved to be one of the most widely planted roses ever. Strangely enough, when it was entered for the All-America Rose Selection trials, it failed to receive an AARS recommendation because it was considered to be a Hybrid Tea and, as such, was too tall to be desirable. However, in recognition of its outstanding qualities, it was made the first of a new class, Grandiflora roses, and re-entered in the trials; a well-deserved recommendation followed.

All too often one hears people say that modern roses cannot match the old ones for scent. In fact, many of the old roses were scentless, and it is only the scented ones that we remember. Some have probably survived in cultivation because of this quality alone. Nevertheless, the Floribunda must take a good deal of the blame for the present-day impression held by so many people. *R. polyantha* is scented, but it seems likely that the other parent of the Polyanthas – probably a China rose – was not. Not many Chinas are noted for their fragrance, and it may well be that, at least in part because of this ancestry, few Floribundas (with notable exceptions, such as 'Elizabeth of Glamis', 'Chinatown' and 'Arthur Bell') have much fragrance. The enormous and ever-growing popularity of the group has led to the idea that nearly all modern roses are scentless, but there are many Hybrid Teas as strongly perfumed as any rose of the past. Moreover, there are signs that scent is being bred back into the Floribunda strain, which will be a bonus all will welcome.

Still looking to the future, the tendency towards larger flowers seems likely to continue, and the term Floribunda may well eventually disappear. All roses, whether Hybrid Teas, Floribundas or shrubs, that bear a number of flowers on each stem will be known simply as cluster-flowering roses; this move is already being discussed at international level. Otherwise, development is likely to be concentrated on new colours and colour combinations. Already a startling breakthrough has been made by the Irish breeder McGredy (now living in New Zealand) with the Floribundas he calls 'hand-painted'. These have variable carmine patterning on silvery-white; 'Picasso' was the first of them, and 'Matangi' so far the best. The American Hybrid Tea 'Double Delight' represents a similar breakthrough.

For listings of Hybrid Musks and other modern shrub roses, see pages 139 and 140; for illustrations, see plates XII, XXIX and XXXV (pp83, 141 and 200); for their uses in the garden, see page 202.

Other shrub roses

Apart from the climbing roses and the Miniatures – whose stories I have left to the end – we are now just about up to the present day in rose history, but I have said very little about modern shrub roses. They are, however, a mixed bag, some descended from old roses and some simply extra-large Floribundas or Hybrid Teas, and there really is no one characteristic which would make them easy to group together. All that would emerge if I tried would be a series of descriptions of individual roses, and I think that these descriptions, or as many as there may be room for, would be more helpful if included when I come to discuss the roses' use in the garden (though some are listed in the next chapter). Just the same, there is one group which does form a distinct family and which cannot be left out of this survey, the Hybrid Musks.

They were given this misleading name by the man who raised them, the Rev Joseph Pemberton of Havering in the county of Essex. His book *Roses, Their History, Development and Cultivation* was published in 1908, which is a pity for it was too early for him to give an account in it of his breeding work. Even the second edition, where a few of the earliest ones are described, says nothing about their background, but some industrious research work has been done by others. From this it is clear that, although the musk rose does figure in the family tree, it only does so some eight generations before the first of the Pemberton roses, and only then because they are descended, as are many other roses, from 'Champney's Pink Cluster' and the Noisette Climbers (which are, to put it mildly, a long way away; over the horizon, really). All the Hybrid Musks may have inherited from their distant forebear is the sweet musk scent of a number of them.

Plate XI: Hybrid Polyanthas
Crossing Polyantha roses with Hybrid Teas resulted in what were first known as Hybrid Polyanthas, but in due course their name was changed to Floribundas. However, it is 'Gruss an Aachen' (top) of 1910, a rose of different parentage but with a Floribunda style of growth, that is considered by some to be the first of the race.
Whether or not this is so, it is a fine rose, but it was 'Else Poulsen' (bottom) and 'Kirsten Poulsen' (centre left) of 1924 which really established the Floribunda as we know it and led to the avalanche of varieties that followed. 'Pinocchio' (centre right), and other roses like 'Fashion' brought double flowers and played an important part in the development of this type in the United States.
See also plates IX, XXV, XXVII and XXVIII (pp73, 126, 135 and 138).

More immediately, Pemberton's roses came from crossing a German rose called 'Trier' with a number of Hybrid Teas, and later with some of his own earlier varieties. 'Trier' was raised in 1908 by Peter Lambert, and was possibly a seedling of a yellow Rambler called 'Aglaia', which Lambert had introduced in 1896. It was a strong, 2–2.5 m (6–8 ft) shrub with semi-double scented blush-pink flowers which shaded to yellow at the petal bases, and was one of a small group known as the Lambertianas, which never achieved much popularity outside Germany.

The results of Pemberton's work were interesting and varied, and between the blush-pink 'Daphne' of 1912 and the salmon-pink 'Felicia' of 1928 he introduced a range of sweet-smelling, very free-flowering and recurrent garden shrubs which in many ways has not been surpassed. The colours varied from the creamy-white of 'Pax' through shades of apricot and pink to the light crimson of 'Nur Mahal'. On many of them truly enormous heads of flowers are produced, especially in the autumn. In a way, they could be said to resemble giant Floribundas, though in many cases they tend to spread out more widely.

'Penelope' is perhaps the best-known and most widely planted of the original Pemberton range, but other breeders since his time have carried on with his work with varieties like 'Wilhelm' of 1934 and 'Will Scarlet' of 1950, which introduced crimson and scarlet colourings respectively, while 'Buff Beauty' added a warm apricot-yellow. In 1954 came the purplish-lilac 'Magenta' from Germany, and the soft pink 'Belinda' and dark red 'Rosaleen' were added by J. A. Bentall, who took over Pemberton's breeding programme after the latter's death.

RAMBLING AND CLIMBING ROSES

It is argued that no rose is a true climber as they do not twine round their supports or make use of tendrils or aerial roots as other climbing plants do. But the more vigorous climbing roses do not go 12 m (40 ft) or even more up a tree by levitation. They hook their ice-axe thorns over twig and branch, and on these haul themselves towards the sky. Tendril or thorn, their function is the same. To me, a climbing rose is a Climber – if, that is, it is not a Rambler, which also climbs. At which point we enter into an area of confusion to one and all. 'How do you tell a Climber from a Rambler?' is a question very often asked, so some sort of definition may be useful at this stage. It must be qualified in all sorts of ways, as will become evident, but in very general terms the answer to the question is as follows.

Ramblers are once-flowering, the blooms being small (sometimes tiny) and carried in clusters or trusses which open comparatively late in the summer. Long new canes with small, glossy leaves grow from the base of the plant in the second half of each year (when the flowering is over) and these bear the best flowers the following summer. The old canes gradually die away. 'Dorothy Perkins' and 'Minnehaha' are long-established examples, and they are hybrids of the species *R. wichuraiana*. This is late-flowering and has single white flowers. It came from eastern Asia in 1891 and is by nature a creeping rose that will spread widely, low over the ground, rooting from the tips of the canes as it goes; but it will scramble up through other shrubs if given the chance. To go back to what I was saying just now, a clematis, tendrils or no, would fall flat on its face if it, too, had nothing to support it.

There is a second quite large group of Ramblers which complicate things by making some new growth from the base but also sending out long, vigorous shoots from higher up. The flowers on these are larger and the clusters smaller, and a few of them do produce the odd bloom or two after the first flush, which tends to be earlier than with the first group. Examples of this kind are 'Albéric Barbier' (1900), 'Emily Gray' (1918) and 'Albertine' of 1921, and the reason for the difference is that they are hybrids from a different species, *R. luciae*, though this is closely allied to *R. wichuraiana* and was at one time thought to be the same.

There are other, more technical characteristics. Practically all Ramblers are what is known as synstylae, meaning that the styles of the flowers are merged into one column above the ovaries. It is from this central column in each flower that the scent comes, and not from the petals as in other roses. It floats freely in the air, too, so that you do not have to bend close to appreciate it.

Climbers have larger flowers and leaves than the Ramblers, may be one-blooming or recurrent, and they make a permanent framework of canes, on the side-shoots of which the flowers are borne. On some varieties a certain amount of new growth will come from low down, on others none. 'Galway Bay' (recurrent) and 'Elegance' (non-recurrent) are climbers. The latter particularly has flowers of Hybrid Tea size and quality. The American Rose Society regards Climbers and Ramblers slightly differently. It recognizes three types of climbing roses: Ramblers with long flexible canes and small flowers borne in clusters; Large-Flowered Climbers, with stiff canes and large flowers borne

Plate XII: Hybrid Musk roses
'Prosperity' (top left), 'Penelope' (top right) and 'Vanity' (bottom right) belong to the Hybrid Musk group raised early this century by the Rev Joseph Pemberton, though they have little but their scent to link them with the true musk rose. They make wonderful hedging shrubs, though 'Vanity' is perhaps a little on the open side and needs to be planted fairly closely. All have two main flushes of bloom, with some flowers appearing in between. The low-growing and very bushy 'Ballerina' (bottom left) came in the late 1930s. It was raised by Pemberton's successor, J. A. Bentall, and though its flower heads are very different from the others, it seems likely that it was a development of work started during the raising of the first group.

in loose clusters; and Pillar Roses, which cannot usually support themselves but do not make excessively long growth and are best used on pillars.

When a rose has the word 'Climbing' added before its name, as in 'Climbing Crimson Glory', it usually means that it is a sport of the bush variety, being derived from a cane that suddenly had the urge to reach for the sky. There are a few exceptions, however, such as 'Climbing American Beauty', which is not derived from 'American Beauty'.

These then are the main groups that most people are likely to see at their local nursery, though the range of Ramblers is likely to be very small. But for the enthusiast there are a number of other races from the past, both Ramblers and Climbers, that are still worth growing, and there are a few roses which stand on their own and do not fit into any group classification. These include the Ayrshire Ramblers, the Noisettes, the Boursault roses and, as an example of a lone customer, the Banksian rose in its various forms, the botanical origin of which is uncertain. All these and some others have their part to play in the story of the rose as a climbing shrub.

The Ramblers

Because they are only once-flowering, and many need special protection from cold in severe climates and are prone to mildew and other diseases, Ramblers are not grown very much nowadays. Possible exceptions are when they are used as weeping standards or tree roses, or in the case of some of the more exuberant varieties, for growing up trees, for which their pliable canes make them ideal. But early in the 19th century they were a brand-new novelty and became enormously popular – remaining so for many years – as they had added a new dimension to rose growing, even if they did have drawbacks.

For a listing of Rambler varieties, see page 142; for illustrations, see plate XXVI (pp130–131) and the photographs on pages 157 and 181; for uses of Ramblers, see page 183.

Two groups were on the scene very early, firstly the Ayrshire Roses, which have had a brief mention already when I discussed the species *R. arvensis*, of which they were hybrids. They were first raised in the 1820s by a breeder named Martin in Dundee, Scotland, from seed that is said to have been imported from America, though *R. arvensis* is a native of Europe. The true Ayrshires bore their mainly white flowers singly, though later hybrids took on a cluster-flowering habit. Among the best were 'Dundee Rambler', with very double flowers, edged pink, the pure white 'Bennett's Seedling', which Thomas Rivers commented on for its toughness in any situation in the garden, and a rose of Rivers's own raising, the dark red 'Ayrshire Queen' (which derived its colour from the Gallica 'Tuscany').

The second early group started its existence in France about the same time as the Ayrshires, and was derived from *R. sempervirens*. Blush-pink 'Adelaide d'Orleans' was one of the most sought after, but of all these roses the one from the second group that has outlasted them all is 'Félicité et Perpétue', still a favourite though dating from 1827. It was raised by A. A. Jacques, gardener to the Duc d'Orleans at Château Neuilly, and named after the Carthaginian martyrs St Felicitas and St Perpetua. Almost evergreen, it has fragrant white double flowers, which it has passed on to its perpetual-flowering dwarf (60 cm; 2 ft) Polyantha-type sport, 'Little White Pet'. In this feat it is not alone among the once-flowering ramblers, for 'Dr W. Van Fleet', a hybrid of *R. setigera*, sported the wonderful repeat-flowering Climber 'New Dawn' in the United States in 1930. 'American Pillar', also a *R. setigera* hybrid (with *R. wichuraiana* and a red Hybrid Perpetual), is another one which has had tremendous staying power, despite its rather harsh and strong pink colouring, but it did not see the light of day until 1902.

R. wichuraiana, together with *R. multiflora* (which we have met already under its other name of *R. polyantha* in the story of the Floribundas), are both extremely hardy and both have enormous families of hybrid Ramblers descended from them. They did not, as species, reach the West from the Far East until the 1880s, though actually there was a *multiflora* hybrid in both Europe and America as early as 1817, even if nobody knew what it was at the time. It had been raised and cultivated in Chinese gardens and was called the 'Seven Sisters Rose', the flowers of which had (and still have) blends of seven colours, from dark lilac-pink to blush-lilac.

However, it was not until over seventy years later that the two species, together with *R. luciae*, began to show what they could do. *R. wichuraiana* far outstripped the others as a favourite among breeders of the time, though *R. multiflora* was the parent of many fine roses such as the fragrant white 6 m (20 ft) 'Rambling Rector', 'Seagull' and the less vigorous 'Goldfinch' of 1907, with clusters of yellow blooms fading rapidly to cream. Sometimes 'Crimson Rambler' is classified as a *multiflora* rather than a *wichuraiana* hybrid, and the answer is that it may have been a cross between the two. This kind of thing happened many times, if not with the species at least with their hybrids, so that placing many in an exact category is difficult to say the least. There is one distinction, however, that the *multifloras* have to themselves, and this is that they alone produced varieties in shades of mauve and purple. The clusters of small flowers on 'Veilchenblau' of 1909 are possibly the nearest to blue of any rose in their later stages, though they open dark magenta, and 'Violette' is crimson-purple with yellow stamens. *R. multiflora* has in its time been extensively used as an understock for other roses.

These, then, are the groups of what might be called the average garden Ramblers, but there are a number of very vigorous species, almost all from the Far East, that can be grown in a garden large enough to cope with their profligacy of growth. The majority have enormous clusters or corymbs of small white flowers, rich in scent, and the biggest can envelop and smother a 9 m (30 ft) tree in a few seasons. These include the Himalayan musk rose (*R. brunonii*) and its very fine form 'La Mortala', which was introduced by A. E. Bunyard after he saw it growing in the Italian garden of that name, *R. filipes* (grown mainly in the superior form 'Kiftsgate') which came from western China in 1908, the late-flowering *R. longicuspis* (which must wish with all its heart that it had been given another name), *R. helenae* from central China (1907) and a number of other roses which are closely allied to and often known as Musk Roses. Not all are completely hardy except in mild winters.

The Climbers

For a listing of climbing varieties, see page 143; for illustrations, see plates XIII, XXX and XXXII (pp87, 145 and 179); see also the photographs on pages 152, 218, 225 and 229; for the uses of Climbers, see page 178.

There is a close link between the early climbing roses and the Ramblers, and frequently the two were intermingled. An example of this is the Noisette group, which are classed as climbers though the original Noisette was raised in 1811 from the China rose 'Old Blush' and the Musk Rose, one of the synstyle Rambler family. A rice grower by the name of John Champney from Charleston in the state of South Carolina was the man who did it and the rose was called in consequence 'Champney's Pink Cluster'. Actually it was more of a strong-growing shrub than a climber and seldom produced a worthwhile second crop of bloom, but from it a nurseryman friend of Champney called Philippe Noisette raised a seedling which became the paler pink 'Blush Noisette'. This, being a second-generation cross from a once-flowering and a repeat-flowering rose, was itself recurrent, and Philippe offered it to his nurseryman brother Louis in Paris, France, who distributed it, and it was in France that the main development of the Noisette rose took place. One of Redouté's most popular plates features 'Blush Noisette' under the name *R. noisettiana*, so it must have been one of the roses in the Empress Josephine's garden at Malmaison, where he did his flower painting.

The Noisettes started life as pink roses, so it is rather strange that the only survivors in this colour seem to be the two American originals. Most of those we now know – many dating from very early on – are white, cream or varying shades of pale orange-yellow, like 'Lamarque' and 'Desprez à Fleur Jaune'. This is a result of 'Parks's Yellow Tea-scented China' being introduced into the breeding line about 1830. White 'Aimée Vibert', with its rich scent, was a little earlier than this in 1828, and the rather tender and less vigorous 'Céline Forestier' in pale yellow followed in 1842.

Nobody, least of all a rose breeder, can let well alone, and hybridizing began between the Noisettes, Bourbons, Hybrid Perpetuals and Tea roses. The proof of how right they were to do so is to be seen in the two most famous results, 'Gloire de Dijon' of 1853 and 'Maréchal Niel', which came eleven years later. If you can get hold of a good strain, the former is still magnificent, with large scented, buff-yellow Tea-type flowers which are among the earliest to open and keep on and on. Dean Hole said of it that, if he could have only one rose, this would be the one. Pale yellow 'Maréchal Niel', though enormously popular in its day, is a rose only for a warm climate or a conservatory in a cool one. It will grow out of doors in certain favoured spots in England, but its big drooping flowers can hardly be relied on to give of their best. The enormously vigorous white 'Mme Alfred Carrière' was a fine but late arrival on the scene in 1879, and by that time the Noisettes were becoming more and more merged with the climbing Teas and gradually fading from popular esteem. Repeat-flowering climbers had, however, arrived.

Historically, the small group known as the Boursault roses should come in now, as our movement from this point will be forwards in time – or more or less, anyway. Traditionally they were supposed to be the result of a cross between *R. chinensis* and another species called *R. pendulina*, the Alpine rose, of about 1830, though according to modern botanical analysis (Mr Gordon Rowley via Mr Graham Thomas) the use of the latter seems unlikely. Nevertheless, they did resemble a double form of the Alpine rose. Their creation is credited to a French amateur raiser, M Boursault, though Thory, in the text accompanying Redouté's plates, tried unsuccessfully to change the name to *R. l'heritiana*, presumably in honour of M l'Heritier, who did so much to help and encourage the young artist.

Though very tough and hardy, few Boursaults survive today, though there seem to be more of them in America than in Europe. I have only seen one of them myself and so must rely on William Paul's description of them as a group; he describes their long, almost thornless canes with few leaves, bearing their flowers in clusters, a mixture of purples and reds and often with muddled petals, though sometimes quartered. On both sides of the Atlantic they had something of a vogue for a limited time, but their hardiness might be of use in

Plate XIII: Old climbing roses
The Chinese Banksian roses, of which the double yellow form R. banksiae lutea is shown (top), have their past wrapped in mystery, though they were almost certainly cultivated varieties when first brought to the West. Rampant and rather tender, they are for warm climates or sheltered walls, as is the famous old Tea-Noisette 'Maréchal Neil' (centre right), which was a favourite in the large conservatories of Victorian times.
The thornless 'Zéphirine Drouhin' (bottom right) is a climbing Bourbon and needs no protection in any but the coldest climates. It flowers well a second time, but 'Gloire de Dijon' (left) is even more prolific with its blooms, with the first showing very early in the summer. It goes back to 1853 and, like 'Maréchal Neil', is a Tea-Noisette.

modern breeding lines if anyone felt like searching out a few to experiment with. The one I have seen is 'Mme Sancy de Parabère', dating from 1874, which has large flowers untypically in a soft pink, but by the turn of the century most others had vanished.

The Banksian rose, known as *R. banksiae* although it is almost certainly a cultivated variety and is thought by some to be a hybrid of *R. laevigata*, was brought originally from western China in 1803 by William Kerr, who found it growing in a Canton garden. It was named after Lady Banks, the wife of Sir Joseph, and the form Kerr brought was the strongly scented double white, *R. banksiae banksiae* or *R. banksiae alba-plena*. The double pale primrose yellow *lutea* followed in 1824, introduced by J. D. Parks for the Horticultural Society of London, and this is the one most popular nowadays. There is in addition a single creamy yellow, *lutescens*, which came to England from La Mortala in Italy, and the single white *normalis*, which could be the oldest of all of them and is possibly the original wild type. Although it is a native of the mountain ranges of western China, the Banksian rose is not considered very hardy in the West and needs a warm climate or a sheltered corner. It is, however, one of our most spectacular climbers, a rampant grower in the right place that will reach 9 m (30 ft) at least (if you have a wall that high) and is smothered very early in the year with its clusters of small white or yellow flowers.

The arrival of another rose, *R. gigantea*, from south-western China and the Shan Hills of Burma in 1888 had a large influence on the climbing roses of the day. With its 13 cm (5 in) flowers of what might be termed blush-yellow, in the right climate it is almost uncontrollable in its growth and will reach 12 m (40 ft) up a tree. It is not a rose for Europe, except in the south, or for other than the southern states of America unless you are very lucky with your weather.

As 'Old Blush' helped to create the Noisettes, so *R. gigantea* took them a stage further, much as the Teas (to which it may be related) influenced the Hybrid Perpetuals, so that large-flowered recurrent Climbers became a reality. Other roses contributed to the mixture as well – climbing Teas and so on, and the Pernetianas – and there were also a number of climbing sports of Hybrid Teas beginning to appear, such as 'Climbing Mme Caroline Testout' in 1901 and 'Climbing Château de Clos Vougeot' in 1920. 'Paul's Lemon Pillar' of 1915 was not a sport but a cross between the Noisette 'Maréchal Niel' and the Hybrid Perpetual 'Frau Karl Druschki', while 'Climbing Hoosier Beauty' was another notable Climber of the early 1920s. Altogether their parentage was a fine old mixture, and as a result some of them were recurrent and some were not. Mostly not.

For a considerable time after this, climbing roses did not advance very much. There were new varieties, of course, but they were not the most attractive proposition from the nurseryman's point of view, especially as gardens became smaller. People might buy dozens of bedding roses, but only one or two Ramblers or Climbers, and as long as they were content with the old varieties there was no incentive to change. However, in the end the public called the tune. They wanted something that flowered more than once and which was a good deal more healthy than many of the old varieties. The demand for Ramblers dropped and the breeders got to work once more.

Just the same, it is only in comparatively recent years that there has been a big selection of recurrent climbing roses and reliable varieties on the market like 'Aloha', 'Golden Showers', 'High Noon' and 'America' from the United

States, 'Pink Perpêtue', 'Handel', 'Galway Bay', 'Swan Lake' and 'Compassion' from the British Isles (a very large number of the best of these being from McGredy) and 'Danse du Feu' ('Spectacular') and 'Danse des Sylphes' from France. From Germany the story is rather a special one, for there Wilhelm Kordes was concentrating mainly on producing a really hardy race of roses and not especially on Climbers. The first stage of this went back a long way to the production in 1919 of a Rugosa × *wichuraiana* hybrid called 'Max Graf', a pink-flowered spreading ground-cover rose, which strangely enough is only nowadays receiving proper recognition. Quite suddenly, in 1940, it performed an almost unheard-of feat in spontaneously giving birth to a completely new and very hardy species, *R. kordesii*, from which Kordes was able to breed countless fine new varieties. These were tough and recurrent, though not by any means all Climbers. Many were shrub roses, but among the very fine Climbers that resulted were 'Karlsruhe' (deep rose-pink), the yellow 'Leverkusen' and – best of all – the glowing red 'Parkdirektor Riggers'.

THE
MINIATURE ROSE

For a listing of Miniature varieties, see page 147; for illustrations, see plates XIV and XXXI (pp91 and 149) and the photograph on page 193; for the uses of Miniatures, see page 191.

In the true Miniature rose everything is in scale; the flowers, the leaves and the canes are all in proportion to the size of the bush, which to my mind should be no more than 15–25 cm (6–10 in) high. It is dainty and certainly merits its alternative name of Fairy Rose.

Many of its characteristics are akin to those of the China roses (including that of being constantly in flower, starting very early in the year) and there is no doubt that it originated in the East. Although it is possible that the first Miniature was not a species and was possibly a sport, it has been given the specific name of *R. chinensis minima*. One theory is that at some unknown time and in some mysterious way Miniatures reached the island of Mauritius in the Indian Ocean, which strangely enough is not all that far from Réunion (Ile de Bourbon), where there grew the Chinas that helped to launch the Bourbon roses on their way. Two China roses on neighbouring islands so far from home would hardly seem to be a coincidence, and though those from which the Bourbons came are generally considered to have reached Réunion via the West, one would have some justification in speculating whether this is true and whether both roses did not in fact arrive there direct from the East.

Be that as it may, from Mauritius the Miniatures moved on, though the dates given for their arrival, first in England, then in France and then in the rest of Europe, conflict. It would appear to have been sometime in the late 18th century, for there is a Miniature included among the roses painted by Redouté. However, it was not until the early 1800s that they became really popular, and then they soon crossed the Atlantic to America – a journey that was to lead to great things in the story of their development. In England, meanwhile, the Miniature rose acquired a new name, *R. lawranceana*, in honour of Miss Lawrance, whose highly successful book on roses had been published in 1799. An illustration in *Curtis's Botanical Magazine* in 1815 shows it as bearing single, blush-pink flowers.

Miniature roses take readily from cuttings, but are not the easiest of plants from which to breed new varieties, as few set seed and the blooms have little pollen. Nevertheless, the number of varieties increased rapidly after their introduction, spurred on in France particularly by the constant craving for novelty in the decoration of their reception rooms by the aristocracy. One does not know whether these were chance seedlings; nevertheless, by 1829, when M'Intosh, gardener to the King of the Belgians, published his book *The Flower Garden*, he was able to describe Miniatures in white, red, crimson and pink, under such names as 'Gloire de Lawrance', 'Caprice des Dames', 'Lilliputienne' and 'Fairy'. In Britain and elsewhere, although there was some interest in the new novelties, they lost out in competition with the much more spectacular Bourbons and the up-and-coming Hybrid Perpetuals.

The vogue for Miniature roses did not last even in France, however, and for a while they almost dropped from sight. Probably they had appealed mainly as something unusual but not to be taken very seriously as an addition to the garden. Then, in 1918, a miniature pale pink rose was discovered by a Major Roulet growing in a pot on the window-sill of a house at Onnens in Switzerland. According to the family who lived there it had come originally from France and had been there many, many years. Major Roulet showed it to his friend M Correvon, a nurseryman in Geneva, who named it *R. roulettii* in his honour. Writing in the *Gardener's Chronicle* in 1922, M Correvon tells how he had just seen it in his garden in full bud under a covering of snow, which shows how wrong were those who had considered Miniatures to be suitable only for pots in a conservatory or salon.

So now the Miniature had yet another name, and it is as *R. roulettii* that the rose that once more popularized the Miniatures is now generally known. Technically, this name is just as invalid as *R. lawranceana*, because Roulet's discovery was almost certainly a cultivated variety, so at best it should be called 'Roulettii'. In any case, it is held by some people to be identical to a French rose called 'Pompon de Paris', which was well known in the 18th century. Others maintain that the latter was a much more bushy grower and that there are other small differences. Whatever the truth of the matter, the little roses had a fresh lease of life after the Swiss discovery.

It did not immediately take off like a rocket. Progress this time was steady but slow, probably because for the first time deliberate breeding programmes were being carried out, with all the trial and error, meticulous selection and prolonged testing of seedlings that this entails. The first of the breeders to show real progress was Jan de Vink of Boskoop in Holland, who crossed *R. roulettii* with the dwarf Polyantha rose 'Gloria Mundi'. In 1930 this produced a crimson-flowered seedling which was even smaller than *R. roulettii* and which he named 'Peon', changed to 'Tom Thumb' when it was introduced to America in 1936. It proved a good parent for other roses, and altogether de Vink put out seven fine varieties, including the still unsurpassed pearly-pink 'Cinderella' and the carmine 'Humpty Dumpty'. The Polyantha rose 'Cecile Brunner', often classed with the Chinas because it closely resembles them, was one of the parents of 'Cinderella'.

A little later the Spanish breeder Pedro Dot entered the field, using Polyanthas, some Hybrid Teas (the Miniature gene being the toughest of the two – in botanical terms, the dominant one – so that the small size was retained) and other Miniatures as seed parents. Probably his most famous varieties were

Plate XIV: Miniature roses (1)
R. roulettii (top left) was the first of the modern Miniatures. It was found by chance growing in a pot in Switzerland, but is of unknown origin except that it had, in miniature, many of the characteristics of the China roses. It may have been a survivor from an earlier vogue for these tiny roses in France, but in modern times it has led to such outstanding varieties as 'Perla de Alcanada' (centre left) and 'Cinderella' (bottom right).
'Baby Masquerade' (top right) is tall-growing, and an example of the introduction of Floribundas into the Miniature strain, leading to bigger flowers and less typically small growth. 'Stars 'n Stripes' (bottom left) is not only the first striped Miniature to achieve real success, but also the first striped rose to be deliberately created, as opposed to occurring as a sport. See also plate XXXI (p149).

'Perla de Alcanada' ('Baby Crimson'), 'Perla de Montserrat' (in the breeding of which he followed de Vink in using 'Cecile Brunner') and 'Estrellita de Oro' ('Baby Gold Star') of 1940. The latter was the first yellow Miniature, for which the Hybrid Tea 'Spek's Yellow' ('Golden Scepter') was crossed with 'Peon'. But his own favourite was 'Si', so called because 'Si' was the answer he had to give again and again when those who had never seen anything so small asked him if it really was a rose. Some ten good varieties came from this distinguished hybridist before his death.

Other European breeders, though not specializing in Miniatures, have produced some first-rate varieties. Meilland of France has 'Colibri', 'Starina' and 'Darling Flame', among others, to his name, while McGredy began a very extensive programme comparatively recently by launching the deep red 'Wee Man', which won a Certificate of Merit from the Royal National Rose Society in 1973. Tantau of Germany's 'Baby Masquerade' is one of the most widely planted Miniatures of all, but although the flowers and leaves remain suitably small and dainty, the bush itself can reach 40 cm (15 in) in height – taller than some low-growing Floribundas. The vigour of one parent – the Floribunda 'Masquerade' itself – may have had its influence here, and certainly the mixing of Floribunda and Hybrid Tea strains with those of the Miniature has resulted more and more in growth that I think is much too tall, or in flowers that are a great deal too large for a very small plant. It is, of course, the search for new colour breaks that has brought this about.

De Vink's 'Peon' ('Tom Thumb') was a sensation in America when it arrived in 1936 – so much so that stock ran out and sales had to be suspended until the 1938 season to build up supplies. However, the United States was not for long to depend on imports from abroad. Dr Dennison Morey and others have produced interesting varieties there, but the man who, above all, has really put the Miniatures on the map on a world-wide scale is Ralph S. Moore of California. Working with great patience and persistence for something like thirty years, he now has a truly remarkable collection of introductions behind him, with yet more to come. He has, too, been responsible for the Miniature rose being grown more widely in the United States than anywhere else, though recognition of its merits in small-scale gardening is gaining momentum everywhere. There are American nurseries supplying Miniatures only, with lists of over 100 varieties, and many amateur gardeners are joining the professional hybridizers in breeding and introducing new Miniatures.

Moore used seeds from a cross between the cluster-flowering Rambler species *R. wichuraiana* and a Tantau-bred Floribunda called 'Floradora' as the mainstay of his early breeding programme, and a small-flowered and not too vigorous pink Climber called 'Zee' to develop climbing Miniatures. He was responsible for the first mauve-coloured varieties, and also pink and white striped Miniatures, but perhaps his greatest achievement so far is to have brought the old Moss roses into his breeding lines. Miniature ever-blooming Moss roses are now a reality, and is more of an achievement than it may seem at first glance. As has already been seen, the Centifolia group (from which the first full-sized Moss rose sported) has long been considered virtually sterile and unable to contribute to rose development. Obviously this cannot be completely so, but as eighteen years' work was necessary before Moore was successful, there were clearly problems that few other breeders would have contemplated facing.

CHAPTER TWO

GREAT ROSES
OF THE WORLD

EACH OF THE ROSES briefly described in the lists that follow are, at the time of writing, available from nurseries, though not necessarily in every country. Anyone, however, in whatever country they live, should be able to obtain without too much difficulty a good representation of every group.

The sizes of the plants when fully grown have been given (where appropriate, height first, then spread) but this was done with some hesitation as they can vary considerably according to climate and other growing conditions. The measurements should be treated with caution and taken as a general pointer only. And again, where the susceptibility of a rose or group of roses to a particular disease is mentioned, it does not automatically follow that it will be equally serious everywhere.

It has already been stressed a number of times that the classification of a number of the roses under races or groups is not easy. For instance, a Rugosa rose crossed with a Rambler might legitimately appear under either heading, and a number of the very vigorous shrubs raised by Herr Kordes in Germany have been classed variously as Shrub Roses, Hybrid Musks and Climbers. National thinking comes into it, too, as in the case of the classification Grandiflora. How this has been dealt with here is explained under the heading of the Floribunda section, but in general, except where I have strong reasons for not agreeing, the roses can be found under the most usually accepted categories. Where there is doubt, the usual practice is to put a rose into the family the attributes of which are predominant. As explained on pages 169 and 170, moves are afoot to rename some categories, and the new names are mentioned after the main headings.

Some of the roses are described as being sports of others. This does not

Plate XV: Roses for foliage
The Alba rose 'Félicité Parmentier' (top left) has, like others of its tribe, soft grey-green leaves which stay attractive after the flowers have gone and make this a useful group for a general shrub planting. The same can be said for the European species R. rubrifolia (top right), and there will be bright red hips as well later on.
The foliage of R. primula (bottom left) from China is scented and also gives some autumn tints, but for real sunset colours in the last months of the year R. virginiana (bottom right) cannot be bettered. This was the first native American species to cross the Atlantic and be planted in European gardens.

mean that they are particularly debonnaire, or even athletic. It means that by some quirk of nature, prodded certainly by a mixed ancestry, a rose bush has produced a cane bearing completely different flowers from the rest. This cane can be used to propagate the new rose by budding, it will come true to type, and is a sport of the first one. 'Chicago Peace' is a sport from 'Peace', and I recently heard of the coppery-pink rambler 'Albertine' putting out a shoot with bright yellow flowers. Looking back into its history, one can see why, as one of its forebears was a Pernetiana. If a rose has the word Climbing in front of its variety name – for example, 'Climbing Cécile Brunner' – it is a climbing sport, and here the habit of growth rather than the flowers has changed. Suddenly it has had a desire to go up and up.

SPECIES ROSES

New classification: Wild Roses. As these are dealt with in some detail in Chapter 1 (to which refer), only a fairly small selection of the pick of them for garden use is included here, together with some of their closely related hybrids of similar character. Except where stated, they are once-flowering, but an indication is given when this is particularly early or late.

R. californica plena Wiry, arching canes; rich pink or light carmine-crimson semi-double flowers; ferny leaves. 1.8 × 1.5m (6 × 5ft).
R. cantabrigiensis R. hugonis × R. sericea. Fragrant pale primrose-yellow single flowers on a big, arching, tangled shrub, followed by some round orange hips. Dainty small leaves. 2 × 2m (7 × 7ft).
R. davidii Open, arching but erect-growing shrub, with deep lilac-rose single flowers with cream stamens. Scarlet hips. Late. 2.75 × 2.5m (9 × 8ft).
R. dupontii R. moschata × a Gallica. Creamy-white single flowers, scented, and fine grey-green leaves. 2 × 2m (7 × 7ft).
R. ecae Looks like a buttercup bush with its small, brilliant yellow flowers. Early. Wiry and erect, with chestnut-coloured canes. 1.5 × 1.2m (5 × 4ft).
  'Golden Chersonese' 1969. A modern hybrid of R. ecae × 'Canary Bird'. Early-flowering, with single bright yellow flowers. Upright habit of growth. 1.8 × 2m (6 × 7ft).
R. farreri persetosa A dense, wide-spreading tangle of thorny shoots bearing miniature ferny leaves and small scented pink flowers in profusion. 1.8 × 2.5m (6 × 8ft).
R. fedtschenkoana Unique, in that its old shoots bear its single white flowers early, and new red-tinted shoots produce more throughout the summer. Beautiful grey-green leaves. 2.5 × 1.8m (8 × 6ft).
R. foetida (R. lutea, Austrian yellow) Arching and open, with startlingly bright single yellow flowers and rich green leaves, liable to black spot. Strange scent. A historic rose. 1.5 × 1.2m (5 × 4ft).
  R. foetida bicolor (R. lutea punicea, Austrian copper) Sport of and identical to R. foetida, except that the single flowers are flame-red with orange-yellow petal reverse. Startling. 1.5 × 1.2m (5 × 4ft).
R. foliolosa Makes a suckering, low-growing thicket, with single pink scented flowers late on. Autumn colour from the leaves. 1.2m (4ft).
R. forrestiana An arching shrub with pink, white-eyed scented flowers with yellow stamens, coming in clusters nestling in leafy bracts. Bright red hips. 2 × 1.8m (7 × 6ft).
R. hugonis Cupped single creamy-yellow blooms in spring, and small black hips. Dense grower, reasonably upright. Dainty foliage. 2 × 1.8m (7 × 6ft).
R. × macrantha hybrids
  'Lady Curzon' 1901. R. rugosa rubra × R. × macrantha. Bushy, tangled shrub with large single pink blooms, the petals attractively crinkled. Scented. 1.8 × 2.5m (6 × 8ft).
  'Raubritter' 1936. R. × macrantha × 'Solarium'. A spreading trailing rose, with massed clear pink, semi-double globular blooms. Dark green leaves. 1 × 1.8m (3 × 6ft).
R. moyesii 'Geranium' 1938. Elegant, upright and open, with long canes bearing bright red single flowers, followed by long orange-red, bottle-shaped hips. 3 × 2.5m (10 × 8ft).
  'Highdownensis' 1928. A moyesii seedling of great beauty. Clusters of single cerise-crimson blooms and spectacular orange-red hips. 3 × 3m (10 × 10ft).
  'Sealing Wax' Similar to 'Geranium', though slightly larger, with cerise-pink flowers.
  'Superba' Typical moyesii growth. Deep crimson double flowers and plum-purple canes. 2 × 1.8m (7 × 6ft).
R. × paulii (R. rugosa repens alba) R. arvensis × R. rugosa. Wide-spreading, with fiercely armed trailing canes and fine grey-green

For further details of these and other rose species, see page 37; for illustrations, see plates I, II, XV and XXXIV (pp40, 46, 94 and 197).

leaves. Massed large single white blooms with silky, crinkled petals and golden stamens. Fragrant. 1.2 × 3.5m (4 × 12ft).

R. × paulii rosea Similar to the above, if a little less vigorous, and with pink, white-eyed flowers.

R. pomifera duplex (*R. villosa*, Wolley Dod's rose) Grey-green, rather downy leaves and rose-pink double flowers. Large, round, bristly dark red hips like huge gooseberries. 3 × 3.5m (10 × 12ft). *R. pomifera* itself, with single flowers, bears more hips.

R. primula (incense rose) Ferny foliage, aromatic on damp warm days, on a twiggy, dense bush bearing multitudes of small, bright yellow single fragrant flowers. Early. 1.8 × 2.5m (6 × 8ft).

R. roxburghii plena (*R. microphylla plena*, chestnut rose) The double pink form of *R. roxburghii*. Flowers open flat, deep pink in the centre paling towards petal edges, followed by prickly hips like chestnuts. Long leaves with many leaflets and grey, peeling bark. 1.8 × 1.2m (6 × 4ft).

R. rubiginosa (R. eglanteria) hybrids

'Fritz Nobis' 1940. 'Joanna Hill' × 'Magnifica'. Exquisite scented double, soft pink flowers in clusters. Bushy grower with mid-green leaves. 1.8 × 1.8m (6 × 6ft).

'Goldbusch' 1954. 'Golden Glow' × *R. rubiginosa* hybrid. Lax shrub with glossy, light green leaves, making a good pillar rose. Coral-pink buds open to semi-double flowers, yellow and fragrant. Recurrent. 1.2 × 1.8m (4 × 6ft).

Penzance Sweet-Briers

All with fragrant foliage and flowers, the latter rather fleeting. Large, thorny, tangled shrubs with autumn hips.

'Amy Robsart' 1893. Pink. 2.5 × 2.5m (8 × 8ft).

'Lady Penzance' 1894. Coppery-yellow. 1.8 × 1.8m (6 × 6ft).

'Lord Penzance' 1894. Buff-yellow. 1.8 × 1.8m (6 × 6ft).

'Meg Merrilees' 1894. Crimson. 2.5 × 2.5m (8 × 8ft).

R. rubrifolia Open and arching, with plum-red new canes, practically thornless, and soft grey-green leaves with a mauve-purple sheen. Very small pink, white-eyed flowers in clusters, and red-brown hips. There is a white form. 1.8 × 1.5m (6 × 5ft).

R. sericea pteracantha (*R. omeinensis pteracantha*) The white four-petalled flowers come early, followed by orange-red hips. Strong canes bear huge flat thorns, red and translucent when young. 2.5 × 1.8m (8 × 6ft).

R. setigera (prairie rose) Trailing canes, with bright mallow-pink fragrant flowers in clusters coming late. 1.2 × 2.5m (4 × 8ft).

R. soulieana Not for a small garden. A mounding shrub with fine grey-green leaves and multitudes of single scented white flowers with yellow stamens, followed by small orange-red hips. 3 × 3m (10 × 10ft).

R. spinosissima hybrids

R. spinosissima altaica (*R. altaica*, *R. grandiflora*) An early, open, arching shrub, with large creamy-white single flowers and black hips. 1.8 × 1.2m (6 × 4ft).

'Double White' Double, globular blooms scented like lily of the valley. 1.5 × 1.2m (5 × 4ft).

'Frühlingsduft' 1949. 'Joanna Hill' × *R. spinosissima altaica*. Tall and arching, with double HT-type flowers in blends of creamy-yellow and apricot. Fragrant. 1.8 × 1.8m (6 × 6ft).

'Frühlingsgold' 1937. 'Joanna Hill' × *R. spinosissima hispida*. Huge arching canes with large leaves, smothered early with big single to semi-double flowers in clusters, creamy-yellow and with yellow stamens. Spectacular and scented. 2 × 2m (7 × 7ft).

'Frühlingsmorgen' 1941. ('E. G. Hill' × 'Catherine Kordes') × *R. spinosissima altaica*. More bushy than 'Frühlingsgold', with lead-green leaves. Large scented single flowers, pale pink merging to pale yellow at the centre, with maroon stamens. Some later flowers and large maroon hips. 1.8 × 1.5m (6 × 5ft).

R. × harisonii (*R. vorbergii*, 'Harison's Yellow') 1830. Probably a *R. foetida* hybrid with a Burnet rose. Fine, rich green leaves on an open-growing shrub, with semi-double bright yellow flowers with yellow stamens. Scented. 1.2m (4ft).

'Stanwell Perpetual' 1838. Possibly a hybrid with a Damask. Many thorns and grey-green leaves. Lax canes with very double soft pink flowers, opening flat and fading near-white. Fine first flush, then spasmodic bloom. 1.5 × 1.5m (5 × 5ft).

'William III' A small, suckering, thicket-forming shrub, with small semi-double magenta-crimson flowers, paler on the reverse. Early. 60cm (2ft).

'William's Double Yellow' Small scented double yellow flowers, loosely formed with green carpels in the centre of each. Prickly. 1 × 1m (3 × 3ft).

R. virginiana (*R. lucida*) A low, tangled, spreading shrub with glossy leaves which give autumn colours of maroon, yellow, scarlet. Cerise-pink single scented flowers. Late. 1.5 × 2m (5 × 7ft).

'Rose d'Amour' (*R. plena*, the St Mark's rose) More compact than the species, and double flowers a clear pink, with colour deeper in the centre. Late summer. 1.2 × 1.8m (4 × 6ft).

R. xanthina 'Canary Bird' (*R. × spontanea*) The best early-flowering single yellow, with beautiful ferny leaves on brown canes. Scented. Bushy and arching. Some die-back possible in some areas. 2 × 2m (7 × 7ft).

GALLICAS

For the history of the Gallicas, see page 54; for illustrations, see plate III (pp50–51).

New classification: Old Garden Roses, Gallicas. Summer-flowering only. Most need watching for mildew on the typically rather rough leaves. Bristly rather than thorny stems and suckering freely.

'Alain Blanchard' 1839. Cupped crimson-purple blooms, mottled maroon, with golden stamens. Rounded leaves and thorns indicate mixed parentage. 1.2 × 1m (4 × 3ft).

'Anaïs Ségales' 1837. Double, quilled flowers, lilac-pink with dark mauve-pink centres. 1 × 1m (3 × 3ft).

'Assemblage des Beautés' Prior to 1790. Full, reflexing flowers with a button eye in near crimson-scarlet. Good foliage. 1.2 × 1m (4 × 3ft).

'Belle de Crécy' Age unknown. Lax in habit, with cerise-pink double flowers with a button eye, changing to soft mauve. Strong scent. 1.2 × 1m (4 × 3ft).

'Belle Isis' 1848. Pale pink flowers with a touch of salmon-pink. Short at 90 × 90cm (3 × 3ft).

'Camaieux' 1830. Blooms on opening are crimson-purple, striped white, moving through stages to mauve, grey and white. 90 × 60cm (3 × 2ft).

'Charles de Mills' ('Bizarre Triomphant') Age uncertain. The alternative name describes well the round flat flowers, crammed with petals and quite unique in blends of deep crimson, wine and purple of a sumptuous richness. 1.5 × 1.2m (5 × 4ft).

'Conditorum' Very old. A compact grower of 1.2 × 1m (4 × 3ft). Loosely-formed magenta-crimson flowers with yellow stamens.

'Cramoisi Picoté' 1834. Small, rosette-type flowers of crimson, fading lighter and mottled, with deeper crimson edging to the petals. 1.2 × 1m (4 × 3ft).

'D'Aguesseneau' 1823. Full flat quartered flowers in strong crimson-scarlet, paling a little at the petal edges. Good foliage. 1.5 × 1.2m (5 × 4ft).

'Duc de Guiche' Age unknown. Outstanding in foliage and flower. Blooms open flat, with imbricated petals in crimson, veined and flushed purple. 1.2 × 1.2m (4 × 4ft).

'Duchesse de Buccleugh' 1846. Large flowers opening flat and quartered in deep purplish-pink, lighter at the edges of the petals. Later-flowering than most. Bushy. 1.5 × 1.2m (5 × 4ft).

'Duchesse de Montebello' Age unknown. Lax, with greyish leaves and cupped blooms of soft pink. 1.5 × 1.2m (5 × 4ft).

'Du Maître d'Ecole' Age unknown. Sturdy, with large leaves and flowers opening flat and quartered. Soft rose-pink, fading to mauve-pink. 1 × 1m (3 × 3ft).

'Georges Vibert' 1853. A compact grower with flat quartered blooms, lightly striped crimson on blush-pink. 1.2 × 1m (4 × 3ft).

'Gloire de France' Age unknown. Lax in growth with double flowers in many shades of mauve, purple and lilac-white. One of the healthiest. 1 × 1m (3 × 3ft).

'Ipsilanté' 1821. Pale pink with a touch of lilac. Quartered flowers. Reasonably strong-growing to 1.2 × 1m (4 × 3ft).

'Jenny Duval' Age unknown. Shapely buds open into very full flowers, blending purple, Parma-violet and soft greyish-violet, sometimes with a cerise flush in hot sunlight. 1.2 × 1m (4 × 3ft).

'La Plus Belle des Ponctuées' Age unknown. Taller than most and bearing hips. Double flowers in bright pink and loosely formed. 1.8 × 1.2m (6 × 4ft).

'Officinalis' (R. officinalis, apothecary's rose, red rose of Lancaster, the old red Damask) Very old. Bushy, with semi-double clear light crimson flowers with yellow stamens. 1.2 × 1.2m (4 × 4ft).

'Perle des Panachées' 1845. Coppery young shoots and leaves. Semi-double, loosely-formed flowers, white, streaked crimson. 90 × 60cm (3 × 2ft).

'Président de Sèze' Prior to 1836. Bushy, with full double flowers in crimson-purple, fading to lilac-white at petal edges. Very striking. 1.2 × 1m (4 × 3ft).

'Rosa Mundi' Prior to 16th century. A sport of 'Officinalis'. Flowers with crimson striping on a pale, blush-pink ground. Otherwise similar. 1.2 × 1.2m (4 × 4ft).

'Surpasse Tout' Age unknown. Cupped, reflexing flowers in near-scarlet, fading cerise-pink, veined darker. 1.2 × 1.2m (4 × 4ft).

'Tricolore de Flandre' 1846. Purplish striping on white; very double, reflexed and with rolled petals. 1 × 1m (3 × 3ft).

'Tuscany' Age unknown. Flat semi-double blooms, opening velvety-maroon with yellow stamens. 1.2 × 1m (4 × 3ft). 'Tuscany Superb' is similar, but with a little larger and more double flowers.

GALLICA HYBRIDS DIFFERING MARKEDLY FROM THE TYPE

'Francofurtana' ('Empress Josephine') Before 1583. Lax and spreading, with large, rather loose double flowers in pink with deeper shadings and good foliage. Outstanding. 1.2 × 1.5m (4 × 5ft).

'Complicata' Age unknown. More nearly resembling a species; will scramble through other shrubs or form a bush 1.8 × 2.5m (6 × 8ft). Good, non-Gallica-like, rather pointed leaves and huge single pink flowers with a white eye.

'Scarlet Fire' ('Scharlachglut') 1952. 'Poinsettia' × R. gallica grandiflora. Long, arching canes bearing big single flowers of blazing scarlet, followed by fine hips. Shrub, pillar rose or short climber. 2.1 × 2.1m (7 × 7ft).

Plate XVI: Bourbon roses
This was the first major group of repeat-flowering roses to be raised in the West, combining features of the recurrent varieties newly arrived from China with, at first, the much more robust growth of the Damasks and then with other groups of roses already established in Europe. Not all Bourbons can, however, be relied upon for a second flush of bloom, though the four shown here – 'La Reine Victoria' (top left), 'Honorine de Brabant' (top right), 'Mme Isaac Pereire' (bottom left) and 'Boule de Neige' (bottom right) – will all repeat well. All, too, make good pillar roses, and the enormously vigorous 'Mme Isaac Pereire' has a scent unsurpassed by any other rose.

DAMASKS

New classification: Old Garden Roses, Damasks. Summer-flowering only, except for the 'Autumn Damask'.

'**Blush Damask**' Age unknown. Early-flowering, with double reflexing flowers, pinkish-mauve, paling at the petal edges. Dense-growing. 1.8 × 1.8m (6 × 6ft).
'**Celsiana**' Before 1750. Flowers loosely-formed, semi-double, large and blush-pink with yellow stamens. Grey-green leaves. 1.5 × 1.2m (5 × 4ft).
'**Gloire de Guilan**' 1949 in the West, but certainly older. Quartered flowers in clear pink. 1.2 × 1.2m (4 × 4ft).
'**Ispahan**' Age unknown. Clusters of large pink, long-lasting double blooms on a robust, upright plant. Long used for the production of attar of roses. 1.5 × 1.2m (5 × 4ft).
'**Léda**' (painted Damask) Age unknown. Double blooms which reflex into a ball, the white petals tipped with crimson. Very dark leaves. 1 × 1m (3 × 3ft).
'**Mme Hardy**' 1832. Beautiful pure white flowers, cupped at first, opening flat and quartered, with a green pointel. Good mid-green leaves. 1.8 × 1.5m (6 × 5ft).
'**Mme Zoetmans**' Age unknown. The blush-pink blooms fade to white, except for their centre petals. Early. 1 × 1m (3 × 3ft).
'**Marie Louise**' 1813. Huge pink blooms, opening flat before reflexing and fading to a lilac-mauve. Arching habit of growth. 1.2 × 1m (4 × 3ft).
'**Oeillet Parfait**' ('La Tour d'Auvergne') 1841. Bright pink blooms, very double, opening flat and fading lighter. Thorny. 1.2 × 1m (4 × 3ft).
'**Omar Khayyam**' Age unknown. Flowers pink, opening flat and quartered. Prickly, with smallish leaves. Said to have come from a rose on the tomb of Omar Khayyham, via a seedling planted on Edward FitzGerald's grave in Suffolk.
'**Quatre Saisons**' ('Autumn Damask', *R. × damascena bifera*) Very ancient. Probably grown at Pompeii. Double pink flowers of poor form, but some borne in autumn. Rounded, light green leaves. 1.2 × 1m (4 × 3ft).
'**St Nicholas**' Found in a Yorkshire garden in 1950, but age unknown. Semi-double cupped flowers in brilliant clear pink, yellow stamens. Red hips follow. 1.2 × 1.2m (4 × 4ft).
'**Trigintipetala**' Very old and used for the production of attar. Loosely-formed double blooms, only borne freely in a warm climate. Otherwise unreliable, but attractive light green leaves. 1.8 × 1.5m (6 × 5ft).
'**York and Lancaster**' (*R. × damascena versicolor*) Before 1551. Said to be the rose from which blooms were picked in the Temple Garden at the start of the Wars of the Roses. Loose double blooms, sometimes blush-white, sometimes pink, sometimes with the odd pink or white petals. Needs good soil. 1.8 × 1.8m (6 × 6ft).

CHINA ROSES

New classification: Old Garden Roses, China Roses. Perpetual-flowering; mostly light and airy shrubs.

'**Comtesse du Cayla**' 1902. Tall and spreading. Loosely-formed semi-double coral-flame flowers with yellow reverse, fading salmon. Dark, bronze-tinted leaves. 1.8 × 1.5m (6 × 5ft).
'**Cramoisi Supérieur**' 1832. A small, neat bush with clusters of globular dark crimson blooms. 90 × 60cm (3 × 2ft).
'**Fabvier**' ('Mme Fabvier') Low-growing with semi-double scarlet flowers, some streaked with white. Good for bedding. 45 × 45cm (18 × 18in).
'**Fellemberg**' ('La Belle Marseillaise') 1857. Spectacular when its clusters of cupped deep crimson-pink blooms cover this big, open bush. 2.5 × 1.8m (8 × 6ft).
'**Hermosa**' ('Armosa') 1840. The cupped soft-pink flowers have a restrained charm, blending with the grey-green leaves. 90 × 60cm (3 × 2ft).
'**Le Vésuve**' ('Lemesle') 1825. Elegant branching shrub with pale pink double flowers of great refinement. 1.5 × 1.2m (5 × 4ft).
'**Mme Eugène Résal**' 1894. A 'Mme Laurette Messimy' sport. Semi-double coral-flame flowers with a yellow reverse, not unlike 'Comtesse du Cayla'. 1.2 × 1m (4 × 3ft).
'**Mme Laurette Messimy**' 1887. 'Rival de Paestum' × 'Mme Falcot'. Semi-double coppery-pink blooms, freely borne. 1.2 × 1m (4 × 3ft).
'**Miss Lowe**' About 1887. An airy open shrub with single crimson flowers that intensify with age. 1.2 × 0.6m (4 × 2ft).
'**Mutabilis**' ('Tipo Ideale') Before 1896, probably hundreds of years before. Unique. Single flowers change from flame to buff-yellow to pink to coppery red. Always in flower. Bronze-tinted leaves. 1 × 1m (3 × 3ft), or 2.5m (8ft) on a wall.
'**Old Blush**' (The common monthly rose) Date unknown. Flowers semi-double, crimson at first, then pink, in clusters on a twiggy bush. In flower till very late. 1.2 × 1.2m (4 × 4ft) or more on a warm wall.
'**Rival de Paestum**' 1836. Loosely-formed white flowers, contrasting with dark, red-tinted leaves. 90 × 60cm (3 × 2ft).
'**Sanguinea**' ('Single Crimson') Age unknown. Single flowers of dark, intense crimson. 1.2 × 1m (4 × 3ft).

For the history of the Damasks, see page 57; for illustrations, see plate IV (p55).

For the history of the China roses, see page 60; for illustrations, see plate V (p58).

Plate XVII: Portland roses

This group – represented here by 'The Portland Rose' itself (top left), which is sometimes known as 'Duchess of Portland', together with 'Comte de Chambord' (bottom left), 'Jacques Cartier' (bottom right) and 'Mabel Morrison' (centre right) – has a very similar historical background to that of the Bourbons. They originated at about the same time and from the same kind of crosses, though in Italy rather than on an island in the Indian Ocean.
They are sometimes called Perpetual Damasks, for there is a strong Damask streak in them, but it is difficult with many of the roses of the 19th century to be quite certain to which group they really do belong. For this reason, 'Mabel Morrison' is often found listed among the Hybrid Perpetuals.

'Semperflorens' ('Slater's Crimson China') 1792. A historic rose, bringing crimson colourings to the West. Not too robust and needs a warm wall, even in a mild climate. Some scent, unusual in a China. 1.2 × 1m (4 × 3ft).

'Serratipetala' ('Rose Oeillet de St Arguey') Age unknown. One of the few roses (apart from some Rugosas) with petal edges serrated like an old-fashioned pink. Crimson, darkening in hot sun. Dark green leaves on an open bush. 1.5 × 1.5m (5 × 5ft).

'Viridiflora' (The green rose) 1855. Open and airy, bearing clusters of blue-green buds opening to strange 'flowers' of green, later streaked with shades of brown. A curiosity only a flower-arranger could love.

BOURBONS

New classification: Old Garden Roses, Bourbons. Except where mentioned, these flower a second time in the autumn, and a number of them have some flowers in between.

'Adam Messerich' 1920. 'Frau Oberhofgärtner Singer' × ('Louise Odier' seedling × 'Louis Philippe'). Quite a modern Bourbon, with globular (though not fully double) pink fragrant blooms. Tall and well-branched. 1.8 × 1.5m (6 × 5ft).

'Boule de Neige' 1867. 'Blanche Lafitte' × 'Sappho' (not the early HT of that name). Red-tinted buds open to the most perfect very double snow-white flowers, richly scented. Upright stance and fine leaves. 1.5 × 1.2m (5 × 4ft).

'Bourbon Queen' ('Reine de l'Ile Bourbon') 1835. Soft magenta-pink flowers, veined deeper, not as double as some, opening flat. Free-flowering, but in summer only. 1.8 × 1.5m (6 × 5ft).

'Champion of the World' ('Mrs De Graw') 1894. 'Hermosa' × 'Magna Charta'. Not quite the champion, but fine, freely-borne light pink globular flowers and sweet scent. Arching growth to 1.5 × 1m (5 × 3ft). Sometimes classed as an HP.

'Commandant Beaurepaire' ('Panachée d'Angers') 1874. One of the most spectacular and free-flowering, but at midsummer only. Cupped blooms, splashed and striped maroon, pink, mauve, purple and scarlet, and very fragrant. Smooth light green leaves. 1.8 × 1.5m (6 × 5ft).

'Ferdinand Pichard' 1921. Quite modern but equals the best. The cupped flowers come in clusters, crimson striping on pink fading to blush-pink. Sweet scent. Light green leaves and well branched. 1.5 × 1.2m (5 × 4ft). Sometimes classed as an HP.

'Great Western' 1838. Possibly named after the famous pioneer steamship. Rich crimson and purple flowers of enormous size and good fragrance. Rarely repeats. 1.5 × 1.2m (5 × 4ft).

'Honorine de Brabant' Age unknown. Possibly a 'Commandant Beaurepaire' sport, but flowers well in autumn. Cupped quartered blooms in lilac-pink, striped and spotted mauve and crimson; scented. 1.8 × 1.8m (6 × 6ft).

'La Reine Victoria' 1872. Beautiful pink flowers with shell-like petals, rounded and cupped; scented. Vigorous but slender, needing support. 1.8 × 1m (6 × 3ft).

'Louise Odier' 1851. Cup-like double flowers, filled with petals of lilac-pink; fine scent. Elegance personified, with its fine foliage. 1.8 × 1.2m (5 × 4ft).

'Mme Ernst Calvat' 1888. Sport of 'Mme Isaac Pereire'. Clear pink with a darker reverse to the sumptuous double blooms. Very fragrant. A lusty grower with coppery young leaves. 2 × 1.5m (7 × 5ft).

'Mme Isaac Pereire' 1880. All the good attributes of its sport (above), but the blooms are deep cerise-pink, often better formed in the second blooming. 2 × 1.5m (7 × 5ft).

'Mme Lauriol de Barny' 1868. Early into flower with silvery-pink quartered blooms on long, arching canes, making it a good pillar rose. 1.8 × 1.5m (6 × 5ft).

'Mme Pierre Oger' 1878. Sport of 'La Reine Victoria' and its equal in every way. Flowers a creamy blush-pink, deepening at petal edges and flushing overall pink in warm sunlight – an inheritance from the China roses. 1.8 × 1m (6 × 3ft).

'Prince Charles' Age unknown. Light madder-crimson double blooms, opening flat and paling with lilac tones. Grey-green leaves and some scent. Midsummer only. 1.5 × 1.2m (5 × 4ft).

'Souvenir de la Malmaison' ('Queen of Beauty and Fragrance') 1843. A cross between 'Mme Desprez' (a Bourbon) and an unknown Tea rose, so really more a Hybrid Tea than a true Bourbon, though Bourbon in habit and usually classed as such. Wide, spreading and bushy. Constant creamy-blush flowers, opening flat and quartered; well scented. There is a climbing sport. 1.2 × 1.2m (4 × 4ft).

'Souvenir de St Anne's' 1950. Sport of 'Souvenir de la Malmaison', but with almost single, very freely-borne flowers in palest blush-pink with a pink reverse. Some scent. 1.8 × 1.2m (6 × 4ft).

'Variegata di Bologna' 1909. Profuse globular quartered fragrant flowers, white with intense crimson-purple striping making a vivid contrast. Tall and needs support. Prone to black spot. 2.5 × 1.5m (8 × 5ft).

'Zéphirine Drouhin' 1868. Famous as the thornless rose, a fine repeat-flowering climbing Bourbon, with coppery young leaves

For the history of the Bourbons, see page 62; for illustrations, see plate XVI (p98).

needing watching for mildew. Loose double cerise-pink fragrant blooms. An old favourite, still holding its own. 4.6m (15ft).

'Zigeunerknabe' ('Gipsy Boy') 1909. Arching and with small, rather rounded leaves for a Bourbon, and very double flat flowers in clusters of the darkest crimson-red. Very striking. Summer-flowering only. 1.5 × 2m (5 × 7ft).

PORTLAND ROSES

For the history of the Portland roses, see page 62; for illustrations, see plate XVII (p101).

New classification: Old Garden Roses, Portlands. Two flushes of bloom with some in between.

'Arthur de Sansal' 1855. Flowers double, opening flat and quartered, crimson-purple with a lighter reverse. 1.2 × 1m (4 × 3ft).

'Comte de Chambord' ('Mme Boll') 1860. Double pink flowers, shading to lilac at the petal edges. 1.2 × 1m (4 × 3ft).

'Jacques Cartier' 1868. Erect and strong in growth. Very double quartered pink flowers of good size. Very free. 1.2 × 1m (4 × 3ft).

'Mabel Morrison' 1878. Sport of 'Baroness Rothschild' and possibly an HP, though resembling a Portland. Pale pink cupped flowers, fading white. Sturdy and upright. 1.2 × 0.6m (4 × 2ft).

'Panachée de Lyon' 1895. A striped Portland, possibly a sport of 'Rose du Roi'. Crimson and purple stripes on strong pink double flowers. 90 × 60cm (3 × 2ft).

'The Portland Rose' ('Duchess of Portland') Earlier than 1809. Probably from an 'Autumn Damask' × 'Slater's Crimson China' cross. Cupped semi-double light crimson flowers on a small upright suckering bush. 60 × 60cm (2 × 2ft).

HYBRID PERPETUALS

For the history of the Hybrid Perpetuals, see page 63; for illustrations, see plate VI (p61).

New classification: Old Garden Roses, Hybrid Perpetuals. Despite their name, not perpetual. Except where mentioned they flower in summer, rest, and then come again.

'Alfred Colomb' ('Marshall P. Wilder') 1865. 'Général Jacqueminot' × seedling? Globular fragrant scarlet-red blooms, shading purple. Dense grower. 1.5 × 1.5m (5 × 5ft).

'American Beauty' ('Mme Ferdinand Jamin') 1875. Very double cupped blooms, deep carmine shading crimson-rose. Very fragrant. Long used in cut-flower trade. 1.5 × 1m (5 × 3ft).

'Baron Girod de l'Ain' 1897. Sport of 'Eugène Fürst'. Medium-sized flowers, double and cupped at centre, outer petals reflexing. Crimson-scarlet, petals edged white. Vigorous. 1.5 × 1.2m (5 × 4ft).

'Baronne Prévost' 1842. Full rose-pink flowers, shading lighter, quartered and with button eye. Scented. 1.5 × 1m (5 × 3ft).

'Empereur du Maroc' 1858. 'Géant des Batailles' seedling. Medium-sized globular, high-centred flowers, opening flat. Crimson-maroon. Vigorous though not large. 1.2 × 1m (4 × 3ft).

'Eugène Fürst' 1875. A 'Baron de Bostetten' hybrid. Large double globular fragrant crimson-red flowers, reverse lighter. 1.5 × 1m (5 × 3ft).

'Fisher Holmes' 1865. 'Maurice Bernadin' seedling? Scarlet shading velvety-crimson. An upright, strong grower. Scented. 1.5 × 1m (5 × 3ft).

'Frau Karl Druschki' ('Reine des Neiges', 'Snow Queen', 'White American Beauty') 1901. 'Merveille de Lyon' × 'Mme Caroline Testout'. From its parentage (HP × HT) almost an early HT. Large pure white blooms from pink-tinted buds. One of the best whites ever. No scent. 1.5 × 1.2m (5 × 4ft).

'Général Jacqueminot' ('General Jack', 'Jack Rose') 1853. Seedling of 'Gloire des Rosomanes'. Fragrant bright scarlet-crimson flowers on long stems. An ancestor of most of the red varieties available today. 1.2 × 1m (4 × 3ft).

'George Arends' ('Fortuné Besson') 1910. 'Frau Karl Druschki' × 'La France'. A real beauty in soft pink with hints of creamy-pink on the reverse. Scented and vigorous. 1.5 × 1m (5 × 3ft).

'George Dickson' 1912. Parentage unknown. Sometimes classed as an HT. Large double blooms in brilliant crimson-scarlet, shading darker and often with weak necks, carried in small clusters at the end of long, ungainly canes. 1.5 × 1m (5 × 3ft).

'Gloire de Ducher' 1865. Parentage unknown. Tall and lax, for wall or pillar. Fragrant double wine-purple blooms and dark green leaves. Only occasional late blooms. 2 × 1.2m (7 × 4ft).

'Heinrich Münch' 1911. 'Frau Karl Druschki' × ('Mme Caroline Testout' × 'Mrs W. J. Grant'). Large double scented soft-pink blooms. Vigorous, but spasmodic repeat only. 1.8 × 1.2m (6 × 4ft).

'Heinrich Schultheis' 1882. 'Mabel Morrison' × 'E. Y. Teas'. A Portland Hybrid Perpetual, with strongly-scented soft-pink very full flowers. Sparse second crop. 1.5 × 1m (5 × 3ft).

'Henry Nevard' 1924. parentage unknown. Very large double blooms, cupped and fragrant, in crimson-scarlet. Dark leaves and robust though not tall. 1.2 × 0.6m (4 × 2ft).

'Hugh Dickson' 1905. 'Lord Bacon × 'Gruss an Teplitz'. As lanky and ungainly as its namesake 'George Dickson'. Crimson-scarlet high-centred flowers. Fragrant. 2.7 × 1.2m (9 × 4ft).

Plate XVIII: Tea roses
The Teas came from China, and they are not as a race hardy in anything other than a warm climate. There are a few exceptions to this, however, of which 'Lady Hillingdon' (bottom) is one. It is nowadays grown in its climbing form more often than as a bush.

Delicate colourings are typical of the Teas, and a number of them – like the very early 'Catherine Mermet' (top left) – had the long centre petals that gave us the high-centred flowers of the modern Hybrid Tea. (The latter originated from hybridization between Tea roses and Hybrid Perpetuals.) The shape of the blooms of 'William R. Smith' (centre) and 'Clementina Parbonifri' (top right) shows strong Hybrid Perpetual influence, and the colour of the latter would suggest that the Pernetianas also had a hand in its birth.

For the history of the Teas, see page 68.

HYBRID PERPETUALS *continued*

'Marchioness of Londonderry' 1893. Very large globular fragrant blush-white blooms on a tall plant needing support. Spasmodic repeat. 1.8 × 1 m (6 × 3 ft).

'Mme Gabriel Luiset' 1877. Blooms silvery-pink, edged lighter. Fragrant. Vigorous, but no repeat. 1.5 × 1 m (5 × 3 ft).

'Mrs John Laing' 1887. 'François Michelon' seedling. Very large double fragrant soft-pink flowers on long stems. An old favourite. 1.5 × 1 m (5 × 3 ft).

'Oskar Cordel' 1897. 'Merveille de Lyon' × 'André Schwartz'. Carmine, very double fragrant blooms, freely borne. 1.5 × 1 m (5 × 3 ft).

'Paul Neyron' 1869. 'Victor Verdier' × 'Anna de Diesbach'. Huge paeony-like flowers of deepest rose-pink. Fine leaves but scent only slight. 1.5 × 1 m (5 × 3 ft).

'Prince Camille de Rohan' ('La Rosière') 1861. Possible hybrid of 'Général Jacqueminot' and 'Géant des Batailles'. Very double cupped flowers of velvety crimson-purple. Poor repeat. 1.2 × 1 m (4 × 3 ft).

'Reine des Violettes' 1860. 'Pius IX' seedling. An HP with the bushy growth of a Bourbon and the flowers of a Gallica. They open flat, filled with cerise-purple petals, that progress through every shade of violet, lilac and purple as they age. Big bush that needs fairly hard pruning and good soil to give its wonderful best. 1.8 × 1.5 m (6 × 5 ft).

'Robert Duncan' 1897. Huge flowers of 70 petals, which are purplish-pink, flushed scarlet, and are carried in clusters. Scented and free. 1.5 × 1 m (5 × 3 ft).

'Souvenir d'Alphonse Lavallée' 1884. Tall and open, needing pegging or a pillar. Dark crimson-maroon. Sweet scent. 2 × 1.2 m (7 × 4 ft).

'Souvenir du Docteur Jamain' 1865. 'Charles Lefèbvre' seedling. Plum-purple blooms, richly fragrant. Needs good soil. 1.8 × 1 m (6 × 3 ft).

'Ulrich Brunner' ('Ulrich Brunner Fils') 1881. Origin uncertain. Large cupped rather loose flowers, very fragrant, in rose-red, becoming carmine. Free and vigorous. 1.8 × 1.2 m (6 × 4 ft).

'Vick's Caprice' 1891. Sport of 'Archiduchesse Elizabeth d'Autiche'. Large double cupped blooms in lilac-pink, striped white and carmine. Scented. 90 × 60 cm (3 × 2 ft).

TEA ROSES

New classification: Old Garden Roses, Tea Roses. Under glass in anything other than a warm climate. Recurrent.

'Catherine Mermet' 1869. Flowers well shaped, large, flesh-pink with petal edges lilac-pink. For a long time widely used by the cut flower trade.

'Devoniensis' ('Magnolia Rose') 1838. 'Elinthii' × a yellow China? Creamy-white with blush centre, large, double and fragrant. 1.5 × 1 m (5 × 3 ft).

'Duchesse de Brabant' ('Comtesse de Labarthe', 'Comtesse Ouwaroff') 1857. Cupped blooms in bright rose-pink, double and very fragrant. Spreading. One of the hardiest.

'Général Schablikine' 1878. Vigorous, with bright, coppery-red blooms. 1.2 × 1 m (4 × 3 ft).

'Hume's Blush Tea-Scented China' (*R. × odorata*) 1809. *R. chinensis* × *R. gigantea*? One of the original Teas. Double flowers in pinkish-white, singly or two or three together. Moderately vigorous.

'Lady Hillingdon' 1910. 'Papa Gontier' × 'Mme Hoste'. A hardy variety. Beautiful long pointed buds open to fragrant apricot-yellow flowers. Bronze tints on leaves. 1.2 × 0.6 m (4 × 2 ft).

'Mme Scipion Cochet' 1873. Mauve-pink blooms, edged soft pink, cupped in form. 1.2 × 1 m (4 × 3 ft).

'Mlle Franziska Krüger' 1880. 'Catherine Mermet' × 'Général Schablikine'. Blended coppery-yellow and pink in large double fragrant blooms with weak necks. Hardy for a Tea. 1.2 × 1 m (4 × 3 ft).

'Maman Cochet' 1893. 'Marie van Houtte' × 'Mme Lombard'. Petals long, pale pink, deepening in the centre, base lemon-yellow. Flower high-centred and fragrant. Leaves dark green. 1.2 × 1 m (4 × 3 ft).

'Marie d'Orléans' 1883. Bright pink blooms, shaded darker, very full and opening flat. Free and vigorous. 1.2 × 1 m (4 × 3 ft).

'Mrs Dudley Cross' ('Dudley Cross') 1907. Pale buff-yellow with a crimson flush in late summer. Slight scent. 1.2 × 1 m (4 × 3 ft).

'Niphetos' 1843. Pointed buds open to large globular, very fragrant white flowers. Top greenhouse rose in its day. 90 × 60 cm (3 ft × 2 ft).

'Rosette Delizy' 1922. 'Général Galliéne' × 'Comtesse Bardi'. Shapely flowers in blends of yellow and apricot, with dark carmine outer petals. Vigorous. 1.5 × 1 m (5 × 3 ft).

'Safrano' 1839. Bud pointed, flower large, semi-double and fragrant. Colour saffron and apricot-yellow. Vigorous and free. An old and historic rose.

'William R. Smith' ('Blush Maman Cochet', 'Charles Dignée', 'Jeanette Heller', 'Maiden's Blush', 'President Smith', 'President William Smith') 1908. 'Maman Cochet' × 'Mme Hoste'. Double flowers of a creamy flesh-pink, paler in the centre and with yellow petal bases. Vigorous and tall, reaching 1.5 m (5 ft), with strong stems and mid-green semi-glossy leaves.

HYBRID TEAS

New classification: Bush Roses, large-flowered. Recurrent. The average height of these has been taken as 75 cm (2½ ft). Where varieties are taller – 90 cm (3 ft) or more – or shorter – 60 cm (2 ft) or below – this is mentioned.

'Admiral Rodney' 1973. Parents not given. Primarily an exhibition rose, with large high-centred blooms in pink which varies from strong to light. Only moderately vigorous, but freely-flowering. Strong fragrance.

'Adolph Horstmann' 1971. 'Dr A. J. Verhage' × 'Colour Wonder'. Blooms deep yellow, edged pink, singly and in small clusters. Slight scent. Semi-glossy mid-green leaves. Vigorous and upright.

'Akebono' 1964. 'Ethel Sanday' × 'Narzisse'. Large high-centred double blooms in light yellow, flushed carmine. Exhibition. Dark glossy leaves. Vigorous and upright; moderately free.

'Alec's Red' 1970. 'Fragrant Cloud' × 'Dame de Coeur'. Very fragrant cherry-red, full and rather globular blooms, singly and several together. Mid-green matt leaves. Vigorous and upright.

'Alexander' 1971. 'Super Star' × ('Ann Elizabeth' × 'Allgold'). Orange-vermilion double flowers opening cupped. Very vigorous and tall, with dark green semi-glossy leaves.

'Allegro' 1962. ('Happiness' × 'Independence') × 'Soraya'. Tall, vigorous and upright, with glossy dark green leaves. Medium-sized bright geranium-red blooms usually in clusters.

'Alpine Sunset' 1974. 'Dr A. J. Verhage' × 'Grandpa Dickson'. Peach-pink flushed yellow, full high-centred blooms, fragrant, singly and in small trusses. Glossy leaves. Healthy.

'Amatsu Omo' 1960. 'Chrysler Imperial' × 'Doreen'. Blooms golden yellow, edged deep orange, very full, high-centred to cupped. Vigorous. Glossy dark green leaves.

'American Heritage' 1965. 'Queen Elizabeth' × 'Yellow Perfection'. Long pointed buds, large, high-centred blooms in an ivory and salmon blend, becoming salmon. Dark leaves. Compact and free.

'American Pride' 1978. Cross between two unnamed seedlings. Striking deep red with rich hue of crushed velvet. Excellent form, disease-resistant and vigorous. Good in hot humid climates.

'Antigua' 1974. 'South Seas' × 'Golden Masterpiece'. Double high-centred blooms borne singly, in blends of apricot. Slight scent. Upright and vigorous.

'Apollo' 1971. 'High Time' × 'Imperial Gold'. Very big double yellow blooms, scented, on stems with few thorns. Dark glossy leaves. Vigorous, upright and tall.

'Apricot Silk' 1965. 'Souvenir de Jacques Verschuren' seedling. Tall, with glossy dark green, bronze-tinted leaves. Long pointed buds open to apricot flowers, moderately full.

'Arianna' 1968. 'Charlotte Armstrong' × ('Peace' × 'Michèle Meilland'). Vigorous and upright, with dark leaves. Large double flowers, carmine-rose suffused coral, high-centred. Slight scent.

'Arlene Francis' 1957. 'Eclipse' seedling × 'Golden Scepter'. Large double high-centred, very fragrant golden-yellow blooms. Dark glossy leaves. Vigorous and free.

'Avon' 1961. 'Nocturne' × 'Chrysler Imperial'. Blooms bright red, high-centred, very large and very fragrant. Vigorous and profuse bloomer.

'Aztec' 1957. 'Charlotte Armstrong' × unnamed seedling. Scarlet-orange double high-centred blooms. Spreading and vigorous in habit.

'Baccara' 1956. 'Happiness' × 'Independence'. Tall and upright, with dark green bronze-tinted leaves. Well-formed blooms, vermilion-red with darker outer shadings. No scent. Dislikes rain, but long the standby of the cut-flower trade for a red rose.

'Bajazzo' 1962. Parents not known. Purplish-red inside, with a white petal reverse. Fragrant, very large and well-shaped. Vigorous and upright. Mid-green leaves.

'Ballet' 1958. 'Florex' × 'Karl Herbst'. Deep pink very double, slightly fragrant blooms. Grey-green leaves. Vigorous and bushy in habit.

'Baronne Edmond de Rothschild' 1968. ('Baccara' × 'Crimson King') × 'Peace'. Vigorous and tall, with dark green leaves. Large full ruby-red blooms with a silvery reverse. Very fragrant.

'Beauté' 1953. 'Mme Joseph Perraud' × unnamed seedling. Very lovely well-formed double flowers, fragrant and in shades of light orange. Vigorous and free, and still one of the best in this colour.

'Belle Ange' 1962. Parents not given. Rose-pink, paler on inside of petals, double and large. Mid-green leaves. Free.

'Bettina' 1953. 'Peace' × ('Mme Joseph Perraud' × 'Demain'). Orange flowers, flushed and veined a deeper orange, double and with short centre petals. Bronzy leaves. Watch for black spot. Vigorous.

'Bewitched' 1967. 'Queen Elizabeth' × 'Tawny Gold'. Deep rose-red blooms, double, fragrant, high-centred. Vigorous and free. Glossy leaves.

'Big Ben' 1964. 'Ena Harkness' × 'Charles Mallerin'. Huge double high-centred fragrant dark velvety-red blooms. Dark leaves. Tall grower.

'Blanche Mallerin' 1941. 'Edith Krause' × 'White Briarcliffe'. Pure white large double

For the history of the Hybrid Teas, see page 70; for illustrations, see plates VIII, IX, XIX, XX, XXI and XXX (pp69, 73, 108, 112, 113 and 145).

high-centred blooms. Fragrant. Glossy leaves. Spreading.

'Blessings' 1968. 'Queen Elizabeth' × unnamed seedling. Full coral-pink flowers, opening cupped, borne several together. Matt leaves. Vigorous, bushy and branching. Ideal bedding rose.

'Blue Diamond' 1963. 'Purpurine' × 'Royal Tan'. Free-flowering. Lavender-mauve, large and double. Strong scent. Dark, coppery leaves.

'Blue Moon' ('Mainzer Fastnacht', 'Sisi') 1964. Seedling × 'Sterling Silver'. Large double high-centred lilac-mauve blooms. Fragrant. Upright and vigorous. The best 'blue' HT so far.

'Bond Street' 1965. 'Radar' × 'Queen Elizabeth'. Very tall and upright, with medium-sized very double blooms, several together in small clusters. Pink, with deeper tones at petal edges. Strong scent.

'Bonsoir' 1966. Seedling × seedling. Peach-pink, very full, well shaped and fragrant. Large glossy dark green leaves. Vigorous and upright. Dislikes rain.

'Bossa Nova' 1964. 'Leverkusen' × 'Buccaneer'. Very deep golden-yellow. Vigorous. Dark green glossy leaves.

'Brandenburg' 1965. ('Spartan' × 'Prima Ballerina') × 'Karl Herbst'. Deep salmon with darker reverse, moderately full. Matt leaves on vigorous, tall plant.

'Brasilia' 1967. 'Perfecta' × 'Piccadilly'. Flowers light scarlet with pale gold reverse. Full. Vigorous and upright, with semi-glossy mid-green leaves.

'Buccaneer' – see Grandifloras.

'Candy Stripe' 1963. Sport from 'Pink Peace'. Blooms very large (60 petals), dusky pink, striped and splashed with off-white or very pale pink. Cupped when open. Fragrant. Upright and bushy. Deep green leaves.

'Caramba' 1967. Parents not given. Blooms red with silver reverse and very full. Vigorous, tall and bushy. Leaves semi-glossy, dark green.

'Carla' 1963. 'Queen Elizabeth' × 'The Optimist'. Tall and upright. Dark leaves and soft pink blooms, shaded salmon, on long stems. Good for cutting.

'Casanova' 1964. 'Queen Elizabeth' × 'Perfecta'. Large, high-centred straw-yellow scented blooms. Dark leaves. Tall and upright habit.

'Century Two' 1971. 'Charlotte Armstrong' × 'Duet'. Dark, rose-red blooms, double and fragrant, deeper colour on reverse. Thorny, upright and tall.

'Charles de Gaulle' 1977. Parents not given. Large fully double blooms in lilac-mauve, richly scented. Compact, bushy grower.

'Charlie's Aunt' 1965. 'Golden Masterpiece' × 'Karl Herbst'. Vigorous, tall and branching, with dark green leaves. Large,

well-shaped light pink flowers with creamy-white reverse. Fragrant.

'Charlotte Armstrong' 1940. 'Soeur Thérèse' × 'Crimson Glory'. Large double fragrant blooms in cerise-red on long stems. Dark leaves, vigorous and free. Check the number of roses in this list of which it is a parent!

'Cherry Brandy' 1965. Parents not given. Blooms light vermilion, shading to gold at petal bases. Shapely, moderately full, opening wide. Mostly one to a stem. Scented. Free and branching, with bronze-tinted leaves.

'Chicago Peace' 1962. Sport of 'Peace' discovered in Chicago. Blooms and growth like 'Peace', but flowers phlox-pink with canary-yellow petal bases.

'Christian Dior' 1959. ('Independence' × 'Happiness') × ('Peace' × 'Happiness'). Large flowers, velvety-scarlet with paler reverse, full and shapely. Tall and upright. Mid-green leathery leaves.

'Chrysler Imperial' 1952. 'Charlotte Armstrong' × 'Mirandy'. Large double, high-centred very fragrant blooms in deep crimson, shading darker. Dark leaves. Compact and free.

'City of Bath' 1969. 'Gavotte' × 'Buccaneer'. Blooms deep candy-pink, paler on reverse, large, very full, fragrant, singly and in clusters. Matt leaves. Vigorous and branching habit.

'City of Gloucester' 1971. 'Gavotte' × 'Buccaneer'. Saffron-yellow shaded gold, with pink tint on outer petals. Tall and branching, with matt leaves.

'City of Hereford' 1967. 'Wellworth' × 'Spartan'. Bushy, branching and tall. Light green matt leaves. Large full globular flowers, rose pink with deeper reverse. Strong scent. Single blooms early, trusses later.

'Clarita' 1972. 'Super Star' × ('Zambra' × 'Romantica'). Flowers deep vermilion-red, large, on strong stems. Deep green glossy leaves. Upright.

'Cologne Carnival' ('Kölner Karneval', 'Blue Girl') 1964. Parents not given. Silvery-lilac, moderately full flowers, opening loosely. Vigorous and bushy with dark glossy leaves.

'Color Magic' 1977. Double creamy-pink high-centred fragrant blooms, ageing cherry-red. Free and healthy, upright and vigorous.

'Colour Wonder' ('Königin der Rosen') 1964. Parents not given. Very full blooms with short petals, orange-salmon with yellow reverse. Not too free. Thorny, vigorous, short-growing. Glossy dark leaves.

'Columbus Queen' 1963. 'La Jolla' × unnamed seedling. Medium-sized flowers, full and shapely, soft pink with magenta-pink reverse. Large glossy leaves. Very tall and vigorous grower.

'Command Performance' 1970. 'Super Star' × 'Hawaii'. Orange-red semi-double

blooms, opening cupped and strongly scented. Upright, with dark leathery leaves.

'Confidence' 1951. 'Peace' × 'Michèle Meilland'. Globular high-centred fragrant flowers in blends of light pink and yellow. Upright and bushy, with dark leaves.

'Coronado' 1961. ('Multnomah' × 'Peace') × ('Multnomah' × 'Peace'). Vigorous and upright, with mid-green glossy leaves. Large, shapely red and yellow bicolour flowers.

'Crimson Glory' 1935. 'Catherine Kordes' seedling × 'W. E. Chaplin'. Double flowers opening cupped, in deep velvety-crimson, shaded darker, with strong fragrance. Spreading growth. Still a favourite, but probably past its best.

'Criterion' 1966. ('Independence' × 'Signal Red') × 'Peace'. Vigorous, tall and branching, with dark green glossy leaves. Well-formed large flowers in rich cerise.

'Curiosity' 1971. A 'Cleopatra' sport. Short, compact grower, with dark green glossy leaves, splashed with cream and white, ruby-red when young. Globular scarlet blooms with gold reverse.

'Dainty Bess' 1925. 'Ophelia' × 'K of K'. medium-sized single fragrant soft rose-pink flowers with darker stamens. Dark leaves, vigorous and free. Floribunda-like.

'Day Dream' 1969. 'Helen Traubel' × 'Tiffany'. Long pointed buds open to large double cupped deep pink flowers. Glossy leaves. Upright and bushy.

'Dame de Coeur' 1959. 'Peace' × 'Independence'. Large full dusky-pink flowers. Vigorous.

'Diamond Jubilee' 1947. 'Maréchal Niel' × 'Feu Pernet-Ducher'. With modern mildew sprays, still one of the best in its colour – a buff, creamy-yellow. Large high-centred sweetly scented blooms. Dark leaves, vigorous and compact.

'Diorama' 1967. 'Peace' × 'Beauté'. Tall, with long stems and dark green leaves. Perfect apricot-yellow blooms, the outer petals flushed pink. Fragrant. Good in autumn.

'Dr Albert Schweitzer' 1961. 'Chic Parisien' × 'Michèle Meilland'. Cerise with paler reverse, large, full, but loosely formed. Vigorous and bushy.

'Double Delight' 1977. 'Granada' × 'Garden Party'. Red and white bicolour, with double globular high-centred very fragrant blooms. Vigorous and hardy.

'Dries Verschuren' 1961. 'Geheimrat Duisberg' × seedling. Pale yellow, reverse bright yellow, full and shapely. Shiny dark green leaves, bronze-tinted. Bushy.

'Duet' 1960. 'Fandango' × 'Roundelay'. Double flowers, opening cupped, fragrant, light pink with reverse darker. Vigorous and branching. Dark green leaves.

'Duke of Windsor' ('Hertzog von Windsor') 1968. 'Prima Ballerina' × unnamed seedling. Large full orange-vermilion blooms borne several together; very fragrant. Bushy with dark green leaves. Not the healthiest of roses.

'Eclipse' 1935. 'Joanna Hill' × 'Fedrico Casas'. Very long petals, opening loosely; golden yellow on strong stems. Dark leaves. Vigorous and branching.

'Eden Rose' 1953. 'Peace' × 'Signora'. Very full, very fragrant blooms, high-centred, then cupped. Tyrian-rose. Dark leaves, glossy, on a vigorous upright plant.

'Eiffel Tower' 1963. 'First Love' × unnamed seedling. Pink full blooms, free and fragrant. Tall and upright, with semi-glossy leathery leaves.

'El Cid' 1969. 'Fandango' × 'Roundelay'. Bud ovoid, opening to large double flowers, high-centred to cupped, orange-red. Vigorous, upright and bushy.

'Electron' – see 'Mullard Jubilee'.

'Elegy' 1971. Parents not given. Large shapely blooms, poppy-red in early stages, then turkey-red. Vigorous and upright.

'Elida' 1967. Parents not given. Blooms vermilion, full and slightly scented. Tall and branching in habit, with semi-glossy mid-green leaves.

'Elizabeth Harkness' 1969. 'Red Dandy' × 'Piccadilly'. Red-tinted buds open to high-centred buff flowers, tinged pink. Fragrant, with semi-glossy leaves. Bushy and vigorous.

'Embassy' 1967. 'Gavotte' × ('Magenta' × 'Spek's Yellow'). Flowers light gold, veined and edged carmine, large, high-centred and fragrant. Tall and upright in habit, with dark green leaves.

'Ena Harkness' 1946. 'Crimson Glory' × 'Southport'. A long-famous crimson-scarlet rose with high-centred blooms, scented only in some strains and with rather weak flower stalks. Dark leaves. Vigorous and bushy.

'Ernest H. Morse' 1965. Parentage unknown. Vigorous, with large dark green leaves. Large well-formed blooms in rich turkey-red, fading duller red but still attractive. Fragrant and very free.

'Eroica' ('Erotica') 1968. Flowers velvety dark red, large, full and very fragrant. Vigorous and upright grower. Semi-glossy dark leaves.

'Etoile de Hollande' 1919. 'General McArthur' × 'Hadley'. Freely-borne cupped dusky-red fragrant blooms. Moderate vigour and branching growth. Mildew likely. Long a favourite and can still be worth growing.

'Fantan' 1958. ('Pigalle' × 'Prelude') × self. Large full, cupped flowers in burnt orange to yellow ochre. Moderately vigorous grower. Leathery leaves.

'Femina' 1963. 'Fernand Arles' × 'Mignonne'. Salmon-pink full flowers. Bronze-tinted mid-green leaves. Vigorous and upright in habit.

Plate XIX: 'Peace' and some of its descendants
It is fitting that a whole page should be devoted to that marvellous rose 'Peace' (top) and two of the many roses that hybridists have produced using it as a parent. In the first generation of 'Peace' crosses, many famous varieties spring to mind, among them 'Rose Gaujard', 'Eden Rose', 'Mischief' and 'Gold Crown'. One of the most lovely (despite its dislike of rain) is 'Royal Highness' (bottom right); with its always immaculate, high-centred blooms, it has won and continues to win award after award at rose shows all over the world.
'Chicago Peace' (centre left) is something different, a sport from 'Peace' named after the city where it was discovered. The crimson and yellow bicolor 'Kronenbourg' was another, and both have their parent's vigour.

'**Feria**' 1968. ('Grand Gala' × 'Premier Bal') × 'Love Song'. Large globular very fragrant coral blooms, suffused pink, on long strong stems. Leathery leaves. Upright, but not too free with its flowers.

'**First Love**' ('Premier' Amour') 1951. 'Charlotte Armstrong' × 'Show Girl'. Medium-sized double well-shaped blooms in shades of rose-pink. Light green leaves. Bushy and free.

'**First Prize**' 1970. 'Enchantment' seedling × 'Golden Masterpiece' seedling. Long pointed buds and very large high-centred fragrant rose-pink flowers, the centre in blends of ivory. Dark leaves; vigorous, upright and free.

'**Flaming Peace**' – see 'Kronenbourg'.

'**Fleet Street**' 1973. 'Kronenbourg' × 'Prima Ballerina'. Flowers rich pink, well-formed, large and fragrant. Vigorous but short-growing. Dark glossy leaves. Not too free with blooms.

'**Florida von Scharbaritz**' 1957. 'Spek's Yellow' × seedling. Strong and upright, with dark glossy leaves. Orange-salmon blooms, borne several together.

'**Forty Niner**' 1949. 'Contrast' × 'Charlotte Armstrong'. Large flowers, cupped and fragrant. A red and yellow bicolour, with dark leaves. Vigorous and upright.

'**Fragrant Charm**' 1969. 'Prima Ballerina' × 'Kaiserin Farah'. Large, high-centred very fragrant rose-red blooms on a plant of moderate vigour.

'**Fragrant Cloud**' ('Nuage Parfumé', 'Duftwolke') 1964. Seedling × 'Prima Ballerina'. Vigorous and bushy, with large dark semi-glossy leaves, coppery when young. Very large double geranium-lake dusky flowers, dulling in colour after a day or two. Strong scent. Very free.

'**Fred Edmunds**' ('L'Arlésienne') 1943. 'Duquesa de Pěnaranda' × 'Marie-Claire'. Large cupped flowers, coppery-orange with good scent. Glossy leaves. Open, branching growth.

'**Fred Gibson**' 1968. 'Gavotte' × 'Buccaneer'. Amber-yellow to apricot-yellow high-centred double flowers, singly and in small clusters. Tall and vigorous, with dark green leaves. Very good in autumn.

'**Friendship**' 1979. 'Fragrant Cloud' × 'Maria Callas'. Strong-growing rugged bush with a profusion of very large coral-red blooms, darkening slightly. Fragrant.

'**Futura**' 1975. Unnamed seedling × unnamed seedling. Loosely double blooms in bright vermilion. Upright and free.

'**Garden Party**' 1959. 'Charlotte Armstrong' × 'Peace'. Ivory to cream, pink-tinged large full, slightly fragrant blooms, loosely formed. Good foliage. Tall and bushy in habit.

'**Garvey**' 1961. 'McGredy's Yellow' × 'Karl Herbst'. Large, rather globular but well-formed blooms in two tones of pink, deeper on reverse. Robust and good in rain. Upright.

'**Gavotte**' 1963. 'Ethel Sanday' × 'Lady Sylvia'. Large double rounded high-centred blooms in silvery-pink. Very dark green leaves. Healthy. Vigorous and branching. Not tall.

'**Gay Gordons**' 1969. 'Belle Blonde' × 'Karl Herbst'. Flowers orange-yellow and red, full, slightly fragrant and free. Glossy dark green leaves. Low-growing and bushy.

'**Gay Paris**' 1960. ('Floradora' × 'Barcelona') × ('Charles Mallerin' × 'Tonnere'). Large well-formed fragrant bright crimson blooms. Bright green leaves, profuse.

'**Gertrude Schweitzer**' 1973. Blooms orange-salmon to light apricot with deeper shadings. Shapely, with long petals, medium-sized, carried singly. Semi-glossy leaves, that are bronze when young. Vigorous and branching.

'**Ginger Rogers**' 1968. 'Super Star' × 'Miss Ireland'. Moderately full and slightly fragrant blooms in salmon-pink. Coppery leaves. Upright and vigorous.

'**Gold Crown**' ('Goldkrone') 1960. 'Peace' × 'Spek's Yellow'. Large high-centred double deep yellow blooms. Glossy leaves. Very sturdy and tall.

'**Golden Masterpiece**' 1954. 'Mandalay' × 'Golden Scepter'. Very large high-centred fragrant golden-yellow blooms. Very glossy leaves. Upright and vigorous.

'**Golden Melody**' ('Irene Churruca') 1934. 'Mme Butterfly' × ('Lady Hillingdon' × 'Souvenir de Claudius Pernet'). Long petals, a high centre, in creamy-buff. Strong scent. Moderate vigour. An old rose but still good.

'**Golden Prince**' 1968. ('Monte Carlo' × 'Bettina') × ('Peace' × Soraya'). Vigorous and upright, with bronzy glossy foliage. Large double high-centred deep golden-yellow flowers, unfading. Fragrant. Free.

'**Golden Scepter**' – see 'Spek's Yellow'.

'**Golden Splendour**' 1962. 'Buccaneer' × 'Golden Sun'. Large double clear light yellow, fragrant flowers. Dark glossy leaves. Vigorous, tall and upright.

'**Golden Times**' 1970. 'Fragrant Cloud' × 'Golden Splendour'. Golden-yellow very full fragrant blooms. Tall and upright, with large matt mid-green leaves.

'**Grace de Monaco**' 1956. 'Peace' × 'Michèle Meilland'. Full globular clear rose-pink fragrant blooms. Tall and branching with matt mid-green leaves.

'**Granada**' ('Donatella') 1963. 'Tiffany' × 'Cavalcade'. Large urn-shaped flowers, scented and in a blend of rose-pink, nasturtium-red and lemon yellow. Leathery and crinkled leaves. Vigorous and upright.

'**Grand'mère Jenny**' 1950. 'Peace' × ('Julien Pontin' × 'Sensation'). Like a smaller

Plate XX: Modern Hybrid Teas (1)

This plate (overleaf) shows some of the outstanding Hybrid Teas introduced for bedding between the years 1946 and 1964. All of them can still be found in most nursery lists despite the thousands of varieties that have been introduced since. That great scarlet rose 'Ena Harkness' (bottom left) has, apart from a tendency to hang its head, a peculiarity in that some strains are scented and some not.

'King's Ransom' (top right) of 1961 ranked as the best yellow Hybrid Tea for bedding well into the late 1970s, and 'Piccadilly' (top left), raised in 1959, has still to be bettered as a red and yellow bicolor.

'Fragrant Cloud' (centre right) is the most recent of the four, and its paeony-like blooms are unmatched among the Hybrid Teas for their rich fragrance.

See also plates VIII, IX, XIX, XXI and XXX (pp69, 73, 108, 113 and 145).

'Peace'. Large flowers, pale yellow suffused and edged with apricot and pink. Vigorous and free.

'Grandpa Dickson' ('Irish Gold') 1965. ('Perfecta' × 'Governador Braga da Cruz') × 'Piccadilly'. Strong and upright, with little spread and dark leathery leaves. Large high-centred light yellow blooms, petal edges sometimes flushed pink.

'Grand Slam' 1963. 'Charlotte Armstrong' × 'Montezuma'. Large cupped flowers in cherry to rose-red. Dark semi-glossy leaves. Upright and well branched.

'Greetings' ('Gruss an Berlin') 1963. Rich, unshaded scarlet high-centred, full flowers. Large dark green leaves, red-tinted when young. Vigorous and bushy.

'Gypsy' 1972. [('Happiness' × 'Chrysler Imperial') × 'El Capitan'] × 'Comanche'. Large double orange-red blooms with slight scent only. Dark green glossy leaves. Vigorous and tall.

'Harriny' 1967. 'Pink Favorite' × 'Lively'. Light pink blooms with salmon shadings and strong fragrance. Dark green healthy leaves. Vigorous.

'Hawaii' 1960. 'Golden Masterpiece' × unnamed seedling. Very long pointed buds open to shapely full coral-salmon blooms, shaded orange. Fragrant. Upright and rather spindly. Copper-green leaves.

'Hawaiian Sunset' 1962. 'Charlotte Armstrong' × 'Signora'. Very large flowers, orange-apricot with a yellow margin. Dark green leaves. Moderately vigorous. Scented.

'Helen Traubel' 1951. 'Charlotte Armstrong' × 'Glowing Sunset'. Pinkish-apricot double flowers. opening flat and very free. Matt green leaves. Fragrant. Tall and upright.

'Heure Mauve' 1963. 'Simone' × 'Prelude'. Robust, dwarf and bushy. Large deep lilac flowers, fading silvery-lilac. Some fragrance. Dark green leaves.

'High Society' 1961. Parents not given. High-centred full glowing red blooms and mid-green leaves. Vigorous grower, but short and bushy.

'Honey Favorite' 1962. Sport of 'Pink Favorite'. Pale yellowish-pink with yellow petal bases. Large double high-centred flowers. Vigorous and upright, with exceptionally healthy mid-green leaves.

'Ideal Home' ('Idylle') 1960. 'Monte Carlo' × 'Tonnerre'. Vigorous and upright, with dark green leaves. Large pink and silver bicolour flowers. Free.

'Indian Chief' 1968. 'Super Star' × unknown variety. Well-shaped currant-red blooms with a golden petal base. Vigorous to less than average height. Dark green leaves.

'Indian Song' 1972. 'Radar' × ('Karl Herbst' × 'Sabrina'). Large blooms, cherry-red and buttercup yellow. Glossy mid-green leaves. Vigorous.

'Intermezzo' 1963. 'Grey Pearl' × 'Lila Vidri'. Medium-sized deep lavender fragrant blooms. Compact and moderately vigorous. Glossy dark green leaves.

'Interview' (formerly 'Interflora') 1970. ('Baccara' × 'Message') × ('Baccara' × 'Jolie Madame'). Large well-shaped vermilion flowers. Vigorous, tall and upright. Mid-green leaves.

'Invitation' 1961. 'Charlotte Armstrong' × 'Signora'. Vigorous and branching, with glossy leaves. Large shapely flowers, rich salmon-pink with yellow petal bases and scarlet veining, opening quickly. Very fragrant. Few thorns.

'Isabel de Ortiz' 1962. Parents not given. Very large, exhibition-form blooms, deep pink with reverse silvery-pink. Scented. Very robust and reasonably free. Dark leaves. Barely tolerates rain.

'Jimmy Greaves' 1971. 'Dorothy Peach' × 'Prima Ballerina'. Large very full well-formed blooms, cerise-red with silver reverse. Exhibition type. Vigorous and bushy.

'John F. Kennedy' 1966. Unnamed seedling × 'White Queen'. Large full well-shaped fragrant white flowers. Healthy dark green leaves. Vigorous and tall.

'John S. Armstrong' – see Grandifloras.

'John Waterer' 1969. ('Karl Herbst' × 'Ethel Sanday') × 'Hannah'. Full deep rose-red blooms, high-centred, singly and several together. Tall and erect. Dark green matt leaves. One of the better modern reds.

'Josephine Bruce' 1949. 'Crimson Glory' × 'Madge Whipp'. Moderate to large cupped dusky-crimson blooms, freely borne. Sprawling growth. Dark leaves.

'Just Joey' 1971. 'Fragrant Cloud' × 'Dr A. J. Verhage'. Light coppery-orange, veined red, paling towards petal edges. Moderately full flowers opening wide. Vigorous, with matt dark green leaves, red-tinted when they are young.

'Kabuki' 1968. ('Monte Carlo' × 'Bettina') × ('Peace' × 'Soraya'). Large high-centred fragrant Indian-yellow blooms. Bronzy glossy leaves. Vigorous and upright.

'Kaiserin Auguste Viktoria' 1891. 'Coquette de Lyon' × 'Lady Mary Fitzwilliam'. Snow-white blooms of 100 petals, with centres tinted yellow. Fragrant. Robust, with matt leaves. Still a favourite in the US.

'Kalahari' 1970. 'Uncle Walter' × ('Hamburger Phoenix' × 'Danse du Feu'). Full deep rose-pink blooms, singly and several together. Light green leaves. Moderately vigorous grower.

'Kentucky Derby' 1973. 'John S. Armstrong × 'Grand Slam'. Urn-shaped blooms in deep red on long stems. Upright, but well branched. Healthy.

'King of Hearts' 1968. 'Karl Herbst' × 'Ethel Sanday'. Bright red high-centred blooms of medium size. Vigorous in growth, with dark leaves.

'King's Ransom' 1961. 'Golden Masterpiece' × 'Lydia'. Blooms a rich, pure yellow, unfading, full, fragrant and very free. Dark green leaves. Vigorous and branching.

'Kordes Perfecta' – see 'Perfecta'.

'Kronenbourg' ('Flaming Peace') 1964. Sport of 'Peace'. All the attributes of its renowned parent, but large blooms red to crimson with an old-gold reverse, the red purpling with age.

'Lady Elgin' ('Thais') 1954. 'Mme Kriloff' × ('Peace' × 'Geneva'). Tall and upright with long-stemmed, well-formed buff-yellow blooms. Fragrant.

'Lady Seton' 1966. 'Ma Perkins' × 'Mischief'. Tall, strong and bushy, with midgreen leaves. Medium-sized very fragrant clear rose-pink flowers.

'Lady Vera' 1976. 'Royal Highness' × 'Christian Dior'. High-centred exhibition-type flowers, though not big. Light pink with darker reverse. Vigorous and bushy.

'Lady X' 1966. Seedling × 'Simone'. Long pointed buds and high-centred double flowers in pale mauve. Some scent. Strong and upright grower.

'La France' 1867. For possible parentage see main text. The first Hybrid Tea. Large globular double flowers in silvery pink, deeper on reverse. Matt foliage. Very fragrant. Nowadays find a good strain if full vigour is to be achieved.

'Lancastrian' 1965. 'Ena Harkness' × unknown variety. Vigorous and upright, with glossy crimson-tinted leaves. Very fragrant. Large rich velvety crimson-scarlet flowers. Good in autumn.

'Lemon Spice' 1966. 'Helen Traubel' × seedling. Large high-centred very fragrant light yellow flowers. Dark leaves. Strong and spreading.

'Lily de Gerlache' 1971. 'Perfecta' × 'Prima Ballerina'. Full cherry-pink strongly scented flowers. Tall and upright. Dark green leaves.

'Lotte Gunthart' 1964. 'Queen Elizabeth' × 'Bravo'. Large paeony-like bright red blooms of up to 100 petals. Leathery leaves. Tall and upright.

'Louisiana' 1975. Unnamed seedling × unnamed seedling. Creamy-white, high-centred blooms on long stems. Slight fragrance. Vigorous, healthy and upright. Free-flowering.

'Lowell Thomas' ('Botaniste Abriel') 1943. 'Mme Mélanie Soupert' × 'Nonin'. Intense golden-yellow blooms, high-centred and freely borne. Compact and bushy.

'Lucy Cramphorn' ('Maryse Kriloff') 1960. 'Peace' × 'Baccara'. Large full well-formed turkey-red blooms, flushed signal-red. Fragrant. Glossy leaves. Upright and sturdy in habit.

'Mme Butterfly' 1918. Sport of 'Ophelia'. Still one of the most immaculate small Hybrid Teas. Perfect high-centred fragrant blooms in light pink, with yellow tints at the centre. Dainty and well branched, but not tall.

'Mme Caroline Testout' 1890. 'Mme de Tartas' × 'Lady Mary Fitzwilliam'. Large globular very double blooms in silvery-pink with deeper carmine shadings. Vigorous and bushy. Now more often grown in its climbing form.

'Mme Edouard Herriot' ('The Daily Mail Rose') 1913. 'Mme Caroline Testout' × a Hybrid Tea. A pioneer in its colour (coral-orange, with scarlet tints), still profuse, though flowers have few petals and are loosely-formed. Huge thorns. Vigorous and more often now grown as a climber.

'Mme René Cassin' 1962. 'Mme Armand Souzy' × 'Impeccable'. Upright, with deep green glossy leaves. Large flowers, cyclamen-pink with silvery-rose veining in the reverse.

'Manuela' 1968. Parents not given. Strong, upright and bushy, with glossy leaves. Large fragrant well-formed cherry-pink flowers.

'Majorette' 1967. 'Zambra' × 'Fred Edmunds'. Flowers orange and bronze, shaded peach, globular to cupped. Dark coppery-bronze glossy leaves. Vigorous and upright.

'Maria Callas' ('Miss All-American Beauty') 1965. 'Chrysler Imperial' × 'Karl Herbst'. Bushy and tall, with dark green glossy leaves. Large very full dark carmine-pink blooms with lighter shades, opening cupped.

'Margot Fonteyn' 1964. 'Independence' × 'Ma Perkins'. Medium-sized cherry-red blooms of good form; scented. Vigorous but not tall.

'Marie Antoinette' 1968. 'Queen Elizabeth' × 'Chrysler Imperial'. Large cupped slightly fragrant pink flowers with a darker reverse. Dark glossy leaves. Vigorous and upright.

'Marla Rubinstein' 1971. 'Sea Pearl' × 'Fragrant Cloud'. Very full coral-pink flowers with deeper reverse. Strong scent. Tall and upright, with matt leaves.

'Matterhorn' 1965. 'Buccaneer' × 'Cherry Glow'. Medium to large high-centred white flowers. Dark leathery leaves. Tall and upright grower.

'Maurice Chevalier' 1959. 'Incendie' × ('Floradora' seedling × 'Independence'). Large shapely fragrant rich red flowers, shaded garnet-red, growing on strong stems. Glossy leaves.

'Medallion' 1973. 'South Seas' × 'King's Ransom'. Huge double flowers in buff-apricot tones, opening loosely. Light green leaves. Inclined to be leggy.

'Mellow Yellow' 1969. A 'Piccadilly' sport. Moderately full blooms, yellow with pink edges. Semi-glossy leaves. Bushy and uniform in growth.

'Melrose' 1963. 'Silver Lining' × 'E. G.

Plate XXI: Modern Hybrid Teas (2)
(Overleaf) Any choice of the best Hybrid Teas of the last few years must be a personal one. In a sense, too, it must be a prediction, for they will not yet have stood the test of time. 'Double Delight' (bottom right) would certainly seem to be a candidate for honours, with its lovely colour blends and strong growth. It is one of quite a small number of American roses that have crossed the Atlantic to the United Kingdom with success, unlike its fellow-countryman 'First Prize' (top right), which is a winner in the States but rarely seen in Britain. The Scottish-bred 'Silver Jubilee' (top left), a healthy, sturdy grower will, on its showing so far, be one of the best roses of the 1970s. The rather older 'Grandpa Dickson' (bottom left) of 1965 can be said to have arrived, its one weakness being a dislike of light soils. See also plates VIII, IX, XIX, XX and XXX (pp69, 73, 108, 112 and 145).

Hill'. Flowers creamy-white, flushed cherry-red, of medium size. Dark leaves. Tall and upright; can be lanky.

'Memoriam' 1961. ('Blanche Mallerin' × 'Peace') × ('Peace' × 'Frau Karl Druschki'). Beautifully-shaped double flowers in the palest pink – almost white. Dark leaves. Moderately vigorous. Dislikes rain.

'Message' ('White Knight') 1955. ('Virgo' × 'Peace') × 'Virgo'. Moderately large blooms, very shapely in bud but opening loosely. The purest white. Vigorous and free. Light green leaves.

'Metropole' 1961. 'Sidney Peabody' × 'Peace'. Large globular fragrant pink flowers on good long stems. Vigorous.

'Michèle Meilland' 1945. 'Joanna Hill' × 'Peace'. Strong-growing but not tall. Shapely double flowers in bright pink, tinted lilac.

'Mirandy' 1945. 'Night' × 'Charlotte Armstrong'. Large double globular blooms, garnet-red, darkening with age. Very fragrant. Sturdy and bushy.

'Mischief' 1961. 'Peace' × 'Spartan'. Salmon to shrimp-pink high-centred double flowers of varying size. Very free and robust.

'Miss All-American Beauty' – see 'Maria Callas'.

'Miss Harp' ('Oregold') 1970. 'Piccadilly' × 'Colour Wonder'. Very full deep bronze-yellow fragrant blooms. Glossy dark leaves. Vigorous and tall.

'Mister Lincoln' 1964. 'Chrysler Imperial' × 'Charles Mallerin'. Large dark dusky-red, very fragrant blooms, shapely at first, opening cupped. Matt dark green leaves. Very tall and vigorous.

'Mrs Oakley Fisher' 1921. A single Hybrid Tea with deep orange-yellow blooms in clusters. Fragrant. Bronze-tinted leaves.

'Mojave' 1954. 'Charlotte Armstrong' × 'Signora'. Apricot-orange, veined darker. Flowers high-centred but open loosely. Rather leggy grower.

'Montezuma' – see Grandifloras.

'Mullard Jubilee' ('Electron') 1969. 'Paddy McGredy' × 'Prima Ballerina'. Cerise-pink very full flowers, borne several together. Fragrant. Bushy and compact, with dark glossy leaves.

'My Choice' 1958. 'Wellworth' × 'Ena Harkness'. Unjustly neglected despite two gold medals. Very double, rather globular blooms in soft pink with a primrose-yellow reverse. Strongly scented. Vigorous and tall.

'National Trust' 1970. 'Evelyn Fison' × 'King of Hearts'. Blooms red, very double, singly and several together. Upright and compact. Dark matt leaves.

'New Style' 1962. ('Happiness' × 'Independence') × 'Peace'. Bright crimson-scarlet flowers, shapely in bud, opening loosely. No scent. Dark green copper-tinted leaves. Vigorous.

'Nocturne' 1947. 'Charlotte Armstrong' × 'Night'. Large double cupped flowers in bright red, shaded crimson. Scented. Dark leaves. Upright and bushy.

'Norman Hartnell' 1962. 'Brilliant' × 'Ballet'. Mid-green matt leaves, copper-tinted when young. Large shapely flowers in cerise-pink, holding their shape well.

'Northern Lights' 1969. 'Fragrant Cloud' × 'Kingcup'. Vigorous and upright, with mid-green matt leaves. Blooms very full and high centred, canary-yellow with a suffusion of rosy-pink on the outer petals. Very fragrant.

'Numéro Un' 1961. Parents not given. Large globular scarlet-red flowers passing to vermilion-red. Bushy even growth and bronzy leaves. Tall.

'Oklahoma' 1964. 'Chrysler Imperial' × 'Charles Mallerin'. Large shapely very fragrant flowers in dark red. Dark matt leaves. Bushy and free.

'Oldtimer' ('Coppertone') 1969. Parentage not given. Very large well-formed, high-centred blooms of rich coppery-bronze.

'Ophelia' 1912. Parents uncertain, but has given rise to almost countless fine sports (see 'Mme Butterfly'). Medium-sized shapely flowers, scented and flesh-pink, tinted yellow. Robust but not tall. One of the classic roses of this century.

'Oregold' – see 'Miss Harp'.

'Oriana' 1970. Parents not given. Very large full red flowers with a creamy-white reverse, mostly singly. Strong and upright, with mid-green leaves.

'Pania' 1968. 'Paddy McGredy' × ('Kordes Perfecta' × 'Montezuma'). Rose-pink, deepening at the petal edges. Bushy in habit and even-growing.

'Papa Meilland' 1963. 'Chrysler Imperial' × 'Charles Mallerin'. Blooms shapely, dark crimson, full and fragrant. Dark leaves which welcome mildew. Vigorous and upright.

'Paradise' 1979. 'Swarthmore' × unnamed seedling. One of the most distinctive roses, developing a most unusual colour combination of striking beauty. As the bud opens its high centre becomes silvery-lavender with each petal brushed with vivid pink. On ageing the lavender deepens and the pink becomes ruby-red. Vigorous and healthy, with large glossy green foliage.

'Pascali' 1963. 'Queen Elizabeth' × 'White Butterfly'. Tall, strong and upright, with semi-glossy leaves. Shapely small to medium-sized flowers in creamy-white with a hint of buff at the centre. The healthiest and most rain-proof white Hybrid Tea.

'Peace' ('Gioia', 'Gloria Dei', 'Mme A. Meilland') 1939. [('George Dickson' × 'Souvenir de Claudius Pernet') × ('Joanna Hill' × 'Charles P. Kilham')] × 'Margaret McGredy'. The world's favourite rose. Huge high-centred blooms, opening cupped, in pale yellow, edged and sometimes flushed pink. Deeper colours in autumn. Very tall, vigorous and outstandingly healthy. Glossy deep green leaves. light pruning only. Very slight scent.

'Peer Gynt' 1967. 'Colour Wonder' × 'Golden Giant'. Canary-yellow full, slightly fragrant blooms. Large matt green leaves. Compact and bushy.

'Percy Thrower' 1963. 'La Jolla' × 'Karl Herbst'. Well-formed fragrant large, rose-pink flowers. Glossy leaves. Vigorous but lax and sprawling.

'Perfecta' ('Kordes Perfecta') 1957. 'Spek's Yellow' × 'Karl Herbst'. Upromising buds open to immaculate very double high-centred flowers, cream, tipped and flushed pink and yellow. Fragrant. Very vigorous and upright, but flower stalks sometimes too weak for bloom size.

'Perfume Delight' 1974. 'Peace' × [('Happiness' × 'Chrysler Imperial') × 'El Capitan']. Huge shapely fragrant blooms in medium pink. Upright and bushy in habit. Matt leaves.

'Peter Frankenfeld' 1966. Parents not given. Strong and upright with dark green leaves. Large shapely slightly scented deep rose-pink blooms on long stems, very good for cutting.

'Pharaoh' ('Pharaon') 1967. ('Happiness' × 'Independence') × 'Suspense'. Large full orange-red blooms. Dark green glossy leaves. Strong and upright.

'Piccadilly' 1960. 'McGredy's Yellow' × 'Karl Herbst'. Still the best scarlet and gold bicolour. Shapely blooms become suffused orange-red as they age. Healthy dark glossy leaves with a bronzy tint. Strong and well-branched habit of growth.

'Pink Favorite' 1956. 'Juno' × ('George Arends' × 'New Dawn'). Large rose-pink high-centred blooms, but needs much disbudding to get full size. Fine leaves; about the healthiest of all Hybrid Teas. Tall and upright grower.

'Pink Peace' 1959. ('Peace' × 'Monique') × ('Peace' × 'Mrs John Laing'). Not, despite its name, a 'Peace' sport, and not much resembling it. Very big, rather loosely-formed double flowers, pink and fragrant. Vigorous and bushy.

'Pink Supreme' 1963. 'Amor' × 'Peace'. Very vigorous, tall and branching, with large light green leaves. Shapely soft pink fragrant blooms with petals attractively waved.

'Portrait' 1971. 'Pink Parfait' × 'Pink Peace'. Large long-lasting double blooms, pink and moderately fragrant. Dark glossy leaves. Healthy and vigorous.

'Precious Platinum' 1974. 'Red Planet' × 'Franklin Engelmann'. Full fragrant cardinal-red blooms, well scented. Glossy dark green leaves. Vigorous.

'President Herbert Hoover' 1930. 'Sensation' × 'Souvenir de Claudius Pernet'. Blends of orange, gold and rose-red in a bloom opening loosely, with fine scent. Vigorous but leggy. Matt dark green leaves.

'Prima Ballerina' ('Première Ballerine') 1958. Unknown seedling × 'Peace'. Shapely, medium-sized double flowers in shades of cherry-pink. Strong scent. Tall and upright.

'Princess' 1964. ('Peace' × 'Magicienne') × ('Independence' × 'Radar'). Very full, globular but high-centred blooms in bright vermilion, not too plentiful. Short-growing but quite vigorous.

'Princess Margaret of England' 1968. 'Queen Elizabeth' × ('Peace' × 'Michèle Meilland'). Large phlox-pink shapely flowers only slightly scented. Matt light green leaves. Strong and upright.

'Princess Paola' 1967. Parents unknown. Flowers pink with a darker reverse, very full and very fragrant. Matt mid-green leaves. Upright and moderately vigorous.

'Proud Land' 1969. 'Chrysler Imperial' × unnamed seedling. Very large, very fragrant deep red blooms of 60 petals. Free. Dark leaves. Upright.

'Red Devil' ('Coeur d'Amour') 1965. 'Silver Lining' × 'Prima Ballerina'. Very vigorous and tall, with healthy dark green leaves. Fine high-centred flowers which hold their form for ever, scarlet with a lighter reverse. Strongly scented.

'Red Chief' 1967. Seedling × 'Chrysler Imperial'. Large shapely very fragrant light red blooms. Dark leathery leaves. Very vigorous, upright and bushy.

'Red Lion' 1964. 'Perfecta' × 'Brilliant'. A tall, slender grower with bronzy-green leaves near the flowers, merging to dark green lower down. Shapely dark cerise-pink blooms, holding well. Scented.

'Red Masterpiece' 1973. ('Siren' × 'Chrysler Imperial') × ('Carrousel' × 'Chrysler Imperial'). Large high-centred deep red blooms with strong scent. Vigorous and upright grower.

'Red Queen' ('Liebestraum') 1968. 'Colour Wonder' × 'Liberty Bell'. Cherry-red flowers, very full, large and borne several together. Vigorous and upright.

'Red Planet' 1970. 'Red Devil' × ('Brilliant' × unnamed seedling). Blooms crimson, very full and borne singly. Dark green glossy leaves. Upright and uniform.

'Rod Stillman' 1948. 'Ophelia' × 'Editor McFarland'. Very fragrant blooms in light pink, flushed orange at the base. Dark leaves. Tall, strong grower.

'Rose Gaujard' 1957. 'Peace' × 'Opera' seedling. Large blooms, high-centred early but many opening split, cherry-red with reverse light pink and silvery-white. A tall, strong, healthy and robust variety. Glossy dark green leaves.

Plate XXII: Alba roses
Of the four Alba roses shown here – 'Celeste' (also known as 'Celestial'; top left), R. × alba semi-plena (top right), 'Maiden's Blush' (bottom left) and 'Königin von Dänemark' (bottom right) – the second is of much the most ancient origin, and may have been spread throughout Europe by the Romans. It is at least possible that it is also the white rose of York, while its double form, R. × alba maxima (the great double white), is the Jacobite rose, adopted as a symbol by Bonnie Prince Charlie and his followers. All are fine, vigorous and not too lax growers, with 'Königin von Dänemark' the most suitable size for a small garden.

'**Royal Albert Hall**' 1972. 'Fragrant Cloud' × 'Postillon'. Cherry-red blooms with pale gold reverse, of classic form and very fragrant. Dark bronze-green leaves. Vigorous and bushy.

'**Royal Dane**' – see 'Troika'.

'**Royal Highness**' ('Königliche Hoheit') 1962. 'Virgo' × 'Peace'. Very shapely soft light pink fragrant blooms, disliking rain. Tall and vigorous, with dark green leathery leaves.

'**Royal Show**' 1973. 'Queen Elizabeth' × unknown seedling. Light red blooms shaded deeper red, one to a stem. Good shape and slight scent. Mid-green glossy leaves. Tall.

'**Samourai**' ('Scarlet Knight') 1966. ('Happiness' × 'Independence') × 'Sutter's Gold'. Double, cupped crimson-scarlet blooms in clusters. Free, vigorous and tall.

'**San Diego**' 1968. 'Helen Traubel' × 'Tiffany'. Very large and shapely fragrant light yellow flowers. Leathery leaves. Bushy and vigorous.

'**Santa Fé**' 1967. 'Mischief' × 'Super Star'. Blooms pink with lighter reverse, large and full. Small matt dark green leaves. Vigorous and upright.

'**Scarlet Knight**' – see 'Samourai'.

'**Seashell**' 1976. Unnamed rose × 'Colour Wonder'. High-centred blooms with frilled petal edges in coral-pink. Cluster-flowering. Healthy and vigorous.

'**Seventh Heaven**' 1966. Seedling × 'Chrysler Imperial'. Well-shaped large flowers, rose-red to cardinal-red. Glossy leaves. Bushy and free.

'**Shannon**' 1965. 'Queen Elizabeth' × 'McGredy's Yellow'. Tall and upright, with rounded glossy mid-green leaves. Full globular bright pink flowers. Late to start.

'**Shot Silk**' 1924. 'Hugh Dickson' seedling × 'Sunstar'. Very fragrant flowers, opening wide, cherry-pink, shading to orange-yellow. Vigorous and low-growing, free and quick to repeat. An old rose but still first-rate. Often grown as a climbing sport.

'**Showtime**' 1969. 'Kordes Perfecta' × 'Granada'. Large double scented pink blooms. Free, vigorous and bushy.

'**Sierra Dawn**' 1967. 'Helen Traubel' × 'Manitou'. Large high-centred fragrant blooms in bright pink blends. Dark, bronzy leaves. Vigorous, upright and bushy.

'**Silent Night**' 1969. 'Daily Sketch' × 'Hassan'. Medium-sized creamy-yellow blooms, suffused pink and carried in trusses. Well-shaped but they dislike rain. Bushy but not tall. Glossy leaves.

'**Silva**' 1964. 'Peace' × 'Confidence'. Large shapely flowers in yellowish-salmon, shaded bright rose-pink, on long stems. Dark glossy leaves. Vigorous and upright.

'**Silver Jubilee**' 1978. [('Highlight' × 'Colour Wonder') × ('Parkdirektor Riggers' × 'Piccadilly')] × 'Mischief'. Full shapely slightly fragrant blooms in coppery-salmon-pink, with peach shadings, mostly borne singly. Healthy, with glossy leaves. Bushy and vigorous.

'**Silver Lining**' 1958. 'Karl Herbst' × 'Eden Rose' seedling. Silvery-pink blooms of good form, the colour deeper at petal edges. Fragrant, free and vigorous.

'**Silver Star**' 1966. 'Sterling Silver' × 'Magenta'. Moderately full lavender blooms, fragrant and free. large matt green leaves. Medium vigour. Bushy.

'**Simon Bolivar**' 1966. 'Roundelay' × 'El Capitan'. Large double high-centred, slightly fragrant flowers in bright orange-red. Dark glossy leaves. Vigorous and upright.

'**Sir Harry Pilkington**' ('Melina') 1973. 'Inge Horstmann' × 'Sophia Loren'. Fragrant blooms of medium size, red with darker shades at petal edges. Not tall, but vigorous and healthy.

'**Song of Paris**' ('Saphir') 1964. ('Holstein' × 'Bayadère') × 'Prelude'. Large shapely silvery-lavender fragrant flowers. Leathery leaves. Upright and moderately vigorous.

'**South Seas**' 1962. 'Rapture' × seedling. Large very shapely flowers in bright coral-pink. Vigorous and bushy.

'**Spek's Yellow**' ('Golden Scepter') 1950. 'Golden Rapture' × unnamed seedling. Large well-shaped flowers, smaller and in clusters in second flush. Fragrant and deep glowing yellow. Sparse leaves. Rather leggy.

'**Stella**' 1958. 'Horstmann's Jubiläumsrose' × 'Peace'. Large rounded well-shaped creamy peach-pink flowers. Tall and upright. Healthy glossy leaves.

'**Sterling Silver**' 1957. Seedling × 'Peace'. Moderately robust plant with medium-sized lilac-mauve flowers, opening cupped. The first really popular modern mauve rose, but better under glass. Strong fragrance.

'**Summer Holiday**' 1968. 'Super Star' × unknown rose. Vermilion-orange-red, with paler reverse, full and fragrant. Semi-glossy leaves. Vigorous and spreading.

'**Summer Sunshine**' 1962. 'Buccaneer' × 'Lemon Chiffon'. Large rich, deep yellow blooms, opening quickly, on very long stems. Semi-glossy dark foliage. Tall and spreading. Weather-proof.

'**Sunblest**' 1972. Parents not given. Unfading golden-yellow slightly scented blooms. Semi-glossy leaves. Tall and vigorous grower.

'**Super Star**' ('Tropicana') 1960. (Seedling × 'Peace') × (seedling × 'Alpine Glow'). Well-shaped light vermilion flowers which appear almost luminous and have a slightly paler reverse. Free-flowering, generally with several blooms to a stem on a robust, upright plant. Matt mid-green leaves. Modern strains unfortunately becoming more and more susceptible to mildew.

'Susan Hampshire' ('Meinatac') 1974. ('Monique' × 'Symphonie') × 'Maria Callas'. Very full fuchsia-pink fragrant blooms. Matt mid-green leaves. Vigorous and upright.

'Sutter's Gold' 1950. 'Charlotte Armstrong' × 'Signora'. Orange-red buds open to large golden-orange scented flowers on long stems. Dark glossy leaves. Vigorous and tall. Outstanding in autumn.

'Swarthmore' 1963. ('Independence' × 'Happiness') × 'Peace'. Large rose-red high-centred, slightly scented blooms on long stems. Dark leaves. Vigorous and bushy.

'Sweet Afton' 1964. ('Charlotte Armstrong' × 'Signora') × ('Alice Stern' × 'Ondine'). Large flowers, high-centred and then cupped, very fragrant, in near-white with blush-pink reverse. Tall, spreading and bushy in habit.

'Tapestry' 1958. 'Peace' × 'Mission Bells'. Blends of bronze, red, yellow and pink. Fragrant. Glossy leaves. Upright and bushy.

'Talisman' 1929. 'Ophelia' × 'Souvenir de Claudius Pernet'. Medium-sized flowers, opening flat, golden coppery-yellow. Light green glossy leaves. Vigorous.

'Tenerife' 1972. 'Fragrant Cloud' × 'Piccadilly'. Deep coral-salmon with pale peach reverse, full and fragrant, borne singly. Glossy leaves. Vigorous and upright.

'The Doctor' 1936. 'Mrs J. D. Eisele' × 'Los Angeles'. Dwarf and bushy, with very large satin-pink blooms. Light foliage. An old favourite for many years.

'Tiffany' 1954. 'Charlotte Armstrong' × 'Girona'. Very fragrant large shapely blooms in Neyron-rose on strong stems. Dark leaves; free and vigorous.

'Tradition' 1964. 'Detroiter' × 'Don Juan'. Fairly vigorous with matt green leaves. Moderately full rich scarlet-crimson flowers, free and quick to repeat. No scent.

'Traviata' 1962. 'Baccara' × ('Independence' × 'Grand'mère Jenny'). Long pointed buds with flowers light crimson on petal margins, merging into white at the base and on the reverse. Dark green leaves; vigorous and very upright.

'Troika' ('Royal Dane') 1972. Seedling × 'Super Star'. Blooms light apricot to orange, edged and veined scarlet, full and fragrant. Vigorous and upright with glossy leaves.

'Tropicana' – see 'Super Star'.

'Typhoon' 1971. 'Colour Wonder' × 'Dr A. J. Verhage'. Orange-salmon, shading to a yellow base, carried singly. Semi-glossy leaves. Strong and upright.

'Vienna Woods' ('Wienerwald') 1974. 'Colour Wonder' × seedling. Large well-formed blooms in light salmon-pink, slow to open. Low, compact and bushy in habit, with healthy leaves.

'Virgo' ('Virgo Liberationem') 1947. 'Blanche Mallerin' × 'Neige Parfum'. Long-petalled snow-white flowers, loveliest in bud stage. Vigorous and bushy, with dark green leaves. Hates rain.

'Waltz Time' ('Saint-Exupéry') 1961. ('Christopher Stone' × 'Marcelle Gret') × ('Holstein' × 'Bayadère'). Large high-centred mauve flowers with silvery tints. Vigorous, bushy and free.

'War Dance' 1961. 'Roundelay' × 'Crimson Glory'. Medium-sized but full orange-scarlet blooms and a robust spreading bush.

'Wendy Cussons' 1963. 'Independence' × 'Eden Rose'? An unending profusion of high-centred double flowers, fragrant and bright cerise-red. Dark leaves on bushy well-branched plant.

'Western Sun' 1965. 'Spek's Yellow' seedling × 'Golden Sun'. Unshaded deep tawny-gold. Flowers full and shapely. Dark leaves; moderate growth.

'Whisky Mac' 1967. Parents not given. Full cupped scented bronze-yellow and apricot blooms, freely borne. Bushy and compact. Matt bronze-tinted leaves. Health suspect.

'White Christmas' 1953. 'Sleigh Bells' × seedling. Large pure white high-centred blooms of 50 petals. Fragrant. Dark leaves. Vigorous but does not like rain.

'White Knight' – see 'Message'.

'White Masterpiece' 1969. Parents not given. Very large double shapely slightly scented pure white flowers. Compact and free-flowering.

'Yankee Doodle' 1976. 'Colour Wonder' × 'King's Ransom'. Yellow and red blends and mainly cluster-flowering. Blooms not large and rather globular. Good in autumn, but hates rain. Healthy.

'Yellow Pages' 1971. 'Arthur Bell' × 'Peer Gynt'. Golden yellow, flushed pale pink, with 64 petals. Bushy and compact with rather small light green leaves.

'Youki San' 1965. 'Lady Sylvia' × 'Message'. A moderate grower with small light green leaves. Flowers white with a greenish tinge, showing red stamens when open. Sweet scent. Does not like rain.

ALBAS

New classification: Old Garden Roses, Albas. Summer-flowering only. Attractive, grey-green leaves.

R. × *alba maxima* (Jacobite rose, the great double white) Age unknown. Upright and vigorous with white double flowers, opening flat. Fine oval hips. 1.8 × 1.5 m (6 × 5 ft).

R. × *alba semi-plena* (white rose of York) Age unknown. A semi-double version of *R.* × *alba maxima*, showing golden stamens.

'Blush Hip' About 1840. Untypically lax and suitable for a pillar or growing through other shrubs. Double pale pink blooms with a green central pointel. 3.5 m (12 ft) canes.

For the history of the Albas, see page 72; for illustrations, see plate XXII (p117).

Plate XXIII: Centifolia roses

Plate XXIII: Centifolia roses

Of uncertain origin, the Centifolias – the original cabbage rose – were developed largely in the Netherlands, and as a result appear more often than any other type of rose in the paintings of the old Dutch masters. Their many-petalled flowers are mostly sterile, but the group has sported freely over the years. 'Chapeau de Napoleon' (top left), with the strange mossy calyx that gave it its name, could hardly be anything other than a sport. If you need a fairly upright grower among the Centifolias, 'Fantin Latour' (top right) is the one. 'De Meaux' (bottom left) and 'Tour de Malakoff' (bottom right) will certainly need some support. The four shown here illustrate well the colour range of this old group.

For the history of the Centifolias, see page 74.

For the history of the Moss roses, see page 75; for illustrations, see plate XXIV (p123).

ALBAS continued

'Celeste' ('Celestial') Late 18th century. One of the finest. Soft pink blooms blend perfectly with the grey-green leaves. 1.8 × 1.2m (6 × 4ft).

'Chloris' ('Rosée du Matin') Age unknown. Darker leaves than typical and few thorns. Blush-pink double blooms. 1.2 × 1m (4 × 3ft).

'Félicité Parmentier' 1836. Short for an Alba, and useful for small gardens. Palest blush-pink flowers, opening in clusters from pale yellow buds. 1.2 × 1m (4 × 3ft).

'Jeanne d'Arc' 1818. A 1.2 × 0.6m (4 × 2ft) counterpart of *R. × alba maxima*.

'Königin von Dänemark' 1826. Fairly lax and open in habit, with clusters of beautiful though small very double flowers, opening scarlet-pink and paling, except for the centre petals. 1.5 × 1.2m (5 × 4ft).

'Maiden's Blush' Before the 15th century. A large shrub with loosely-formed, scented blush-pink flowers. An old favourite, as is the very similar 'Great Maiden's Blush'. 1.5 × 1.2m (5 × 4ft) and 1.8 × 1.5m (6 × 5ft) respectively.

'Pompon Blanc Parfait' 1876. Long flowering season, producing neat, small blush-pink pompon blooms with button eyes over many weeks. 1.5 × 1.2m (5 × 3ft).

POSSIBLE ALBA HYBRIDS

'Mme Legras de St Germain' Prior to 1848. Possibly Noisette blood. White double flowers, opening flat, with yellow-flushed centres, fading white. Thornless and lax. 1.8 × 1.8m (6 × 6ft).

'Mme Plantier' 1835. Creamy double blooms with green pointels on a rather rambling shrub. Pillar rose or arching, undisciplined bush. 1.5 × 1.8m (5 × 6ft).

CENTIFOLIAS

New classification: Old Garden Roses, Provence (Centifolias). Summer-flowering only. Generally lax and sometimes rather gaunt growers, with lovely but drooping flowers and leaves.

'Blanchefleur' 1835. Very full blooms of creamy blush-pink, fading white. Coarse leaves. 1.5 × 1m (5 × 3ft).

'Bullata' Before 1815. Large globular pink flowers and exceptionally large wrinkled (bullate) leaves. 1.2 × 1.2m (4 × 4ft).

R. × centifolia (Cabbage rose, rose of Provence, *R. provincialis, rose des peintres*) Pink typically globular flowers, richly scented. 1.5 × 1.2m (5 × 4ft).

'Châpeau de Napoleon' (*R. × centifolia cristata*) 1826. Also known as the 'Crested Moss', but not a Moss rose, though it has a mossy growth on the sepals which gives it the effect of an old-fashioned cocked hat. Otherwise a typical pink Centifolia. 1.5 × 1.2m (5 × 4ft).

'De Meaux' Before 1800. One of the three babies of the Centifolias, with small leaves and flowers, opening to pompon shape in pink, deepening in the heart. 1.2 × 1m (4 × 3ft).

'Fantin Latour' Age uncertain. Named after the French flower painter. Profuse clusters of pale, blush-pink very double flowers, opening flat. More erect and bushy than most, and one of the very best. 1.8 × 1.5m (6 × 5ft).

'Juno' 1847. Large, sometimes quartered double flowers in blush-pink and with a button eye. Greyish leaves. Lax, but reaching 1.2 × 1.2m (4 × 4ft).

'La Noblesse' 1856. Rich pink blooms, later than most, spreading the flowering period of a collection. 1.5 × 1.2m (5 × 4ft).

'Petite de Hollande' ('Petite Junon de Hollande', 'Pompon des Dames', 'Normandica') Age unknown. Companion to 'De Meaux', more compact and flowers a softer pink. 1.2 × 1m (4 × 3ft).

'Robert le Diable' Age unknown. Reflexing flowers in blends of deep violet and purple, fading to grey. Occasional petals cerise and scarlet, colouring best in hot weather. Late-flowering and lax in growth. 1.2 × 1m (4 × 3ft).

'Spong' 1805. Another of the small ones, with clear pink flowers. 1.2 × 1m (4 × 3ft).

'The Bishop' Age unknown. Many-petalled cerise-maroon flowers with lilac-pink reverse, paling to an attractive greyish-mauve as blooms age. Unusually glossy leaves. 1.5 × 1m (5 × 3ft).

'Unique Blanche' ('White Provence', 'Vierge de Cléry') 1775. White flowers open cupped and the petals then reflex round a button eye. A sport of *R. × centifolia*, but more compact in habit. 1.2 × 1.2m (4 × 4ft).

'Variegata' ('Dometil Beccard') Before 1845. Double blooms, striped pink on a white ground, not long-lasting but plenty of them. 1.5 × 1.2m (5 × 4ft).

MOSS ROSES

New classification: Old Garden Roses, Moss Roses. Except where noted, summer-flowering only.

'Capitaine John Ingram' 1856. Free-flowering, rather late. Full blooms in mottled dark crimson with lighter reverse. 1.5 × 1.2m (5 × 4ft).

'Common Moss' (*R. × centifolia muscosa*) 1727. The original Moss and still unsurpassed. Pink globular blooms with button eyes. 1.2 × 1.2m (4 × 4ft).

'**Duchesse de Verneuil**' 1856. Bright pink flowers with a paler reverse and button eye; bright green leaves. 1.5 × 1.2m (5 × 4ft).

'**Général Kléber**' 1856. Probably the best-loved pink Moss, with double flowers, opening flat with button eyes. Good green moss and some hips. 1.5 × 1.2m (5 × 4ft).

'**Gloire des Mousseux**' 1852. Clear pink flowers, paling with age, many up to 13cm (5in) across. Light green moss. 1.2 × 1m (4 × 3ft).

'**James Mitchell**' 1861. Early-flowering, the magenta-crimson flowers (fading to lilac-pink) small but perfect. Brownish moss. 1.5 × 1.5m (5 × 5ft).

'**Louis Gimard**' 1877. Globular flowers of many tones, light crimson and lilac predominating. Very double and profuse. 1.5 × 1m (5 × 3ft).

'**Monsieur Pélisson**' ('Pélisson') 1848. More bushy than most, with double pink blooms, opening flat. 1.2 × 1.2m (4 × 4ft).

'**Mousseline**' ('Alfred de Dalmas') 1855. A compact grower with smallish blush-pink double flowers. Fully recurrent. 1.2 × 1.2m (4 × 4ft).

'**Mousseux du Japon**' ('Moussu du Japon') Age uncertain. Flowers a magenta rose-pink, fading to greyish-lilac, less shapely than most. Unique in that the purplish stems and the leaves are mossed. 60 × 60cm (2 × 2ft).

'**Nuits de Young**' 1851. Slender and open growth, with deep, velvety-maroon flowers, showing yellow stamens. The darkest Moss. 1.5 × 1m (5 × 3ft).

'**Oeillet Panachée**' 1888. Small leaves and small double blooms, opening flat, purple striping on a blush-pink ground. 1.2 × 1m (4 × 3ft).

'**Shailer's White Moss**' (*R. × centifolia muscosa alba*) 1788. A 'Common Moss' sport, the cupped white blooms blush-tinted when young. Open and lax. 1.2 × 1m (4 × 3ft).

'**William Lobb**' ('Duchesse d'Istrie', 'Old Velvet Moss') 1855. Tall and can be used as a short climber or pillar rose. Profuse double blooms open crimson-purple with a lighter reverse, and fade to mauve-lavender. Green moss. 1.8 × 1.8m (6 × 6ft).

DAMASK MOSS ROSES

The moss on these is coarser than on the other Mosses and often brownish.

'**Blanche Moreau**' 1880. 'Comtesse de Murinais' × 'Quatre Saisons Blanc Mousseux'. Rather sprawling, but fine double creamy-white flowers, dark leaves and brown moss. Recurrent. 1.8 × 1.2m (6 × 4ft).

'**Comtesse de Murinais**' 1843. Quartered flowers, opening flat; blush-pink, fading white. 1.8 × 1.2m (6 × 4ft).

'**Deuil de Paul Fontaine**' 1873. Cupped crimson-purple flowers with many tones of purple, maroon and cerise at the heart. Reddish moss. 1 × 1m (3 × 3ft).

'**Quatre Saisons Blanc Mousseux**' (*R. × damascena bifera alba muscosa*, 'Perpetual White Damask Moss') 1835. Mainly of historical interest as the blooms are poorly shaped. Lax, with coarse brownish-green moss. Recurrent. 1.2 × 1.2m (4 × 4ft).

RUGOSAS

New classification: Shrub Roses, repeat flowering. Although very old in origin, most are quite modern hybrids, and so are included under the classification of modern garden roses. Really are perpetually in flower, though two main flushes. Only single and a few semi-double varieties bear hips, and only those hybrids near to the species have the fine, healthy Rugosa leaves.

'**Agnes**' 1900. *R. rugosa* × *R. foetida persiana*. Rather lanky and open in habit. Double pompon flowers in a blend of yellow and orange distinguish it from the others. Unpredictably recurrent. 1.8 × 1.5m (6 × 5ft).

'**Alba**' (*R. rugosa alba*) Age unknown. A bushy, rounded shrub with fine leaves. Large scented single white flowers, followed by large orange-red rounded hips. 1.8 × 1.8m (6 × 6ft).

'**Belle Pointevine**' 1894. Rich pink fragrant flowers, pointed in the bud, opening flat and semi-double. Few hips. 1.5 × 1.5m (5 × 5ft).

'**Blanc Double de Coubert**' 1892. Pure white semi-double blooms in great profusion, but seldom hips to follow. Less bushy than some. 1.8 × 1.5m (6 × 5ft).

'**Conrad Ferdinand Meyer**' 1899. A 'Gloire de Dijon' hybrid. Large silvery pink flowers, shapely at first, informal later. Formidable thorns rather than Rugosa spines and gaunt growth, needing careful placing. Scented. 2.5 × 1.5m (8 × 5ft). Watch for rust.

'**Dr Eckener**' 1930. A modern hybrid with HT-style scented flowers in yellow and pink blends. Rangy in habit and very thorny. 2.7 × 2.5m (9 × 8ft).

'**Fimbriata**' ('Dianthaflora', 'Pheobe's Frilled Pink') 1891. *R. rugosa* × 'Mme Alfred Carrière'. Interesting parents produced a beautiful rose. Soft pink, scented carnation-like blooms with serrated petal edges. 1.5 × 1.2m (5 × 4ft).

'**F. J. Grootendorst**' ('Grootendorst', 'Nelkenrose') 1918. *R. rugosa rubra* × 'Mme Norbert Lavavasseur'. Small crimson flowers in clusters, with frilled petal edges. Scentless. Makes a rather open bush. 1.5 × 1.5m (5 × 5ft). 'Grootendorst Supreme' is a darker crimson sport.

For the history of the Rugosas, see page 75; for illustrations, see plate XXXIII (p185).

Plate XXIV: Moss roses
There are some Damask Moss roses, but the main group appeared as sports of the Centifolias. In habit of growth – lax and a bit leggy, with large, drooping leaves – and in the type of flower, they are mostly indistinguishable from the Centifolias except for the so-called 'moss' on the flower stems and calyx.
'William Lobb' (top right) is a very large one and is best grown as a pillar rose or as a semi-climber on a wall. The others, 'James Mitchell' (bottom left), 'Général Kléber' (bottom right) and 'Common Moss' (top left), will all need some support, but are of more manageable proportions. The last is one of the very earliest, dating from the beginning of the 18th century, and is still one of the best.

'**Frau Dagmar Hastrup**' ('Frau Dagmar Hartopp') 1914. *R. rugosa* seedling. One of the loveliest single roses, the clearest pale pink with cream stamens. Fragrant, with large crimson hips later. 1.5 × 1.5 m (5 × 5 ft).

'**Hansa**' 1905. Double crimson-purple flowers, not everyone's colour, but borne with great freedom. 1.5 × 1.5 m (5 × 5 ft).

'**Max Graf**' 1919. *R. rugosa* × *R. wichuraiana*. A most un-Rugosa-like rose, trailing flat on the ground. Shiny green leaves make good ground-cover, spangled with clusters of single bright scented flowers. Late.

'**Nova Zembla**' 1907. Sport of 'Conrad Ferdinand Meyer' and identical except that the flowers are creamy-white with soft pink tints. 2.5 m × 1.5 m (8 × 5 ft).

'**Parfum de l'Hay**' ('Rose à Parfum de l'Hay') 1903. A Damask × 'Général Jacqeminot' × a Rugosa. More mauve than 'Roseraie de l'Hay' and not as robust, but otherwise quite similar. 1.2 × 1.2 m (4 × 4 ft).

'**Pink Grootendorst**' 1923. A strong, clear pink sport of 'F. J. Grootendorst' and otherwise similar. 1.5 × 1.2 m (5 × 4 ft).

'**Roseraie de l'Hay**' 1901. Endless velvety wine-red double blooms, loosely-formed in clusters, sweetly scented. No hips. Dense and bushy. 1.8 × 1.5 m (6 × 5 ft).

'**Ruskin**' ('V.F.1', 'John Ruskin') 1928. *R. rugosa* × 'Victor Hugo'. Strongly-scented very double flowers of crimson-scarlet, but needing sunny weather to give their best. Long, lax canes and informal habit, needing pillar or tripod. 1.8 × 3 m (6 × 10 ft).

'**Sarah Van Fleet**' 1926. *R. rugosa* × 'My Maryland'. Cupped light pink double blooms, richly scented, in clusters on an upright bushy shrub. 2.5 × 1.5 m (8 × 5 ft).

'**Scabrosa**' Pre-1939. Uncertain parentage. The largest hips and magenta-pink flowers of all the Rugosas. Bushy. 1.2 × 1.5 m (4 × 5 ft).

'**Schneezwerg**' ('Snow Dwarf') 1912. White semi-double flowers in clusters, with golden stamens. Free, bushy, with many small leaves just missing true Rugosa quality. Orange-red hips. 1.8 × 1.5 m (6 × 5 ft).

'**Thérèse Bugnet**' 1950. [(*R. acicularis* × *R. rugosa kamtchatica*) × (*R. amblyotis* × *R. rugosa plena*)] × 'Betty Bland'. Square-tipped dark red buds open to large double red flowers, fading pink. Long shoots. Very hardy. 1.8 × 1.5 m (6 × 5 ft).

'**Vanguard**' 1932. (*R. wichuraiana* × *R. rugosa alba*) × 'Eldorado'. Very large double orange-salmon flowers. Will reach 3 m (10 ft) as a climber, or make a bush 1.5 × 1.5 m (5 × 5 ft). Summer-flowering only.

'**Will Alderman**' 1954. (*R. rugosa* × *R. acicularis*) × a Hybrid Tea. Clear rose-pink double flowers, large, well-shaped and strongly scented. Upright and bushy. 1.2 × 1 m (4 × 3 ft).

New classification: Bush Roses, Polyanthas. All of these are recurrent and some are almost continuously in bloom.

'**Baby Faurax**' 1924. Clusters of small flowers in lavender-purple, fragrant and freely-borne. 30 cm (1 ft).

'**Bloomfield Abundance**' 1920. Flowers indistinguishable from 'Cécile Brunner' (see below), save for the feather-like extensions to each sepal. It grows to 2.5 × 2.5 m (8 × 8 ft), with small clusters of bloom in summer and vast corymbs later. The parentage is often given as Paul's lemon-yellow rambler 'Sylvia' × 'Dorothy Page Roberts', a 1907 coppery-pink HT from Dickson, but it seems as unlikely as a lamp post sprouting leaves that any such cross would almost exactly duplicate a bloom as unique as that of 'Cécile Brunner'. Much more probably, 'Bloomfield Abundance' is a sport of the latter, which is why it is included here.

'**Cameo**' 1932. Sport from 'Orléans Rose'. Salmon-pink semi-double cupped flowers, fading orange-pink, in clusters. 40–45 cm (15–18 in). There is a climbing sport.

'**Cécile Brunner**' 1881. *R. multiflora* × 'Mme de Tartas' and hence a Tea-Polyantha. A dainty, wiry plant with thimble-sized soft pink flowers, HT-shaped in bud, opening confused. 60 cm (2 ft).

'**Clotilde Soupert**' ('Mme Melon du Thé', 'Mme Hardy du Thé') 'Mignonette' × 'Mme Damaizin'. Recommended only for a warm climate if blooms are to open properly. Very double, cupped, blush-pink, deeper in the heart. 60 cm (2 ft).

'**Gloire du Midi**' 1932. Sport of 'Gloria Mundi'. Brilliant orange-scarlet double, cupped flowers. Vigorous and bushy in habit. 45 cm (18 in).

'**Jenny Wren**' 1957. 'Cécile Brunner' × 'Fashion'. Orange-coral-pink flowers, fading paler, well shaped in bud but opening loosely. 1.2 × 0.6 m (4 × 2 ft).

'**Little White Pet**' ('Belle de Teheran') 1879. Included here for its Polyantha-type growth, but actually a sport of the rambler 'Félicité et Perpétue'. Red buds produce clusters of white flatish pompon-style flowers, making a mound of bloom. Dark, rather pointed leaves. 60 × 60 cm (2 × 2 ft).

'**Margo Koster**' 1931. A 'Dick Koster' sport. Quite large salmon-pink flowers, cupped and with slight fragrance. Good as a pot-plant. 45 cm (18 in). There is also a climbing sport.

'**Nathalie Nypels**' ('Mevrouw Nathalie Nypels') 1917. 'Orléans Rose' × ('Comtesse du Cayla' × *R. foetida bicolor*). Semi-double rose-pink flowers, fragrant despite China parentage. Dwarf and spreading. 60 cm (2 ft).

'**Paul Crampel**' 1930. Bright orange-

For the history of the Polyanthas, see page 76; for illustrations, see plate X (p77).

scarlet double flowers, cupped on opening. Very showy. 60 cm (2 ft).

'Perle d'Or' 1883. *R. multiflora* × 'Mme Falcot'. A Tea-Polyantha. Resembling 'Cécile Brunner' in many ways, but more robust in habit and the buds are yolk-yellow, intense at the heart, paling as they open. 1.2 × 1 m (4 × 3 ft).

'The Fairy' 1932. Sport of the rambler 'Lady Godiva', but a Polyantha in habit. Soft pink globular blooms in large sprays. Glossy bright green leaves. 75 cm (2½ ft).

'Yesterday' 1972. ('Phyllis Bide' × 'Shepherd's Delight') × 'Ballerina'. Officially a Floribunda-Polyantha, and rather resembling a small China rose. Airy growth. Sprays of semi-double lilac-pink flowers with orange stamens. 1 m (3 ft).

'Yvonne Rabier' 1910. *R. wichuraiana* seedling × a Polyantha. Double white flowers with a hint of yellow in the centre. Scented and vigorous. 1.2 × 1 m (4 × 3 ft).

FLORIBUNDAS

For the history of the Floribundas, see page 77; for illustrations, see plates IX, XI, XXV, XXVII and XXVIII (pp 73, 80, 126, 135 and 138).

New classification: Bush Roses, cluster-flowering. With these the flowers are generally smaller than those of Hybrid Teas, quite often single or semi-double, and carried in sprays or trusses. The average height has been taken as 75 cm (2½ ft), and where they are taller or shorter this has been noted; but things are not quite as simple as that. An increasing number of Floribundas have larger, Hybrid-Tea-type flowers, and these are known as Floribundas HT-type in Britain. Those that combine flower size with, generally, a much taller habit of growth than the average, are Grandifloras in the United States and in some other places, so a rose can, in fact, be a Hybrid Tea or a Floribunda in one country and a Grandiflora in another, provided that it tends to produce clusters of fair-sized blooms rather than flowers one or two to a stem.

To get over this problem and to keep, I hope, the maximum number of people happy, where there is conflict the varieties are cross-referred under the appropriate headings. The actual descriptive note is included under the classification of the country of origin, and it may appear under Floribundas or Grandifloras and, less frequently, under Hybrid Teas. This is one area where the new system of classification will be more than welcome.

'Adair Roche' 1969. 'Paddy McGredy' × 'Femina' seedling. Fl-HT. Full flowers, pink with a silver reverse. Mid-green glossy leaves. Upright and vigorous.

'Alamein' 1963. 'Spartan' × 'Queen Elizabeth'. Scarlet semi-double blooms in very large trusses. Vigorous and bushy.

'Alison Wheatcroft' 1959. Sport of 'Circus'. Deep apricot flowers, flushed crimson, large and semi-double. Fragrant and tall.

'Allgold' 1958. 'Goldilocks' × 'Ellinor Le Grice'. Golden-yellow unfading double flowers in medium and small trusses. Bushy but dwarf in habit, with glossy, extremely healthy leaves.

'America's Junior Miss' 1964. 'Seventeen' × 'Demure' seedling. Fragrant double soft coral-pink blooms. Strong and bushy. Sometimes incorrectly called 'Junior Miss'.

'Anabell' – see 'Korbell'.

'Angel Face' 1968. ('Circus' × 'Lavender Pinocchio') × 'Sterling Silver'. Large blooms with wavy petals, opening flat. Deep mauve-pink and very fragrant. Glossy leaves. Upright and vigorous.

'Anna Louisa' 1967. 'Highlight' × 'Valeta'. Double soft pink flowers. Low-growing, vigorous and bushy.

'Anna Wheatcroft' 1959. 'Cinnabar' seedling. Large light vermilion flowers, opening flat. Mid-green leaves. Bushy and strong.

'Anne Cocker' 1969. 'Highlight' × 'Colour Wonder'. Small full light vermilion blooms in good trusses. Very long-lasting when cut. Glossy leaves. Upright and bushy.

'Apricot Gem' 1977. Parents not given. Very large double blooms in apricot, flushed yellow, on medium-sized trusses. Vigorous and bushy.

'Apricot Nectar' – see Grandifloras.

'Arabian Nights' 1964. 'Spartan' × 'Beauté'. Large light salmon-orange double fragrant blooms. Tall and upright.

'Arthur Bell' 1965. 'Clare Grammerstorf' × 'Piccadilly'. Large semi-double yellow flowers, fading paler and strongly fragrant. Strong and tall with fine, dark green leaves.

'Ascot' 1962. 'Brownie' × seedling. Semi-double coral-salmon flowers on a dwarf, spreading bush with large mid-green leaves.

'Baby Bio' 1977. 'Golden Treasure' × unnamed seedling. Double golden-yellow blooms. Mid-green leaves. Strong and bushy.

'Bahia' 1973. 'Rumba' × 'Tropicana'. Small clusters of long-lasting double orange-red blooms. Low-growing and bushy. Small light green leaves.

'Bangor' 1972. 'Jubilant' × 'Marlena'. A small bush with large, open flowers in bright carmine-pink. Good foliage and hardy.

'Betty Prior' 1935. 'Kirsten Poulsen' × unnamed seedling. Dark carmine buds and single carmine-pink flowers, fragrant and profuse. Bushy and vigorous.

'Bon Bon' 1973. 'Bridal Pink' × unnamed seedling. Semi-double flowers in pink and white blends, of HT-form when young. Vigorous low, spreading habit of growth. Mid-green leaves.

'Bonfire Night' (previously 'Bonfire') 1969. 'Tiki' × 'Variety Club'. Moderately full orange-scarlet flowers with lighter reverse. Dark green leaves; bushy and compact.

'Bonnie Hamilton' 1976. 'Anne Cocker' × 'Allgold'. Double orange-vermilion blooms. Not tall, but strong and bushy. Red-tinted young leaves.

'Border Gold' 1966. 'Allgold' × 'Pigmy Gold'. low and bushy, with profuse bloom. Very double deep golden flowers.

'Busy Lizzie' 1969. ('Pink Parfait' × 'Masquerade') × 'Dearest'. Soft pink double blooms in moderate trusses. Not tall. Compact. Mid-green semi-glossy leaves.

'Cairngorm' 1972. 'Anne Cocker' × 'Arthur Bell'. Double flowers orange and gold, overlaid salmon-pink, with paler reverse. Upright and vigorous, with semi-glossy leaves.

'Cathedral' – see 'Coventry Cathedral'.

'Centurion' 1975. 'Evelyn Fison' × seedling. Large double crimson blooms, opening cupped. Upright, with dark matt leaves.

'Chanelle' 1958. 'Ma Perkins' × ('Mrs William Sprot' × 'Fashion'). Semi-double flowers, shapely in bud and opening cupped and fragrant. Cream, blending into soft yellow at petal bases. Bushy and vigorous.

'Charles Dickens' 1970. 'Paddy McGredy' × 'Elizabeth of Glamis'. Fl-HT. Flowers rosy-salmon with a darker reverse. Dark green semi-glossy leaves. Upright and vigorous in habit.

'Charleston' 1963. 'Masquerade' × ('Radar' × 'Caprice'). Large semi-double flowers, yellow flushed crimson, turning crimson. Glossy mid-green leaves. Vigorous. Watch for black spot.

'Charm of Paris' 1965. 'Prima Ballerina' × 'Montezuma'. Fl-HT. Bushy and tall, with abundant glossy dark green leaves. Shapely clear pink fragrant flowers.

'Chinatown' ('Ville de Chine') 1963. 'Columbine' × 'Clare Grammerstorf'. A Floribunda-shrub that reaches 1.2–1.5m (4–5ft). Large double blooms in trusses, golden yellow, occasionally flushed pink, and strongly scented. Vigorous and healthy, with bright green glossy leaves.

'Circus' 1956. 'Fandango' × 'Pinocchio'. Double flowers opening cupped, predominantly yellow but flushed pink, salmon and sometimes scarlet. Matt leaves. Vigorous and bushy in habit.

'City of Belfast' 1967. 'Evelyn Fison' × ('Korona' × 'Circus'). Velvety-scarlet full blooms with slightly frilled petals. Upright and branching, with glossy leaves.

'City of Leeds' 1965. 'Evelyn Fison' × ('Spartan' × 'Red Favourite'). Tall and bushy, with large dark green leaves. Rich salmon double blooms in well-spaced trusses.

'Cocorico' 1951. 'Alain' × 'Orange Triumph'. Large semi-double flowers, opening flat and fragrant. Geranium-red. Glossy leaves. Vigorous and upright.

'Comanche' – see Grandifloras.

'Contempo' 1970. 'Spartan' × ['Goldilocks' × ('Fandango' × 'Pinocchio')]. Double well-formed blooms, singly and also in medium-sized trusses, showing blends of orange and coppery gold. Vigorous and bushy in habit.

'Copper Pot' 1968. Seedling × 'Spek's Yellow'. Blooms orange-yellow with a deeper reverse, moderately full. Dark green bronzy leaves. Tall and upright.

'Cordula' 1973. 'Europeana' × 'Marlena'. Semi-double long-lasting scarlet flowers, opening flat and very freely borne. Leaves red-tinted when young, then mid-green. Vigorous grower.

'Courvoisier' 1969. 'Elizabeth of Glamis' × 'Casanova'. Fl-HT. Flowers ochre-yellow, very double, borne singly and several together. Scented. Glossy leaves. Moderately vigorous grower.

'Coventry Cathedral' ('Cathedral') 1971. ('Little Darling' × 'Goldilocks') × 'Irish Mist'. Fl-HT. Light orange-vermilion with a paler reverse, moderately full, in large and small trusses. Showy but some blooms marred by spotting. Upright and branching, with semi-glossy leaves.

'Cupid's Charm' 1964. 'Little Darling' × 'First Love'. Profuse medium-sized fragrant salmon-pink blooms. Strong and bushy.

'Dairy Maid' 1957. ('Poulsen's Pink' × 'Ellinor Le Grice') × 'Mrs Pierre S. du Pont'. Single cream flowers, fading white; buds yellow splashed carmine. Tall.

'Dame of Sark' 1976. ('Pink Parfait' × 'Masquerade') × 'Tabler's Choice'. Double blooms, golden-yellow flushed scarlet. Glossy leaves. Vigorous, tall and upright.

'Dearest' 1960. Seedling × 'Spartan'. Large double flowers, pink with a touch of salmon, opening flat in large trusses. Sweet scent. Dark leaves; bushy, branching growth. Not at its best in rain.

'Diablotin' 1961. 'Orléans Rose' × 'Fashion'. Strong and branching with dark green leaves and small-petalled cupped geranium-red flowers.

'Dominator' 1962. 'New Yorker' × 'Sweet Repose'. Strong and upright, with healthy mid-green leaves. Blooms semi-double, pink with white shadings.

'Dorothy Wheatcroft' 1961. Parents not given. A Floribunda-shrub. Very tall and vigorous, with matt leaves. Large semi-double orange-scarlet flowers, opening flat in big trusses.

'Dreamland' ('Traumland') 1959. 'Cinnabar Improved' × 'Fashion'. Double flowers in soft peach-pink with slight scent. Low-growing and bushy.

'El Capitan' 1959. 'Charlotte Armstrong' × 'Floradora'. Large full high-centred cherry-red blooms and glossy leathery foliage. Vigorous grower.

127

'Elizabeth of Glamis' ('Irish Beauty') 1963. 'Spartan' × 'Highlight'. Large coral-salmon flowers, shapely in bud, opening flat and sweetly scented. Of great beauty where it does well, but not as robust or healthy in areas with cold heavy soil.

'Else Poulsen' 1924. 'Orléans Rose' × 'Red Star'. One of the first Floribundas in the modern style. Single flowers in good trusses, opening flat on long stems. Bright rose-pink. Dark glossy bronzy leaves. Vigorous and bushy in habit.

'Elysium' 1961. Parents not given. Vigorous and tall, with glossy mid-green leaves. Very large cupped flowers in palest vermilion. Fragrant.

'English Holiday' 1977. 'Bobby Dazzler' × 'Goldbonnet'. Full HT-shaped bright yellow blooms with some red splashes. Glossy light green leaves. Free and hardy.

'English Miss' 1977. 'Dearest' × 'Sweet Repose'. Very double blooms of 60 petals, pale pink, ageing deeper. Strong scent. Dark purple leaves, turning dark green. Upright and vigorous.

'Escapade' 1967. 'Pink Parfait' × 'Baby Faurax'. Semi-double flowers opening flat, large, fragrant and lilac-rose, paling almost to white in centres. Glossy light green leaves. Vigorous and well branched.

'Esther Ofarim' ('Matador') 1970. 'Colour Wonder' × 'Zorina'. Fl-HT. Brilliant blends of orange-red and yellow in the double flowers. Dwarf, bushy and compact. Matt leaves.

'Europeana' 1963. 'Ruth Leuwerik' × 'Rosemary Rose'. Very double deep crimson blooms in huge trusses, barely supported by the canes, especially after rain. Vigorous and well branched. Dark leaves.

'Eurorose' 1973. 'Zorina' × 'Redgold'. Double flowers, shapely in bud, opening flat, yellow-ochre flushed red. Vigorous but short and bushy.

'Evangeline Bruce' 1971. 'Colour Wonder' × 'Sea Pearl'. Full flowers, yellow, edged and flushed pink. Tall and upright with matt mid-green foliage.

'Evelyn Fison' 1963. 'Moulin Rouge' × 'Korona'. Double scarlet-red blooms, quite unfading and rain-proof, freely borne. Rather small very glossy leaves. Vigorous and bushy.

'Eye Paint' 1976. ('Little Darling' × 'Goldilocks') × ['Evelyn Fison' × ('Coryana' × 'Tantau's Triumph')]. A Floribunda shrub. Small single scarlet blooms with white eyes and paler reverse in large and small trusses. Semi-glossy leaves. Tall, vigorous and very bushy in habit.

'Fabergé' 1969. Seedling × 'Zorina'. Large double high-centred blooms, light peach-pink, the reverse with yellow tints. Dark leaves. Very vigorous, tall and bushy.

'Fairlight' 1965. 'Joybells' × seedling. Upright, with dark coppery foliage. Semi-double buds open coppery-orange, turning rich deep pink with salmon shadings.

'Fashion' 1949. 'Pinocchio' × 'Crimson Glory'. Peach-pink buds open to coral-salmon double flowers. Vigorous and bushy but prone to rust in some areas. Its colour, new at the time, set a fashion.

'Fervid' 1961. 'Pimpernel' × 'Korona'. Flowers, in glowing scarlet, open flat. Mid-green leaves. Tall, vigorous and upright.

'Feurio' 1955. 'Rudolph Timm' × 'Independence'. Double orange-scarlet medium-sized blooms. Bright green leaves. Dwarf, bushy growth.

'Fidélio' 1964. ('Radar' × 'Caprice') × 'Fire King'. Turkey-red double high-centred flowers with a crimson reverse. Leathery leaves. Vigorous and upright.

'Fire King' 1958. 'Moulin Rouge' × 'Fashion'. Very double flowers, shapely in bud and opening flat. Fragrant. Reddish orange-scarlet, reverse lighter. Vigorous and spreading.

'First Edition' 1976. 'Zambra' × ('Orléans Rose' × 'Goldilocks'). Very large trusses of coral-salmon flowers, double and opening loosely with some colour fade. Mid-green leaves. Erect and strong-growing.

'Floradora' 1944. 'Baby Château' × *R. roxburghii*. Not quite so many offspring as 'Charlotte Armstrong', but they cover a range from 'Queen Elizabeth' down to Miniatures, so its record is, in its way, equally remarkable. Medium-sized cupped double cinnabar-red blooms in medium-sized clusters. Upright and bushy.

'Fragrant Delight' 1978. 'Chanelle' × 'Whisky Mac'. Semi-double very fragrant salmon-pink blooms. Red-tinted glossy leaves. Healthy and vigorous.

'Franklin Engelmann' 1970. 'Heidelberg' × ('Detroiter' × seedling). Double bright scarlet blooms. Matt dark green leaves. Vigorous grower.

'Frensham' 1946. Seedling × 'Crimson Glory'. Big enough for a hedging shrub. Semi-double crimson-scarlet flowers, opening informally, in large clusters. Bright shiny leaves, subject to mildew. Wide-spreading.

'Friesia' ('Korresia', 'Sunsprite') 1974. Parents not given. Double bright yellow, very fragrant blooms in good trusses. Semi-glossy leaves. Vigorous and compact. One of the best yellows.

'Garnette' 1947. ('Rosenelfe' × 'Eva') × 'Heros'. Very double garnet-red rosette flowers with small tough petals, making it long-lasting when cut. Bushy, with holly-like dark green leaves. Less likely to mildew under glass. 'Carol' is a similar but pink sport.

'Geisha Girl' 1965. 'Gold Cup' × 'McGredy's Yellow'. Tall, but bushy and uniform, with mid-green leaves. Large flowers open flat, golden-yellow with occasional red streaks on reverse in the early stages. The yellow fades to cream.

'Gene Boerner' 1968. 'Ginger' × ('Ma Perkins' × 'Garnette Supreme'). Very double, rather globular blooms in deep pink. Strong and upright.

'Ginger' 1962. 'Garnette' seedling × 'Spartan'. Large double, cupped flowers, fragrant and orange-vermilion. Compact and bushy in habit.

'Glenfiddich' 1976. Seedling × ('Sabine' × 'Circus'). Double blooms in golden-amber that seem to do best in cool climates. Dark green leaves and healthy, bushy growth.

'Glengarry' 1968. 'Evelyn Fison' × 'Wendy Cussons'. Fl-HT. Large full vermilion blooms, many borne singly. Compact and bushy, with light green semi-glossy leaves.

'Golden Slippers' 1961. 'Goldilocks' × unnamed seedling. Double flowers, opening flat, in orange-flame with a golden reverse, the colour fading paler. Fragrant. Low-growing and well-branched.

'Golden Treasure' ('Goldschatz') 1965. Parents not given. Moderately full deep yellow flowers. Glossy leaves. Vigorous in growth and tall.

'Goldgleam' 1965. 'Gleaming' × 'All-gold'. Small dark green glossy leaves on a medium to tall bush. Large deep lemon-yellow flowers, carried mainly singly.

'Goldilocks' 1945. Unnamed seedling × 'Dubloons'. Double, rather globular flowers in deep yellow, fading cream. Vigorous, bushy and low-growing.

'Grace Abounding' 1970. 'Pink Parfait' × 'Circus'. Creamy-white semi-double flowers. Light-green semi-glossy leaves. Bushy and uniform in habit.

'Greenfire' 1958. 'Goldilocks' × unnamed seedling. Moderately vigorous, with small matt green leaves. Semi-double pale canary-yellow flowers with golden anthers. Some scent.

'Gruss an Aachen' 1909. 'Frau Karl Druschki' × 'Franz Deegen'. Included here in deference to the school of thought that holds this to be first Floribunda – with a Hybrid Perpetual and a Hybrid Tea as parents! Certainly a Floribunda style of growth, with very double flattish pompon flowers, flesh-pink, fading creamy-white. Low-growing and bushy in habit.

'Gypsy Moth' 1970. Seedling × seedling. Fl-HT. Full rosy-salmon flowers. Fragrant. Dark glossy leaves. Vigorous and branching.

'Haakbergen' 1962. Parents not known. Light green leaves, the colour deepening with age. Large full canary-yellow flowers, fading cream, with cherry-red markings on the outer petals.

'Hansestadt Bremen' 1958. 'Ama' × 'Fanal'. Very large double deep salmon-pink blooms. Dark leathery foliage. Strong and bushy in habit.

'Happy Anniversary' 1961. ('Incendie' × 'Chic Parisien') × ('Floradora' × 'Sondermeldung'). Very large salmon-pink blooms and dark green glossy leaves. Moderately vigorous and upright.

'Harry Edland' 1976. ('Lilac Charm' × 'Sterling Silver') × ['Blue Moon' × ('Sterling Silver' × 'Africa Star')]. Fl-HT. Very fragrant deep lilac double blooms and dark green leaves. Strong and bushy.

'Hassan' 1961. 'Tivoli' × 'Independence'. Large double glowing scarlet flowers in big trusses. Light green glossy leaves. Vigorous.

'Heat Wave' ('Mme Paule Guisez') 1958. Unnamed seedling × 'Roundelay'. Large double, cupped orange-scarlet flowers. Dark semi-glossy leaves, rather rounded. Vigorous and bushy.

'Heinz Erhardt' 1962. 'Lilli Marlene' × 'Lys Assia'. Dwarf and bushy with small leaves, shaded copper. Large full dark red flowers with crimson shadings.

'Highlight' 1957. Seedling × 'Independence'. Medium-sized double blooms in large trusses, bright orange-scarlet and scented. Upright and vigorous.

'Honey Gold' 1957. 'Yellow Pinocchio' × 'Fashion'. Moderately vigorous with rather small leaves. Well-formed pale aureolin-yellow blooms, deeper colour in the centres, in small trusses.

'Honeymoon' 1960. 'Clare Grammerstorf' × 'Spek's Yellow'. Double canary-yellow flowers, shapely in bud and opening flat. Heavily veined dark green leaves. Bushy.

'Iceberg' ('Fée des Neiges', 'Schneewittchen') 1958. 'Robin Hood' × 'Virgo'. Lightly pruned makes a fine shrub. Double white flowers with some fragrance in large and small trusses all over the bush. Vigorous slender branching growth and dainty pointed leaves.

'Iced Ginger' 1971. 'Anne Watkins' seedling. Fl-HT. Ivory-white double blooms, tinted coppery-pink and with a pink reverse and yellow petal bases. Semi-glossy light green leaves. Upright and strong.

'Ice White' 1965. 'Mme Léon Cuny' × ('Orange Sweetheart' × 'Tantau's Triumph'). Tall and upright with healthy dark green leaves. Semi-double pure white blooms, opening flat.

'Independence' ('Kordes Sondermeldung', 'Reina Elisenda', 'Geranium') 1951. 'Crimson Glory' × 'Baby Château'. Double, cupped vermilion-scarlet flowers with outer petals darker. Vigorous, but now replaced by better roses, though it introduced a new colour range and so is of interest.

'Irish Mist' 1967. 'Orangeade' × 'Mischief'. Fl-HT. Shapely orange-salmon flowers. Small dark green leaves and strong branching growth.

'Ivory Fashion' 1958. 'Sonata' × 'Fashion'. Very large fragrant creamy-white flowers with amber stamens, opening flat in medium trusses. Dark leaves. Vigorous, but not tall.

'Jan Spek' 1965. 'Clare Grammerstorf' × 'Faust'. Bushy and branching, with dark green leathery leaves. Rosette small-petalled flowers, yellow, fading cream.

'Jazz Fest' 1971. 'Pink Parfait' × 'Garnette'. Cerise semi-double HT-type blooms, singly and in clusters. Vigorous and spreading habit.

'Jean de la Lune' ('Moon Magic', 'Yellow Glow') 1965. ('Orléans Rose' × 'Goldilocks') × ('Fashion' × 'Henri Mallerin' seedling). Large lemon-yellow cupped flowers. Low-growing and bushy, with matt leaves.

'Jimminy Cricket' 1954. 'Goldilocks' × 'Geranium Red'. Orange-red buds open to double blooms in blends of pink, orange and coral. Vigorous and well branched.

'John Church' 1964. 'Ma Perkins' × 'Red Favourite'). Fl-HT. Large double fragrant orange-scarlet blooms in smallish trusses. Red leaves turning light green. Vigorous but rather irregular growth.

'Joyfulness' ('Frohsinn') 1963. 'Horstmann's Jubilaumsrose' × 'Circus'. Strong and tall, with dark glossy leaves. Large flowers, peach flushed pink at petal edges.

'Jubilant' 1965. 'Dearest' × 'Circus'. Double flowers which open flat, salmon-pink in bud, opening peach with silvery tones at petal edges. Bronzy leaves.

'Judy Garland' 1978. [('Super Star' × 'Circus') × ('Sabine' × 'Circus')] × 'Pineapple Poll'. Blooms yellow in the centre with red outer petals, the whole turning red. Fragrant. Dark green semi-glossy leaves. Vigorous and bushy in habit.

'Kerryman' 1971. 'Paddy McGredy' × ('Mme Léon Cuny' × 'Columbine'). Fl-HT. Full flowers, pink with deeper edges. Small trusses. Bushy and compact with semi-glossy leaves.

'Kim' 1970. ('Orange Sensation' × 'Allgold') × 'Elizabeth of Glamis'. Double canary-yellow flowers. Dwarf, compact and bushy with light green matt leaves.

'King Arthur' 1967. 'Pink Parfait' × 'Highlight'. Fl-HT. Very full salmon-pink flowers on a well-branched bush with matt mid-green foliage.

'Kirsten Poulsen' 1924. 'Orléans Rose' × 'Red Star'. One of the first modern-style Floribundas. Single bright scarlet flowers and leathery leaves. Tall and vigorous.

'Kiskadee' 1973. 'Arthur Bell' × 'Cynthia Brooke'. Large double yellow long-lasting blooms and quick repeat. Glossy leaves. Upright and strong.

'Korbell' ('Anabell') 1971. 'Zorina' ×

'Colour Wonder'. Fl-HT. Flowers salmon-orange with deeper petal edges. Copper-tinted young leaves, turning mid-green. Vigorous and upright.

'Korresia' – see 'Friesia'.

'Korona' 1935. Parents not given. Large trusses of bright orange-scarlet semi-double blooms. Vigorous; sometimes blackish markings on leaves, which is quite natural.

'Korp' ('Prominent') 1971. 'Zorina' seedling. Fl-HT. Very full flowers, bright red with scarlet reverse. Upright and bushy, with matt medium-green leaves.

'Kortor' ('Tornado') 1973. 'Europeana' × 'Marlena'. Rich red semi-double blooms, free and continuous. Dark green leaves on low-growing bushy, compact plant.

'Lagoon' 1969. 'Lilac Charm' × 'Sterling Silver'. Lilac-pink semi-double flowers. Tall and spreading, with coppery dark green leaves.

'Lavender Princess' 1960. 'World's Fair' seedling × 'Lavender Pinocchio'. Fragrant lavender flowers and leathery dark green leaves on a strong, upright bush.

'Lilac Charm' 1961. parentage not given. Large semi-double blooms, pale lilac-mauve with red anthers, fading in bright sunlight. Short bushy grower.

'Lilli Marlene' 1959. ('Our Princess' × 'Rudolph Timm') × 'Ama'. Semi-double bright crimson blooms in large trusses. Dark bronzy leaves. Vigorous and branching.

'Little Darling' 1956. 'Capt. Thomas' × ('Baby Château' × 'Fashion'). Double, cupped fragrant blooms, blending yellow with soft salmon-pink. Dark glossy leaves. Very vigorous and bushy.

'Lively Lady' 1969. 'Elizabeth of Glamis' × 'Super Star'. Fl-HT. Full light vermilion flowers on an upright, tall grower with small semi-glossy leaves.

'Liverpool Echo' 1971. ('Little Darling' × 'Goldilocks') × 'München'. Hybrid-Tea-style flowers in pale salmon-pink. Semi-glossy light green leaves. Vigorous.

'Living Fire' 1972. 'Super Star' × unknown. Full orange flowers, shading to scarlet and with golden-yellow petal bases. Healthy dark green leaves. Strong and upright.

'Lübeck' ('Hansestadt Lübeck') 1962. Parents not given. Orange-red blooms in large trusses. Dark green leaves. Very vigorous and tall.

'Macspash' 1979. [('Little Darling' × 'Goldilocks') × {'Evelyn Fison' × ('Coryana' × 'Tantau's Triumph')} × ('John Church' × 'Elizabeth of Glamis')] × ['Evelyn Fison' × ('Orange Sweetheart' × 'Frühlingsmorgen')]. Large semi-double pink blooms with a white eye, pale pink at frilled petal edges. Glossy mid-green leaves. Strong and bushy.

'Magenta' 1954. Yellow seedling × 'Lavender Pinocchio'. Tall and lax, sometimes classed as a Hybrid Musk. Clusters of double 'old rose' flowers, rosy-magenta to deep mauve and strongly scented. Dark leaves. Will need support.

'Manx Queen' ('Isle of Man') 1963. 'Shepherd's Delight' × 'Circus'. Tall and moderately bushy, with dark green leaves, exceptionally healthy. Flowers gold with orange-tipped petals.

'Ma Perkins' 1952. 'Red Radiance' × 'Fashion'. Cupped shell-pink flowers, sometimes flushed apricot. Still hard to beat in its colour range. Vigorous, with dark leaves.

'Margaret Merril' 1977. ('Rudolph Timm' × 'Dedication') × 'Pascali'. Double blooms, white tinted with mother of pearl, singly and several together. Strong fragrance. Mid-green grey-tinted leaves. Free-flowering, a vigorous grower and hardy.

'Marielle' 1963. 'Independence' × seedling. Vigorous and free. Large scarlet flowers and dark green leaves, copper-tinted when they are young.

'Marjorie Anderson' 1972. 'Fragrant Cloud' × 'Sea Pearl'. Large cyclamen-pink double blooms, opening flat. Vigorous but not too quick to repeat.

'Marlena' 1964. 'Gertrud Westphal' × 'Lilli Marlene'. Low-growing and compact, with double orange-scarlet blooms and glossy dark green, bronzy foliage.

'Mary Sumner' 1975. ('Orangeade' × 'Margot Fonteyn') × ['Elizabeth of Glamis' × ('Little Darling' × 'Goldilocks')]. Double orange-salmon flowers. Very vigorous, tall and upright, with glossy bronze-tinted leaves.

'Masquerade' 1949. 'Goldilocks' × 'Holiday'. Yellow buds open to semi-double yellow flowers, turning salmon-pink and then a not very attractive bronze-red. All the colours appear at one time on the strong, tall-growing branching bush. Dark leaves.

'Matador' – see 'Esther Ofarim'.

'Matangi' 1973. {('Little Darling' × 'Goldilocks') × ['Evelyn Fison' × ('Coryana' × 'Tantau's Triumph')]} × 'Picasso'. Orange-vermilion blooms with a silver eye and reverse. Vigorous and upright. Glossy dark green exceptionally healthy leaves.

'Megiddo' 1970. 'Coupe de Foudre' × 'S'Agaro'. Fl-HT. Moderately full scarlet-red blooms; dark green foliage. Tall and upright.

'Meipuma' ('Scherzo') 1973. 'Tamango' × ['Sarabande' × ('Goldilocks' × 'Fashion')]. Flowers vivid orange-vermilion with a silver reverse, full and opening flat. Spreading and bushy.

'Memento' 1979. 'Bangor' × 'Korbell'. Cerise-pink flowers with a carmine-rose reverse. Mid-green glossy leaves. Vigorous and bushy.

'Meteor' 1957. 'Feurio' × 'Gertrud Westphal'. Large, very double orange-scarlet flowers, opening flat. Light green leaves. Low-growing.

'Michelle' 1969. Seedling × 'Orange Sensation'. Flowers porcelain-rose with darker reverse; fragrant. Vigorous grower. Light green leaves.

'Minnie Watson' 1965. 'Dickson's Flame' × 'Dickson's Flame'. Semi-double light pink blooms and glossy leaves. Compact and bushy in habit.

'Molde' 1966. Parents not given. Low-growing and branching, with glossy dark green leaves and flowers of brilliant scarlet.

'Molly McGredy' 1968. 'Paddy McGredy' × ('Mme Léon Cuny' × 'Columbine'). Fl-HT. Blooms cherry-red with a silver reverse, large, in medium-sized trusses. Dark glossy leaves. Upright and bushy.

'Moon Maiden' 1970. 'Fred Streeter' × 'Allgold'. Very double creamy-yellow fragrant flowers and semi-glossy dark leaves. Tall and branching.

'Moonraker' 1967. 'Pink Parfait' × 'Highlight'. Fl-HT. Large flat creamy-white blooms and light green leaves. Vigorous, tall and branching.

'Moulin Rouge' ('Sans Souci') 1953. 'Alain' × 'Orange Triumph'. Cupped double blooms in rose-red, on large trusses. Glossy leaves and upright bushy growth.

'News' 1970. 'Lilac Charm' × 'Tuscany Superb'. Moderately full blooms opening flat in glowing beetroot-purple. Mid-green matt leaves. Bushy and compact.

'Nana Mouskouri' 1975. 'Red Gold' × 'Iced Ginger'. Fl-HT. Double creamy-white blooms, pink-flushed in the bud. Bushy and upright in habit.

'Oberon' 1955. 'Nymph' × seedling. Fully double salmon-apricot flowers in large trusses. Bushy and free.

'Old Master' 1973. [{'Evelyn Fison' × ('Tantau's Triumph' × 'Coryana')} × ('Hamburger Phoenix' × 'Danse du Feu')] × ['Evelyn Fison' × ('Orange Sweetheart' × 'Frühlingsmorgen')]. Blooms moderately full, carmine with a silver eye and reverse, in medium-sized trusses. Bushy with bronzy-green leaves.

'Orangeade' 1959. 'Orange Sweetheart' × 'Independence'. Large semi-double flowers in deep, bright vermilion rather than orange. Colour darkens with age. Robust and branching, with dark leaves.

'Orange Korona' 1959. 'Bergfeuer' × 'Independence'. Vigorous and upright with plentiful mid-green leaves. Flowers glowing orange-scarlet.

'Orange Sensation' 1960. Parents not given. Very large trusses of cupped flowers in orange-vermilion, deeper at petal edges. Light green leaves. Very sweet scent. Vigorous and spreading wide.

'Orange Silk' 1967. 'Orangeade' × ('Ma Perkins' × 'Independence'). Large full blooms in orange-vermilion. Vigorous and bushy, with semi-glossy dark green foliage.

'**Overture**' 1960. (Seedling × 'Lavender Pinocchio') × 'Prelude'. Short and moderately vigorous. Healthy. Double blooms lavender, shaded mauve. Fragrant.

'**Paddy McGredy**' 1962. 'Spartan' × 'Tzigane'. Fl-HT. Very large HT-type globular flowers, singly and in small trusses, strong rose-pink and fragrant. Dark leaves. Compact and low-growing.

'**Paint Box**' 1963. Seedling × 'St Pauli'. Strong, tall and branching, with dark green leaves. Flowers open flat, red and golden-yellow, changing to deep red with age.

'**Pantomime**' 1962. 'Ma Perkins' × 'Karl Herbst'. Fl-HT. Large full flowers in rich cerise-pink, mottling to deeper tones with age. Good fragrance. Bushy habit.

'**Peach Glow**' 1960. 'Goldilocks' × 'Fashion'. Double, cupped warm peach-coloured blooms and leathery green leaves. Upright and compact.

'**Peggy Netherthorpe**' – see Grandifloras.

'**Permanent Wave**' ('Duchess of Windsor', 'L'Indéfrisible', 'Mevrouw Van Straaten Van Nes', 'Mrs Van Nes', 'Van Nes') 1932. An 'Else Poulsen' sport. Large semi-double flowers with waved petals in bright carmine. Dark glossy leaves. Vigorous and bushy.

'**Pernille Poulsen**' 1965. 'Ma Perkins' × 'Columbine'. Dwarf and compact with mid-green leaves. Large salmon-pink flowers, opening wide, fading lighter. Fragrant.

'**Picasso**' 1970. 'Marlena' × ['Evelyn Fison' × ('Orange Sweetheart' × 'Frühlingsmorgen')]. Carmine flowers with deeper blotches and silvery reverse. The first of this original McGredy strain, bushy and compact. Smallish leaves.

'**Picnic**' 1976. 'Southseas' × unnamed seedling. China-pink blooms with a yellow flush on the reverse. Leathery leaves and strong growth, branching wide.

'**Pineapple Poll**' 1970. 'Orange Sensation' × 'Circus'. Full, fragrant double flowers, orange-yellow, flushed red. Small glossy leaves. Low and bushy.

'**Pink Bountiful**' 1945. 'Juanita' × 'Mrs R. M. Finch'. Large very double pink blooms and dark leaves on a vigorous, branching bush.

'**Pink Chiffon**' 1956. 'Fashion' × 'Fantasia'. Large very double blush-pink blooms in small trusses. Fragrant, but dislikes rain. Moderately vigorous. Glossy leaves.

'**Pink Parfait**' – see Grandifloras.

'**Pink Rosette**' 1948. Parents not given. Very double rosette-type flowers in soft pink. Dark leaves. Dwarf and bushy.

'**Pinocchio**' ('Rosenmärchen') 1940. 'Eva' × 'Golden Rapture'. Small double cupped salmon-pink blooms, edged deeper. Fragrant. Leathery leaves. Vigorous and bushy. A prolific parent of early Floribundas in the US.

'**Playboy**' 1976. 'City of Leeds' × seedling. Almost single blooms, orange-scarlet with a golden-yellow reverse. Glossy leaves, bronze-tinted early. Bushy and compact.

'**Poppy Flash**' 1970. ('Dany Robin' × 'Fire King') × ('Alain' × *R. chinensis mutabilis*). Moderately full flowers, brightest vermilion with a lighter reverse. Upright, bushy and compact. Glossy leaves.

'**Princess Michiko**' 1965. 'Spartan' × 'Circus'. Tall, upright and vigorous, with dark green leaves. Large flowers in coppery-orange, changing with age to dull red.

'**Priscilla Burton**' 1978. {'Maxi' × ['Evelyn Fison' × ('Orange Sweetheart' × 'Frühlingsmorgen')]} × {('Little Darling' × 'Goldilocks') × ['Evelyn Fison' × ('Coryana' × 'Tantau's Triumph')] × ('John Church' × 'Elizabeth of Glamis')}. Large semi-double flowers, deep carmine with a white eye. Deep green leaves. Vigorous and bushy.

'**Prominent**' – see 'Korp'.

'**Queen Elizabeth**' – see Grandifloras.

'**Red Dandy**' 1959. 'Ena Harkness' × 'Karl Herbst'. Fl-HT. Shapely double blooms, velvety rose-red with a lighter reverse. Small clusters but plenty of them. Healthy. Tall, vigorous and branching.

'**Red Glory**' 1958. 'Gay Lady' × ('Pinocchio' × 'Floradora'). Large cherry-red semi-double blooms, cupped to flat, in domed clusters. Glossy leaves. Tall and bushy.

'**Red Gold**' 1966. ('Karl Herbst' × 'Masquerade') × ('Faust' × 'Piccadilly'). Fl-HT. Flowers golden-yellow, edged cherry-red, in large trusses. Tall and branching, with semi-glossy, rather small leaves.

'**Red Pinocchio**' 1947. 'Yellow Pinocchio' seedling × 'Donald Prior'. Large double velvety carmine-red cupped blooms. Bushy and profuse.

'**Rob Roy**' 1969. 'Evelyn Fison' × 'Wendy Cussons'. Fl-HT. Scarlet-crimson shapely blooms, borne several together. Dark green semi-glossy leaves. Upright, strong-growing and well branched.

'**Rodeo**' 1960. 'Obergartner Wiebicke' × 'Spartan'. Full blooms, bright red and slightly fragrant. Light green leaves. Low and bushy.

'**Roman Holiday**' 1966. ('Pinkie' × 'Independence') × 'Circus'. Blooms high-centred in bud, opening cupped, orange with yellow petal bases, becoming dark red. Dark leaves. Low-growing and bushy.

'**Rosemary Gandy**' 1957. 'Tabarin' seedling × 'Jolie Princesse' seedling. Semi-double cupped flowers, lemon-yellow suffused pale coppery-red at the edges. Fragrant. Vigorous and upright.

'**Rosemary Rose**' 1945. 'Grüss an Teplitz' × seedling. Camellia-shaped flat very double blooms in bright currant-red. Very large trusses. Dark, purplish new foliage, turning very dark green and likely to mildew. Vigorous and bushy.

Plate XXVII: Modern Floribunda roses (2)
'First Edition' (top left) is a top rose in the United States, but is little known in Europe – a pity, for it is a fine variety. 'Coventry Cathedral' (top right) has succeeded in moving from its homeland across the Atlantic in the opposite direction, under the alternative name of 'Cathedral', and it seems to be making a good show in other countries as well. Tall-growing 'Southampton' (bottom left) has both attractive flowers and, above all, almost complete freedom from the common rose ills. It makes an outstanding hedging variety, while, at the other end of the scale, little 'Stargazer' (bottom right) typifies the modern breeding trend towards bushy but low-growing Floribundas for the small garden. See also plates IX, XI, XXV and XXVIII (pp73, 80, 126 and 128).

'Rosenelfe' ('Rose Elf') 1939. 'Else Poulsen' × 'Sir Basil McFarland'. Double high-centred fragrant flowers of silvery-pink. Light green glossy leaves. Strong and bushy.

'Rose of Tralee' 1963. 'Leverkusen' × 'Korona'. Fl-HT. Robust and branching, with small dark green leaves. Large deep pink blooms, shaded salmon. Small trusses.

'Rose Parade' 1974. 'Sumatra' × 'Queen Elizabeth'. Coral-peach cupped double blooms. Dark matt leaves. Vigorous and compact in habit.

'Ruby Lips' 1958. 'World's Fair' × 'Pinocchio'. Large semi-double deep rose-red blooms, shading lighter towards centre. Bushy and vigorous.

'Rumba' 1959. ('Poulsen's Bedder' × 'Floradora') × 'Masquerade'. Very small and double rosette blooms, yellow edged red. Small leaves and dwarf growth. Cheerful at first, but flowers do not age well.

'Ruth Leuwerick' 1960. 'Käthe Duvigneau' × 'Rosemary Rose'. Large turkey-red blooms. Fragrant. Bushy and vigorous.

'St Pauli' 1958. 'Masquerade' × 'Karl Herbst'. Very vigorous and tall, with large leathery leaves. Semi-double flowers in carmine, splashed and fading to pale yellow.

'Salmon Marvel' 1958. 'Red Pinocchio' × 'Signal Red'. Small sprays of orange-salmon double flowers. Bushy.

'Sarabande' 1957. 'Cocorico' × 'Moulin Rouge'. Large semi-double scarlet-red flowers on a spreading, branching plant. Dark healthy leaves. Not too tall.

'Saratoga' 1963. 'White Bouquet' × 'Princess White'. Very large double gardenia-shaped fragrant white blooms. Glossy leaves. Vigorous.

'Satchmo' 1970. 'Evelyn Fison' × 'Diamant'. Double bright scarlet flowers, which hold their colour well. Bushy and compact. Dark leaves.

'Scarlet Queen Elizabeth' 1963. 'Korona' seedling × 'Queen Elizabeth'. Large orange-scarlet double blooms, opening cupped. Dark semi-glossy leaves. Tall, vigorous and upright, but does not really resemble 'Queen Elizabeth' in flower or growth.

'Scented Air' 1965. 'Spartan' seedling × 'Queen Elizabeth'. Tall and upright, with small dark green leaves. Large full salmon-pink fragrant flowers, lasting well.

'Scherzo' – see 'Meipuma'.

'Sea Pearl' 1964. 'Perfecta' × 'Montezuma'. Fl-HT. Tall, upright and vigorous, with large shiny leaves. Fragrant blooms, shapely in bud, opening wide, in orange-pink with a light yellow reverse. Larger than most.

'Seven Seas' 1970. 'Lilac Charm' × 'Sterling Silver'. Very full lilac blooms in small trusses. Dark green matt leaves. Bushy and compact in habit.

'Shepherdess' 1966. 'Allgold' × 'Peace'. Fl-HT. Semi-double flowers, yellow flushed pale salmon. Medium vigour and branching. Glossy bronze-tinted dark leaves.

'Shepherd's Delight' 1957. 'Masquerade' seedling × 'Joanna Hill'. Large semi-double blooms in a mixture of flame and yellow. Dark leaves. Vigorous and tall.

'Sir Lancelot' 1966. 'Vera Dalton' × 'Woburn Abbey'. Large semi-double apricot-yellow flowers. Matt, light green leaves. Moderately vigorous and well branched.

'Snowline' 1970. Parents not given. Very full white flowers in large and small trusses. Dark green leaves. Bushy and compact.

'Soleil' 1958. Parents not given. Clusters of semi-double cinnabar-red large flowers. Light green leaves. Vigorous and bushy.

'Sonia' ('Sweet Promise') 1970. 'Zambra' × ('Baccara' × 'Message'). Small, shapely double blooms, some singly, in light rose-pink. Light green leaves. Vigorous and tall in habit.

'Southampton' 1971. ('Anne Elizabeth' × 'Allgold') × 'Yellow Cushion'. Double flowers, apricot-orange flushed scarlet, singly and several together. Vigorous and upright. Exceptionally healthy semi-glossy dark green leaves.

'Spartan' 1955. 'Geranium Red' × 'Fashion'. Large shapely orange-red blooms, shaded coral, singly and in trusses. Strong fragrance. Dark glossy leaves. Vigorous and tall in habit.

'Stargazer' 1977. 'Marlena' × 'Kim'. Low-growing, compact and bushy, with matt mid-green leaves. Single bright orange-scarlet blooms with golden centres in medium-sized trusses.

'Stephen Langdon' 1971. 'Karl Herbst' × 'Sarabande'. Fl-HT. Large, shapely deep scarlet blooms in large and small trusses. Matt dark green leaves, red when young. Upright and bushy.

'Strawberry Ice' 1977. [('Goldilocks' × 'Virgo') × ('Orange Triumph' × 'Yvonne Rabier')] × 'Fashion'. Double creamy blooms with light carmine petal edges. Semi-glossy leaves. Tall and bushy.

'Stroller' 1969. 'Manx Queen' × 'Happy Event'. A gold and cerise bicolour, moderately full. Dark glossy leaves. Strong and bushy in habit.

'Sunbonnet' 1967. 'Arlene Francis' × ('Circus' × 'Sweet Talk'). High-centred double yellow blooms with a greenish tinge. Dark leaves. Low and bushy.

'Sunday Times' 1970. ('Little Darling' × 'Goldilocks') × 'München'. Flowers deep pink with a lighter reverse. Dwarf, compact and mounding in habit. Small dark green semi-glossy leaves.

'Sunfire' 1974. 'Super Star' × 'Zorina'. Full, well-formed vermilion blooms. Bushy, vigorous and healthy.

'Sunsilk' 1973. 'Pink Parfait' × 'Redgold' seedling. Fl-HT. Blooms pure lemon-yellow, full and slightly fragrant, many borne singly. Strong and upright. Semi-glossy leaves.

'Sunsong' – see Grandifloras.

'Sunsprite' – see 'Friesia'.

'Sweet Vivien' 1963. 'Little Darling' × 'Odorata'. Large semi-double pink flowers with light yellow centres. Small dark leaves. Low-growing and bushy.

'Taora' 1970. Seedling × 'Super Star'. Flowers signal-red with cherry reverse. Double. Bushy and compact, with semi-glossy leaves.

'Tamango' 1967. ('Alain' × *R. chinensis mutabilis*) × ('Radar' × 'Caprice'). Large very double flowers, rose-red shaded crimson. Large trusses. Vigorous and well branched.

'Telstar' 1963. 'Rosemary Gandy' × 'Masquerade'. Flowers orange and yellow, heavily flushed scarlet with age. Upright and tall, with dark green bronzy foliage.

'The Sun' 1974. ('Little Darling' × 'Goldi-locks') × 'Irish Mist'. Double, cupped blooms, vermilion with a lighter reverse. Semi-glossy leaves. Vigorous, tall and upright in habit.

'Tip Top' 1963. Parents not given. Dwarf, bushy and compact, with matt mid-green leaves. Profuse salmon-pink double flowers.

'Tombola' 1966. 'Amor' × seedling. Flowers deep salmon to carmine pink, shaded gold. Large glossy dark green leaves. Moderately vigorous and upright.

'Toni Lander' 1959. 'Independence' × 'Circus'. Blooms full, rich salmon edged scarlet. Vigorous and uniform.

'Tony Jacklin' 1972. 'City of Leeds' × 'Irish Mist'. Double orange-salmon blooms. Leathery mid-green foliage. Vigorous.

'Topsi' 1972. 'Fragrant Cloud' × 'Fire Signal'. Brilliant orange-scarlet semi-double flowers, very freely borne. Dwarf, bushy and compact. Semi-glossy leaves. Watch out for black spot.

'Tornado' – see 'Kortor'.

'Travesti' 1966. 'Orange Sensation' × 'Circus'. Flowers yellow, flushed cherry-red and with a yellow reverse. Dark leaves. Vigorous and branching.

'Trumpeter' 1977. 'Satchmo' seedling. Bright orange-scarlet-vermilion blooms and a low-growing compact bush.

'Variety Club' 1965. 'Columbine' × 'Circus'. Very strong and tall, with dark green glossy leaves. Shapely flowers, pink blended on cream and yellow.

'Vera Dalton' 1961. Seedling × 'Queen Elizabeth'. Compact and bushy, with dark green foliage. Healthy. Flowers semi-double, pale camellia-rose.

'Violet Carson' 1963. 'Mme Léon Cuny' × 'Spartan'. Fl-HT. Double flowers, soft salmon with a silvery reverse. Dark glossy leaves. Compact and bushy.

For the history of the Grandifloras, see page 79; for illustrations, see plates XXVIII, XXIX and XXXV (pp138, 141 and 200).

'Vogue' 1951. 'Pinocchio' × 'Crimson Glory'. Shapely cherry-red blooms in trusses. Glossy leaves. Upright and bushy. A full sister to 'Fashion'.

'Warrior' 1977. 'City of Belfast' × 'Ronde Endiablée'. Double scarlet-red blooms, singly and in trusses, free and continuous. Deep green leaves. Hardy and vigorous.

'White Spray' 1968. Seedling × 'Iceberg'. Small fragrant pure white flowers, well formed and good trusses. Free and branching.

'Woburn Abbey' 1961. 'Masquerade' × 'Fashion'. Strong, tall and bushy, with small dark green leaves, not mildew-proof. Cupped double flowers, changing from deep cadmium-orange to yellow at petal base; rather crowded in trusses.

'World's Fair' ('Mina Kordes') 1939. 'Dance of Joy' × 'Crimson Glory'. Large semi-double fragrant blooms, deep crimson fading scarlet. Dark leaves. Vigorous and bushy in habit.

'Yellow Queen Elizabeth' 1964. Sport of 'Queen Elizabeth'. Fl-HT. Not quite as vigorous as its parent, but still very tall. Same type of flowers in pale orange-yellow.

'Zambra' 1961. ('Goldilocks' × 'Fashion') × ('Goldilocks' × 'Fashion'). Flat semi-double blooms in large trusses, orange with a yellow reverse. Low and spreading and not too healthy.

'Zorina' 1963. 'Pinocchio' seedling × 'Spartan'. Large, double, cupped blooms. Red. Glossy leaves. Upright in habit and best in a greenhouse.

GRANDIFLORAS

New classification: Bush Roses, cluster-flowering. All of these are recurrent. Average height 1.1 m (3½ ft).

'Apricot Nectar' 1956. Seedling × 'Spartan'. Tall, with strong stiff stems and light green leaves. Shapely blooms open to paeony form and are very large. Light apricot, the edges tinted pink.

'Aquarius' 1971. ('Charlotte Armstrong' × 'Contrast') × ['Fandango' × ('World's Fair' × 'Floradora')]. Large double flowers, pink and long-lasting. Dark leathery leaves. Upright and bushy.

'Arizona' 1975. 'Fred Howard' × ('Golden Scepter' × 'Golden Rapture'). Full urn-shaped orange-red blooms in good trusses, but not too quick to repeat.

'Bienvenu' 1969. 'Camelot' × ('Montezuma' × 'War Dance'). Large shapely, very double flowers in orange-red. Matt green leaves. Vigorous.

'Buccaneer' 1953. 'Golden Rapture' ('Max Krause' × 'Capt. Thomas). Full, slightly fragrant bright yellow blooms. Very tall. Matt mid-green leaves.

These are classified as
Floribundas in Britain, but
as three of the four varieties
in the painting originated in
the United States, it seems
reasonable to use the
terminology of that country.
Like 'Peace' (plate XIX)
among the Hybrid Teas,
'Queen Elizabeth' (top)
must be the most popular
rose of all time in its
particular group, difficult
though it may be to place in
the garden because of its
height. With careful
pruning it makes a fine
hedge, and the flowers last
for ever in water.
'Camelot' (left centre) and
'John S. Armstrong'
(bottom left) are an
outstanding pair for the back
of the border (for the most
distinctive thing about
almost all Grandifloras is
their height), while
'Prominent' ('Korp';
right), can be used if a splash
of brightness is needed).
See also plates XXIX and
XXXV (pp141 and 200).

For the history of the
Hybrid Musks, see page 81;
for illustrations, see plate
XII (p83).

GRANDIFLORAS *continued*

'Camelot' 1964. 'Circus' × 'Queen Elizabeth'. Large double flowers, opening cupped and fragrant, in salmon-pink. Glossy dark leaves. Free.

'Candy Apple' 1975. 'Jack O'Lantern' × seedling. Bright cherry-red cupped double blooms. Well branched with dark matt leaves and good repeat.

'Carrousel' 1950. Seedling × 'Margy'. Dark red medium-sized fragrant blooms and dark leaves. Bushy and profuse.

'Cherry Vanilla' 1974. 'Buccaneer' × 'El Capitan'. Large cream flowers with pink petal edges, semi-double and loosely formed. Well branched and healthy.

'Commanche' 1968. 'Spartan' × ('Carrousel' × 'Happiness'). Strong and bushy with orange-red flowers, well formed and then opening cupped.

'El Capitan' 1959. 'Charlotte Armstrong' × 'Floradora'. Large double shapely cherry-red blooms in small trusses. Slight scent only. Bushy in habit.

'Golden Scepter' – see 'Spek's Yellow' under Hybrid Teas.

'Hocus Pocus' 1975. 'Fandango' × 'Simon Bolivar'. Semi-double cupped flowers, orange-red with darker shadings. Semi-glossy leaves. Free and bushes out well.

'John S. Armstrong' 1961. 'Charlotte Armstrong' × seedling. Large double high-centred currant-red flowers, some opening cupped. Dark semi-glossy leaves. Bushy.

'Lucky Lady' 1966. 'Charlotte Armstrong' × 'Cherry Glow'. Bushy, with dark glossy leaves. Flowers large, double, shapely, light pink with a darker reverse.

'Montezuma' 1955. 'Fandango' × 'Floradora'. Large double high-centred flowers in a unique blend of orange and brick-red. Semi-glossy leaves. Very vigorous and branching well. Does not like rain.

'Mount Shasta' 1963. 'Queen Elizabeth' × 'Blanche Mallerin'. Very large double fragrant white flowers, opening cupped. Grey-green leaves. Strong and bushy.

'Olé' 1964. 'Roundelay' × 'El Capitan'. Medium-sized fragrant orange-red flowers, high-centred in bud, then cupped. Glossy leaves.

'Nitouche' 1975. Seedling × 'Whisky Mac'. Rounded double blooms shapely and with waved petals in small trusses and singly. Light salmon-pink. Dark green leaves. Below average height, but vigorous and hardy.

'Peggy Netherthorpe' 1974. 'Voeux de Bonheur' × 'Chic Parisien'. Blush-pink shapely blooms on long stems, but below average Grandiflora height. Vigorous nevertheless.

'Pink Parfait' 1960. 'First Love' × 'Pinocchio'. High-centred blooms, opening flat, in blends of cream and peach-pink with

apricot reverse. Mid-green leaves. Rather slender canes, but well branched.

'Queen Elizabeth' 1945. 'Charlotte Armstrong' × 'Floradora'. Large cupped china-pink flowers on long stems and long-lasting when cut, some coming singly, on an enormously tall and upright bush. Dark leathery leaves which are exceptionally healthy.

'Prominent' – see 'Korp' under Floribundas.

'Roundelay' 1954. 'Charlotte Armstrong' × 'Floradora'. Medium-sized flowers, opening flat, fragrant and currant- to cardinal-red. Dark leaves. Very good repeat.

'Scarlet Knight' – see 'Samourai' under Hybrid Teas.

'Scarlet Queen Elizabeth' – see Floribundas.

'Smooth Sailing' 1977. 'Little Darling' × 'Pink Favorite'. Coppery-salmon medium-sized blooms, rather globular. Glossy mid-green leaves. Bushy and healthy.

'Sonia' – see Floribundas.

'Starfire' 1958. 'Charlotte Armstrong' × ('Charlotte Armstrong' × 'Floradora'). Large double flowers, shapely in bud, opening cupped and fragrant. Very large trusses. Glossy leaves.

'Stella' – see Hybrid Teas.

'Sunsong' 1976. 'Folie d'Espagne' × ('Zambra' × 'Danish Pink'). Globular blooms of up to 70 petals, changing colour through various orange shades. Upright in habit, vigorous and healthy.

HYBRID MUSKS

New classification: Shrub Roses, recurrent. Two main flushes of bloom, but there are generally some flowers in between.

'Ballerina' 1937. Large clusters of small single soft pink flowers with a white eye, resembling apple-blossom. Vigorous, bushy and spreading. 1 m (3 ft).

'Belinda' 1936. Huge corymbs of fragrant soft pink blooms. Erect in growth and suitable for hedging. 1.5 × 1.2 m (5 × 4 ft).

'Bishop Darlington' 1926. 'Aviateur Blériot' × 'Moonlight'. Semi-double cupped very fragrant creamy-pink blooms with primrose overtones. Bronzy leaves. 1.5 × 1.5 m (4 × 4 ft).

'Bloomfield Dainty' 1924. 'Danaë' × 'Mme Edouard Herriot'. Pointed orange buds open to small single flowers of canary-yellow. Fragrant. 1.5 × 1 m (4 × 3 ft).

'Buff Beauty' 1939. Fully double scented buff-apricot-yellow blooms in clusters on arching canes with dark leaves. 1.5 × 1.5 m (5 × 5 ft).

'Clytemnestra' 1915. 'Trier' × 'Liberty'. Copper buds and small ruffled buff-salmon flowers in clusters. Dark leaves. Vigorous and spreading. 1 × 1.2 m (3 × 4 ft).

'**Cornelia**' 1925. Fragrant terracotta to coppery-pink blooms, fading lighter, in large sprays. Dark leaves. Spreading. 1.5 × 1.8m (5 × 6 ft).

'**Danaë**' 1913. 'Trier' × 'Gloire de Chédane Guinoisseau'. One of the babies of the Pemberton group. Clusters of semi-double orange-yellow flowers, fading cream. Lax. 1 × 1m (3 × 3 ft).

'**Daphne**' 1912. Semi-double blush-pink blooms in clusters. 1.2 × 1.2m (4 × 4 ft).

'**Felicia**' 1928. 'Trier' × 'Ophelia'. Clusters of silvery-pink blooms, blended salmon-pink. Bushy and compact in habit. 1.5 × 1.5m (5 × 5 ft).

'**Francesca**' 1922. 'Danaë' × 'Sunburst'. Fine scent and rather loosely-formed flowers in yellow and apricot tints, fading cream. Robust, long-stemmed growth. 1.8 × 1.8m (6 × 6 ft).

'**Kathleen**' 1922. 'Daphne' × 'Perle des Jeannes'. Big trusses of small single blush-pink blooms among coppery leaves. Open growth. Rain can spot flowers. 1.5 × 1.5m (5 × 5 ft).

'**Moonlight**' 1913. 'Trier' × 'Sulphura'. Enormous trusses of semi-double creamy flowers with golden stamens. Dark leaves and dark wood. Very fragrant. 1.8 × 1.2m (6 × 4 ft). Will scramble into a small tree.

'**Nur Mahal**' 1923. Hybrid Musk seedling × 'Château de Clos Vougeot'. Semi-double blooms in bright crimson on a low-growing bushy shrub. Less scent than most. 1.2 × 1.2m (4 × 4 ft).

'**Pax**' 1918. 'Trier' × 'Sunburst'. The largest flowers of all the Pemberton Musks, semi-double, creamy-white and spectacular. Rich scent. 1.8 × 1.8m (6 × 6 ft).

'**Penelope**' 1924. 'Ophelia' × seedling. Large and bushy, the dark green leaves having a bluish tinge. Semi-double scented flowers in creamy-apricot in very large trusses. Sometimes autumn show disappointing, but there can be very big individual sprays of bloom. 1.8 × 1.2m (6 × 8 ft).

'**Prosperity**' 1919. 'Marie-Jeanne' × 'Perle des Jardins'. Scented creamy-blush rosette flowers, fading white. 'Pink Prosperity' is similar but bright pink. Sturdy. 1.5 × 1.2m (5 × 4 ft).

'**Rostock**' 1937. 'Eva' × 'Louise Catherine Breslau'. Buds pink and yellow, opening to large shapely light pink blooms in clusters. Slight fragrance only. Dark glossy leaves. Bushy. 1.5 × 1.2m (5 × 4 ft).

'**Sangerhausen**' 1938. 'Ingar Olsson' × 'Eva'. Large cupped light red blooms in clusters on long stems. Large leathery leaves. Slight scent. 1.2 × 1.2m (4 × 4 ft).

'**Trier**' 1904. An 'Aglaia' seedling. Included mainly for historical interest, as the ancestor of all Hybrid Musks. Semi-double fragrant blush-white flowers, merging to yellow at the base. Lax. 2 × 1.8m (7 × 6 ft).

'**Vanity**' 1920. 'Château de Clos Vougeot' × seedling. Single to semi-double blooms in trusses on an open shrub. Bright pink with sweet scent. 1.8 × 1.8m (6 × 6 ft).

'**Wilhelm**' ('Skyrocket') 1934. 'Robin Hood' × 'J. C. Thornton'. Dark pointed buds in clusters open to semi-double dusky crimson-red flowers with only slight scent. Huge trusses. Red hips. 1.8 × 1.5m (6 × 5 ft).

'**Will Scarlet**' 1948. Sport of 'Wilhelm' in near-scarlet with a white eye; otherwise similar. 1.8 × 1.5m (6 × 5 ft).

MODERN SHRUB ROSES

New classification: Shrub Roses, recurrent and non-recurrent. Too mixed a bag for any general points to be made.

'**Angelina**' 1975. ('Super Star' × 'Carina') × ('Clare Grammerstorf' × 'Frühlings-morgen'). A small rounded shrub. Semi-double slightly cupped light carmine-pink flowers, paling towards the centre. Light green leaves. Recurrent. 1.5 × 1.2m (5 × 4 ft).

'**Adelaide Hoodless**' 1972. Parents not given. Clusters of semi-double red blooms, opening flat and long-lasting. Tall and spreading. Hardy. 1.5 × 1.2m (5 × 4 ft).

'**Bonn**' 1950. 'Hamburg' × 'Independence'. Sometimes classed as a Hybrid Musk. Upright and bushy, with large loosely-formed semi-double orange-scarlet flowers in large trusses. Recurrent. 1.5 × 1.2m (5 × 4 ft).

'**Butterfly Wings**' 1978. 'Dainty Maid' × 'Peace'. Very large semi-double slightly fragrant flowers, opening wide. Ivory-white, tipped carmine, carried in trusses. Glossy mid-green leaves. Upright and branching. Recurrent. 1.2 × 1m (4 × 3 ft).

'**Cappa Magna**' 1965. 'Tenor' seedling. Blooms velvety red, semi-double, large and in large trusses. Vigorous, tall and upright. Glossy dark green leaves. 1.5m (5 ft).

'**Cerise Bouquet**' 1958. *R. multibracteata* × 'Crimson Glory'. A great arching, informal shrub with long canes and small grey-green leaves. Massed clusters of semi-double cerise-crimson scented flowers. Summer only, but long season. 1.8 × 2.4m (6 × 8 ft).

'**Clair Matin**' 1962. 'Fashion' × [('Independence' × 'Orange Triumph') × 'Phyllis Bide']. Cupped semi-double pink flowers in clusters. Slight scent only. Lax shrub or pillar rose. Recurrent. 1.5 × 2m (5 × 7 ft).

'**Cocktail**' 1957. ('Independence' × 'Orange Triumph') × 'Phyllis Bide'. Single crimson blooms with a primrose centre. Semi-glossy, rather small leaves. Recurrent. Vigorous to 1.2m (4 ft) but may die back in winter.

For more information on modern shrub roses, see pages 81 and 202; for illustrations, see opposite and also plate XXXV (p200).

Plate XXIX: Modern shrub roses (1)
One tends to think of modern shrub roses as being constantly in flower, but three of those illustrated here – 'Constance Spry' (top left), 'Cerise Bouquet' (top right) and 'Fritz Nobis' (bottom left) – all bloom only at midsummer, though over a long period. 'Constance Spry' has another resemblance to the old roses, in that its huge pink blooms might almost be those of a Centifolia. All make large, informal shrubs, or if trained on wires would be suitable for hedging.
'Fred Loads' (bottom right) is very different, a gigantic Floribunda in style which, with quite hard pruning, will grow as tall as 'Queen Elizabeth' (plate XXVIII) but much more spread out because its trusses of blooms are so much bigger.
See also plate XXXV (p200).

'**Constance Spry**' 1961. 'Belle Isis' × 'Dainty Maid'. Very large double rose-pink blooms in the old style, but in summer only. Dark green leaves on robust, arching shrub. 1.8 × 1.5 m (6 × 5 ft).

'**Erfurt**' 1939. 'Eva' × 'Réveil Dijonnais'. Nearly single pink flowers with a white eye and yellow tints, in clusters. Fragrant. Recurrent. Sprawling growth. 1.8 × 2.1 m (6 × 7 ft).

'**Frank Naylor**' 1976. [('Orange Sensation' × 'Allgold') × {('Little Lady' × 'Lilac Charm') × ('Blue Moon' × 'Magenta')}] × [{('Clare Grammerstorf' × 'Frühlingsmorgen') × ('Little Lady' × 'Lilac charm')} × {('Blue Moon' × 'Magenta') × ('Clare Grammerstorf' × 'Frühlingsmorgen')}]. A unique blend of small fragrant single deep maroon-crimson flowers with a golden eye, on a bushy shrub with the darkest green leaves. Recurrent. 1.2 × 1.2 m (4 × 4 ft).

'**Fountain**' 1971. Parents unknown. Rich, velvety-red fragrant double flowers, singly and in small trusses. Vigorous and very upright, with dark leaves, reddish when young. Recurrent. 1.5 × 1 m (5 × 3 ft).

'**Fred Loads**' 1967. 'Orange Sensation' × 'Dorothy Wheatcroft'. Large semi-double vermilion-orange blooms in huge trusses. Fragrant. Semi-glossy light green leaves. Very tall and well branched. Recurrent. 2 × 1.5 m (7 × 5 ft).

'**Goldbonnet**' 1972. ('Anne Elizabeth' × 'Allgold') × 'Golden Showers'. Lemon-yellow blooms with a lighter reverse, moderately full, singly and in small clusters. Dark leaves. Vigorous and bushy. Recurrent. 1.2 m (4 ft).

'**Golden Wings**' 1956. 'Soeur Thérèse' × (*R. spinosissima altaica* × 'Ormiston Roy'). Single pale yellow blooms with a deeper colour in the centre and amber stamens. Large and fragrant, and really continuously borne. Matt light green leaves. Vigorous and bushy. 1.8 × 1.5 m (6 × 5 ft).

'**Gustav Frahm**' 1958. 'Fanal' × 'Ama'. Large trusses of double, cupped glowing crimson-scarlet flowers, darker at the petal edges. Recurrent. Vigorous and upright. 1.2 m (4 ft).

'**Heidelberg**' ('Gruss an Heidelberg') 1959. 'Sparrieshoop' × 'World's Fair'. A spreading shrub or short climber. Large double bright crimson blooms, reverse lighter, in clusters. Glossy deep green leaves. Recurrent. Vigorous. 1.8 × 1.5 m (6 × 5 ft).

'**Joseph's Coat**' – see Large-flowered Climbers.

'**Kassel**' 1957. 'Hamburg' × 'Scarlet Else'. Spreading shrub or short climber. Large semi-double fragrant orange-scarlet blooms. Dark leaves. Recurrent. 2 × 1.8 m (7 × 6 ft).

'**Lady Sonia**' 1961. 'Grandmaster' × 'Doreen'. Vigorous, upright and branching. Large double flowers, shapely, deep buttercup-yellow. Recurrent. 1.2 m (4 ft).

'**Lavender Lassie**' 1959. Parents not given. Rosette old-style flowers of 65 small petals in huge sprays. Lilac-pink with slight scent. Recurrent. Light green glossy leaves. Vigorous, but canes may need support because of the weight of the flowers. 1.2 m (4 ft).

'**Marjorie Fair**' 1976. 'Ballerina' × 'Baby Faurax'. Vigorous and bushy, the equivalent of 'Ballerina' but with the small single flowers deep carmine with a lighter eye. Recurrent. 1 × 1 m (3 × 3 ft).

'**Marguerite Hilling**' ('Pink Nevada') 1959. A pink sport of 'Nevada' (which see), and identical but for the colour.

'**Nevada**' 1927. Reputed Moyesii × HT cross, but some doubt. No doubt about magnificence; the finest garden shrub, rose or not, there is. Arching and mounding, with plentiful rather rounded dark leaves. Huge creamy-white single flowers cover every cane in the first flush. Some repeat later. 2 × 2.5 m (7 × 8 ft).

'**Nymphenburg**' 1954. 'Sangerhausen' × 'Sunmist'. Salmon-pink flowers, shaded orange, semi-double and with sweet scent. Recurrent. Will climb. 1.8 × 1.8 m (6 × 6 ft).

'**Rainbow**' 1974. 'Vera Dalton' × 'Buccaneer'. Flowers coral-orange with pink and yellow shading, semi-double and cupped. Upright, rather open growth. Recurrent. 1.2 × 1 m (4 × 3 ft).

'**Réveil Dijonnais**' 1931. 'Eugène Fürst' × 'Constance'. Semi-double flowers, opening flat, in brilliant cerise-scarlet with a golden eye. Profuse with some repeat. Will climb. 1.8 × 1.8 m (6 × 6 ft).

'**Saga**' 1972. 'Rudolph Timm' × ('Chanelle' × 'Piccadilly'). Buff paling to white, the edges of the petals tipped pink. Semi-double. Recurrent. Strong and bushy. 1.5 m (5 ft).

'**Sparrieshoop**' 1953. ('Baby Château' × 'Else Poulsen') × 'Magnifica'. Large single pink fragrant blooms. Glossy leaves. Vigorous and spreading. 1.8 × 1.8 m (6 × 6 ft).

RAMBLERS

New classification: Climbing roses, non-recurrent. Summer-flowering only.

'**Albéric Barbier**' 1900. *R. luciae* × 'Shirley Hibberd'. Yellow pointed buds open to double flowers, first pale yellow, fading cream. Fragrant and with fine healthy glossy leaves lasting into winter. 7.5 m (25 ft).

'**Albertine**' 1921. *R. luciea* × 'Mrs Arthur Robert Waddell'. Profuse coppery-pink double flowers with a rich scent. Very vigorous and branching. Dark green leaves; some mildew likely. 6 m (20 ft).

For the history of the Ramblers, see page 84; for illustrations, see plate XXVI (pp130–131) and the photograph on page 181.

'American Pillar' 1902. (*R. wichuraiana* × *R. setigera*) × a red HP. Many large clusters of big single flowers, vivid carmine-pink with a white eye. Leathery, glossy leaves. 6m (20ft).

'Baltimore Belle' 1843. *R. setigera* × a Gallica hybrid. Very double blush-white blooms in clusters. Fragrant. 5.5m (18ft).

'Bobbie James' 1961. Parents unknown. Small semi-double cupped creamy-white flowers in big trusses. Fine leaves. Very vigorous to 7.5m (25ft).

'Breeze Hill' 1926. *R. wichuraiana* × 'Beauté de Lyon'. Very double cupped fragrant blooms in flesh, pink and apricot blends, paling buff-pink. Bushy and branching. 5.5m (18ft).

'Crimson Shower' 1951. 'Excelsa' seedling. Pompon-style small crimson flowers in big trusses. Light green glossy leaves. An improvement on 'Excelsa'. Vigorous grower to 3m (10ft).

'Dr W. Van Fleet' 1910. (*R. wichuraiana* × 'Safrano') × 'Souvenir du Président Carnot'. Large clusters of china- to flesh-pink blooms, fading lighter, mainly on old wood, so prune lightly. Dark green leaves. 4.5m (15ft).

'Dorothy Perkins' 1901. *R. wichuraiana* × 'Mme Gabriel Luizet'. Probably the most famous rambler ever, despite its mildew. Double rose-pink blooms in profuse clusters. Dark glossy leaves. 4.5m (15ft).

'Emily Gray' 1918. 'Jersey Beauty' × 'Comtesse du Cayla'. Double buff-yellow flowers in clusters. Dark bronze-tinted leaves. 4.5m (15ft).

'Excelsa' ('Red Dorothy Perkins') 1909. Rose-red to crimson cupped double blooms in large clusters. Glossy leaves. 5.5m (18ft).

'Félicité et Perpétue' 1827. A Sempervirens sport. Red-tinted buds open singly and in clusters to enchanting pompons of white. Slight fragrance only. Dainty leaves, almost evergreen. 4.5m (15ft).

R. filipes 'Kiftsgate' The best form of *R. filipes*, found at Kiftsgate Court, Gloucestershire. Enormously vigorous; for large gardens only. Huge corymbs of many hundreds of small creamy-white strongly-scented flowers and tiny red hips. 9 × 6m (30 × 20ft).

'Fortune's Double Yellow (*R.* × *odorata pseudindica*, 'Beauty of Glazenwood', 'Gold of Ophir', 'San Rafeal Rose') 1845. Needs mild climate. Semi-double scented orange-yellow flowers, flushed salmon-red. 4.5m (15ft).

'François Juranville' 1906. *R. wichuraiana* × 'Mme Laurette Messimy'. Salmon-pink large flowers, fading light pink; yellow petal bases. Scented. Glossy leaves. 7.5m (25ft).

'Goldfinch' 1907. 'Hélène' × unknown. Clustered small semi-double slightly fragrant yellow blooms, fading white. 4.5m (15ft).

'Jersey Beauty' 1899. *R. wichuraiana* × 'Perle des Jardins'. Single buff-yellow flowers, fading cream, in clusters and very fragrant. Leaves last into winter. Occasional late blooms. 5.5m (18ft).

'Rambling Rector' A multiflora rambler. Clusters of small white semi-double blooms. 6m (20ft).

'Ramona' ('Red Cheroke') 1913. *R. anemonoides* sport. Clematis-like blooms in crimson-lake with paler pink reverse. Exceptionally lovely, but needs mild climate. Early. 4.5m (15ft).

R. longicuspis (*R. lucens*) Species. Large corymbs of small white blooms followed by tiny red hips. Late. Very vigorous and fine glossy leaves. 6m (20ft).

'Rose-Marie Viaud' 1924. A Multiflora rambler, seedling of 'Veilchenblau'. Profuse clusters of semi-double blooms, amethyst to violet and scentless. No thorns; light green glossy leaves. 4.5m (15ft).

'Sanders's White Rambler' 1912. Rosette flowers, fragrant and in large clusters. Very free. Fine glossy leaves. One of the healthiest. 4.5m (15ft).

'Seagull' 1907. About the best of the medium-sized white ramblers. Single flowers with golden stamens in large clusters. Good foliage. 4.5m (15ft).

'Seven Sisters' (*R. multiflora platyphylla*, *R. grevillei*) 1817. Flowers large for a Multiflora, carried in clusters. Seven different shades of crimson, lilac, pink and lilac-white. Rampant. 9m (30ft).

'The Garland' ('Wood's Garland') 1835. *R. moschata* × *R. multiflora*. Sometimes classified as a Hybrid Musk. Medium-sized semi-double fragrant blush-pink blooms with a hint of yellow, fading white. Large clusters. 3m (10ft).

'Veilchenblau' ('Violet Blue') 1909. 'Crimson Rambler' × unknown. Small cupped semi-double blooms in trusses, violet-blue with a white centre and occasional white streaks. Scented. Glossy mid-green leaves and few thorns. 4.5m (15ft).

'Wedding Day' 1950. *R. sinowilsonii* hybrid. Yellow buds open to single white star-like flowers, flushed and spotted pink as they age. Scented. 6m (20ft).

CLIMBERS

New classification: Climbing roses, recurrent and non-recurrent.

NOISETTE CLIMBERS AND RAMBLERS
These are all recurrent.

'Aimée Vibert' ('Bouquet de la Mariée', 'Nivea') 1828. 'Champney's Pink Cluster' × *R. sempervirens* hybrid. Beautiful rich green glossy leaves. Medium-sized pure white double flowers produced in small clusters. Scented. 4.5m (15ft).

For the history of the Climbers, see page 85; for illustrations, see plates XIII, XXX and XXXII (pp87, 145 and 179).

'Alister Stella Gray' ('Golden Rambler') 1894. Small clusters early, large heads later, of yellow buds opening to pale yellow fragrant flowers, fading white. 4.5 m (15 ft).

'Blush Noisette' 1817. A seedling of 'Champney's Pink Cluster'. Scented blush-pink flowers in clusters, with a hint of lilac. Very free and continuous. 3 m (10 ft).

'Céline Forestier' 1842. Best grown on a warm wall. Small double flowers in clusters, pale orange-yellow, deeper at the centre. Fragrant. 4.5 m (15 ft).

'Desprez à Fleur Jaune' ('Jaune Desprez', 'Noisette Desprez') 1830. 'Blush Noisette' × *R. × odorata ochroleuca*. Double flowers that open flat with a button eye, yellow shaded apricot. Scented. Not reliably hardy. 5.5 m (18 ft).

'Gloire de Dijon' 1853. Tea rose? × 'Souvenir de la Malmaison'. Could be a climbing Tea, but habit more that of Noisettes. A historic rose, one of the first with buff-yellow HT-type flowers, double and scented, borne very early and continuously. Essential nowadays to get a good strain to have it at its best. 4.5 m (15 ft).

'Lamarque' ('Général Lamarque') 1830. 'Blush Noisette' × 'Parks's Yellow Tea-scented China'. Small double fragrant white blooms with pale yellow centres, in clusters. Needs a warm wall. 4.5 m (15 ft).

'Mme Alfred Carrière' 1879. Pink-tinted white double, cupped blooms, large for the class and fragrant. Fine mid-green leaves. Profuse first flush and seldom without flowers later. 7.6 m (25 ft).

'Maréchal Niel' 1864. 'Chromatella' seedling? A Tea-Noisette, anyway. Pointed buds open to large double loosely-formed flowers with weak stalks. Hardy only in warm areas; otherwise a greenhouse rose. 4.5 m (15 ft).

'William Allen Richardson' 1878. Sport of 'Rêve d'Or'. Not completely hardy. Small yellow-buff fragrant blooms with a hint of apricot. Free early, less so later. 3.5 m (12 ft).

LARGE-FLOWERED CLIMBERS

Except where mentioned, these flower more than once, but the second flush of bloom rarely equals the first. Despite catalogues' claims, few climbers are really perpetual.

Apart from a number which are nowadays more often grown in climbing form than as bushes, the wide range of climbing sports of Hybrid Teas and Floribundas has not been included in this list. As a recognition that there are some roses equally good in both spheres, I have put in 'Climbing Blessings', but there are, of course, many others. Their flowers and foliage can be taken as conforming to that of their bush equivalent, but though most will put on a good show of bloom in early summer, by no means all of them do as well later. Some, in fact, only flower once in a season. There are few if any Floribundas grown mainly or exclusively as climbing sports, but some, such as 'Climbing Iceberg', are outstanding in this form.

'Aloha' 1949. 'Mercedes Gallart' × 'New Dawn'. Unpromising buds open to the most lovely very double pink flowers in the old style, quite unaffected by rain and strongly fragrant. Very healthy glossy leaves. Good repeat. 3 m (10 ft), or use as a 1.5 m (5 ft) shrub.

'Altissimo' 1965. 'Ténor' × unknown. Sturdy, with large dark green leaves. Single 10 cm (4 in) flowers in deep red with crimson tones which hold well. 3.5 m (12 ft).

'Amadis' ('Crimson Boursalt') 1829. A china rose × *R. pendulina*. Large semi-double cupped blooms, deep purple shaded crimson. Whitish wood turns red-brown. Thornless. 2.5 m (8 ft).

'America' 1976. 'Fragrant Cloud' × 'Tradition'. Large double fragrant blooms in peachy-apricot. Very recurrent. Glossy mid-green leaves. Healthy. 3 m (10 ft).

'Bad Neuenahr' 1958. Parents not given. Large very double, cupped, fragrant scarlet blooms in clusters. Dark leaves. To 1.8 m (6 ft) on wall, or grow as shrub.

R. banksiae lutea Large sprays of very small globular pale yellow double flowers, borne on thornless old wood, so prune to a minimum. Very vigorous, but not hardy. Spring-flowering only. 7.5 m (25 ft). There are single-flowered yellow and white Banksian roses as well, also the double white *R. banksiae banksiae*. Not, in this case, large-flowered, but otherwise in character.

'Bantry Bay' 1967. 'New Dawn' × 'Korona'. Blooms pink and semi-double, in widely-spaced trusses. Semi-glossy leaves. 3 m (10 ft).

'Blairi No 2' 1845. Bronze-tinted foliage on hardy, arching stems laden with double cerise-pink blooms, paling towards petal edges. Scented. Summer only. 5.5 m (18 ft).

'Blaze' 1932. 'Paul's Scarlet Climber' × 'Gruss an Teplitz'. Very similar to its first parent, but more reliably recurrent in autumn and with some scattered bloom during the summer.

'Blessings, Climbing' Sport of the bush rose. Soft coral-pink, fragrant and a good repeat. 6 m (20 ft).

'Casino' 1963. 'Coral Dawn' × 'Buccaneer'. Large double soft yellow flowers; fragrant. Matt leaves. 3 m (10 ft).

'Cécile Brunner, Climbing' 1894. Sport of the bush rose and more commonly grown. Enormously vigorous with massed blooms early and sporadic repeat. 6 m (20 ft).

'Chaplin's Pink Companion' 1961. 'Chaplin's Pink' × 'Opera'. Silvery-pink double flowers in clusters. Glossy leaves. Fragrant. 4.5 m (15 ft).

Plate XXX: Climbing sports
All these roses – 'Climbing Mme Caroline Testout' (top), 'Climbing Shot Silk' (right) and 'Climbing Etoile de Hollande' (bottom) – began life as bush Hybrid Tea varieties. Climbing forms appeared as sports, and now this particular trio are much more often grown in this form. They are certainly among the best of such sports. Care is needed with this group as a whole because a number of them flower with much less freedom than they did as bushes.
There are climbing forms of Floribundas as well as Hybrid Teas, and 'Masquerade' (plate XXV) grown in this way has long been a favourite. More recently, 'Iceberg' (plate XXV) has shown tremendous potential. Do not prune any of them in their first year, or they may revert to their bush form.

'**Compassion**' 1972. 'White Cockade' × 'Prima Ballerina'. Double pale orange-salmon blooms with lighter reverse; very fragrant. Dark green leaves, glossy. 2.5 m (8 ft).

'**Copacabana**' 1967. 'Coup de Foudre' × unnamed seedling. Vermilion blooms, deeper colour at petal edges, full and compact, in trusses. Glossy dark green leaves. 1.8 m (8 ft).

'**Copenhagen**' 1963. Seedling × 'Ena Harkness'. Healthy leaves with coppery shadings. Blooms very double and shapely, fragrant and rich scarlet. 3 m (10 ft).

'**Danse des Sylphes**' 1959. 'Danse du Feu' × ('Peace' × 'Independence'). Rich red, suffused geranium-red, in clusters. Matt leaves. 4.5 m (15 ft).

'**Danse du Feu**' ('Spectacular') 1953. 'Paul's Scarlet Climber' × unnamed Multiflora. Double flowers, opening cupped to flat, fragrant and bright scarlet, dulling later. Glossy leaves and good repeat. 3 m (10 ft).

'**Dr J. H. Nicolas**' 1940. 'Charles P. Kilham' × 'George Arends'. Large very double rose-pink blooms, several in a cluster. Very fragrant. 3 m (10 ft).

'**Don Juan**' 1958. 'New Dawn' seedling × 'New Yorker'. Full velvety dark red, very fragrant blooms, and dark green glossy leaves. 3 m (10 ft).

'**Dornröschen**' 1960. 'Pike's Peak' × 'Ballet'. Large fragrant double flowers, salmon to light red, reverse yellow. Large clusters. 2.5 m (8 ft).

'**Dortmund**' 1955. Seedling × *R. kordesii*. Large clusters of very big single flowers, bright crimson-red with a white eye. Dark glossy leaves. 3 m (10 ft).

'**Dreaming Spires**' 1973. 'Buccaneer' × 'Arthur Bell'. Golden-yellow blooms, singly and in clusters. Fragrant. Dark green leaves. 2.5 m (8 ft).

'**Etude**' 1964. A 'Danse du Feu' cross. Double deep salmon-pink blooms, lasting well. Small dark green leaves. Long laterals. 3 m (10 ft).

'**Fugue**' 1958. 'Alain' × 'Guinée'. Bright crimson-red semi-double blooms. Glossy leaves. 3 m (10 ft).

'**Galway Bay**' 1966. 'Heidelberg' × 'Queen Elizabeth'. Large salmon-pink double flowers in clusters. Good repeat. Semi-glossy leaves. 2.5 m (8 ft).

R. gigantea (*R. odorata gigantea*) Red-tinted leaves and large fragrant loosely-formed lemon-white flowers. For a warm climate; summer only. 7.5 m (25 ft).

'**Golden Showers**' 1956. 'Charlotte Armstrong' × 'Capt. Thomas'. Large golden-yellow flowers, opening loosely, singly and in clusters. Some fragrance. Dark glossy leaves. 2.5 m (8 ft).

'**Grand Hotel**' 1973. 'Brilliant' × 'Heidelberg'. Blooms HT-shaped, opening cupped, in unfading bright scarlet, shaded darker. Dark green glossy leaves. 2.5 m (8 ft).

'**Guinée**' 1938. 'Souvenir de Claudius Denoyel' × 'Ami Quinard'. Very dark maroon-crimson blooms, large and double and very fragrant. 6 m (20 ft).

'**Handel**' 1965. 'Columbine' × 'Heidelberg'. Dark green glossy leaves with coppery shades. Double flowers opening cupped, cream flushed rosy-pink at the petal edges. 4.5 m (15 ft).

'**Helen Knight**' 1977. *R. ecae* × *R. spinosissima altaica*. Like a climbing *R. ecae*, with bright buttercup-yellow single flowers and small ferny foliage. Spring only. 3 m (10 ft).

'**Joseph's Coat**' 1964. 'Buccaneer' × 'Circus'. Shrub or semi-climber. Dark green leaves. Double flowers, opening wide, golden-yellow and orange, flushed cherry-red at the petal edges. Recurrent. 1.8 m (6 ft).

'**Lady Hillingdon, Climbing**' 1917. Sport of the bush rose. Coppery foliage and orange-yellow Tea rose flowers. Recurrent if on warm wall. 6 m (20 ft).

'**Lawrence Johnston**' ('Hidcote Yellow') 1923. 'Mme Eugène Verdier' × *R. foetida persiana*. Fragrant semi-double loosely cupped blooms in bright yellow. Only spasmodic repeat. 6 m (20 ft).

'**Leverkusen**' 1954. *R. kordesii* × 'Golden Glow'. Double light yellow shapely flowers in big clusters. 2.5 m (8 ft).

'**Mme Grégoire Staechelin**' ('Spanish Beauty') 1927. 'Frau Karl Druschki' × 'Château de Clos Vougeot'. One of the earliest roses in flower, laden with large, rather loosely-formed double pink flowers with sometimes crimson splashes on the reverse. Spring only. 6 m (20 ft).

'**Mme Sancy de Parabère**' 1874. A Boursault climber. Large semi-double fragrant light violet-pink blooms, opening wide with short centre petals. Spring only. 3 m (10 ft).

'**Maigold**' 1953. 'Poulsen's Pink' × 'Frühlingstag'. Semi-double bronze-yellow fragrant blooms, opening flat. Glossy healthy leaves. Bushy to 3 m (10 ft). Summer only.

'**Malaga**' 1971. ('Danse du Feu' × 'Hamburger Phoenix') × 'Copenhagen'. Double fragrant blooms salmon-pink with carmine reverse. Large dark green leaves, semi-glossy. 2 m (7 ft).

'**Mermaid**' 1918. *R. bracteata* × a yellow Tea rose. Huge single sulphur-yellow flowers with amber stamens. Small clusters perpetually borne. Fierce thorns and glossy, almost evergreen leaves. No pruning. Not completely hardy. 9 m (30 ft).

'**Morgengruss**' 1962. Parents not given. Large, full blooms, light pink tinted yellow. Glossy light green leaves. 4 m (14 ft).

'**Morning Jewel**' 1968. 'New Dawn' × 'Red Dandy'. Rich pink semi-double blooms over a long period. Glossy leaves. 3 m (10 ft).

'New Dawn' 1930. Sport of 'Dr W. Van Fleet'. Blush-pink double blooms borne with great freedom. Good repeat. 6m (20ft).

'Parkdirektor Riggers' 1957. *R. kordesii* × 'Our Princess'. Medium-sized double flowers in glowing crimson. Large trusses and dark glossy leaves. One of the best. 4.5m (15ft).

'Paul's Lemon Pillar' 1915. 'Frau Karl Druschki' × 'Maréchal Niel'. Pale lemon-yellow buds open to large, very double globular near-white fragrant flowers. Summer only. 6m (20ft).

'Paul's Scarlet Climber' 1916. 'Paul's Carmine Pillar' × 'Rêve d'Or'. Sometimes classed as a Rambler. Profuse unfading cupped double blooms in scarlet-crimson. Seldom recurrent. 4.5m (15ft).

'Phare' 1961. 'Danse du Feu' × ('Floradora' × unnamed seedling). Freely-borne large double crimson-red blooms. Dark green glossy leaves. 3.5m (12ft).

'Piñata' 1977. Unnamed seedling × unnamed seedling. Short ovoid buds and high-centred full double blooms borne in clusters of three to ten. Yellow with vermilion overlay changing to vermilion over most of the petal. 3.5m (12ft).

'Pink Perpêtue' 1964. 'Danse du Feu' × 'New Dawn'. Double blooms pink inside and carmine-pink on reverse; fragrant. Freely borne. Rather small but plentiful dark green leaves. Good repeat. 3.5m (12ft).

'Ritter von Barmstede' 1960. Parents unknown. Deep pink very full flowers, quick to repeat. Glossy light green leaves. 2.5m (8ft).

'Rosy Mantle' 1970. 'New Dawn' × 'Prima Ballerina'. Deep rose-pink double blooms in clusters. Slight fragrance. Dark green glossy leaves. 3m (10ft).

'Royal Gold' 1957. 'Climbing Goldilocks' × 'Lydia'. Full, deep yellow fragrant blooms. Semi-glossy leaves. 2.5m (8ft).

'Santa Catalina' 1970. 'Paddy McGredy' × 'Heidelberg'. Soft, warm pink semi-double blooms, opening wide. Dark green semi-glossy leaves. 2.5m (8ft).

'Schoolgirl' 1964. 'Coral Dawn' × 'Belle Blonde'. Large double apricot-orange flowers and glossy dark green leaves. 4.5m (15ft).

'Sombreuil' 1850. A climbing Tea rose. Creamy-white large, very double blooms, opening flat and sometimes pink-tinted. Scented. 6m (20ft).

'Spectacular' – see 'Danse du Feu'.

'Stadt Rosenheim' 1961. Double orange-red fragrant blooms in clusters of up to 10. Glossy light green leaves. 2.5m (8ft).

'Swan Lake' 1968. 'Memoriam' × 'Heidelberg'. Large, very full and high-centred white blooms, tinged with pink. Semi-glossy mid-green leaves. 3m (10ft).

'Sweet Sultan' 1958. 'Independence' × 'Honour Bright'. Large single flowers in large clusters, crimson shading to maroon. Very fragrant. 2.4m (8ft).

For the history of the Miniatures, see page 89; for illustrations, see plates XIV and XXXI (pp91 and 149) and the photograph on page 193.

'Sympathie' 1964. Very full velvety red fragrant blooms. Mid-green glossy leaves. 3.5m (12ft).

'Tempo' 1974. 'Climbing Ena Harkness' × seedling. Large fully double intense dark red blooms, singly or in small clusters. Profuse and continuous, 4.5m (15ft).

'White Cockade' 1969. 'New Dawn' × 'Circus'. Large double fragrant white blooms. Glossy mid-green leaves. 2.5m (8ft).

MINIATURE ROSES

New classification: Miniature Roses, bush and climbing. All these are recurrent, beginning early and finishing late. Unless otherwise stated, the height is 25–30cm (10–12in).

'Angela Rippon' ('Ocaru-Ocarina') 1976. Double salmon-pink blooms in good clusters. Compact and bushy.

'Angel Darling' 1976. 'Little Chief' × 'Angel Face'. Mauve semi-double flowers with yellow stamens, loosely formed. Bushy in habit.

'Baby Darling' 1964. 'Little Darling' × 'Magic Wand'. Small orange to orange-pink moderately full flowers. Glossy dark green leaves. Bushy.

'Baby Masquerade' ('Baby Carnival') 1956. 'Tom Thumb' × 'Masquerade'. Similar in effect to 'Masquerade', but colours less harsh. Bushy and tall at 40cm (15in).

'Baby Ophelia' 1961. (*R. wichuraiana* × 'Floradora') × 'Little Buckaroo'. Small cupped shell-pink flowers, suffused apricot, with yellow bases. Free and fragrant. 20–25cm (8–10in).

'Bambino' 1953. 'Perla de Alcanada' sport. Shapely rose-pink flowers with a slight fragrance. Compact.

'Beauty Secret' 1965. 'Little Darling' × 'Magic Wand'. Flowers crimson-red, high-centred and very fragrant. Glossy leaves. Vigorous and bushy.

'Bit o' Sunshine' 1956. 'Copper Glow' × 'Zee'. Large semi-double clear yellow blooms, sometimes flushed red. Up to 45cm (18in) tall.

'Cinderella' 1953. 'Cécile Brunner' × 'Tom Thumb'. Very double (50–60 petals) small flowers in blush-pink. Upright, bushy and thornless.

'Colibri' 1959. 'Goldilocks' × 'Perla de Montserrat'. Small double bright orange-yellow blooms. Dwarf and bushy, with dark green leaves. 23cm (9in).

'Coralin' 1955. 'Méphiste' × 'Perla de Alcanada'. Large coral-red to orange-red blooms and light green, bronze-tinted leaves. 30–40cm (12–15in).

'Cricri' 1958. ('Alain' × 'Independence') × 'Perla de Alcanada'. Very double, well-formed flowers, salmon shaded coral.

147

'Cuddles' 1978. 'Zorina' × seedling. Deep coral-pink fully double petite flowers of excellent substance and form.

'Darling Flame' 1971. ('Rimrosa' × 'Josephine Wheatcroft') × 'Zambra'. Double vermilion flowers. Bushy to 35 cm (14 in).

'Donna Faye' 1975. 'Ma Perkins' × 'Baby Betsy McCall'. Very double blooms in soft pink, holding shape well. Upright in habit and healthy.

'Dresden Doll' 1975. 'Fairy Moss' × unnamed Moss rose. Clusters of quite large, very double soft pink blooms; heavily mossed. A breakthrough, but large for a miniature at 60 cm (2 ft).

'Dwarf King' ('Zwergkönig') 1957. 'World's Fair' × 'Tom Thumb'. Full fragrant carmine blooms, opening flat, in small clusters. Glossy leaves. 20–25 cm (8–10 in).

'Easter Morning' 1960. 'Golden Glow' × 'Zee'. Quite large double flowers in ivory-white. Good glossy foliage. Vigorous.

'Eleanor' 1960. (R. wichuraiana × 'Floradora') × (seedling × 'Zee'). Blooms coral-pink, full and slightly scented. Glossy mid-green leaves. Upright.

'Elfin Charm' 1974. (R. wichuraiana × 'Floradora') × 'Fiesta Gold'. A bushy, compact grower with phlox-pink very double flowers.

'Fashion Flame' 1977. 'Little Darling' × 'Fire Flame'. Large very double flowers in coral-orange. Bushy.

'Fire Princess' 1969. 'Baccara' × 'Eleanor'. Small very double orange-red flowers. Very free. 23 cm (9 in).

'Frosty' 1953. (R. wichuraiana × unnamed seedling) × self. Very small greenish-white flowers with button eyes. Spreading.

'Gloriglo' 1977. Seedling × 'Over the Rainbow'. A startling colour combination of brilliant glowing orange on the inside of the petals and creamy-white on the outside. Good flower form.

'Gold Coin' 1970. 'Golden Glow' × 'Magic Wand'. Very full canary-yellow blooms (52 petals) in trusses. Compact and bushy. Light green leaves.

'Golden Angel' 1975. 'Golden Glow' × unnamed seedling. Flowers of HT form with 60–70 petals, some coming singly. Bright yellow. Spreading growth. 35 cm (14 in).

'Gold Pin' 1974. Bushy and spreading, with bright golden-yellow double flowers, large for the size of the plant.

'Green Diamond' 1975. Unnamed seedling × 'Sheri Anne'. Rose-tinted buds, changing to soft green. Some blooms fail to open. A novelty, and not showy.

'Green Ice' 1971. (R. wichuraiana × 'Floradora') × 'Jet Trail'. Novelty, with apricot buds opening into white double blooms which then change to a cool soft green.

'Gypsy Jewel' 1975. 'Little Darling' × 'Little Buckaroo'. Very double but loosely-formed deep pink blooms, large for a miniature. Some scent.

'Happytime' 1974. (R. wichuraiana × 'Floradora') × ('Golden Glow' × 'Zee'). Climber. Flowers yellow flushed red. Vigorous grower. Good early flush, with some repeat.

'Judy Fischer' 1968. 'Little Darling' × 'Magic Wand'. Freely-borne small double rose-pink flowers. Dark bronzy leaves. Bushy. 20–25 cm (8–10 in).

'June Time' 1963. (R. wichuraiana × 'Floradora') × [('Etoile Luisante' seedling × 'Red Ripples') × 'Zee']. Small double light pink blooms with a deeper reverse. Compact. 23–30 cm (9–12 in).

'Lavender Lace' 1970. 'Ellen Poulsen' × 'Debbie'. Very full mauve-lavender blooms in good trusses. Small light green leaves.

'Little Buckaroo' 1956. (R. wichuraiana × 'Floradora') × ('Oakington Ruby' × 'Floradora'). Small bright red, white-centred blooms, moderately full and with some scent. Glossy bronze-tinted leaves. Vigorous to 33–40 cm (13–15 in).

'Little Flirt' 1961. (R. wichuraiana × 'Floradora') × ('Golden Glow' × 'Zee'). Full fragrant orange-red flowers with reverse yellow. Light green leaves. 40 cm (15 in).

'Little Sunset' 1967. Seedling × 'Tom Thumb'. Small flowers with yellow-based salmon-pink petals. Free. Light green leaves. 30–40 cm (12–15 in).

'Lollipop' 1959. (R. wichuraiana × 'Floradora') × 'Little Buckaroo'. Bright red with petal bases sometimes white. Blooms small and full, with 30–40 petals. Glossy leaves. 35 cm (14 in).

'Magic Carrousel' 1973. 'Little Darling' × 'Westmont'. Similar to 'Toy Clown', but more distinctive. Petals white, edged brilliant red. High-centred bloom.

'Mary Marshall' 1971. 'Little Darling' × 'Fairy Princess'. Outstanding coral-orange flowers with yellow base. Perfect pointed HT-type buds.

'Mona Ruth' 1959. [('Soeur Thérèse' × 'Wilhelm') × (seedling × 'Red Ripples')] × 'Zee'. Small double rosy-crimson flowers. Leathery leaves.

'Mr Bluebird' 1960. 'Old Blush' × 'Old Blush'. Small semi-double flowers in variable shades of lavender-blue. Compact and bushy in habit. Unusual parents for a miniature. 30–40 cm (12–15 in).

'My Valentine' 1975. 'Little Chief' × 'Little Flirt'. Rich red double flowers with pointed petals. Bushy. Bronze-tinted leaves.

'New Penny' 1962. (R. wichuraiana × 'Floradora') × unnamed seedling. Salmon blooms turn pink with age; moderately full and fragrant. Dark leaves. Branching habit of growth.

Plate XXXI: Miniature roses (2)
'Dresden Doll' (top) was not the first Miniature Moss rose to be raised in the United States by Ralph Moore, but it is certainly the best so far, even if its growth is more on the scale of a Polyantha than a Miniature, with flowers of a size to match.
A great deal of the breeding of Miniatures nowadays involves the use of Floribundas, which has meant a tremendous increase in their colour range. 'Darling Flame' (centre left), 'Toy Clown' (centre right), 'Easter Morning' (bottom left) and 'Little Flirt' (bottom right) are examples of what has been achieved, not only with colours, but with an improvement in the substance and shape of the flowers when compared with the original Miniature, R. roulettii (plate XIV). It is a pity, however, that the original daintiness has been lost in some cases.
See also plate XIV (p91) and the photograph on page 193.

'Nozomi' 1972. 'Fairy Princess' × 'Sweet Fairy'. A climber or ground-cover rose. Flowers single, pearl-pink, fading white in trusses on long canes. Small pointed dark green leaves. Non-recurrent.

'Over the Rainbow' 1972. 'Little Darling' × 'Westmont'. Red and pink with gold base and reverse. Well-formed flowers.

'Perla de Alcanada' ('Baby Crimson', 'Pearl of Canada', 'Titania', 'Wheatcroft's Baby Crimson') 1944. 'Perle des Rouges' × *R. roulettii*. Semi-double bright carmine blooms. Dark glossy leaves. Compact.

'Perla de Montserrat' 1945. 'Cécile Brunner' × *R. roulettii*. Semi-double pink blooms, edged pearly-pink. Dwarf and very compact. 23 cm (9 in).

'Pink Cameo' ('Climbing Cameo') 1954. ('Soeur Thérèse' × 'Wilhelm') × 'Zee'. Small double rich rose-pink blooms in clusters. Long season. Leaves small and glossy. Climbs to 1.5 m (5 ft).

'Pink Heather' 1959. (*R. wichuraiana* × 'Floradora') × ('Violette' × 'Zee'). Very small double lavender-pink blooms, scented. Small glossy leaves. 20–25 cm (8–10 in).

'Pompon de Paris' ('Pompon Ancien') Before 1838. Bright pink double flowers on a twiggy, bushy plant. 23 cm (9 in). The climbing sport will reach 2.5 m (8 ft).

'Pour Toi' ('For You', 'Para Ti', 'Wendy') 1946. 'Eduardo Toda' × 'Pompon de Paris'. Semi-double, with white petals tinted yellow at base. Very bushy. 15–20 cm (6–8 in).

'Prince Charming' 1953. 'Ellen Poulsen' × 'Tom Thumb'. Bright crimson, large and full. Red-tinted leaves. Bushy habit. 20–25 cm (8–10 in).

'Red Cascade' 1976. Climber or trailer. Cherry-red blooms, cupped then flat, in clusters. Good repeat. Good in hanging basket. 1.2 m (4 ft).

'Rise 'n' Shine' 1977. 'Little Darling' × 'Yellow Magic'. Clear yellow well-shaped blooms. Bushy. 35 cm (14 in).

'Robin' 1956. 'Perla de Montserrat' × 'Perla de Alcanada'. Rich red blooms of 60–70 petals in clusters. Vigorous and bushy. Matt dark leaves.

'Rosmarin' 1965. 'Tom Thumb' × 'Decapo'. Small double globular blooms in soft light pink with light red reverse. Glossy light green leaves.

R. roulettii (*R. chinensis minima*, 'Fairy Rose', *R. lawranceana*, 'Roulettii') Small single to semi-double rose-red flowers with petals often pointed. Bushy.

'Royal Ruby' 1972. ('Garnette' × 'Tom Thumb') × 'Ruby Jewel'. Globular red blooms, some singly and most in clusters. Tall at 45 cm (18 in).

'Royal Salute' 1976. 'New Penny' × 'Marlena'. Full carmine-pink blooms in trusses; very free. Vigorous, dwarf and compact with coppery leaves.

'Scarlet Gem' ('Scarlet Pimpernel') 1961. ('Moulin Rouge' × 'Fashion') × ('Perla de Montserrat' × 'Perla de Alcanada'). Orange-scarlet very full blooms, freely borne. Vigorous and branching. 30–40 cm (12–15 in).

'Sheri Anne' 1974. 'Little Darling' × 'New Penny'. HT-style buds open flat in big clusters. Orange-red. Large dark green leaves. 40 cm (15 in).

'Simplex' 1961. *R. wichuraiana* × 'Floradora'. Delightful single, with apricot buds opening white with prominent yellow stamens. 40 cm (15 in).

'Small World' 1975. 'Little Chief' × 'Fire Princess'. Dazzling orange-red flowers, double, some borne singly and some in clusters. Tiny at 15 cm (6 in).

'Snowcarpet' 1980. 'New Penny' × 'Temple Bells'. A spreading, ground-hugging Miniature rose for banks and rock gardens. Repeat-flowering, with trusses of white 4 cm (1½ in) short-petalled, very double blooms. Small glossy leaves.

'Stacey Sue' 1976. 'Ellen Poulsen' × 'Fairy Princess'. Flowers of 60 petals, soft pink, in sprays of five and some singly. Low and spreading. 18 cm (7 in).

'Starina' 1965. ('Dany Robin' × 'Fire King') × 'Perla de Montserrat'. Double, well-formed vivid orange-scarlet flowers, long-lasting when cut. Vigorous.

'Stars 'n Stripes' 1976. ('Little Chief' × unnamed seedling) × ('Little Darling' × 'Ferdinand Pichard'). Red and white striped semi-double flowers. Tall at 60 cm (2 ft) and bushy.

'Strawberry Swirl' 1978. 'Little Darling' × unnamed Miniature seedling. Deep orange-red intermixed with white. Very double high-centred bloom. 40 cm (15 in).

'Toy Clown' 1966. 'Little Darling' × 'Magic Wand'. Small semi-double flowers, opening cupped, white edged red. Small leathery leaves. Bushy.

'Wee Man' 1973. 'Little Flirt' × 'Marlena'. Blooms signal-red, semi-double. Vigorous and spreading. Semi-glossy light green leaves. 40 cm (15 in).

'White Angel' 1972. White double flowers, opening flat and star-shaped. Fragrant. Bushy spreading growth.

'Windy City' 1974. ('Little Darling' × 'Little Darling') × (*R. wichuraiana* × unnamed seedling). Very full HT-style blooms. A red and white bicolour. Tall spreading growth. 90 cm (3 ft).

'Yellow Doll' 1962. 'Golden Glow' × 'Zee'. Blooms light yellow to cream, very full and fragrant. Light green leaves. Spreading. 23 cm (9 in).

'Zinger' 1978. 'Zorina' × 'Magic Carrousel'. Pointed buds opening to a brilliant crimson shading to scarlet; bright yellow centre. 20 cm (8 in).

CHAPTER THREE

THE
ROSE GARDEN

WHILE THERE ARE MANY early references to roses being grown in gardens, the rose garden – that is, a garden designed around and dominated by roses – would appear to be a relatively modern development, less than 200 years old. One can find references here and there earlier than this to what may or may not have been rose gardens; King Childebert was supposed to have had one near Paris as early as AD 550, and there was Charlemagne, of course, but there are no real details to enable one to reach a conclusion as to what they were like. Ancient China quite possibly had rose gardens, but all that is known for certain is that the Chinese cultivated the rose long before this was done in the West. They may simply have grown the rose along with all the other plants in their gardens.

Insel Mainau, West Germany
The gardens of Insel Mainau – an island in Lake Constance (Bodensee), where the frontiers of West Germany, Austria and Switzerland meet – are formal and Italianate in design. Massed plantings of bush and standard roses are heightened by the traditional use of wooden pergolas for Ramblers and Climbers.

THE BIRTH OF
THE ROSE GARDEN

So, while it is perfectly possible that there were thousands of rose gardens all over the place, all traces of which have vanished, the first one of note for which there is considerable documentation was that of the Château de Malmaison, about 12 km (8 miles) from Paris and not far from Versailles. Its owner and its creator was the Empress Josephine, wife of Napoleon I, who had a passionate love of flowers and purchased Malmaison, with its several hundred acres of grounds, in 1799. These grounds she first had landscaped by a Scot, Thomas

153

Blaikie, while she was gathering about her a team of expert botanists, gardeners and horticulturists to advise her in the planting and to help her to run things afterwards. They included André Dupont, after whom *R.* × *dupontii* was named – a rose that, as I mentioned earlier, may well have been raised in the château gardens.

Though there were other and more exotic plants and flowers at Malmaison, and quite a collection of rare birds and animals too, it seems certain that the *roseraie* or rose garden was Josephine's favourite. She set out with great determination, using diplomatic channels where necessary, to collect for it samples of every species and variety of rose then known from every country where it could be found. Her thoroughness in this is well illustrated by the fact that, despite hostilities between France and Britain, a certain Mr Kennedy was granted immunity to bring roses for her garden from England. When divorced from Napoleon in 1809, Josephine (whose second name, incidentally, was Rose) moved permanently to Malmaison and was able to devote all her time to this remarkable garden.

It is not known exactly how many different roses made up the final collection, but it would certainly seem to have topped two hundred. In 1912 Jules Gravereaux of Paris published a monograph, *Les Roses de la Malmaison*; despite considerable research, he admitted to it being incomplete, but it contained 107 Gallicas alone. That we know as much as we do about what was grown there we owe to one man, Pierre Joseph Redouté.

Josephine and Redouté

Born at St Hubert in the Ardennes, Redouté acquired his love of flowers at a very early age through his friendship with a local priest who was a keen botanist and herbalist and who taught the boy to use his eyes to discover the beauties of the woodlands and fields they roamed together. Redouté's father was much away from home, for he and other members of the family were travelling artists who moved from town to town in northern France, painting scenery for the theatres and at times carrying out church decoration. So the son and the wise priest spent much time together which was, in due course, to shape the young Pierre Joseph's life.

Showing the family aptitude for drawing, at quite an early age he followed in the footsteps of his father and his uncles until his work took him to Paris. In his spare time from scene painting and set designing in theatres of the French capital, he would wander for hours in the Jardins des Plantes, sketching the flowers there. This led to his friendship with the distinguished botanist Charles l'Heritier de Brutelle, who recognized in the young man a rare skill in depicting, and a singular feeling for, the plants and flowers he studied so carefully. M l'Heritier took him under his wing and became his patron.

With such an influential man behind him, Redouté was able to visit England, where he studied the techniques of engraving, learning much from Bartolozzi about stipple work, which he was to use in his own work later on. Back once more in France and with a growing reputation as a botanical artist, he was commissioned to carry out some plates for the prestigious *Collection des Velins* under the supervision of the leading botanical painter of the day, M van Spaendonk, and he was also appointed drawing master to Queen Marie Antoinette. In 1805 Empress Josephine decided that Redouté was the man to make a permanent record of the flowers she grew, though it was not – rather surprisingly in view of her known preferences – her roses on which he made his start. Until the final one appeared in 1817, he was engaged, working in watercolour, on the eight volumes of *Les Liliacées*, a masterpiece in its own right dealing with the whole lily family. The roses did, however, come next, but there is sadness in the fact that the publication of the first set of his plates for *Les Roses* did not come about until 1817, three years after the Empress's death.

They were enormously successful, for here for the first time was a man who delighted in combining considerable (though not infallible) botanical accuracy with a technique and feeling for composition that made each drawing into a work of art. The three volumes of *Les Roses* depict 170 of the Malmaison roses, and a smaller edition brought out later between 1824 and 1830 added a further eleven, though these may not have been from the gardens of the Empress.

Though many of the names have been changed as a result of later research or botanical whim, it is still possible to identify most (but by no means all) of the varieties Redouté painted, and quite a number of them are still available today. Others have regrettably vanished beyond recall, for the rose treasure-house that was Malmaison declined rapidly under Josephine's heirs. Today, there is nothing left there of that great collection, but two wonderful legacies were passed on for later generations. First were Redouté's plates, which have been reproduced again and again over the years, decorating walls as pictures in their own right and everything else imaginable – even, in the present day, down to table mats. The following is, unfortunately, apocryphal:

> Napoleon and Josephine
> They both sat down to dine;
> Their table was set splendidly;
> They had the best of wine.
> But something marred the picture
> And left it incomplete;
> They really needed table mats
> In front of every seat.
> 'I have an inspiration!'
> They both cried out in chorus,
> 'We'll send for old Redouté,
> And he will paint some for us.'

Following the fashion

Secondly, and more importantly for the rose-lover, the rose garden had been born. Where top people led, others followed (keeping up with the Bonapartes), and soon every château had its rose garden. At the end of the Napoleonic Wars the fashion spread elsewhere on the Continent, to the British Isles, and in due course to America, but it was still a fashion fad of the rich, of the owners of big houses. This casual attitude changed of course when people realized the beauty that had been created for their pleasure, but it was to be a very long time before rose gardens were to be found other than in the grounds of the stately homes of the nobility, or at any rate the wealthy. This was an era of cheap and plentiful labour, of vast greenhouses and conservatories for the more exotic plants, of rolling lawns and yew alleys, of walled gardens heavy with the scent and ablaze with the colours of summer. And of toiling workers who could make even the most intractable soil grow the Gallicas, Damasks, Centifolias and Moss roses by digging into it barrowloads of the manure that was ready and waiting in the stable yard.

A nurseryman named Lee, of Hammersmith in London, introduced standard (tree) roses from France to England in 1818, and these were a great and eagerly sought-after novelty which were used to line rose walks, their popularity increasing with the introduction of the recurrent Bourbons and later Hybrid Perpetuals. The growing enthusiasm for the rose was greatly helped by other remarkable nurserymen as well. One such was Thomas Rivers of Sawbridgeworth in Hertfordshire who, in 1837 (the year in which Queen Victoria came to the English throne), published the first edition of *The Rose Amateurs' Guide*. This, only sixteen pages in length, was really a guide to the roses in his nursery, and he himself described it as a supplement to his descriptive catalogue. There is some information on rose culture, but its main interest today is in its descriptions of some 700 varieties of roses which he could offer. Of these, there were no less than 122 varieties of Gallica (a reflection of the Malmaison pattern), but all the main groups were represented up to but not including the Hybrid Perpetuals, the introduction and rise of which can be traced through later editions. One-third of Rivers's roses were available in standard (tree) form, in marked contrast to present-day taste. Except for old and uncatalogued varieties offered at £2.10s.0d per hundred, the cheapest roses were one shilling each, and the most expensive was the new Macartney rose 'Hardii', at 10s 6d. (For American readers, a shilling at that time was worth about 22 cents and £1 about $4.45.)

Other great rose nurserymen who made their mark in or about this period were Prince of New York state, from whom Thomas Jefferson bought his roses, Lane of Berkhamsted and Adam Paul of Cheshunt and later Waltham Cross, all in Hertfordshire. It was the latter's son, William Paul, who wrote at the age of twenty-five and published in 1848 *The Rose Garden*, which is still one of the greatest books in rose literature. It was far more than the catalogue so many of its predecessors had been, for in it he deals extensively with the early history of the rose, even if some of his ideas on it have been superseded. On the roses of his time he is unbeatable, and on planning and making a rose garden he is brimming with ideas. Soil preparation, planting, cultivation, pruning and all the other operations necessary for a rose grower to know, and also the equipment needed to carry them out, are all described in great detail. Like Rivers, he also provides a marvellous source of information about hundreds of varieties, which he divides into summer (once-flowering) and autumnal roses (his term for recurrent), and he actually advises the complete disbudding of the autumnal kinds such as Bourbons to ensure a fine crop of flowers in late summer. The first edition of the book had colour plates, but because of the cost these were later dropped. The instructive and delightfully decorative wood engravings in the text were, however, retained until the final printing in 1903.

Robert Buist ran a seed store in Philadelphia rather than a nursery, but *The Rose Manual*, written by him to encourage ladies to grow roses, was the first book published in the United States to deal exclusively with the rose. It is fairly local in its appeal and, while containing quite a lot of useful general advice, concentrates in the main on the roses then available to his customers in the eastern States, which is hardly surprising in view of its origin and does in fact give it a value all its own. Samuel B. Parsons's *Parsons on the Rose* of 1869 is far more comprehensive on the practical side of rose growing and covers a good deal of the history of roses too, though the author admits that he

Parc de Bagatelle, France
The Bagatelle rose gardens in Paris, laid out in 1907, were the first in the world designed to test roses under garden conditions and to give awards based on their performance. A feature of the formal layout is the metal tripods on which Climbers and Ramblers are grown. The yellow rose in the foreground is the Hybrid Tea 'Belle Blonde'.

borrowed much of his material from earlier French works. A little later, yet another American nurseryman, H. B. Ellwanger of Rochester NY, joined the lists with perhaps the best work of that period from the New World, *The Rose*, which had descriptions of 956 varieties based on the author's own experience with them, and which was revised periodically over the next thirty years.

These are only a few of the early books among a flood – good, reasonably good and frankly bad – that appeared during the last century. One other that might be mentioned was Mrs C. F. Gore's *The Rose Fancier's Manual* of 1838, which, it transpired, she had translated with very little change from Boitard's *Manuel Complet de l'Amateur de Roses* but without any acknowledgement as to its true source. It is, however, one of the most comprehensive books on the French roses of the period, but the point I am making is that, good, bad or indifferent, these books sold in prodigious quantities. Few had less than two printings, and though there is no information as to the size of each edition of any of them, the total must have been well into the tens of thousands. It was possibly much higher, and most if not all of the people who bought the books probably did so because they grew roses already or wanted to start doing so. They were spreading knowledge and enthusiasm for the rose ever wider, even though the garden plans so often featured in them would be difficult to accommodate in less than five or six acres and the scale of planting described echoed this thinking.

An extensive and annotated bibliography, giving details of the most important rose literature of the last 150 years, will be found on page 268.

Rosarians united

Another great influence in the Victorian period was the formation of rose clubs and societies, large and small, to which anyone who loved the rose could belong. These clubs and societies organized rose shows to attract and to educate the public in what they were missing. The National Rose Society (later to become Royal) in Britain was founded as early as 1876, which was a period when it would seem to have been impossible to move in an English rose garden without falling over a dignitary of the Church, bending to sniff the fragrance of his favourite flower. The leading spirits of the society from the beginning were Canon (later Dean) Reynolds Hole, as first president, with the Rev Honywood d'Ombrain, assisted by Mr Edward Mawley, as joint secretaries, and the amount of energy and time they expended in encouraging the growing of (and particularly the showing of) roses makes one wonder, with due deference to their calling, whether their parishioners could possibly have received the same amount of attention. For in addition to their other activities, these clergymen wrote books on roses – in the case of Dean Hole, a classic. His *Book About Roses* is both informative and full of charm and wit, which led to phenomenal sales. D'Ombrain edited *The Rosarian's Year Book*, the forerunner of the Society's *Annual*, and also wrote a paperback, *Roses for Amateurs*.

Then there was the Rev A. Foster-Melliar, whose pen produced a very comprehensive if slightly stolid work (at least when compared with the Dean's book) in which he gives a very much qualified welcome to the newly emerging Hybrid Teas. Lastly, the Rev Joseph Pemberton of the Hybrid Musks, produced a book illustrated with nine lithographs of roses of the most exquisite delicacy and an equally fine coloured frontispiece of a dog rose.

The American Rose Society came a little later, started in 1899 by a small number of growers whose main interest was the growing of roses under glass for the cut-flower trade. Under the guidance of Robert Pyle, and particularly that of Dr Horace McFarland, it grew and prospered and became open to all. McFarland at the time headed the major horticultural printing firm in the United States, and he edited, illustrated and printed the first *American Rose Annual* in 1916. He continued to edit it from that initial issue for a further twenty-nine years.

Spreading the word

The Victorians at times must have had difficulties in fitting the vigorous and undisciplined growth of the roses of their time into the otherwise rigid formality of the bedding schemes they so loved. This is probably one reason why the rose garden was often separated from the rest, though I will be suggesting another one shortly. It was largely through the work of that great revolutionary among British garden designers, Gertrude Jekyll, and of her companion in many an enterprise, William Robinson, that the rose became freed from these fetters of convention. To them both, roses were garden plants to be used as and where they fitted best. Theirs was 'natural' gardening, and Miss Jekyll liked nothing better than a wild, uninhibited scramble of Ayrshire or Multiflora ramblers taking over a corner of a garden, wandering where they would, or smothering an arch or pergola till it vanished from sight. Hers and William Robinson's, too, was still big garden thinking, and many of the ideas they advocated would not now be practicable, but to their flexibility of mind we owe a great debt.

All their thoughts, inevitably as it must seem by now, were set out in two great books, Jekyll's *Roses for English Gardens* (with Edward Mawley contributing a good deal about exhibiting roses) and Robinson's *The English Flower Garden*. *Roses for English Gardens* had another section by yet a third hand that was a real sign of the times and the leisured classes to whom it was clearly directed. This was on 'English Gardens on The Riviera', for the roses had to bloom there before the English milords returned home after wintering on the Mediterranean coast.

The best of all these writers had the virtue of being both informative and immensely readable, and some extracts from their works from about 1860 to the turn of the century will give a small flavour of their style of writing as well as throwing a light on how different things were in their day. Here is Dean Hole rebuking a friend for not looking after his roses properly:

> You have taken no trouble which deserves the name; and as to expense, permit me to observe that your fifty rose trees cost you £4, and your sealskin jacket £20. You don't deserve beautiful roses, and you won't have any until you love them more.

On another occasion the price of roses came up again:

> 'How do you afford,' I enquired from another, 'to buy these new and expensive varieties?'
> 'I'll tell you,' he said, 'how I manage to buy them. *By keeping away from the beer shops!*'

Shirley Hibberd, who perhaps because of his lack of clerical qualifications has not even had a mention yet, gives us in *The Rose Book* of 1864 a haughty reminder of the scale on which roses were grown at the big country houses: 'Fifty in a batch,' he says, 'may look fine, but ten clumps of five each may have a very paltry appearance unless the Rosarium is on so small a scale as to be

Mixed plantings at Zweibrücken Rosarium, West Germany
Zweibrücken Rosarium demonstrates many ways in which roses can be used. Recently, an informal aspect has been added, with other species used to mingle with the roses. This modern preference for mixed planting has its origins in the naturalistic theories first popularized by Gertrude Jekyll and William Robinson. Here, in an attractive corner, delphiniums supply the missing colour in the rose spectrum.
See also the photograph on page 215.

beyond the reach of criticism.' This sort of attitude was reflected in the rose names of his time, and raisers must have sought out every Baron, Baroness, Count, Countess, Duke, Duchess, Emperor, Kaiser, King, Queen, Prince, Princess, Lord and Lady, and sundry military nobs, to name their new varieties after. At least one-third of the many hundreds of new varieties put on sale towards the end of the last century paid deference in their naming to a member of the upper classes. This did not, however, save them from oblivion, and of William Paul's recommendations for 1875–1876 – seventy-six varieties in all and mostly Hybrid Perpetuals – the only one whose name is still familiar is the Bourbon 'Commandant Beaurepaire', which, expert though he was, Paul listed as a Gallica.

Shirley Hibberd almost rivals Dickens in his descriptions of Victorian towns, but he does not allow the smoke-polluted atmosphere to defeat him in growing his roses:

This brings us to the choice of roses for town culture; and here let me give a reason in favour of dwarf plants, and it is this, that in very smoky places they may be covered with bell-glasses, as recommended by Mr Cranston in his excellent shilling book.

When the neighbouring brewery sends out its blackest clouds abroad at certain hours of the day; when the floor-cloth factory diffuses a more than ordinary amount of gaseous poison, then the bell-glasses would screen the roses from the worst of the blacks and keep a moisture about them beneficial to their foliage and swelling blooms, and the glasses could be removed at night, early morning, or at such other times as the nature of the district might warrant.

This allowed you to grow your roses within four miles of the General Post Office! Hibberd puts forward an interesting theory, which fortunately need not now be put to the test:

It so happens that the services of a rose pilot may be had at a very low rate of expenditure – a pilot as trustworthy as any of the old blue-jackets that bear the Trinity mark. It is the common China rose, which is the most susceptible of all roses to the influence of smoke and the fumes of chemical works. As towns enlarge and shed heavier clouds of soot upon the suburban gardens they intend shortly to destroy, the common China rose is the first to feel the shock, the first to succumb to it. It is a fuligometer, that is, a measurer of soot; or to coin a neater phrase, a fumometer, a measurer of smoke, and its indications are as reliable as those of the magnet or the pole-star.

Putting down pests

Present-day methods of pest and disease control are discussed on pages 254 to 258.

As far as I know, the ancient writers – I am thinking now about the Greeks and Romans and even of those of a much later period – do not deal with the problems of greenfly (aphids) or other insect pests on roses. Presumably there have always been aphids, and perhaps they were just accepted as an inevitable evil or pinched off the young shoots without thinking it worth making a note about them. If they were there in those far off times, and if every greenfly born since were to be put end to end – well, it would take a lot of pairs of tweezers to do it. There is no doubt that there were aphids in Victorian gardens, and we will stay with Hibberd for advice about them, which comes under the heading of June in the Garden.

Aphis will probably abound out of doors, and the best remedy will be water. Ply them with the full force of one of Reid's or Warner's engines every evening, and if this does not dislodge and scatter and exterminate the vermin, resort to the use of tobacco water.

Procure the strongest shag tobacco, pour boiling water on it, in the proportion of half a gallon of water to every ounce of tobacco; when cold and clear, distribute by means of the finest rose of an engine.

I am not prepared to advise the use of *hot water*, but I would recommend all experimental rosarians to ascertain how high a temperature roses will bear without injury, for there is nothing more certain to destroy aphis than immersion in water heated above 150°, it is even more effective than tobacco.

There would appear to be a contradiction here, as Hibberd first suggests experiment and then gives the answer which would make it unnecessary, even if you were prepared to sacrifice one or two roses from your batches of fifty! Some forty years later, Foster-Melliar dealt with another pest:

Bear in mind, however, that, next to the aphis or greenfly, certain small moths are the commonest enemies of rose plants and if any such innocent flutterers should be seen amongst them, they should be hunted and destroyed.

Earliest in appearance amongst the moth larvae is what is generally known as the black grub. This is the larva of the pretty and delicate-looking moth, the Tortrix. As soon as there is any warmth in April, dormant buds on standard stocks should be examined at least every other day with a magnifying glass, spectacles or pince-nez being best, for both hands will be required.

Where a tiny heap of dust is seen upon the bud, the destroyer is within. I have found the point of an ordinary quill toothpick is the most efficacious instrument for dislodging the intruder.

When dealing with 'Canary-coloured fly' (leaf hopper?), sulphur and snuff was the mixture to be dusted on the leaves, and it was best to catch a leaf-cutting bee with a butterfly net; readers were, however, advised to take heed of this warning: '*It possesses a sting.*'

From insects to rose diseases, about which *Amateur Gardening* of 1899 had this to say: 'Black Spot: this pest may be held in check by carbonate of copper compound, using three ounces of carbonate of copper, one quart of ammonia and fifty gallons of water.' The fifty gallons is further indication that the amateur gardener of that day worked on a grander scale than now, but this is one of the earliest references to coping with the problems of black spot that I have found. Paul, for instance, makes no reference to it and it was really supposed to have become prevalent, as I mentioned elsewhere, after Pernetiana roses became so popular, with their markedly unresistant parent, *R. foetida*. 1899 is, however, really too early for this, so clearly it was about some degree before the yellow roses made their mark. For rose canker (probably what we now call crown gall or rose gall), *Amateur Gardening* gives this recipe:

All this knotty excrescence should be cut away, and also all decayed wood and bark. Then dress the wood with either Bordeaux mixture, sulphate of iron, two ounces dissolved in a gallon of water, or sulphide of potassium, one ounce to twelve gallons of water. If none of these are at hand, rub the part with flowers of sulphur. After (whichever is used), make a poultice of equal parts of clay and cow manure and bind the wound.

Paul on winter care wrote:

It is an excellent plan to wash the stems of rose trees in Winter, which is the time of leisure in the garden. A mixture of cow dung, soot and lime, two parts to one part of each of the former, serves for this purpose. This will destroy insects which may have sheltered in the bark, and also the moss and lichen which often grows there. It will further soften the bark and favour the swelling of the stem.

Old roses in a country garden
A good example of the blending of the soft colours of old shrub roses into an informal border of other plants and shrubs is seen at Tyninghame, east of Edinburgh.

In view of the grandeur of scale of gardening operations then, it is a pity that no dimensions were given in the following advertisement: 'R. Wheeler's Five Guinea Greenhouse. Glazed painted and fixed. Complete.' It would hardly seem to have been suitable for Hibberd's pot-grown roses, for he says:

> In February they are all turned out of their pots, their roots moderately shortened, and their shoots cut back to five or six buds. They are then repotted in a mixture of half turfy loam and half-rotted stable dung, the stuff being rammed into the pots with a wooden rammer. They are then packed as close together as possible in a bed of cocoa-nut dust and so left to the middle of April.
>
> A large dung bed is then made up by throwing long dung together, four or five feet deep . . . on this, when beaten smooth with a fork, the pots are placed and packed to their rims with cocoa-nut dust.

Paul tells us how to rid a greenhouse of greenfly:

> Today you will see a few stalking up and down the shoots; disregard them for a week and you will have thousands. To avoid the unpleasant situation of being enveloped in a dense cloud of tobacco smoke, the following plan is adopted in many places.
>
> A portion of tobacco, judged sufficient for the size of the house, is mixed with an equal portion of damp moss, and placed in a fine wire sieve, over charcoal embers. This gradually smoulders away, and the house is filled to perfection. In a large house [not, I think, Wheeler's] a sieve at each end is advisable.

Here are a few more miscellaneous gleanings from Paul and others, which give the flavour of rose growing in the late 19th century:

> Of other roses wanted may be instanced striped Hybrid Perpetuals, which may probably be obtained by bringing the most constant-flowering varieties of that group in union with Rosa Mundi, or any of the French striped roses . . .

> The old stuffed scarecrow, which served so well as a scarecrow in my boyish days, is of no avail against the superior intelligence of modern birds . . .

> Roses like water overhead as much as they do at the root, and Reid's engine is just the thing to refresh them with on summer evenings, when the operator will find just as much delight in splashing the cool, sparkling spray about, as the roses will in accepting it. It is just the sort of job to enjoy a cigar over . . .

There is a nice vignette from Paul on going to a show:

> In packing, each plant should stand clear of the other, and all free from contact with the sides of the van. A careful person ought to accompany them, as the pace at which they travel should be a walking one. Attention John! From home to the place of exhibition, *all* depends on you. You must neither trot, gallop nor canter. If you do, the consequences will be disastrous. Put your horse to its correct walking pace, having reckoned up beforehand the time he will require for the journey.

Finally, Dean Hole in full flight on the first London show that started his campaign to bring roses to every home and garden:

> In the days of the Great Stench of London, the Naiades ran from the banks of Thamesis, with their pocket-handkerchiefs to their noses, and made a complaint to the goddess Flora, how exceedingly unpleasant the dead dogs were, and that they couldn't abide 'em – indeed they couldn't. And Flora forthwith, out of her sweet charity, engaged apartments at the Hall of St James's, and came up with 10,000 roses, to deodorise the river, and to revive the town.

A ROSE GARDEN –
OR A GARDEN WITH ROSES?

Such is the variety of form, size and colour of the flowers, and such is the range in the habit of growth of the bushes if you bring in the miniatures, the species, other shrub roses and the climbers and the ramblers, that it would be almost impossible to produce a garden that was not beautiful using roses alone. However, the now commonly-held idea that roses should not be mixed with other plants almost certainly goes back to writers like Foster-Melliar, whose works, as we have seen, had such great influence at the end of the last century. They advocated roses on their own and at times virtually decreed it, but they looked at things from the point of view of fanatical exhibitors and thought about their roses almost exclusively in terms of the prizes they might win. Here is Foster-Melliar on the subject:

> It is odd to notice how generally those Rose lovers who do not exhibit are set against Rose shows, and have hardly a good word to say for them. According to these critics the least lovely of Roses are most shown and encouraged, the manner of exhibition is faulty, the grace and beauty of the flowers are lost and the public taste is generally led astray.

They appreciated their beauty, of course, and Dean Hole perhaps saw their possibilities rather more than most of the others as garden plants pure and simple. Certainly William Robinson did, for he said:

> Shows, too, have had a bad effect on the Rose in the garden, where it is many times more important than as a show flower. The whole aim of the man who showed Roses was to get a certain number of large blooms grown on the Dog Rose . . . at the least cost.

Unfortunately the 'should not be mixed' of the rest of them was interpreted as 'cannot be mixed' in the popular mind, though they were right within their rather narrow horizons. For roses grown for showing by a serious as opposed to an occasional exhibitor should be on their own, as they need special care which is much more difficult to give if they are spread about. Also, the most commonly used 'Chinese hat' bloom-protectors, used by exhibitors to keep rain off the flowers so that they are not damaged, can make an ordinary garden for ten days or so before a show look more like a street market in Old Peking than a place for peaceful enjoyment.

But roses, if some thought is given to the choice of varieties, mix very happily with other plants, and can also be enhanced by them. Conversely, other plants will mix with roses in what is predominantly a rose collection. Fewer and fewer people nowadays have plots large enough for them to be able to create a rose garden in the old sense, complete with arbours, pergolas and so on, so combining roses with other things makes sense from that point of view alone. (Though a small and less grandiose rose garden can be created in only a few square yards if your terrain gives you a little help.)

Planning a rose garden
If you are going to take the design of your garden seriously, one important point must be borne in mind: the surroundings must be taken fully into account. These will be different every time, and nobody can give positive

advice to an individual owner without first seeing what the features of the setting may be. So do not expect that all your problems will be solved by reading what follows. I could, for instance, say that nothing is more spectacular than massed climbing roses as a screen, but that would not be much help if the only place you could put them would hide a wonderful view, or if there is nothing in your garden for them to climb up and no space for a pergola or whatever else you would like to have. A bed of miniature roses may sound enchanting, but will hardly do if what you need is something to hide a grain silo a quarter of a mile away. A fast-growing cupressus (cypress) might be the right answer, and you could grow a rambler rose up through it.

So all that can sensibly be done here is to discuss the potentialities of as many situations as possible for both large and small gardens, so that what may suit your particular one can be picked out and adapted if necessary to its setting, size and shape. First, however, a few general points which will apply whatever your garden may be like. And also a definition.

All roses need the sun, so if you have a shady part of the garden choose something else to grow there. To do well, roses must have sunlight, or what passes for it in some climates, for a reasonable proportion of the day – though not necessarily for a full twelve hours if you happen to live in a part of the world where such a thing is likely. In shade, a rose will become spindly in its efforts to reach the light, and if the shade comes from overhanging trees it will have their roots to contend with, too. Some varieties of climbing roses are recommended in nursery catalogues for north walls (or for south walls in the southern hemisphere), and they will have been chosen because they will give a reasonably satisfactory performance there, but they will be nothing like as spectacular as they would be in full sun. So give your roses the limelight due to any star of the garden.

Roses will grow in most kinds of soil, but do best in good, middle-of-the-road loam. They are not over-fond of chalk or lime, and will not show their full vigour or live as long in dry, sandy soil except for some of the shrub roses like the Rugosas and the Spinosissimas, which will grow in anything short of the heat-shield of a space rocket. At the other end of the scale, none of them like to have their roots swimming about in water like the tentacles of an octopus. Good drainage is essential, and where the old wives' tale came from that they must have clay to do well, nobody seems to know.

If your soil is not ideal, there are many things you can do to make it a great deal better, and these will be gone into in some detail when I come to discuss cultivation, in chapter 5. For the moment I will just say that the initial preparation of the site will involve a good deal of labour, and certainly it will be necessary to apply extra mulches and fertilizers afterwards if the land is poor. All of which will be unwelcome news to the less enthusiastic gardener who would prefer to spend his or her time playing dominoes with ladybirds (ladybugs), but it will be more than worth it. If, on the other hand, you choose just to put the roses in and hope for the best, you will get blooms of a sort, but you will never know just what they could have been like.

As Rudyard Kipling said:

> Our England is a garden
> And such gardens are not made
> By singing 'Oh how beautiful!'
> And sitting in the shade.

Roses in a mixed border
This country house garden gives proof, if proof were needed, that roses can be mixed attractively in a border with other shrubs and herbaceous plants.

A good, honest wind now and again will not hurt roses, but do not plant them in a position you know to be draughty, such as a narrow space between the walls of two houses. They will not like this and will show it by their poor performance.

Choosing your roses

On the question of just which roses to plant, on the choice of varieties, there is only one word for the enormous numbers that are available, even among single classes such as Hybrid Teas and Floribundas: bewildering. And there is only one way of making sure that you get what you want; see as wide a selection as possible growing and fully established in garden conditions, preferably over a full year or more. From these you can safely make your choice, or confirm that a rose you have been thinking of buying really does live up to what you have heard about it. It is the only way you will be able to discover for yourself how well and continuously particular varieties bloom, how vigorous and healthy they are, whether the flowers stand up to rain, whether they hold their colour well as they age, and whether they shed their petals cleanly when the end comes.

Are they upright and perhaps leggy growers? Do they bush out well, with good foliage covering the plant properly – or do they sprawl all over the place? These are other questions that will be answered if you actually see them growing, and with shrub roses particularly an assessment of the ultimate size and habit of growth is absolutely vital. Half the charm of many of them would be spoiled – particularly so with the species that have long, arching, flower-laden canes – if they had to be cut back because too little space was allowed for them. It is quite impossible to describe a rose adequately in words in a book or nursery list, and the colour printing of mass-produced catalogues often does less than justice to many roses, particularly the red ones – or by the same token may be overly optimistic. More will be said later about the advantages and disadvantages of the various ways of buying your bushes, but however you buy, do try to see the actual thing first. There are plenty of show gardens about in which the varieties are labelled, many of them run by local or national garden societies. A number are described and many more listed in chapter 4.

There are two handy, authoritative and unbiased reference works that can be useful. The American Rose Society publishes each year a *Handbook for Selecting Roses*, which gives a national rating for each variety for North America, based on individual reports from hundreds of rosarians. Top rating gives a maximum of 10 points, and while they may not be exact for every particular garden, they do give an indication of overall quality and how well the rose may be expected to perform. A rose with a rating of 9 or above is considered superior, between 8 and 9 very good, and so on down the scale. Beginning in 1978, ratings in the 'Proof of the Pudding' section of the *American Rose Annual* are given for both garden and exhibition value. The second small book, for readers in the British Isles, is *Roses – A Selected List of Varieties*, published by the Royal National Rose Society. While not giving ratings, it does give brief descriptions of a very large number of roses of all kinds which have been carefully chosen for their garden qualities. It is brought up to date every few years, but good as both these guides are, seeing the varieties actually growing and in bloom is still the best way of making the right choice for the particular site you have in mind.

Naming names

So much for the general points, but I did promise a definition; here it is, and none too soon, for I have already referred to shrub roses a number of times without attempting to answer the question most often asked about them, which is: 'What exactly is a shrub rose? Are not all roses shrubs?' To which the answer can only be: 'Yes, they are.' Shrub rose is a convenient term, though a completely artificial one with no botanical justification, which has been chosen to describe those roses which grow too large for most bedding schemes – larger, that is, than the average Hybrid Tea or Floribunda – but it does also take in all the old roses from the Hybrid Perpetuals backwards in time, whatever size they may be. Some authorities exclude the Hybrid Perpetuals, and as they are half-way towards the Hybrid Teas there is an argument for saying they are a borderline case. However, anything that grows like the Hybrid Perpetual 'Reine des Violettes' can hardly to my mind be anything other than a shrub rose if the Bourbons count as such.

With modern shrub roses, size is the main criterion. 'Peace', if grown as it should be, lightly pruned and reaching 1.5 m (5 ft) or more in height, is both a shrub rose and a Hybrid Tea, and the Floribundas 'Chinatown', 'Fred Loads' and, if allowed to develop its full potential, 'Iceberg', are shrub roses, too. So are members of the Hybrid Musk group, though there are one or two not all that big. Not, as can be seen, a very precise definition, but as will surely have been realized by now, nothing to do with roses is ever precise. It is people who try to make the classifications and definitions and to fit the rose to them. Even in Scotland you would not find a more dedicated non-conformist than the rose, but the classifiers and definers do not give up. They have more in store for us in the not too distant future, though in this case it is a brave attempt to simplify things for the average gardener.

Roses have changed over the years, are still changing, and will almost certainly continue to do so, but the names by which we have continued to call the different groups – Hybrid Teas, Floribundas and so on – have remained static, or nearly so. Grandiflora in America and the unbelievably clumsy Floribunda Hybrid-Tea-type in the British Isles have been added comparatively recently, but they really are little help in describing to the layman who has never grown roses just what he is buying. The terms Floribunda and Grandiflora do not even have a botanical justification.

I commented earlier on the growing difficulty in distinguishing between the larger-flowered Floribundas and Hybrid Teas, so these two names are going to vanish, and there will be other changes as well, with a first tentative toe in the water in 1978 and a gathering momentum from that time on. Panic among those who resist change for whatever reason is probably unnecessary, as it is sure to be a number of years before the new rulings filter down from officialdom, through the nursery trade and then on to the customer, but change there will be. This has been decreed by the World Federation of Rose Societies, which means that it will be universal, and is based on proposals, with some amendments, put forward by the Council of the Royal National Rose Society of Great Britain. The thing for the diehards to remember is that the new ideas are designed to help, and changes have only been made where there was a concensus of opinion from all countries that there was a real need for it. The rose family is confusing enough without having names for groups within it which mean little or nothing. So what exactly is happening?

Firstly, there are to be three main groups: Wild Roses, covering the species and those kinds closely resembling them; Old Garden Roses, covering anything other than species and which pre-date the introduction of Hybrid Teas; and Modern Garden Roses, which term covers hybrids produced since then which, once again, do not resemble species. The Old Garden Rose classification remains much as it is, the individual group names such as Gallica, Alba, Centifolia and so on being retained, and the Wild Roses or species have been left alone, too. The only exception in both cases (and this applies to Modern Garden Roses as well) is that the Federation has subdivided them logically into climbers and non-climbers, and both of these yet again into recurrent and non-recurrent varieties.

In the listings in chapter 2 are noted the new classifications of the various groups.

Thus far, nothing very drastic, covering, of course, the area where there has been least change in the roses. It is in the subdivisions of the Modern Garden Roses that there will be more differences. There will be a Shrub Rose category, which will conform to the definition I gave a page or two back except that the old roses will be excluded, there will be Miniature Roses and there will be Bush Roses. The latter will be made up of Large Flowered (corresponding to the present large-flowered Hybrid Teas), Cluster Flowered (corresponding to the Floribundas and Grandifloras) and Polyanthas (unchanged).

So there you have it. Read it twice and it will not seem nearly so complicated. It will even begin to make sense, and just how it will work out in practice we will see in due course. However, it is time we were getting back to the rose in the garden.

ROSES
FOR BEDDING

Since more people use roses for bedding than anything else, it is logical to begin with this and then to progress onwards to find out just what other exciting possibilities there are.

Planning your rose beds

Rose beds can, of course, be of any shape or size – round, triangular, square, oblong, oval or with an irregular, informal outline – and which of these you choose will to a large extent be decided by the amount of space you have available and how it is laid out. If you pick on a square or a circle, it is best for practical reasons not to make it too big. The less you have to tread on a rose bed the better, particularly on heavy soils, and if dead-heading, spraying, mulching, cutting flowers for the house and hoeing can be carried out without (unless your legs are remarkably short) having to put more than one foot on the bed to reach the farthest roses, so much the better. Apart from trampling down the soil, after rain you would get very wet legs, whatever length they were, so the beds should not really be more than 1.2 m (4 ft) across. If you have set your heart on a much larger circular bed, this can be achieved by dividing it into segments with paths running in to the centre and with perhaps a different variety of rose in each segment. Large square beds can in the same way be divided into smaller squares by paths.

A well-planned rose border
A mixed rose border at Duxford Mill, Cambridgeshire, shows exemplary planting, graded in height with the taller roses kept to the back, where they belong.

The best surround of all for a rose bed is grass, but informal paving stones or gravel run it a close second, provided that the gravel is in one of the many tones of grey. Grey is a colour that sets off roses particularly well, and I will come to grey-leaved plants to grow with roses presently. In the meanwhile, paving does have obvious advantages over grass in wet weather, and as a compromise paving stones can be set at intervals into the grass, as long as they are about 1 cm (½ in) below its level so that the grass can still be cut without breaking mower blades on the paving. Gravel has two disadvantages. It will, in due course, need weeding, and if there is grass bordering it on the side away from the rose bed, stones can easily get kicked on to this and once again the mower may suffer. Gravel must be laid on a proper foundation, too, or it will gradually vanish into the earth.

Choosing bedding roses

Now as to the roses themselves. For bedding, Floribundas will give greater continuity of bloom and generally speaking will stand up to rough weather better than Hybrid Teas. With many of the latter, there may be several weeks' pause between each flush, though they will put up a fine display over long periods. One can argue convincingly in favour of either type, as one can with anything where personal preference must play a large part. It is, however, best not to try to get the best of both worlds by planting both Hybrid Teas and Floribundas together in one bed as their flowering habits are so different.

Assuming that you do stick to either one or the other for a particular bed, there are also a number of arguments against mixing your varieties. There can be up to about three weeks' difference between the flowering peak of one variety of Hybrid Tea and another (or one Floribunda and another) so that, while mixing will spread the period when there is some colour, the overall effect will be patchy at certain times. There may be considerable height variations, too, which can look rather odd, so if you do want to mix your roses, pick those of reasonably uniform height and plant them in groups of not less than five bushes of each variety. And make sure that the colours will blend into a harmonious whole.

Unless the bed is a very large one, do not choose tall, leggy roses for it. Choose a type which is compact and bushy, and which covers the ground well. Tall roses have their place, which can be for a hedge or for the back of a bed which is against a wall or fence. Do not plant roses which sprawl – or Floribundas which have huge trusses of flowers which are weighed down almost to the ground after rain – too close to the edge of a bed which borders on a path. Once again, wet legs and feet would be the result, for a good-sized truss of a Floribunda such as 'Europeana' after a heavy shower can be reckoned to tip the best part of a pint of water into your shoes if you brush against it.

Sprawling varieties like this bring up the question of how close together roses should be planted in a bed. Those which are very lax, or which branch out widely but with strong, rigid canes, naturally take up more space than the others and you will need less of them – an attraction if you have a one-way wallet. If you have seen them growing before you buy, you can form your own judgement about the closeness of planting, but as a general guide, a distance of about 45–60 cm (18–24 in) between plants will suit in the majority of cases in cool climates and areas with hard winters. This will be enough to prevent the roots of one rose robbing those of its neighbours of nourishment,

172

will allow for proper air circulation, and will enable weeding, spraying and mulching to be carried out in reasonable comfort and with reasonable efficiency. If they are not too close, it will also, in climates where this may be needed, make protective earthing up in winter an easier operation.

Much farther apart than 60 cm (24 in) and the bed will look under-planted, unless you are going in for the other sort of underplanting, which I will come to in a moment. Even the many dwarf-growing Floribundas in which breeders are beginning to specialize for small gardens should in most cases be kept to the same average distance, for what they may lack in stature they make up for in spread. However, rosarians living in warmer climates – such as the southern or western United States, Australia, New Zealand, South Africa and so on – will know (and others can, by visiting public and private gardens in the areas, easily see) that roses thrive to a degree that can only make less fortunate growers green with envy. Everything is more or less doubled in scale, and you can have a full bed with a spacing of 1–1.5 m (3–5 ft).

The question of height has now cropped up a number of times, and while it is best to keep to reasonable uniformity in the main planting of rose beds, a *planned* variation in height can still be achieved if you want it. If you are lucky enough to have a garden on several levels this will be less important as you will have your variation built in and will not have to do anything about it. In a completely flat garden, on the other hand, a number of rose beds of equal height will benefit from something which will cause the eye to move up and down for a change. While I do not willingly admit that any rose beds could be monotonous without this diversion, it must be said that they could come close to it. Standard (tree) roses or pillar roses are the answer.

A standard makes an ideal centre-piece for a circular rose bed, or a row of standards (either full, half or quarter height) can be planted at about 1.8 m (6 ft) intervals down the centre of a long, narrow one. If pillar roses are used instead, they will need rather more space around them as there is – or should be if they are properly trained – more growth lower down. The varieties chosen for either standards or pillars can be a complete contrast in colour from those used in the beds, or can be in blending tones.

For the use of pillar roses, see the photograph of Bagatelle on page 157 and the photograph on page 218.

Other roses for bedding

There are a number of roses other than Hybrid Teas and Floribundas that can be used for bedding, and though some of them will be that little bit more difficult to buy, they will bring with them, in addition to their beauty, the satisfaction of having something in your garden which everyone else has not got as well. A bed of one or other of the low-growing China roses such as 'Fabvier' (scarlet) or 'Hermosa' (pink), or others of similar type which are often classified as Chinas – such as 'Perle d'Or', 'Cécile Brunner' (the sweetheart rose) with its thimble-size pink blooms, or 'Little White Pet' – will be constantly in flower, though they would not be ideal for a very large planting. They have an airy and delicate charm and, apart from 'Fabvier', the muted colours best appreciated on a small scale.

For the use of China roses, see the photograph on page 193.

These are rarely troubled by disease on their dainty, pointed foliage, but you would have to face up to spraying against possible mildew if you chose as an alternative one or other of the shorter-growing Gallicas. Despite this, I have never seen anything more attractive than a massed bed of 'Officinalis' against an old, rough stone wall in a friend's private garden – even though it has only one season of bloom. The shorter Musk roses 'Danaë' in creamy yellow, 'Thisbe' (buff yellow), or the modern 'Ballerina' – in effect supercharged Floribundas – are wonderful for bedding, though one must be prepared to accept as true the old saying that whatever colour a Pemberton Musk sets out it ends up white. They do fade.

When writing about their place in history, I mentioned that Hybrid Perpetuals in their heyday before the turn of the century were often pegged down. This is a way of using for bedding types of roses that are generally too tall for it, for if left to themselves the long canes of most Hybrid Perpetuals – sent up, as you may remember, in late summer and early autumn – will bear flowers just at the top in the following year. They can be pruned but will shoot up again, and pruning wastes a lot of good growth which can be put to use by pegging. This can be done in two ways.

In the first, which strictly speaking is not really the pegging from which the operation gets its name, the roses are first planted about 1 m (3 ft) apart. Stakes are then driven into the ground at more or less regular intervals of about 1.2 m (4 ft) each way over the whole of the bed, leaving 30 cm (1 ft) of each stake showing above the ground. A galvanized nail is driven into the top of each, and from these wire of the sort you would use for training climbing roses is strung, backwards and forwards, both along the sides of the bed at right angles to it, and diagonally across it, until you have formed what could be called a flat wire frame 30 cm (1 ft) from the ground.

When the long canes of the roses grow, do not prune them except to remove the soft tips which frosts would kill. Instead, bend them over one at a time, outwards all round the plant, away from its centre, taking care not to overdo things and snap any of them off, and tie the canes to the wires. Roses planted on the outsides of the bed should have their canes fanned out inwards. Space out all the canes as evenly as possible.

The canes from one rose will overlap those of others, but this is intended and desirable if the full effect you are aiming for is to be achieved. In spring, all the side buds will produce flowering shoots instead of remaining dormant, just as the canes of a climber will if you train them horizontally. The explanation is simple. Growth-regulating hormones are produced in the vegetative growth. These move downwards and inhibit the development of the buds on the lower part of the cane. When the cane is trained horizontally, the growth regulators still move vertically downwards and inhibit the development of the buds on the lower side of the cane, but do not prevent those on the upper side springing into life and creating flowering shoots other than just at the cane ends. Many plant responses are controlled by substances manufactured within the plant in this way. Stimulated, each shoot bears blooms, and a solid carpet of leaves and flowers covers the frame, hiding it from view. And not only do the roses produce far more blooms, they also produce them at a height where they can be more easily appreciated.

As many Hybrid Perpetuals rest for quite a while between their first and second flushes, a late-flowering but not too vigorous clematis can be trained on the frame as well to fill in the colour time-gap, though it (or they) must be religiously cut back early each spring to prevent a massive and unsightly tangle of dead-looking stems developing over the years. The flowering of the clematis and the roses may well overlap to some extent, so choose your colours carefully. The vivid purple of the old favourite *Clematis* 'Jackmanii'

Ground-cover roses
Ground-cover roses displayed in the garden of the Royal National Rose Society, St Albans: In the foreground is the wide-spreading 'Nozomi', with the rather taller-growing 'Raubritter' behind it. It might seem that these roses would be suitable for bedding, but their habit of growth is too informal and irregular. Their best use is for banks and other 'difficult' areas.
See also plate XXXVI (p203).

would not look well with purplish-red roses, though it would with white or pink ones. No rose would clash with white or soft blues, so the clematis varieties 'Marie Boisselot' (white), 'Perle d'Azur' (light blue) or 'Margo Koster' (pink) would all be right for colour and provide a breathtakingly lovely combination, before flowering on their own into late summer.

There is one great disadvantage of such a frame for tying down, apart from the labour of making it and the work each year in dealing with the new rose growth. It can be hell to weed. The alternative, the real pegging, is considerably better from this point of view because you do not have both the wires and the canes to push a long-suffering hand through. Instead of fixing them to wires, the canes are tied individually to either metal or wooden pegs, driven into the ground at appropriate spots. You may have to put in a certain number of new pegs each year to accommodate new growth, but all in all this is an easier way to peg down Hybrid Perpetuals if you only have three or four (or even only one) to deal with.

Pegging down need not, of course, be confined to Hybrid Perpetuals. It can be tried with any lanky rose that is reasonably flexible, or even used as a novel way of displaying climbing roses in a bed instead of on a wall or fence. A frame is probably the answer with these, as the length of the canes may make it necessary to tie each one in several places.

Edging the rose beds

Though by no means essential, the right edging around rose beds can be as a frame to a picture. Many of the dwarf-growing, mound-forming annuals are suitable – including sweet alyssum (*Alyssum maritimum*) – and there are a large number of other less usual perennials which can be tried, such as *Anaphalis yedoensis* (grey furry leaves and unobtrusive tufty whitish 'everlasting' flowers) and its variant *A. triplinervis*, or *Pterocephalus parnassi* (*Scabiosa pterocephala*) with tiny pink scabious-like blooms on 2.5 cm (1 in) stems. The early-flowering yellow alyssum, *Alyssum saxatile*, provided that it can be kept tidy and you have the light soil which suits it best, will flower before the roses, and its grey foliage will look well with them afterwards.

Any plant with grey or grey-blue leaves provides a colour lacking in the rose spectrum, perhaps the best of all being lavender – one of the dwarf forms like 'Munstead Dwarf' if either the rose bed or the roses themselves are small. Not only the leaves but the flowers give a new colour dimension, as will the delicate-looking blooms of some of the geraniums – the real ones of the genus *Geranium*, that is, not those gaudy monsters the pelargoniums – such as 'Johnson's Blue', used most effectively as an edging to a number of the beds at the gardens of the Royal National Rose Society just outside London. There are other blue- and mauve-flowered forms which are equally suitable, and apart from the colour, the deeply cut leaf form of these herbaceous perennials contrasts attractively with the rose foliage. The violet-blue of the large-flowered *Campanula carpatica* 'Jewel' looks well, too.

For the use of grey foliage and blue flowers, see the photographs on pages 152, 160 and 163.

Miniature roses forming a 20 cm (8 in) hedge are a strong recommendation for edging, but not if the main planting of the bed is of tall or lax roses which would keep the Miniatures in the shade most of the time. They, like all roses, must have sunlight, so leave a strip of soil at the edge of the bed at the very least 45 cm (18 in) wide in which the Miniatures can grow without having to fight their way upwards in search of light.

Underplanting

Finally, before leaving the subject of bedding roses, the question of under-planting them with something else must be thrashed out. I use the word thrashed, because this is a subject which raises strong arguments both for and against. Straightaway I should say that I am not really in favour of it, for reasons which I will give in a minute, but will try to give, as far as is possible in the circumstances, as balanced a view as possible.

The strongest reason for using other plants between the rose bushes is that a newly-pruned rose bed resembles nothing so much as a barrier designed to halt a charge of infantry. Even I can see that anything that will help to divert the eye, either by leaf or flower, from all those bleak-looking prickly stumps is a decided advantage. Violas are the most usual recommendation and probably there is nothing better – and they do flower early. On poor but well-drained soil I have seen helianthemums used successfully, particularly the grey-leaved varieties, and I myself acquired, quite by chance, a ground cover of scillas, which seeded freely and were quite impossible to get rid of despite yearly hoeing of the foliage. So I gave up and enjoyed the sky-blue sheen over the rose bed in spring.

The scillas must, however, have robbed the roses of a good deal of food and transpired a share of the moisture from the earth through their leaves. Any underplanting will do this, in the same way that weeds will, and we do not put up with weeds for this reason among others. And if your soil is of the light, sandy kind where mulching is essential, how do you do it without smothering the other plants? A hoe or chemical weed-inhibitors are likely to be impossible to use, and hand weeding is the only alternative with all the woe that this entails. Finally, despite what I said a while back, there will be times when you have to step on the beds – to get in the right position to pull out suckers, perhaps – which would do the underplanting very little good.

When it comes to using other plants with bedding roses I prefer to opt for something bigger – interplanting rather than underplanting. Not, I should say, for beds isolated in a lawn, but one against a wall can be greatly enhanced by a bush of grey-green rosemary, the silver-leafed *Senecio greyii* (cut back regularly in late spring to curb its tendency to straggle), common sage, or by clumps of rue (*Ruta graveolens*) or *Stachys lanata* (lamb's tongue or lamb's ears) strategically placed. Where old roses are used, try planting white lilies nearby; their upright formality makes a good foil. Brigadier Lucas Phillips in the RNRS *Rose Annual* tells how he interplants his Floribundas with dwarf evergreen azaleas, which sounds an idea worth trying. I have not actually seen it, but the colour of one must follow that of the other, and certainly the rose beds would look better in winter.

A last thought on bedding, really the final one this time – and obvious on the face of it, though surprisingly easy to overlook while making decisions about planting, when colour is usually the first consideration. Under a window that is likely to be open in the summer, plant scented roses – of the colour you want, too, of course. It is a funny thing about scent. A very well-known rose grower told me not long ago that most people who visit his nursery say that they want nothing but scented roses. They go out to the fields to make their choice, and often come back to his office with a list on which only a small proportion of the roses are strongly scented, though such were there if the customers' eyes had not got the better of their noses. Colour wins every time.

USING
CLIMBING ROSES

Though climbing and rambling roses are similar in many ways, there are places in the garden where Climbers can be used but Ramblers should not, largely because of the likelihood (if not certainty) of mildew on Ramblers if air circulation around and through them is not good. Even if precautions are taken, a number of them, particularly the hybrids, will get mildew anyway, and their other main drawback is that they only flower once. Just the same, there are uses to which they can be put for which they are infinitely superior to Climbers, so when discussing the function of both in the garden, it seems best to keep them separate, even though there will be a degree of overlap.

The basic thinking behind the use of climbing roses, though I risk being accused of making a second obvious statement in the course of four paragraphs, is to give height and hence variety to your rose plantings – a greater height than standard roses can give. While doing this, they will cover walls and fences, hide unsightly sheds and tree stumps, cover arches and pergolas, form hedges if trained on wires between upright poles and climb trees. The less vigorous ones make pillar roses or can be grown as free-standing, lax shrubs – not, of course, their true role, but one they adapt to very well.

Covering walls

Taking the above list of uses in order, Climbers on walls come first, and the walls can be either those of your house or else those surrounding or dividing your garden. To grow them so that they will give the maximum display of flowers, so that they will bloom low down and not just at the top, the canes must be fanned out and kept as near to the horizontal as possible so that the side shoots will grow and bear bloom, just as in pegging down. In due course a framework is built up which will cover the wall, moving upwards each year as new growth is made after pruning. This kind of training is particularly important with certain roses ('Paul's Lemon Pillar' is an example) which rarely if ever produce new growth from ground level once established. With them, even if properly trained, it may be necessary to plant bush roses or some other low shrub to hide the far from beautiful gnarled and ancient lower canes.

It follows from the above that roses must have plenty of wall space. If your windows are tall and close together there will be problems, the answer to which is to choose one of the less vigorous Climbers such as 'Golden Showers', 'Joseph's Coat' or that pearl among scented pinks, 'Aloha'. These are the roses in fact that you would otherwise choose for pillars and which will do better than most with the minimum of training, not going much above 2.5 m (8 ft). As an alternative, many of the stronger-growing Bourbons, like 'Mme Isaac Pereire', will do well against a wall as semi-climbers. Others will be mentioned when we come to discuss shrub roses, but I might enlarge a little on one rather special one here. This is the China rose of unknown origin called 'Mutabilis'. It is by no means common and is more often grown by those with a taste for the unusual as a medium-sized shrub, but as a Climber it will reach about the same height as 'Golden Showers'. The remarkable range of colour in its semi-double flowers, changing from buff-yellow to a rusty red, with many intermediate tones, always causes comment and admiration.

The origins of 'Mermaid' (top) go back to 1918, so it is on the borderline between the new and old Climbers. Nevertheless, it is very much a rose of today, coming into flower rather later than most but going on and on right into the autumn. Its fine foliage, almost evergreen, is inherited from R. bracteata and is a great asset; its thorns are formidable.
'Handel' (left), 'Danse du Feu' ('Spectacular'; right) and 'Golden Showers' (bottom) represent the modern trend in climbing roses, with well-branched growth which, though vigorous, is not too rampant, so that they can be contained within a reasonable space. The least rampant is 'Golden Showers'. All flower well a second time, and 'Handel' – rather a slow starter – will eventually need a bigger wall than the others.
See also plates XIII and XXX (pp87 and 145).

For the traditional use of Climbers on walls, see the photographs on pages 225 and 229.

On the question of colour, when making your choice of roses, bear in mind the colour of your brickwork, wall rendering and paintwork. A buff-coloured rose such as 'The Alchymist' would be rather a waste of time against a buff wall, as would a white rose against white rendering, and roses in certain shades of red might well clash horribly with the red of bricks.

The colour stability of the blooms of Climbers is important, too, because if they become less attractive as they age, dead-heading is a problem 4.5 m (15 ft) or more above the ground. Also important is resistance to rain, for no one likes their house to look, after a wet day, as if it were festooned with small, soggy brown-paper bags. So select carefully and do not be beguiled by seeing the roses just at their peak of perfection. 'Danse du Feu' ('Spectacular') came into the world to great acclaim and may be taken as an example of what I mean. It is a tremendously profuse bloomer, repeats later on, and the flowers when they first come out are a magnificent fiery-red. But for how long? A few days at most and they lose their glow and become faded and muddy-looking, with a reluctance to shed their dead petals after rain.

There are more and more climbing roses being bred nowadays which are repeat-flowering, which is a welcome advance, but it must be said that few of those so far introduced put on the same show second time round as they do in the first flush. Be cautious in accepting assurances that a Climber is 'perpetual', that it is always in flower, as very few even approach this ideal. The single yellow 'Mermaid' comes as close to it as any, though I would describe its flowering as spasmodic rather than perpetual. It does, however, have a great asset in that it takes a very long time to shed its leaves (due to its *R. bracteata* parentage) and I have even seen it described as evergreen. It is not that, but the bare canes of a long-established climbing rose in winter can make the walls of a house look as if they have suffered the worst attentions of a mad Victorian plumber, so that any that do hold on to their leaves are to be welcomed.

If you choose only repeat-flowering Climbers, you will miss some beauties from the past. There are old recurrent roses, such as 'Gloire de Dijon', 'Mme Alfred Carrière' or 'Mrs Herbert Stevens', all of which have survived on the sheer quality of their performance, but what about 'Mme Grégoire Staechelin', whose massed, huge pale pink flowers, with a deeper reverse and deeper pink veining, bring to us the sunlight of Spain from which it came? Though once-flowering only, it is something not to be missed, and there is a way of getting the best of both worlds. Simply grow another type of climbing plant such as clematis, or the old-fashioned (and scented) kind of sweet peas up through the roses, making your choice from Climbers which flower at a different time. As an alternative, grow the roses up through another wall shrub, and if this is evergreen, like for instance some of the later-flowering ceanothus (in areas where they are hardy) such as 'Autumnal Blue', so much the better. The other shrub does not, of course, have to flower after the roses, and there is no lovelier combination than white or pale yellow roses with the tufts of powder-blue ceanothus flowers of earlier varieties. You will not increase colour continuity in this way, but what you will achieve over quite a long period will be more than worth it.

Climbing roses, in combination with other things or on their own, can give beauty to any building you choose to live in, even if it resembles a Pecksniff design (stolen from one of his pupils) for a workhouse. Harriet Beecher Stowe knew what they could do. Of Uncle Tom's Cabin she wrote: 'The whole front

A Rambler in an old apple tree
The very vigorous Rambler 'Wedding Day', a hybrid of R. sinowilsonii, is one of many of this group ideal for growing up through the branches of a stalwart tree. The more rampant of them will think nothing of climbing 12 m (40 ft) or even more.

of it was covered with a large scarlet bignonia and a native multiflora rose, which entwisting and interlacing, left scarce a vestige of rough logs to be seen.' *R. multiflora* is not, of course, native to the United States, and while she could have been referring to one of its hybrids, they were not widely distributed by 1850, when *Uncle Tom's Cabin* was first published. It is more than likely that what she had in mind was the Cherokee rose or the Macartney rose.

Other uses for Climbers

Paths lead from one part of a garden to another, and what could be better than one being turned into a tunnel of scented roses by a pergola? Its size and structure must depend on the size of your garden, your ambition, and the amount of money in your bank. It can, by anyone who can handle a hammer and saw, be quite easily built from rustic poles. This will be the cheapest way, but it will last a great deal longer if the pillars are brick-built, preferably using second-hand, mellowed bricks. On the other hand, they will be more difficult to train the roses on at first, a wooden structure (if it is not to blow over in the first gale) having bracing struts at the side to which the canes can be tied in. For brick pillars, select roses which make plenty of new basal growth, and consider the possibility of trellis-work fixed about 5 cm (2 in) out from the surface for the formative years of the rose.

For photographs of pergolas, see pages 152, 211, 218 and 221.

If you cannot, perhaps for space reasons, accommodate a pergola, try its truncated cousin, a rose arch, using it to lead into a rose garden, to frame your front gate, or to give interest to a gap in a hedge which leads to a hidden vegetable plot or secluded corner. For this, rustic poles can again be used, but strength and rigidity are very important. The sheer weight of a fully-grown Climber, to say nothing of its wind-resistance, can be enormous. For an arch, a rose (or roses) with reasonably flexible canes should be used as it will be much easier to train it to go in the right direction, and a rose arch is meant to be walked through without having the clothes grabbed at by self-willed thorny laterals as you pass.

Pillar roses, the less strong-growing Climbers, can, as we have seen, make centre-pieces for rose beds, but they can also be used for specimen planting in a lawn, or else to lighten an otherwise uninteresting corner where two hedges meet. And if you have only a tiny patio garden a pillar rose (without its pillar) can still be given an honoured place, by growing it in a large tub if there is no bare earth. Make sure, however, that you choose the sunny side of the patio, and train the rose on a strong trellis if there is not a suitable wall.

I mentioned earlier in passing that many Climbers can be grown as shrubs, either lax and rambling, or quite compact with the less volatile varieties. Some training and almost certainly some support will be needed for the first few years if they are to be kept reasonably under control. This need not necessarily consist of staking, and I have used successfully a group of relatively short-lived cytisus (brooms), which were already about half-way through their natural lifespan, on which to start off 'Albertine' (actually a Rambler but with many of a Climber's attributes) into its role as a shrub. The broom gave support up to about 1.8 m (6 ft), and the new canes of the rose were trained in on each other each year until the whole thing became self-supporting and the brooms breathed their last, their job done. This was, of course, an enormously vigorous rose, but something like 'Aloha' will stand on its own quite happily, with only the minimum of cutting back to keep it balanced.

USING
RAMBLER ROSES

Much of what I have said about Climbers applies to Ramblers as well, provided always that they are kept away from walls and close-boarded fences. They are excellent for pergolas and easy to train, colour continuity (if you think this important) being obtained by alternating the planting with recurrent Climbers. By far the biggest group of Ramblers, the Wichuraiana hybrids, and also the so-called Musk Ramblers, do not come into flower until summer is well advanced, and so will take over when the early-flowering Climbers are resting and preparing for their second flush of bloom. Colour will have an unbroken run.

Ramblers are equally good for arches, open-work frames of any sort, and for wandering like Kurdish nomads through other shrubs in something which has been deliberately designed as – and has not accidentally become – a wild garden. There is one thing, however, at which they excel: growing up trees. The more adventurous Climbers can be used for tree-climbing, too, but the easily guided canes of most Ramblers make them easier to train in the right direction initially, and when once established, their flexibility allows their huge sprays of small flowers to hang down gracefully from the tree's branches and display their full beauty. They can give an old apple or holly tree – not something which in the summer would draw the eye as iron filings to a magnet – a new dimension.

For a photograph of a Rambler in an old apple tree, see page 181.

A word of caution, however. The big Musk Ramblers, *R. brunonii* and its hybrids, *R. filipes* 'Kiftsgate', *R. longicuspis* and the like, which will scent the air for yards around in addition to turning a tree into a creamy-white waterfall of blossom, are often quoted as the ideal roses for this purpose. They are, but, by heaven, you need a tall, tough tree to take them! They can go up to 9–12 m (30–40 ft), and do not think that they will not – fast too, and not just straight up. A medium-sized tree would be smothered in a few years, if it did not collapse under the weight of the rose first. I have had it happen to me, and untangling the remains was like spending an hour or two inside a pincushion. I have not, however, made the mistake of putting a thorny Rambler of whatever size up an apple tree which has to be climbed to pick the apples.

For weeping standards, see page 190; for ground-cover roses, see page 204.

I will now leave Ramblers in the garden for the moment, but I will be coming back to them again when discussing weeping standards and also their use as ground-cover roses.

ROSES
FOR HEDGES

Let me start by defining a hedge. There are two kinds. Those which surround a garden are best if they form an all-year-round screen, are capable of reaching 2 m (7 ft) tall if you grow opium poppies or marijuana in your flower-beds and 1.2–1.5 m (4–5 ft) if you do not, are child-, animal- and neighbour-proof, reasonably compact, and preferably decorative as well. Hedges for dividing a garden internally should, above all, be decorative, may well be no more than 30 cm (1 ft) tall, and may or may not incorporate some of these other qualities.

How does the rose fit these requirements? In all except the very first one, extremely well. No rose keeps its leaves for twelve months of the year; no rose is evergreen. But as a compensating factor the flowers on a rose hedge will, throughout the summer and well into the autumn, be, shall we say, more noticeable than those of a privet or laurel. Let us take the perimeter hedge, the screening roses, first.

Rose hedges as screens

There can be little doubt that the Rugosa group of shrub roses is the best of all for this if one keeps to the hybrids which most nearly resemble the original wild *R. rugosa*. Of them, *R. rugosa alba*, 'Roseraie de l'Hay' and 'Scabrosa' are the pick, to which can be added 'Frau Dagmar Hastrup' (Hartopp) if you need something reaching only 1.2 m (4 ft) instead of 1.5–1.8 m (5–6 ft). The very fragrant flowers of these are all single, with the exception of 'Roseraie de l'Hay', and the colours are, in order, white, wine-red, pinky-mauve and pale pink with cream stamens. They will keep coming without cease right through the summer season and, on all but the double varieties, are followed by very large red hips. 'Scabrosa' has the largest blooms of any Rugosa, fully 10 cm (4 in) across. The wonderful, completely healthy foliage starts to unfold early, covers the plants to the ground, and in autumn turns yellow before it falls, to reveal a mass of the most spiny stems imaginable, which would deter the boldest intruder.

Rugosas do send out suckers if they are on their own roots, but even without these they can spread to quite a width if left to their own devices. However, selective pruning in winter can help to keep them to 1–1.2 m (3–4 ft) wide for a hedge, and they can in fact be clipped over with shears. This is not to suggest that you should aim for a neat, squared-off finish, as one would expect to achieve with privet, beech or holly. Roses do not grow in the right way for that, and would not flower anything like as well if you attempted it. A great deal of their charm for hedge work is in their informality, so follow their natural contours as much as possible, giving them at most a light trim.

Apart from those I have mentioned, there are other Rugosas you can try, though in general they will tend to be rather more open at the base of the bushes and less compact growers generally. They include 'Belle Pointevine' (semi-double, pink), the lovely 'Blanc Double de Coubert' (double, white), 'Hansa' (crimson-purple), and the four members of the Grootendorst 'family' – 'F. J. Grootendorst', 'Pink Grootendorst', 'White Grootendorst' and 'Grootendorst Supreme' – with large trusses of tiny, carnation-like, scentless flowers in red, pink or white. 'Schneezwerg', with small white flowers like those of a Japanese anemone and orange-red hips, is one further one which can be recommended without reserve, but for hedges on their own avoid the tall-growing 'Conrad F. Meyer', its white sport 'Nova Zembla', and 'Sarah Van Fleet' – Rugosa hybrids quite unlike the other roses we have been discussing – unless you plan to put something else in front of them to hide their fiercely armoured and rather gaunt stems. They are also far less healthy than the other Rugosas, and the first two of them particularly are tough customers to train properly or to prune unless you, yourself, are suitably armoured as well. With their lovely flowers, they have their place, but not to my mind in a

Plate XXXIII: Rugosa roses
The original Rugosa rose goes far back into history and was the ramanus rose of Japan, though it also came from other parts of the Far East. Most of the hybrids, like those shown here, date from about the turn of the century, and among the best of those with characteristic rugose leaves and the typical Rugosa flowers is 'Roseraie de l'Hay' (bottom right). It is very sweetly scented, as are most of them, but not the Grootendorst group of hybrids, of which 'Pink Grootendorst' (bottom left), with its frilled blooms, is the most attractive example. 'Frau Dagmar Hastrup' (top) illustrates yet another flower form. Less tall than the others, it bears the biggest hips of the family, which only appear on those varieties with single or semi-double flowers. Although they have many other uses, Rugosas make ideal rose hedges.

hedge. Rugosas will, by the way, make useful screens even on the coast, as their tough, brilliant green foliage stands up well to salt-laden winds, even if the flowers are rather less happy.

The older, Pemberton-type Hybrid Musks can also be used with great advantage for perimeter hedges, though they are much less regular in growth than the Rugosas and certainly cannot be clipped over in the same way. Varieties like 'Buff Beauty' (apricot-yellow), 'Cornelia' (coppery-apricot-pink), 'Felicia' (pink), 'Francesca' (apricot-yellow), 'Nur Mahal' (magenta), 'Penelope' (creamy-pink), 'Prosperity' (ivory) and 'Pink Prosperity' will all form reasonably bushy plants up to 1.5–1.8 m (5–6 ft) tall with a profusion and continuity of bloom hardly matched by any other rose. They do, however, have a tendency to send out very long shoots in quite unexpected directions in late summer, bearing enormous heads of flowers which only a barbarian would dream of cutting off to keep his hedge tidy-looking. All the Pemberton Musks go well together, so a hedge of mixed varieties is well worth trying, excepting only 'Pax' (creamy-white), which is really too lax, the lovely single pink 'Vanity', which is nothing like compact enough, and the few dwarf ones like 'Danaë'.

The more modern Hybrid Musks like 'Wilhelm', 'Will Scarlet' and 'Hamburg', with their habit of growth more closely resembling tall Floribundas, have their trusses of bloom mainly at the top and are grand for growing behind and peering over the kind of wall, about 60 cm (2 ft) high, which is often to be found dividing a garden from the highway. This is one place, too, to use the taller Floribundas proper, and even 'Queen Elizabeth' can be tamed into semi-submission in such a place. If closely planted and pruned hard yearly to no more than 60 cm (2 ft), it should not exceed the height of a tall man, will bush out better than it usually does, have flowers not solely for viewing from the bedroom windows, and make a good screen with its fine foliage.

But back to the Hybrid Musks for a minute. In the gardens of the Royal Horticultural Society at Wisley in Surrey, they are grown in a way I have not seen elsewhere, being trained, believe it or not, like climbers on an openwork fence supported by uprights. In this way, their width is kept down to little more than 45 cm (18 in), and a better and more colourful hedge it would be hard to imagine. True, late summer still produces the usual vagrant shoots which have to be controlled – though not, in this august place, by a barbarian – if the path beside them is not to be obstructed.

The *R. rubiginosa* (*R. eglanteria*) hybrids or Sweet Briers, such as 'Lord Penzance', 'Lady Penzance' and 'Amy Robsart', which one sees often on lists of hedging shrubs, are treated at Wisley in the same way and with equal success, though they are far less colourful than the Musks and only flower once. Lovely but fleeting blooms at midsummer, scented foliage and a dazzling display of small scarlet hips are their chief attractions, but in any but a very large garden they take some accommodating if given their heads. Nothing could get through their thorny stems into any garden, whether large or small, but in the latter there might not be much room left for whoever was there already.

Rose hedges within the garden

For internal hedges of medium height which are not intended primarily for screening but rather to form a decorative feature, there are few things to beat the taller Floribundas such as 'Iceberg' or else 'Chinatown', which is an upright grower but carries its fine foliage right to the ground (more or less), and the large double yellow blooms of which are strongly scented into the bargain. For extra density (remembering that it will also take up more space) staggered planting can be used, the roses being put in alternately (in a zigzag) along two centre-lines about 30 cm (1 ft) apart. Two or more varieties can be mixed if they blend well together.

'Peace', deep red 'Uncle Walter' or vermilion 'Alexander' are Hybrid Teas which will serve the same purpose as the Floribundas for hedging, or else modern shrub roses like 'Lavender Lassie' (actually pink, without a hint of lavender, and needing some staking until established due to the weight of the enormous flower heads) and 'Fountain', which has crimson blooms. On the whole I favour Floribundas rather than Hybrid Teas because of their better continuity. In a hedge, one is really after as much colour as possible and not individual quality in each bloom.

Moving downwards, I am not sure at what height a hedge ceases to be one and turns into a row of plants. *The Concise Oxford Dictionary* defines a hedge, rather strangely, as 'Fence of bushes or low trees, *living or dead*' (my italics), but it gives no height limit in either direction. 'Bush' must be the operative word, and the box hedges of the Tudor knot gardens were not much more than 30 cm (1 ft) high, so Polyanthas and the taller Miniature roses must qualify too. There are not all that many Polyanthas still on the market, but one that is, 'The Fairy', with huge heads of small, pale pink double flowers, makes a first-rate low hedge for lining a path – and, considering its restrained colour, a surprisingly showy one. It looks even better interplanted with lavender. Another very recent Polyantha-type Floribunda – light and airy in habit, and with more than a hint of lavender in its own flowers – is the rather taller 'Yesterday'. In appearance, it could easily be grouped with the China roses. Of the Miniatures, 'Gipsy Jewel', 'Fire Princess', 'Wee Man', 'Shooting Star' or 'Windy City' are suitable, either planted in a single line or staggered.

Climbers and ramblers, trained on a long framework of rustic poles, must not be forgotten, though whether they qualify in the strictest sense as hedges I am not sure. Possibly not (as if it mattered), but they will make the most attractive dividing line, barrier or what you will between different parts of the garden. However, apart from the usual careful and constant attention needed to keep them from being rather bare low down, they will not always grow exactly where you want them to fill gaps higher up, so do not expect to achieve an impenetrable screen – just something to delight the eye.

I have deliberately left mentioning the use of the more upright-growing Gallica roses for hedges until last, as I am not sure how good a thing it is. An example often mentioned is the hedge of the deep pink and near-white striped 'Rosa Mundi' at Kiftsgate Court, a show garden near Chipping Camden in Gloucestershire. I have, of course, seen this, and in flower it is something never to be forgotten. But afterwards? 'Rosa Mundi', and all other Gallicas, are once-flowering only. They put on an unrivalled display for a month or more, but their rather rough foliage is never at any stage their strongest point and it does not age attractively. Also, with the possible exception of the rather lax-growing 'Gloire de France', one of the most free-flowering of the family, the very double blooms of which shade from purplish-mauve to pale lilac at the petal edges, they will need frequent spraying to keep mildew in check. At this point it will certainly be recalled that I suggested Gallicas for bedding, and on the face of it the objections I have just raised might seem to apply to that use as well. But with bedding it is easier to arrange things so that other plants nearby distract the eye. A hedge, by its very nature, tends to be more isolated, so that when the flowers are over the leaves become of prime importance and if they are not up to scratch one cannot help but notice them.

Far be it for me to suggest that nobody should try a Gallica hedge. There will be great rewards, and the more twiggy, upright varieties like 'Rosa Mundi' do have the advantage that they, like the Rugosas, can be clipped over lightly with shears in winter to keep them shapely. Again like the Rugosas, if they are on their own roots they will sucker freely, which can be a distinct advantage in thickening up a hedge. When this has been achieved a spade driven into the ground, straight down and about 30 cm (1 ft) away on each side along the length of the hedge will sever suckers that are heading in the wrong direction and make them easy to pull out. So, apart from the flowers, there are advantages with Gallicas and I think that the deciding factor as to whether you use these roses must be the importance of the hedge in your scheme of things. If it is only one of a number of hedges, fine; but if it occupies a place of major importance in a small garden, careful thought is needed.

STANDARD
OR TREE ROSES

A standard or tree rose is one in which a bush variety (or rambler or climber in the case of a weeping standard) is budded into the top of a single, long, strong, straight cane which is growing up from the understock, the rest of the canes having been cut away. The stem of a standard is thus in one with the roots, and all the nourishment from the soil must pass up it to the cultivated variety at the top. In dealing with bedding, I have already discussed a number of the uses to which these roses can be put. I mentioned the idea of planting them in a line down the centre of a long, narrow rose bed, but it can equally well be a bed of other plants. Their function will be the same: to give height.

One would not think that, with their long bare stems, standards alone could be used for screening an unsightly fence, but they can, most effectively, provided that you have a wide flower bed in front of it. Make use of the three different heights of standards stocked by many nurseries, and about 45 cm (18 in) from the fence plant your first row of full standards – with 1.05 m (3½ ft) stems – about 90 cm (3 ft) apart, though this distance must depend to some extent on the size of the head the variety of rose is likely to make. Something like the enormously vigorous Floribunda 'Iceberg' should have another 30 cm (1 ft) or even more added – and at the risk of being a bore about it, I will say once more (and for the last time), that you should see before you buy so that you can judge for yourself. The roses, when in full growth, will reach about 1.8 m (6 ft) high.

In front of this first row of standards, plant a second row of half-standards – which have about 60 cm (2 ft) of clear stem – staggering the planting if you wish, and in front of this again a row of quarter-standards (with half as much

Parc de la Grange, Switzerland
This panoramic view shows the successful use of weeping standards to break up, and give height to, a rather flat geometric layout.

188

stem). If you have space and any money left to do it with, finish things off in the front with compact-growing bush roses, or perhaps a lavender hedge. The results will be something that will be the talk of the neighbourhood, if not the county – a sloping bank of solid colour which will make your fence just a memory until it is once more leering at you between the stems when winter comes around again. One reminder, however, for those who live in climates cold enough to necessitate standard roses being laid on their sides and buried for winter protection. Temper your enthusiasm with the thought of the amount of work you will be letting yourself in for, and be prepared for losses even with the best of treatment.

Standards as specimens

In addition to combining them with roses and other plants in flower beds, standards make fine specimen plantings on their own, perhaps as a focal point in a lawn. For this purpose it is hard to better a weeping standard, even if the best ones are created from the once-flowering Wichuraiana Ramblers. They will, or should be, budded on to 1.8 or 2.5 m (6 or 8 ft) stems, and the long, lax canes hang down all round quite naturally – in time right to the ground – smothered in bloom from latish in the summer for many weeks. They are weeping but anything but mournful. Weeping standards are not used very frequently in the United States, but when they are they are budded on to 2–2.5 m (7–8 ft) understocks and then supported by a heavy pipe and umbrella-like frame, over which the canes are trained. In a few gardens, such as the Rose Hills Memorial Park in Whittier, California, the frames may be 3–4 m (10–12 ft) in diameter, forming a kind of one-post pergola.

For the use of weeping standards, see the photograph overleaf.

The Ramblers with much stiffer growth such as 'Albertine', and the comparatively small selection of Climbers which are also sold as weeping standards, will need some training – bullying, in some cases – to make them weep properly, and special wire 'umbrellas' – like those just mentioned, only smaller – can be bought for this purpose for attaching to the top of the very strong stake any weeping Rambler should have. New growths are tied in to this wire frame to persuade them to go downwards against their natural inclination, and the best you can expect is a very beautiful but possibly exuberantly lopsided result.

For the training of weeping standards, see page 251.

Other roses which grow exceptionally large heads, in the way that 'Iceberg' does, make equally good specimens of a different kind. Most nursery lists concentrate on Hybrid Teas and Floribundas for standards, so you may well have problems finding anything else ready made and have to resort to carrying out your own bud-grafting (see chapter 5) if you want to try to be more original. Not that original is really the right word, for, as described earlier, around the turn of the century standards of many of the old roses – Mosses, Centifolias and some of the Albas – were common and there were, in fact, many more standards grown then than now.

For budding, see page 262.

Budding a shrub rose on to a standard stem may well be the best way of coping with the larger ones in a small garden, and in Britain the near-species 'Canary Bird', for which as a shrub one must allow a space about 2–2.5 m (7–8 ft) across, probably sells more in standard form than in its natural state. It is one that is quite easy to get, and a few other shrub roses such as the Hybrid Musk 'Ballerina' have recently joined it in the market place. There is great scope for an enterprising grower to extend the range indefinitely, though I must confess that as far as most standard Hybrid Teas and Floribundas are concerned, I side with that great gardener William Robinson, who wrote in *The English Flower Garden*: 'But the rose must not come back to ugly ways, in roses stuck – and mostly starving – on the top of sticks . . . roses should be closely massed, feathering the ground . . .' Only the weeping standards and some shrub roses justify such unnatural treatment.

ROSES FOR
THE PATIO GARDEN

For the cultivation of roses in containers outdoors, see page 260.

Inevitably in a discussion about roses in the garden, there must be some overlap between the different sections, and at least one use of roses on a patio – that of climbers – has been mentioned already. All roses can be grown in tubs – though I would not recommend a 3×3 m (10×10 ft) species for a patio – provided that they are in a good growing medium, have good drainage and, for anything other than Miniatures, the tubs are at least 45 cm (18 in) deep and about the same across. Obviously the tall and more leggy Hybrid Teas and Floribundas are best avoided, as is planting in a sunless spot, which can make even a bushy rose into a lanky one. Long troughs – an Egyptian sarcophagus would be ideal – can be placed against patio walls, or a series of them can be formed into a low wall along an open side, remembering only to leave a space for you to get in. Pillar roses can be used on the pillars, if any, but always, if you are among those who like to share your food with mosquitoes and have a barbecue, keep the roses away from the heat and smoke.

A large patio can even accommodate a standard rose grown in a large tub, the only problem being the firm fixing of the stake which all standards need for support. Wind-rock will probably not be such a problem as it is in the open, but gusts can still come from unexpected directions, and the soil in the tub is unlikely to be either deep enough or firm enough to take the strain. A galvanized metal or wooden brace, fitted into the tub and firmly fixed before the soil goes in when the rose is planted, is quite easy to make, and the stake is attached to this. If you are quite sure that you will not want to move the rose about, you can experiment by lifting one of the paving stones forming the floor of the patio and seeing if bare earth lies underneath. If the foundations are extensive, all you can do is put the paving stone back and use a tub.

MINIATURE
ROSES

The fact that Miniature roses are so often sold in pots – the only way, in fact, in which many people have seen them at all – has led to the idea that they are house-plants pure and simple. An additional reason for this belief is the tiny size and fragile look of the flowers of many of them. A puff of harsh north wind and a touch of frost, and anything so dainty must surely wither away.

Nothing, however, could be farther from the truth. With a good deal of help, and provided that fairly exacting conditions are fulfilled, miniature roses *can* be grown indoors, but for the moment we are concerned with them in the open garden, where they are certainly as tough as any other rose and considerably more robust than some that are many times their size.

For the cultivation of Miniatures indoors, see page 260.

Primarily in what follows, I am concerned with those Miniatures which grow 20–25 cm (8–10 in) tall at the most. Those which grow taller than this, anything from 30–45 cm (12–18 in) or even more (like 'Baby Masquerade', 'Easter Morning', 'Little Flirt' and 'Beauty Secret') are, as far as garden use is concerned, really interchangeable with the shorter-growing Floribundas. In some, the flowers themselves are not all that much smaller (though the leaves are generally true to type) and I would classify them as having progressed backwards. A pity, but there it is, and if we rose growers want new colours and other features in Miniature roses which only crossing with Floribundas can give us, we will have to pay the penalty.

Uses of Miniatures

Miniature roses can be used, as has been seen, for edging rose beds or for lining a path, and the taller ones come into their own for bordering something as wide as a drive. However, in these days when every other person one meets has an aching back and once bent down is unable to rise again, problems arise in appreciating the true beauty of the flowers. Standing rigidly erect and looking, with down-turned eyes, from a height of 1.5 m (5 ft) plus is not the answer. The mass effect can be admired, but that is all, and while there is nothing wrong with this, the mountain can be brought to Muhammad simply by raising the beds. There are a number of ways in which this can be done.

For the sides of paths a brick or stone wall (its height depending on your back), with a well-drained planting trough built into the top of it, is a very good answer – the kind of thing I suggested for surrounding a patio garden. If you have, or decide to make, a sunken garden, a development of this idea can be tried. The sides surrounding the central area can be formed into terraces, with brick or stone retaining walls, each succeeding level being perhaps 30 cm (1 ft) higher than the last. The terrace beds can be any width you wish, enough to hold only one row of Miniatures, or much more if you intend to carry out a proper bedding scheme. Miniature standard roses can be used to add variety, or the miniature climber-cum-ground-cover rose, 'Nozomi', with its white star-like flowers, be allowed to meander downwards over the walls themselves.

'Nozomi' will, however, need watching, for a reason that applies to most of the other miniature climbers, of which a rapidly growing selection of varieties is becoming available. They are of considerable vigour, and many will reach 1.5 m (5 ft) or more in height. In fact, 'Climbing Pompon de Paris', the rose from which in its original bush form it is possible that all Miniatures originated some 200 years ago, will make a fair attempt to cover the side of a house, which may be an extreme case but illustrates graphically the point I am making. In general, Miniature climbers make much bigger plants in relation to the bush varieties than most full-sized climbers will make in relation to Hybrid Teas or Floribundas. They are none the less beautiful for that, but if you plan to lay out a miniature rose garden, complete with arches and pergolas, of the kind we will come to in a minute, the eventual size of the

Miniature rose beds
Miniature roses growing in raised beds at the Royal National Rose Society's garden at St Albans; China roses are largely used for the background planting, since their airy growth does not overwhelm their smaller cousins.
See also plates XIV and XXXI (pp91 and 149).

climbers should not be forgotten. 'Nozomi' will cover a lot of ground if allowed its head, so leave plenty of space for it if you plan to use it for a terraced bed. Cutting back will do no great harm if it gets too ambitious, but as with the large species shrub roses, it is a pity to spoil a good thing through lack of forethought.

Miniature roses make good plants for a rock garden, the upright stance of the bushes making a useful contrast to the low, creeping habit of many alpines. A majority of the better-known alpines are spring-flowering, and a rock garden can become rather colourless later in the year, so that the bright colours of the Miniature rose flowers – which in a good year and the right climate will continue to appear until late autumn – are more than welcome. Planted in groups of three or four, they will make even more impact. A rock garden will give the good drainage the roses need, but when planting them it is important to make sure that they have an unrestricted root run into good soil. The rocks will keep it cool and moist, which is ideal, but it must be there in the first place, as Miniature roses will not thrive on the near starvation diet that suits something like a rock rose (*Helianthemum*) – which is, of course, no relation.

Miniature bedding schemes
So far, with the exception of the terrace bed planting, the suggested uses for Miniatures could be described as trimmings on the cake, an extra decoration to enhance something else. However, a miniature rose garden using them alone brings them, mixed metaphor or not, off the cake and right to the front of the stage. First of all, considerable thought must be given to the site. It must, naturally, be sunny, and it is best if it is not isolated in a wide-open space like the middle of a lawn. As a centre-piece for the sunken garden mentioned just now it could be most effective, but the best choice of all is, once again, one in which it is possible to view it, even if only from one side, from something not too far below normal eye level. This is, after all, how you would expect to look at any other garden where a proportion of the flowers will reach 1–1.2 m (3–4 ft) and many will be much taller. The flat top of a bank is a good place, or you could construct a raised garden surrounded by dry-stone walls about 1 m (3 ft) tall.

The small-size beds can be laid out just as in any other rose garden in patterns of squares, circles or triangles, or any other shape that takes your fancy – even a heart-shape if you are romantic. But the question of the paths between them, if they are to be in scale, needs consideration. If you have cut the beds into the surface of a lawn, you will have grass between them already, but ideally these paths should not be more than about 22 cm (9 in) wide, and if so how are you going to cut the grass? With scissors? And what about the balancing act that would be necessary to get to the central beds for weeding or cutting flowers for the house? If you do want to use grass, there must be a compromise based on the width of your lawnmower, but this will be less obvious if you have a fairly large layout overall. Just the same, fine grass cut to bowling-green smoothness really is needed (again with scale in mind), for which a mower with a cylinder blade (rather than the rotary type) and a reasonably equable climate are essential.

In places where the midday sun scorches the earth and where grass is usually left much longer in order for it to survive at all, constant watering would be needed, which could become something of a chore. Since the idea of such a garden is that it should give the maximum of enjoyment with the minimum of hard work, it would be better and certainly easier to use small paving stones for your paths, or else fine stone chippings, once again compromising a little on the ideal width for reasons of easy access. Ordinary gravel would probably be too coarse.

For the rest, plant out your garden as you would a full-scale one with bedding roses, either of the Floribunda or Hybrid Tea type, for you can get fair imitations of either kind among the Miniatures. True, they mostly tend to be cluster-flowered, but some have the shapely, high-centred blooms of the typical Hybrid Tea. Miniature standards can be used as centre-pieces, but pillars and pergolas will be a little more difficult in view of the vigour of what will be growing up them. The most rampant climbers can be trained horizontally along a surrounding small-scale fence or trellis, and a good deal of cutting back of laterals can be done without much harm.

When choosing your varieties for a bedding scheme, remember the guidelines used for larger roses, such as selecting those with a degree of uniformity in ultimate height if you are using more than one kind. With Miniatures, however, equally important is the size of the flowers. 'Baby Gold Star', 'Persian Princess' and 'Starina', for instance, have blooms which can reach 5 cm (2 in) across, and they do not look well with the dainty 2.5 cm (1 in) or even smaller flowers of 'Beauty Secret', 'Kara', 'Small World' or 'Cinderella'. In general, those Miniatures sold in pots will be from cuttings and on their own roots, which means that the plants themselves will not be as large as those which have been bud-grafted. This is no bad thing, and is, if anything, to be preferred. They will lack nothing in vigour, unlike some of the more highly bred Hybrid Teas and Floribundas when raised in the same way, but will simply keep to the size the good Lord intended.

Most of the practical reasons I put forward against underplanting bedding roses do not apply with Miniatures. You will not at any time be trampling on the beds, for suckers will not come from a rose on its own roots, and weeding will almost certainly have to be by hand rather than with a hoe, so the only discouragement I can give is to say that it will be difficult to find anything small enough. Once again nature provided an unasked-for answer for me, as I happen to live in a place where wild mauve and white violets seed themselves freely all over the garden. And they do look good among the tiny roses.

APPLICATIONS OF SHRUB ROSES

Here, and indeed elsewhere in this book, I am using the definition of a shrub rose which has been current for a number of years, so the garden uses of both the old and the new will be covered. To keep some sort of order in things, it will probably be best to take them group by group as far as possible, though where one or more groups mix well with others this will also be mentioned.

To start with, two popular misconceptions: that all shrub roses grow too large for the average garden, and that all of them only flower once and must for some strange reason be dismissed on that account. Anyone who has read this far will have realized by now that neither of these two things is true, but even those roses which are not recurrent will give you weeks of concentrated glory. If a nagging doubt as to whether they are worth while still persists, drop the word roses and just think of them as garden shrubs, as you would with once-flowering lilacs, mock-orange (*Philadelphus*) or rhododendrons. They will certainly equal, if not out-perform, any of these.

Using species roses

The species roses were the first on the scene, and so should come first in this review, though it will also include some of their more recent hybrids which follow them in flower form and habit of growth. It is unfortunate that, in view of the point I have just been making, small garden owners (owners of small gardens, that is) run straight into a size problem with many of these, though there are some species like *R. ecae* which are not particularly large, as a reference back to chapters 1 and 2 will show. However, this might be a good place to make an important point about size which applies to roses in general and not just to the wild ones.

The vigour and size of different specimens of any one variety can vary, in some cases startlingly, according to climate, soil, whether it is on its own roots and how well it is looked after. In some cases there will be no discernible reason, and all any writer can do is to give an indication of what the size is likely to be under average conditions, though I am not quite sure what these may be! In other words, no one can give a definite dimension, and as an example from my own garden I will cite a bush of the long-popular Flori-bunda 'Orangeade'. All the books and catalogues rightly give the average height as about 75 cm (2½ ft), but my particular rose regularly reaches 1.4 m (4½ ft) and bushes out to the width of a good Floribunda shrub. It is growing with other roses which behave perfectly normally. There is no logical explana-tion for it.

But back to the species roses in the garden. A fairly large number of species have been described in some detail in chapter 1 and so, though I may well say something more about some of them and some others may be introduced as we go along, I will now concentrate mainly on how to grow species to their best advantage in fairly general terms. Species or near species, such as the magnificent hybrid 'Complicata', can take their place in general shrub plantings provided always that they have their fair share of sun. In time they will weave their way in and out of their neighbours and, if these and the roses have been carefully selected, will garland them with bloom when the other shrubs are resting. In autumn, when otherwise there might be no sign of colour anywhere, scarlet rose hips will light up the dark days, even after the leaves have gone, which inspired these lines from Tennyson:

> Wearing his wisdom lightly, like the fruit
> Which in our winter woodland looks a flower.

Of the species particularly noted for their display of hips as the year draws to its close, the Moyesii group must come first in any list. In them the fruit may be up to 8 cm (3 in) long, and just as showy are two close relatives, *R. holondonta* (*R. moyseii rosea*) and *R. highdownensis*, on the last of which the hips are offset by purplish-tinted leaves. *R. forrestiana* carries clusters of the brightest scarlet imaginable, and others to make a note of are *R. davidii*, *R.*

Plate XXXIV: Roses for hips
The flowers of these four species roses, R. spinosissima altaica (top left) from Siberia, R. roxburghii (top right) and R. moyesii (bottom left), both from the Far East, and the European R. pendulina (bottom right), are shown in the painting as well as the hips, but they do not appear at the same time. The hips decorate the shrubs from late summer onwards, with R. moyesii and its many hybrids putting on an especially spectacular display. The hips of R. roxburghii have, for obvious reasons, given rise to the alternative names of chestnut rose and burr rose.

196

woodsii, the single-flowered Rugosas of course, *R. rubrifolia*, *R. virginiana* and the comparatively modern hybrid 'Scarlet Fire' ('Scharlachglut'). The hips on 'Frühlingsmorgen' are deep maroon and those of *R. soulieana* tiny, multi-tudinous and orange. The Chinese species *R. sweginzowi* has the long, bottle-shaped hips of the Moyesii group, and those of *R. setipoda* are also elongated, a shape which contrasts markedly with the rounded, bun-shaped, black and shiny fruit of *R. spinosissima altaica* and *hispida*. And it is worth remembering when choosing the form you want that the hips of the apple rose, *R. pomifera*, from which it gets its name, do not come as freely on *R. pomifera duplex*, which is the one most frequently stocked by nurseries.

Finally two other roses, though they are not species. In a summer in which they have a chance to ripen properly, the hips of the Hybrid Musk 'Penelope' turn an attractive soft coral-red, and *R.* × *alba semi-plena* is worth growing for its large pendulous clusters of hips, too. *R. virginiana* and *R. primula* are two which, in company with the Rugosas, give a shrub planting autumn colour from their leaves as well.

Except in the wild garden, which if you have space for such a thing is not likely to be in the immediate vicinity of the house, mixing species in with other shrubs has certain advantages. There are some, such as 'Canary Bird' and 'Golden Chersonese', whose very attractive foliage has staying power and looks well in all its stages, but there are many others which become distinctly untidy as the season advances, and if they have companions of a different genus, preferably evergreens, this messiness is to a large extent disguised. Something like a holly, Mexican orange (*Choisya ternata*) or *Garrya elliptica* (silk-tassel bush) will give the wandering rose canes a support for their elbows and make a suitably contrasting backcloth for the delicate rose colours.

Species certainly come into their own for specimen planting if you choose those which age reasonably tidily. Nothing in the garden will put on a finer display in early summer than the pale yellow 'Frühlingsgold' or else 'Nevada', literally vanishing under its huge creamy-white flowers with some further bloom in late summer as well. If they are set in a lawn, a circle should be cut out no less that 1 m (3 ft) in diameter to take them – or a square of about the same area, which will be easier than a circle to cut round with a mower. This should be kept free of weeds at least until such time as the growth of the rose gives an excuse for saying that it is no longer possible and that they are being smothered anyway. A little cutting back and training may be needed in the first few years to keep the new rose reasonably symmetrical, for the longer it is given to become lopsided the more difficult it will be to get it back on an even keel. It is not a question of clipping it to formality, but of giving it gentle guidance, and a specimen leaning at a drunken angle is not really at its best. Once it has established itself, it can be – should be – left alone.

Back among the poets again, Gray had this to say:

> Full many a flower is born to blush unseen,
> And waste its sweetness on the desert air.

And before I had learned my lesson a number of my spring-flowering species roses – and other early-blooming shrubs as well – came into this category. My dry, sandy soil almost completed the desert picture, but the real trouble was that I had planted them where they could not be seen from the house or even when approaching it from the road. I forgot that the weather early in the year is not always such as to tempt one to a casual stroll into tucked-away corners where *R. spinosissima altaica*, *R. sericea pteracantha* or plain old 'Canary Bird' might be opening their wonderful flowers to an audience too busy with nest-building to notice them.

Using old garden roses

For the use of old roses in the border, see the photograph on page 163.

The Albas and Damasks can, perhaps, be discussed together, as they both form big bushes suitable for general shrub planting. The second of the two groups are much more lax growers, and so are better in front of the tough, upright Albas. They contain varieties with stronger colours, too, which can be shown off to advantage against the soft, grey-green Alba foliage. This is an outstanding Alba asset, and varieties like the white-flowered *R. × alba maxima* and *R. × alba semi-plena*, 'Maiden's Blush' and 'Celeste' ('Celestial') make fine specimen bushes. The shorter-growing – 1.2 m (4 ft) – but equally lovely 'Félicité Parmentier', whose rosette flowers open from the palest of yellow buds to soft blush-pink, is for the front of the border.

Gallicas have already been discussed fairly fully as bedding and hedging plants, but they are by no means a uniform race. Apart from the short, fairly compact and upright growers like 'Charles de Mills' and a number of others, space should certainly be found for the lax, flower-laden canes of the deep purple-maroon 'Cardinal de Richelieu' or the sumptuous, rich pink of 'Empress Josephine' ('Francofurtana'). Neither of these is likely to top 1.2 m (4 ft), except in very favourable climates, for they will be borne down by the weight of the clustered flowers, so spreading to a width of twice their height or more. Keep them well forward in any shrub planting, remembering however that they will not just spread out backwards and sideways and so should not be too close to the edge. The spectacular Gallica hybrid 'Scarlet Fire' ('Scharlachglut') is clearly a throwback to something else and quite untypical. More nearly resembling a species, it should be thought of as a meandering, large, informal shrub, but if this takes it beyond your limits of space, try it as a pillar rose or trained along a fence as a climber.

The Centifolias and Moss roses, which can be taken together as they are very similar in many ways, have some of the loveliest blooms of all, crammed with petals and scent, but they do need more help from the gardener if they are to be seen at their best. A lax rose which nevertheless keeps its flowers upright can be left to itself. One in which the flowers also hang naturally downwards so that their beauty can only be fully appreciated while lying flat on the ground needs attention, and such is the case with the large-flowered Centifolias particularly. *R. × centifolia* itself and 'Bullata' are examples, and they most certainly need staking and tying in so that their globular blooms can be properly admired. This helps, too, to lessen a certain gauntness of habit by bringing the canes closer together so that they are masked by the large, pendulous leaves.

There are some Centifolias, however, which are comparatively upright. 'De Meaux' is one, and has miniature flowers of typically globular shape in the early stages, opening to flat pompons in soft pink. Of the bigger growers, 'Fantin Latour' is reasonably rigid and less inclined to hang its head, though even it will benefit from at least one stake. Its very double flowers in pastel pink should not be missed if twenty stakes were called for, and there is equal through different charm in the Moss rose 'William Lobb'. The flowers here

pale from crimson-purple to lavender-grey, and the very thorny canes will top 1.8 m (6 ft) so that they must be well staked, make use of a pillar, or it can be trained as a short climber on a wall.

So, too, can the more vigorous of the Bourbon roses, though none of them can be described as weaklings. A characteristic of most is thick, strong canes, though these tend to wander at will and not stay upright as a matter of course. They make good pillar roses, and one group, slenderer growers than most, do need support if their flowers are not to brush the ground. This includes the trio 'La Reine Victoria' (pink cupped blooms with shell-like petals), its sport 'Mme Pierre Oger' (paler, but whose flowers blush deeper in the sun, a trait inherited from the China rose side of its ancestry) and the pink 'Louise Odier', all of which will go up to 1.8 m (6 ft). 'Boule de Neige', unsurpassed among pure white double roses, grows more naturally erect, is sturdy enough on its own, and holds its blooms well displayed.

There are, however, those which do not quite reach climbing status but still make very large shrubs which you would like to have if only there was space for them. Butchering by pruning is not to be thought of and a pillar may be hardly adequate, so a variation of it should be tried. Erect a 1.8 m (6 ft) narrow-based pyramid of larch poles with cross-pieces bracing the sides to give it strength, and train the Bourbons over this. There will be much more to tie the canes to than on a pillar, and they can be spread out much more widely, taking for preference a spiral course round the pyramid. This is an ideal arrangement for specimen planting, for which it is naturally best to choose a variety that really does put on a good display of bloom in the autumn as well as at midsummer. Avoid varieties like 'Bourbon Queen' (pink) and 'Commandant Beaurepaire' (striped), using the recurrent striped 'Honorine de Brabant' or pink 'Mme Ernst Calvat' in their place. The latter is a sport of the equally suitable deep madder-pink 'Mme Isaac Pereire', perhaps the most richly scented Bourbon of all, with huge, very double blooms which are even better late in the year than at the beginning, when some can be malformed. As a climber it may reach 4.5 m (15 ft) on a wall.

I hope that the above has not been taken as a condemnation of 'Bourbon Queen' and 'Commandant Beaurepaire', for both are beautiful roses which more than earn their place in the garden, mixed in with other shrubs like the Albas or Damasks. It is just that they concentrate their effort into one flush only, which is not so satisfactory when a rose is standing on its own. I mentioned 'Boule de Neige' as a good, erect-growing Bourbon, and there are other smaller ones which will do this equally well. The rather exaggeratedly-named but none the less beautiful 'Champion of the World' in pink, the crimson and white striped 'Ferdinand Pichard' and 'Souvenir de la Malmaison' (large flowers opening flat in a creamy blush), which can get pretty big and of which there is a climbing form, are examples.

The colours of all the Bourbons go well together, ranging as they do from white through the palest pink to stronger pink, crimson, mauvish-purple and deep maroon, so that a complete border of mixed varieties is something which should be tried, and they go equally well with most of the other old roses. One of the most striking striped varieties, however – 'Variegata di Bologna', whose globular, quartered, very fragrant flowers are a mixture of white and deep crimson purple – is so susceptible to black spot that it should be banished to a lonely life on its own somewhere.

For the use of tripod supports, see the background of the photograph on page 163.

Plate XXXV: Modern shrub roses (2)
'Chinatown' (top left) is, like 'Fred Loads' (plate XXIX), a Floribunda-shrub, but in this case more bushy and not so tall; it is often described as being as tall as a short rose grower! The full flowers are very sweetly scented and rather resemble those of 'Peace' (plate XIX).
'Nevada' (bottom left), in contrast, carries its blooms along every arching cane, and at their peak their profusion needs to be seen to be believed. It needs space to spread, so for something more restrained 'Golden Wings' (top right) could be chosen. This is seldom without its sweetly scented single blooms, whereas 'Nevada' does not always give even a fitful second display.
'Dortmund' (bottom right) is fully recurrent, and is one of those in-between roses – either a huge, rambling shrub or a short climber suitable for a pillar.

201

The more lax Bourbons can also be pegged down in the same way as Hybrid Perpetuals, though not necessarily for bedding as they have a natural tendency to branch anyway. It is simply a way of helping them to cover more ground and so using less of them if your finances are not what you would wish them to be. The Hybrid Perpetuals in general consort well with Bourbons in a mixed planting, and the flowers of the older ones are of similar shapes and colourings. The rather lanky Hybrid Perpetual growth will be effectively hidden by that of the older group, though there is at least one Hybrid Perpetual which can rival any Bourbon for bushiness. This is 'Reine des Violettes', a Hybrid Perpetual which grows like a Bourbon and has flat, quartered flowers more nearly resembling those of a Gallica!

The shorter-growing China or China-type roses were covered under bedding, but there is a small range of much larger ones, mostly with the same open, dainty style of growth, which can be mixed with other shrubs where a lightness of touch is needed: 'Fellemberg' ('La Belle Marseillaise'), with clusters of small, cupped, crimson-pink flowers; 'Comtesse du Cayla', with loosely-formed coral-flame blooms and coppery foliage; and the China-type of uncertain ancestry 'Bloomfield Abundance', which resembles a 2.5 m (8 ft) 'Cécile Brunner' since its minute pink flowers are identical save for the long, feathery sepals which give them an added charm. In late summer this latter one will send up enormous corymbs of flowers bearing as many as a hundred blooms on each.

The remarkable, multi-coloured 'Mutabilis' ('Tipo Ideale' or *R. turkestanica*) can, as we have seen, reach 2.5 m (8 ft) also, though only as a climber. Otherwise it is for the front of the border; and for the very front, or as a rock garden rose, there is the enchanting 60 cm (2 ft) 'Little White Pet', which is actually a dwarf sport of the Rambler 'Félicité et Perpétue' and has the same clusters of red-tinted buds which open almost without cease right through to the autumn into small rosettes of creamy-white. Another perpetual rose of the same height and for the same kind of place has semi-double rose-pink fragrant blooms. This is 'Natalie Nypels', which I once heard a nurseryman pronounce to a customer as 'Natalie Nipples', though fortunately he did not use the possessive form of Natalie.

The Musk roses and Rugosas have both been dealt with fairly fully as hedging roses, but both groups can be used as specimen plants as well. And there is one quite enchanting and little-known Rugosa which must be mentioned as it is in a class of its own. I am referring to 'Fimbriata', also called 'Dianthiflora' and, rather charmingly, 'Phoebe's Frilled Pink'. It will reach 1.5 m (5 ft) in time, but has a delicacy and refinement which is not usually associated with this robust group. The flowers are soft pink, frilled at the edges like the much later Grootendorsts, but not so double and opening out flat like small carnations. I have seen it, kept to a height of about 1 m (3 ft), as a delightful companion for columbines (aquilegias).

Using modern shrub roses

Modern shrub roses are a somewhat motley crew, and their uses just as varied as their form of growth and flower. They range from the super-big Floribunda types like 'Berlin', orange-vermilion 'Dorothy Wheatcroft', red and yellow 'First Choice' and vermilion 'Fred Loads' to the great rambling, arching 'Cerise Bouquet' – actually more crimson-red than cerise and a hybrid of

Plate XXXVI: Ground-cover roses
'Max Graf' (top left), a Rugosa × Wichuraiana hybrid, represents the Rambler type of ground-cover rose, which spreads across the earth, rooting where its canes touch the soil. R. × paulii (bottom left), which has a pink form as well, is a variety with a single central crown, but sends its very long canes outwards rather than upwards, covering a wide area with its dense and attractive foliage.
Classed as a Miniature, 'Nozomi' (top right) is really anything but that, except in flower and leaf size, and follows the growth pattern of 'Max Graf'. So, too, does the most recently introduced of the four, 'Temple Bells' (bottom right), a useful addition to this rapidly expanding group. Their sprawling growth is excellent for covering banks and other difficult areas.
See also the photograph on page 175.

R. multibracteata and the Hybrid Tea 'Crimson Glory' – which would add distinction to any general shrub planting. So, too, would 'Claire Matin' or 'Fritz Nobis', both pearly-pink, or 'Nymphenburg' of a warmer salmon-pink with orange shadings. 'Goldbusch' is a peach-yellow lax shrub or pillar rose, and 'Constance Spry' (from the Gallica 'Belle Isis' and the Floribunda 'Dainty Maid') has huge pink flowers which could be those of a Centifolia. Like 'Fritz Nobis' and 'Cerise Bouquet', 'Constance Spry' is not recurrent, but probably the majority of modern shrub roses are. One which does go on and on is 'Golden Wings' from America, and this makes a 1.5 m (5 ft) wide-spreading but not too lax shrub, with large, pale yellow, scented single flowers with amber stamens, not unlike those of the climber 'Mermaid'. These are borne almost without cease in small clusters among fresh green foliage which is exceptionally healthy.

One could go on and on making recommendations, but the range is so enormous and diverse that it is impossible to generalize about them in groups as one can with most of the older types. All one can say is that there is at least one modern shrub rose which will fill any spot you have in mind.

ROSES FOR
GROUND COVER

Many gardens have places where it is difficult to decide what to plant. The kind of thing I have in mind is a bank infested with lank, untidy grass which the mower finds difficulty in dealing with. Spring bulbs are one answer, but after their brief spell of flowering there will be dying foliage for many weeks and then rough grass once more. So why not, provided that it gets adequate sun, cover it with ground-hugging roses? Unless the bank is enormous, no more than three or four would be needed; a small area, and one would suffice. And the place you put them does not have to be a bank. Any piece of ground which you wish to make beautiful with the minimum of trouble will do.

For illustrations of ground-cover roses, see Plate XXXVI (overleaf) and the photograph on page 175.

There are two groups of roses that are especially suitable, each with a slightly different way of going about it. The first, represented by *R. × paulii*, vanishes almost out of sight early in the year beneath its white, scented single flowers lit by their golden stamens. This, and its pink form, *R. × paulii rosea*, grows no more than 1.2 m (4 ft) high, but spreads out its fiercely thorned canes, covered with Rugosa-type foliage, for 3.5 m (12 ft) or more all round. Only a steel-skinned bat could live in the prickly gloom beneath them, and certainly no weed. A *R. × macrantha* hybrid, 'Raubritter', not quite so vigorous, spreads out over the ground in the same way, flowers slightly later, and has globular clear pink flowers like smaller versions of the Bourbon 'La Reine Victoria'.

It will have been realized from the measurements I have given that these three do form fairly high mounds in time, and it may be that this is not precisely what you want. You may be looking for a real ground-hugger, and if so we come back to the Ramblers, to *R. wichuraiana*. It is not always realized that this, from which so many of our garden roses are descended, is by nature a plant that creeps along the ground, rooting as it goes where the canes touch the earth. There is thus no limit, other than a man-made one, to how far it will go, and it must be cut back when it reaches the outer limits of its allotted territory. It will make quite a thick carpet, its shiny leaves looking well at all times and showing off to perfection the star-like, single white flowers which appear quite late in the summer. For a change of colour (to quite a strong pink) 'Max Graf' can be tried, which is a *R. wichuraiana* hybrid with a Rugosa.

It is an interesting but as far as I know unexplained fact that the two most often recommended ground-cover roses are Rugosa hybrids, for *R. × paulii* is one, too, though nothing about the rest of the family suggests a liking for prostrate growth. Other ramblers can be tried as well as *R. wichuraiana* itself, and 'Temple Bells' is one of the group which is beginning to make a name for itself in this way. So, too, is the Japanese 'Nozomi'.

It should be emphasized, I think, that these ground-cover roses will not make an impenetrable mat of growth in five minutes. Several seasons must pass before they will begin fully to carry out their function, and until that point has been reached there will be weeds amongst them. So before planting try as far as possible to eliminate perennial horrors like couch-grass (quack grass), which, once established, will put on its spiked shoes and race off over any piece of neglected ground and be almost impossible to get rid of. It will continue to send up its green spears through what appears to be an impenetrable tangle of other plants, and would survive, I am convinced, in a small boat in the middle of the Atlantic ocean. If you do not clear this and others of like kind away, you will be plunging your hand into such a thorny tangle in order to try to get rid of them later that you will rue the day you planted the roses. The thorns on *R. × paulii* would penetrate the skin of a rhinoceros!

CHAPTER FOUR

ROSE GARDENS
OF THE WORLD

**Yatsu-Yuen Rose
Garden, Japan**
*At first glance, this rose
garden, in the Chiba
Prefecture near Tokyo,
could be in Europe or North
America, for there is no sign
of the traditional elements of
Japanese garden design. In
fact, roses are not much used
in traditional Japanese
gardens and are considered
rather 'Western' flowers.
Perhaps the most
remarkable features of this
garden are the vigour of the
bush roses and the close
planting of the standards.*

NO TWO PEOPLE would ever agree as to which are the most beautiful,
imaginative or historically interesting rose gardens in the world. Each
person will have his or her favourite, reflecting probably their own particular
enthusiasms within the world of roses. A complete list of all the gardens, large
and small, in every country would go on for ever, but in this chapter are listed
as many as can be fitted into a reasonable compass. The risk must be run of
offending those left out.

The listings are preceded by fuller descriptions of some of the most important gardens, many of them national collections of great historical interest.
In them can be seen practical examples of all the various ways of growing roses·
– and the roses themselves, of course, in all their matchless beauty and endless
variety. One must be grateful to the cities whose parks departments have
created many of them and keep them so meticulously, and to the various
organizations, a number of them voluntary, that run the others.

National or international rose competitions or *concours* take place in many of
the gardens each year, often in conjunction with a rose festival which attracts
thousands of visitors. Gold and other medals and awards are made to the best
roses; these are of value to the raisers in promoting new varieties and are
intended to serve as a guide to the public who may buy them. This they do,
but only up to a point, for the rules of judging vary enormously from garden
to garden and from country to country. Awards may be for the performance
of the roses when the appointed judges have gathered together on a single day
during the summer, or they may be for careful and detailed assessment of the
plants over a period of years.

There can be little doubt as to which of these two alternatives is of most value to a potential grower, but, in addition to this, the climate in which a garden is situated must play a big part. A gold medal in Madrid, California or the south of France may be given to a variety that would be a complete failure in the cooler, damper conditions of the British Isles, Holland or northern Germany. Awards from The Hague or the Royal National Rose Society would be a better guide there, and of course the converse applies. Awards based on prolonged trials at a number of centres, as is the case with the All-America Rose Selections, can obviously be more meaningful than single-centre assessments, but even they may not tell you the varieties that will do best in the particular climate and soil of your district. So, as I have emphasized many times, there is no substitute for going yourself to see the roses growing – preferably at various times during the season.

The descriptions and listings that follow span the world (though with an obvious bias towards the English-speaking parts of it), for I do not imagine that you will only want to visit rose gardens to see which varieties grow best in your own neighbourhood. It is always interesting, if you have the chance, to see how other people do things – and maybe to imagine how you might have done them differently.

AUSTRALIA

In spite of what I said above about the work of parks departments, unfortunately very few Australian civic bodies have seen fit to provide large-scale support to public rose gardens. The largest areas of formal rose plantings are generally to be found in the various cemeteries, especially the one at Springvale, Victoria. There are no trial grounds, as there is not yet any patent protection for raisers.

NEW SOUTH WALES
Nellie Melba Memorial Rose Garden, Sydney. Part of Sydney Botanical Gardens. At one time it had a slope with Climbers trained on low horizontal frames, but these have deteriorated.

QUEENSLAND
New Farm Rose Garden, near central Brisbane. Thousands of plants, mainly bush varieties. Attractive, unusual pergolas.

SOUTH AUSTRALIA
Veale Rose Garden, Adelaide. Beautiful formal garden. Massed planting of cluster-flowering varieties about a sunken garden with pools, lawns and paths.

TASMANIA
Hobart Botanical Gardens. Beds with massed plantings of separate varieties on a sloping site, making a wonderful sight when they are viewed down the slopes or up from the Derwent River.
Rose Society of Tasmania Garden, Ho-

bart. A pretty rose garden with timber arches and massed beds. It is still developing and expanding.

VICTORIA
Alistair Clark Memorial Rose Garden, St Kilda, near Melbourne. Established 1950 but not yet adequately developed.
Benalla Rose Garden, north of Melbourne. A beautiful rose garden on both sides of the Hume Highway. Mass plantings and pillars.
Royal Botanical Gardens, Melbourne. A new rose garden featuring species, old roses and modern varieties displaying the history of the rose.
Springvale Necropolis, east of Melbourne. A magnificent display, mainly of 75 cm (30 in) standards, many of them cluster-flowering varieties. 20,000 plants.
Victorian State Rose Garden, Werribee Park Estate, east of Melbourne. Still at the planning stage, this will eventually be the most spectacular rose garden in Australia. It is intended to include all types of settings, fountains and pergolas.

CANADA

Centennial Rose Garden, Burlington, Ontario

The Royal Botanical Gardens at Hamilton cover about 2,000 acres altogether, and administratively part of this vast complex (if one can use a rather prosaic word for such a beautiful creation) is the Centennial Rose Garden situated in Hendrix Park at Burlington, 10 miles away. It was created in 1967 to celebrate Canada's 100th anniversary of Confederation, and in it over 2,800 modern varieties are represented, plus about 450 shrub roses, all arranged according to their botanical classifications.

Though the main plantings are of modern bedding roses, among the old ones in three special beds are a fair representation of species and their hybrids, Damasks, Centifolias, Bourbons and Hybrid Perpetuals. There are some modern shrub roses, too. Around the periphery of the rose garden climbing and rambling roses grow on free-standing supports, and others are trained on wires along a pergola, which leads to a pavilion with a tiled pyramid roof. Clematis and other climbing plants can also be found there.

This is very much a working as well as a pleasure garden. New varieties are tested there for three years, particular attention being given to their hardiness in the cold Canadian winters. Hybrid Teas, Floribundas and Grandifloras all need winter protection, though many of the old roses have been found to be tougher. Experiments with different methods of cultivation for both these and the other kinds are carried out all the time.

Jackson Park Rose Test Gardens, Windsor, Ontario

These were established in 1967, like the rose garden at Burlington, to celebrate Canada's first 100 years. The garden is circular, laid out as a huge compass bowl, the points of entry being at the cardinal points: north, south, east and west. The beds fill each quadrant in the form of eight concentric rings with grass paths in between, and at the centre, mounted on a 7.5 m (24 ft) plinth, is a Lancaster bomber, a war memorial to the airmen of Windsor.

There are about 12,500 roses altogether – mainly Hybrid Teas and Floribundas – in something over 450 varieties. All are numbered, and a catalogue is available giving the names and numbers for quick reference. The outer perimeter of the circle features climbing roses on individual frames in the form of elongated inverted cones, interspersed with lighting standards so that the gardens can be enjoyed even after the sun goes down.

Evaluation of the roses is carried out annually by the Windsor chapter of the American Rose Society and unsatisfactory varieties replaced. Altogether about 20,000 rose bushes are planted throughout the whole of the Windsor parks system, and the city has formally adopted the title City of Roses.

BRITISH COLUMBIA
Butcharts Gardens, Victoria. Contains an English-style rose garden with many old roses as well as new.

ONTARIO
Centennial Rose Garden, Burlington – see full description above.
Dominion Arboretum and Botanic Gardens, Ottawa. Includes extensive display gardens of roses.

Jackson Park Rose Test Gardens, Windsor – see full description above.
Royal Horticultural Gardens, Niagara Falls. Many rose plantings will be found within this general garden.

QUEBEC
Connaught Park Rose Garden and Memorial Park Rose Garden, Montreal. Both include extensive plantings of Hybrid Teas and Floribundas.

FRANCE

La Roseraie de l'Hay-les-Roses, Paris

This is one of the two main rose gardens of Paris, though a third, the Jardin des Plantes, does offer many interesting roses, even if many of them are sadly mislabelled through lack of expert staff. The Roseraie de l'Hay is about three miles south of the French capital on a hill overlooking the valley of Brièvre and the Parc de Sceaux. Having been founded by a fanatical collector of old roses, Jules Gravereaux, in 1893, it can claim to be the oldest surviving roseraie in the world. By 1899 M Gravereaux had gathered together some 3,000 species and varieties.

Since his time, the garden's fortunes have waxed and waned, but it is now established once more as one of the finest rose gardens in the world. On entering, the eye is immediately mesmerized by the cascades of colour on the metal-framed arches that are such a feature. 'Paul's Scarlet' and 'Dr W. Van Fleet' seem to be everywhere, and from a central pathway other paths fan out, running under pergolas of yet more Ramblers and Climbers. More again are on pillars and tripods throughout the gardens.

Of particular interest are a number of special beds or groups of beds featuring among them a re-creation (as far as is possible) of the Empress Josephine's Malmaison collection, species roses, beds tracing the history of the rose from its earliest beginnings, roses from the Far East, and the other old rose groups – though of course Hybrid Teas and Floribundas have their place too. A rose museum completes the picture.

La Roseraie d'Orléans

The beautifully laid out 1½ acres of the rose garden at Orléans have a selection of 520 different rose varieties, made up of 5,600 Polyanthas and Floribundas, 3,250 Grandifloras (France, as well as the United States, being a country where this classification is used), 263 standards, including six weeping ones, 80 Miniature roses, and no less than 530 Climbers and Ramblers. The latter are wonderfully displayed on a large pergola, on trellis-work screens and on pylons, and are of particular interest because the district around Orléans was the birthplace of so many of them. Among other raisers working in the field, between 1900 and 1914 René Barbier used *R. wichuraiana* and its close relative *R. luciae*, which had been introduced from Japan, in the breeding of 'Albéric Barbier', 'François Juranville', 'Alexandre Girault', 'Léontine Gervais', 'Albertine' and 'Primevère', all of which can still be found in the garden, amongst a wealth of others.

These and the Polyanthas, many of which were also raised by nurserymen of the region, make this roseraie of special interest for anyone who is looking for a unique historical collection from the fairly short period they represent. A yearly rose *concours* for many kinds of roses – but with a special emphasis on Climbers with small and medium-sized flowers – is held in conjunction with the gardens, and awards are made to outstanding roses.

La Roseraie du Parc de Bagatelle, Paris

This is, most conveniently, set in the Bois de Boulogne, only two miles from the centre of Paris. In 1907 the municipality of the French capital purchased the estate of the Château de Bagatelle to preserve it as an open space, and it was

Parc de la Tête d'Or, France
The Floribunda 'Sarabande' is used to provide colour in this combination of water and statuary at the Parc de la Tête d'Or in Lyon. A new garden, opened in 1964, it is nevertheless sited in an area where rose breeders made history at the turn of the century.

A photograph of the Bagatelle rose garden appears on page 157.

then that the gardens were laid out by the director of the Paris parks, Jean Forestier, aided by the knowledge and experience of Jules Gravereaux, founder of the Roseraie de l'Hay.

Paved paths and carefully clipped box hedges surround the main plantings of Hybrid Teas and Floribundas, which include many grown as standards, while around the periphery are Climbers, Ramblers and many of the older varieties – Hybrid Perpetuals and Teas among them – and species. Though other gardens had established gold medal awards at an earlier date – 1883 in the case of the Royal National Rose Society in Britain – Bagatelle was the first to decide to give them purely on the performance of the roses under garden conditions and not for the pick of the blooms on a certain single day or when exhibited at a show.

La Roseraie du Parc de la Tête d'Or, Lyon

Lyon is an appropriate place for one of the world's finest rose gardens, for it was around this city at the end of the 19th century and the beginning of the 20th that so much of the history of our modern roses was made. The name of Pernet-Ducher alone should make it a place of pilgrimage for all rose lovers.

A photograph of the Tête d'Or rose garden appears overleaf.

It was not, however, until 1964 that the present gardens were opened on a fine site with tall trees as a background and bordered along one side by a wandering stream, over which there are a number of foot-bridges. A central pergola and fountain with surrounding statuary is complemented by two further pergolas to the east and west. Under these, with climbing roses scrambling up their Grecian columns, one may wander among the beds of Hybrid Teas and Floribundas, or else branch out over the lawns – being careful, for they are strict here, to follow the paths of stepping stones that are set into the grass!

At Lyon a *concours* is held annually for the selection of *La Plus Belle Rose de France*, which is restricted to French-raised varieties. It is a pity in a way that Lyon is so far south, for although some wonderful roses have been winners over the years, they rarely seem to do well or to make their mark in more northerly climates.

La Roseraie de Saverne, near Strasbourg

In its original form and location the garden was first planted in 1900, with a particularly fine display of Ramblers of the period on pergolas, arches and pylons, and such was its success that by 1904 it was decided that it must be enlarged. New roses were presented to it by, among others, the notable hybridist and nurseryman Peter Lambert, whose introductions figure in the early story of the Hybrid Musks. The garden continued to prosper, and then actually changed its nationality after the First World War, when Alsace was returned to France. In 1925, an international *concours* for new roses was instituted, with varieties sent to it in that first year from French, Belgian, Dutch and Portuguese raisers.

By 1962, it was realized that the soil in which the roses were planted had become exhausted, and the plants were suffering as a result. Complete replacement would have been a mammoth task, and it was decided that a new site should be chosen, and a suitable spot, that of the present gardens, was found to the north-east of Strasbourg. Today it contains something like 20,000 roses and examples of the latest introductions are added all the time – in the 1977–78 season, for instance, about 500 of them in 25 different varieties and about 20 new standards.

The setting is of pine and some deciduous trees, with gravelled paths between the lawns and beds of Hybrid Teas and Floribundas. Ramblers arch over the paths on metal supports, and ramble over a gazebo beside one of the formal ponds. Corinthian columns have been placed at strategic points.

La Roseraie de Schiltigheim, Strasbourg

The garden is situated on the outskirts of the city, and was created out of a plot of waste ground in 1926. It is maintained and cared for entirely by the 300 or so members of the Strasbourg society *Les Amis des Roses* – all amateurs – and their subscriptions to the society pay for most of the upkeep.

There are areas of grass, but most of the beds are divided one from another by broad gravel paths, edged with low-growing foliage plants. In them are displayed some 3,000 roses in about 160 varieties, with new award-winners added each year. On a pergola and numerous arches is a fine selection of Climbers, and great use is made of standard roses to give a variation in height to the central plantings of bedding Hybrid Teas and Floribundas.

June of each year sees the garden's festival of roses, enlivened and enriched by music, a pageant and other activities. Instruction on planting and pruning – and other rose-growing activities – is given at the appropriate times of year.

GERMAN DEMOCRATIC REPUBLIC (EAST GERMANY)

Sangerhausen Rosarium

First conceived by the nurseryman and breeder Peter Lambert in 1897 and opened in 1903, Sangerhausen Rosarium (which is about 50 miles west of Leipzig) is one of the oldest of the major rose gardens and can certainly claim, with some 6,500 different species and varieties growing there, to have the most comprehensive collection of old roses in the world. The idea behind it has always been to seek out and preserve those roses from the past which would otherwise have vanished, and many of the varieties to be found there cannot now be seen anywhere else. In the 31 acres of the gardens there are, for instance, over 100 varieties of Moss roses, about 400 different Hybrid Perpetuals, close on 140 individual Gallicas, and both the white and double pink forms of *R. rubrifolia*. The latter can be seen in a hedge of about 800 species and their near relatives, which runs along one side of the garden. Early Teas, Noisettes, Damasks, Albas and all the rest are fully represented elsewhere in the plantings.

The more modern parts of the garden – more land has had to be taken in from time to time – has been landscaped with informal beds among trees and other ornamental shrubs. But the low box hedges surrounding the geometric earlier plantings in the French manner, radiating out from a fountain, are still there. Multitudes of Climbers and Ramblers are displayed on tripods rather than pillars. Each summer there is a two-day festival, and on the more serious side a Rose Research Institute was opened at Sangerhausen in 1936.

GERMAN FEDERAL REPUBLIC (WEST GERMANY)

Insel Mainau, Lake Constance

This is unique in its setting on the island of Mainau in Lake Constance (Bodensee), and is complete with a 200-year-old Baroque castle. In Italian style, stone steps flanked by statuary lead down from a wide terrace to the rose garden, where gravelled paths and paved areas separate massed plantings of Hybrid Teas and Floribundas (in both bush and standard form), flanked by wooden pergolas for Climbers and Ramblers.

A photograph of the Insel Mainau rose garden appears on page 152.

Westfalenpark Deutsches Rosarium, Dortmund

When the original rosarium at Sangerhausen, now in East Germany, became difficult of access to those living in West Germany, the German Rose Society decided to create another one. For it they chose the city of Dortmund, which was already, through the work of an energetic and enterprising parks department, renowned as a city of roses, and work on the new gardens started in 1969. Westfalenpark occupies about 173 acres, of which, up to the present time, some 25 acres have been planted with roses.

The gardens are on a south-facing slope and are divided into areas representing each country in which rose breeders are at work. These are divided yet again into beds for each individual breeder, who is asked to send ten plants of each of his new varieties. Thus a complete range of his products, all carefully labelled, can be seen together and easily compared by visitors with those of his competitors, and their respective merits assessed. In the early 1970s additional beds were added to display the best roses in different colour groups, regardless of breeder, so that once again these could be compared.

Apart from these plantings of modern roses, there is a representative collection of species and other old roses, which were presented to the German Rose Society (whose headquarters this is) by Wilhelm Kordes and by friends of the society in England and Switzerland. Small greenhouses are used for those varieties, such as the old Climber 'Maréchal Niel', that are too tender to be grown out of doors.

Zweibrücken Rosarium

In a magnificent tree-fringed setting on the southern side of the city park, with a large ornamental lake nearby, is this wonderfully comprehensive collection of roses of every kind. All are there: species, Gallicas, Damasks, Centifolias, Moss roses and all the rest – Climbers, Ramblers, as well as modern Floribundas and Hybrid Teas, together with a large representation of French roses and of Miniatures. In 1964 the garden celebrated its first fifty years of existence, and nowadays there are about 60,000 roses in some 2,000 different varieties, the beds set in sweeping lawns or broad paved areas. Fountains and pools are everywhere.

Over the last few seasons the beauty of the roses has been greatly enhanced by the addition of many other carefully chosen plants to mingle with them. Before the first wild roses bloom in late April, spring flowers can be seen in profusion, and irises and lilies add their charm in May and later. This is, without doubt, one of the loveliest gardens in Europe.

Zweibrücken Rosarium, West Germany
This view of Zweibrücken Rosarium, West Germany, shows the lake which is such a feature of the setting. Of all the European rose gardens, this makes the finest use of both still and moving water. The rosarium is about 20 miles east of Saarbrücken. See also the photograph on page 160.

HOLLAND

Westbroekpark, The Hague

First laid out in the 1920s, this is situated between The Hague and the seaside town of Scheveningen. It is a 50-acre public park, and the rose beds were only planted in 1961. Some 60,000 roses can be seen in bloom at the height of their flowering season, set in a glade of cool green lawns where people can wander at leisure, pausing when they feel like it in the shade of long-established trees to reflect that Holland is not just a land of bulb fields. The municipal parks department, which runs the gardens, regards them as a permanent rose show.

Separated from the main gardens, and not open to the general public, are the International Trial Grounds. Gold medals and the Golden Rose of The Hague award are given to outstanding new varieties, which are inspected regularly. There is a second competition also for established varieties, which is held in June or July each year. This embraces Hybrid Teas, Floribundas, shrub and Miniature roses and those with the greatest fragrance, and is judged on one day only by an international jury made up of both amateur and professional rosarians. It is, however, the beds of Hybrid Teas and Floribundas in the park that most visitors come to see.

There is another very extensive display and test garden in Holland at the Agricultural Institute at Wageningen, near Arnhem. Amstelpark, Amsterdam, is a fine park of about 9½ acres containing a rose garden that has (among other roses) something like 120 species. For earlier colour there is an iris garden and a rhododendron valley.

ITALY

The Rose Garden of Rome

The original rosarium was in the ruins of the Emperor Nero's palace, the Domus Aurea, but it was partially destroyed in the Second World War. When restoration work was considered, it was realized that the site would not be large enough to allow for possible future expansion, and a new one was chosen on the Via di Valle Murcia, backed by the Palatine Hill, one of the seven hills on which Rome was founded.

As with so many of the national gardens, the main layout is a huge half-circle, though in the Roman context one tends to think of it as an amphitheatre, a parallel given greater weight by the fact that the ground rises slightly towards the back, with ruins and pine trees beyond. Along a perimeter path can be found 200 different climbing and rambling roses and in front of them species and other old types, so that together they ring the main central plantings of Hybrid Teas and Floribundas. There are something like 1,000 varieties in all.

The trial or competition grounds are in a separate plot, and the pre-war practice of making awards only to Italian-raised roses was abolished in 1953. Gold medals are now given each year for the best Hybrid Tea and the best Floribunda, regardless of the country of origin.

Another Italian rose garden that is well worth a visit is farther north, in Lombardy – the garden of Villa Reale at Monza.

NEW ZEALAND

New Zealand National Rose Society Trial Ground, Palmerston North
Opened in 1969 and centrally situated (and thus accessible from most parts of the country), the Palmerston North trial grounds are the first to be established in the Southern Hemisphere. Though under the auspices of the New Zealand Rose Society, the gardens are looked after by the city parks department, and are in fact formed from a section of a park of nearly 50 acres, the Esplanade. Six bushes of each new seedling variety from both professional and amateur breeders are submitted for the two-year trials, except in the case of Climbers, when three plants are considered sufficient. Something like 100 varieties take part in each trial.

As is inevitable in what is primarily a trial ground, there is a certain formality in the layout, but close by are the lovely Dugald Mackenzie Rose Gardens, also part of the Esplanade. Here what most strikes the visitor from overseas – as it does in Madrid – is the size to which the roses grow. 1.5–1.8 m (5–6 ft) and almost as much across is nothing out of the ordinary for a well-grown Hybrid Tea, and ones that are tall in any climate, such as the crimson 'Uncle Walter', are rampant climbers. If left to themselves, four or five flushes of bloom are usual, over a flowering period that lasts from October to May. With so short a period of dormancy, summer pruning is often practised – as it is by many New Zealand gardeners – simply to give the bushes a rest and a chance to build up to an autumn display that can only be described as spectacular.

Lady Norwood Rose Gardens, Wellington. Forming part of the Botanic Gardens, a flat area in what is basically a sloping site, the focal point of the rose gardens is a fountain and pool. From this, four wide paths radiate outwards to where a fine display of Climbers on wooden pergolas and brick colonnades forms the outer perimeter.

A total of some 3,600 Hybrid Teas and Floribundas, some grown as standards, are displayed in beds of varying shapes and sizes, set in large grassy areas between the paths. There is, in addition, a trial ground for new varieties, and in the annual Rose Week the garden is floodlit.

Mona Vale, Christchurch. The only important rose garden in the South Island, this is comparatively small and in it is set a house in the Edwardian style. There are about 400 roses, ranging from species through the latest Hybrid Teas and Floribundas to Miniatures. Trial beds in the garden are maintained by the Canterbury Rose Society.

Parnell Rose Garden, Auckland. Established in 1934, this garden of 14 acres has some 4,500 roses in 400 different varieties, including a good selection of recently-introduced Hybrid Teas and Floribundas and a small selection of old roses.

Rogers Rose Garden, Hamilton. This garden was named after Dr Denis Rogers, one-time mayor of Hamilton and president of the Rose Society, and was established in 1971 in time for the World Convention of Rose Societies, which took place in New Zealand that year. It occupies an attractive 3½-acre site on the east bank of the Waikato River, where 3,500 roses are planted in irregularly-shaped beds, backed by native trees and shrubs – deliberate informality in planning that breaks away from the traditional Victorian concept of a rose garden.

Sloping down from a main highway, great splashes of strong colour can be seen by passing motorists. There are many popular varieties, a trial ground, and a bed of old roses transplanted from old-established pioneer homesteads. The setting and layout make it one of New Zealand's loveliest rose gardens.

Te Awamutu Rose Garden. This garden is situated not far to the south of the city of Hamilton and, though by no means large, has earned a reputation for the high quality of its roses since its beginnings in 1969. Administered by the local authority, it was created by a community effort.

The circular garden has a central fountain featuring sculptured stainless steel birds in flight, and surrounding it are about 2,500 Hybrid Teas, Floribundas and Grandifloras, which thrive in what are ideal climatic and soil conditions. Modern varieties from hybridists the world over are represented, and provide visitors with a blaze of colour from the beginning of the flowering season early in November until the end of May.

SOUTH AFRICA

The Municipal Rose Gardens, Cape Town

This is, in fact, two gardens, the upper main planting and the smaller lower garden. The former is laid out in a square, with paths running concentrically within it between the beds and others radiating out from the centre. Refreshingly different, the focal point in the middle is not a pool or fountain, but the all-too-rarely-seen pink shrub rose or semi-climber 'Clair Matin', which is a real beauty. Each of the surrounding 20 beds contains one variety of Hybrid Tea, with an emphasis on scented varieties. Separated a little outside the square are two long beds of 'Super Star'.

The main garden was planted in 1937, but the lower one goes back to 1893. Basically a circle, but with an additional path looping out below it, it contains Floribundas. A number of these, such as 'Impala', 'Kalinka', 'Florian' and 'Minuetto', are not so familiar north of the Equator. The invaluable if ubiquitous 'Iceberg' does, however, form the centre-piece.

There is a large rose garden, with an impressive design, at Johannesburg Botanic Gardens, but the roses here were sadly not in good condition when last seen. Let us hope that they have been improved by the time this book appears. Jamieson Park in Durban and Princes Park in Pretoria are also worth a visit by any rose lover.

SPAIN

Rosaleda del Parque de Oeste, Madrid

Those who do not vote for Geneva (see below) as the loveliest rose garden might well choose this one instead, but it must be said that its climate gives it an edge over many others. Though much watering has to be done to take full advantage of it, 'Paul's Scarlet Climber' will reach 6m (20ft) and more in height and 'Climbing Peace' will be smothered in bloom – just two examples of what many a more northern grower must envy. In (relatively) gloomy England, my 'Climbing Peace' produced just one bloom in five years.

The Madrid garden itself is fan-shaped or semicircular, with a backcloth of dark green conifers, and one enters at the pivot of the fan up wide steps flanked by cypress trees. Ahead is the central path, with a fountain marking its mid-point and another beyond it, inside the perimeter of the circle. Behind this is a group of statuary. A grass bank planted with terraced beds of Floribundas is topped by a long, curved, iron-framed pergola, which becomes a tunnel of scent and colour in summer. Below, in the body of the garden, are the beds of Hybrid Teas and Floribundas from all countries of the world, interspersed with standards of incredible size and with pillar roses. As might be expected in the land that gave birth to Pedro Dot, Miniature roses figure prominently, and all varieties are clearly labelled to help the visitor. Madrid is the scene of yet another international competition for new roses.

To the south, in Seville, the 7-acre Parque de los Principes de España has a bed featuring varieties raised by the Spanish breeders Pedro Dot and Cipriano Comprubi. It is surrounded by a pergola of climbing roses and circular beds of Hybrid Teas and Floribundas.

Pillar roses in Portugal
Pillar roses are used to remarkable effect in this private garden at Sintra, near Lisbon. The use of one variety only on this long rose-walk is unusual and certainly successful.

SWITZERLAND

La Roseraie du Parc de la Grange, Geneva

This would, without doubt, receive many votes as the most beautiful rose garden in Europe. It is approached over the lawns of the breathtaking, mile-long Quai Gustave Ader on the banks of Lake Geneva, which is planted along its entire length with bush and standard roses in carefully blended colours. This dates from 1936 and the rose garden itself, in the Parc de la Grange, from 1945.

Laid out on three levels, one can look down over the whole panorama, which is floodlit at night during the summer, from a pergola and stone patio at the top. Immediately below are Rambler-covered grey stone walls, and an ornamental pool and fountain add to the peace of the scene. The lower level is planted in the main with floribundas, the line of the beds being broken with Ramblers on pylons and weeping standards. 'Paul's Scarlet Climber', 'Albertine' and 'Golden Rambler' are much in evidence. On the upper terraces are Hybrid Teas and once again standards and weeping standards. One finds that many of the varieties from many countries are sadly no longer in commerce, for the parks department does its own budding, thus keeping many very lovely roses of the past in being.

The garden nurseries (not open to the public) are the setting for the annual *Concours International des Roses Nouvelles de Genève*, attended by an international panel of rose judges. This is the climax to the Geneva Rose Week, during which, in the floodlit park, ballet is performed in the open air – a setting for it that is pure fairyland.

The Parc de la Grange rose garden is shown in the photograph on page 189.

UNITED KINGDOM

City of Belfast Rose Trial Gardens

The setting of these gardens is the beautiful 130-acre Sir Thomas and Lady Dixon Park, just outside the city. This was once the private estate of the late Sir Thomas and was presented by his wife to the Belfast corporation. When the Rose Society of Northern Ireland was founded in 1964, the idea for the trial gardens – first mooted by Sam McGredy in 1960 – became a reality through the co-operation of the other great Ulster nursery firm of Dickson, the Northern Ireland Ministry of Agriculture, the Belfast City Council and the Rose Society itself. The first planting took place in the winter of 1964, and since that time awards have been made to new roses by a specially invited international panel of judges, including gold medals and the Uladh Award for fragrance. Belfast Rose Week coincides with the judging, and ties in with the society's summer show, so it is quite an occasion.

The rose gardens, on a gentle slope, cover 11 acres and contain over 20,000 roses, but they are not devoted only to the roses on trial. Past award winners and other popular Hybrid Teas and Floribundas can be found in large display beds surrounding the trial area, set off by plantings of trees and shrubs. The formal entrance to the gardens is via a recently constructed patio, on both sides of which are planted shrub roses, and it is intended to increase the collection of these. Climbers feature on a circular structure of wire on timber uprights.

The Royal National Rose Society Garden, England
This general view of part of the RNRS gardens at St Albans shows bedding Hybrid Teas and the pergola in the background. The Polyantha-type Rambler sport 'The Fairy' borders the pool.
See also the photographs on pages 175 and 193.

Mottisfont Abbey, Hampshire

The abbey lies in the wooded valley of the River Test, near Romsey. Though parts of the mellow building date back to the 13th century, the rose garden is very new. Here are extracts from a letter which appeared in *The Observer* newspaper in November 1972: 'The National Trust is in the process of establishing a national collection of these [old] roses of all varieties. The Winchester Centre of the Trust has undertaken to pay for these roses and I invite your readers . . . to assist us. Roses may be sponsored at £1 per rose.' Over £1,000 was subscribed, and under the direction of Graham Thomas, then gardens adviser to the National Trust, planting within the confines of an enormous square walled garden was begun in the winter of 1972–73.

The garden, now almost fully established, shows the history of the rose up to the end of the 19th century. Species are confined to the wide perimeter beds, and though quite limited in range, include many Burnets and *R. foetida* and its two sports. There are many other roses in these outside beds, too, including a range of Rugosas, while old Ramblers and Climbers cover the walls.

The centre of the garden is laid out symmetrically, with large borders surrounded by low box hedges and divided by a central walk and paths of gravel or grass; there is an ornamental pond in the middle. Old apple trees dotted here and there give support to the more rampant of the Bourbons, and Albas, Damasks, Hybrid Perpetuals, Gallicas and China roses make up the bulk of the collection.

Queen Mary's Rose Garden, Regent's Park, London

Dating from 1931, this is London's rose garden, only a few minutes' walk from Baker Street station on the London Underground. It was never planned to be a comprehensive collection, and though there are some shrub roses – particularly modern ones – and some Ramblers and Climbers, emphasis is on display beds of Hybrid Teas and Floribundas, old varieties being replaced by new periodically. The intention is to publicize British-grown roses.

Entering by the gate close to the restaurant and turning left, one passes on the right a series of long beds of Floribundas and Hybrid Teas, closely planted and one variety to a bed. In the background, across a wide stretch of grass, are shrub roses, particularly varieties of the Moyesii group. The path continues past more beds along the side of the lake until, at a slightly higher level, the garden's focal point is reached. Here, from a central round bed, others radiate out concentrically, with the lake below them on one side. Near the circumference of the circle is a ring of wooden pillars about 3 m (10 ft) high; growing up these, and trained along the ropes looped between them, are an assortment of Ramblers, *R. longicuspis, R. filipes* 'Kiftsgate' and 'Silver Moon' among them. More shrub roses hide behind the railings that border the road and screen from outside this vast circle of bedding roses.

If you leave the gardens by the nearby gate and turn left, there is a considerable planting of species behind the railings there, but they are so overshadowed by the trees as to be far from what they should be. Much more rewarding is to turn left inside the gardens and, keeping to the right, take the winding path where herbaceous plants are intermingled with shrub roses (including a quite enormous 'Complicata'). At the end one emerges near an ornamental fountain, with a broad walk lined with beds of Hybrid Teas and Floribundas leading back towards the lake.

The Royal National Rose Society Garden, St Albans

The RNRS gardens are shown in the photograph on page 221.

This, the headquarters of the society, is on the face of it an unpromising site, high up and exposed to all the winds that blow, and completely flat. All of this emphasizes the skill with which these disadvantages have been overcome. The clever use of screening evergreen trees, through which the old white Ramblers scramble, of plantings of tall shrub roses, pillars and arches, and above all of the long, brick-pillared pergola leading in a half-circle away from the round ornamental pond with its fountain – these are examples without parallel of how a level garden can be given height and interest. The glory of the pergola, smothered in bloom just after midsummer, has to be seen to be believed.

The main idea of the garden is to display for both members of the society and the public a representative selection of every type of rose, and to show how to grow them at their best. There are close on 1,000 kinds in the display gardens. Among the species, the Burnet roses, the Cinnamomeae and those of the New World are particularly well represented. There is a fine collection of shrub roses both old and new, a large number of them around the perimeter of the garden, but also in an area specially devoted to them. Beds cut in the lawns show the best and the newest of Hybrid Teas and Floribundas, and in a small sunken garden a wide selection of Miniatures are grown on low terraces.

Of great interest to visitors are the trial grounds for assessing new roses for possible awards. Unlike those of most other world rose gardens, the public can wander along the beds to inspect them and make their own judgements. Top award is the President's International Trophy, which is only given to a really outstanding variety and is by no means awarded every year; a rose must have already won a gold medal from the society in order to qualify.

Sissinghurst Castle, Kent

Situated in the heart of the countryside, the garden of Sissinghurst was the creation of the well-known gardening writer the late Vita Sackville-West and her husband Sir Harold Nicolson. It is now managed by the National Trust.

Though large for what was once a private garden, one does not – except from certain viewpoints – have an impression of great size, for it is divided into a series of smaller units. These are separated by either walls or hedges, and each has its own theme. It is not a garden of roses only – though there are large numbers of them – but it is included here as a marvellous example of how they, particularly the older ones and the Climbers and Ramblers, can and should be fitted into their setting and used with other plants.

One part of the garden does form a rose garden as such, on the mellowed brick walls of which is a fine old specimen of the deep red 'Climbing Etoile de Hollande' and the tender, clematis-flowered 'Anemonoides' among a number of others. The old, single-flowered Hybrid Tea 'Mrs Foley Hobbs' is one of the more rarely seen of the other roses at Sissinghurst, and the robust and hardy Hybrid Perpetual 'Ulrich Brunner' is pegged down in exemplary fashion, consorting well – if a little surprisingly – with the nearby 'Golden Wings' and *R. rugosa alba*.

Elsewhere too, roses – carefully blended into their surroundings – catch the eye wherever one turns. The vivid red 'Allen Chandler' grows all of 6 m (20 ft) up the main brick tower, from which one can look out over the whole panorama. 'Nevada' adds the glory of its huge creamy flowers to the White Garden, 'Harison's Yellow' to the Spring Garden.

223

Wisley Garden, Surrey

Wisley is just off the A3 trunk road between Esher and Guildford, about 25 miles from London. It is the country garden of the Royal Horticultural Society, and as such one can see there every kind of tree, shrub and plant imaginable in a lovely wooded setting. Although it is not primarily a rose garden, roses are particularly well represented.

For many years Hybrid Teas and Floribundas have been grown in huge beds, one row on either side of a broad grass walk leading up to the Pavilion on Battleston Hill, with Climbers and Ramblers on pillars linked by ropes behind them, forming a second double row. More recently, in a less exposed spot in a dip below and sheltered by tall hedges, two complete new rose gardens have been added. One is of the very latest Hybrid Teas and Floribundas in fairly small groupings, the other of shrub roses both old and new, intermingled with herbaceous plants. It is here that the unique hedge of Hybrid Musks and Sweet Briar hybrids trained on wires between wooden uprights can be found.

Shrub and other roses are also used in many other parts of the garden. There is quite a substantial collection of old roses on top of the hill beyond the Pavilion, and more from all periods in the walled gardens between the Alpine meadow and the house. On the edge of the meadow, too, one of the Far Eastern Musk ramblers goes 12 m (40 ft) or more up and over several trees, smothering them in cascades of white blossom late in the summer.

Apart from the most important rose gardens described above, there are countless gardens open to the public in Britain in which roses can be seen as part of a mixed planting or on their own in rose gardens of varying size and interest. In fact, few gardens can be found that do not have some roses, but I have tried to pick out a number of the best in which they are a main feature, or else where there are special collections either of old or new roses, or of both. These are listed below. Some of these gardens are privately owned, and not all are open to the public every day. The times of opening of others may change periodically, so it is as well to check in advance that you will be able to get in before setting out to see them.

ANTRIM
City of Belfast Rose Trial Gardens – see full description above.

BERKSHIRE
Orchard Cottage, Cookham. 500 bush roses but excluding Climbers and shrub roses.
Savill Garden, Windsor Great Park, nr Egham. Extensive beds of Hybrid Teas, Floribundas and modern shrub roses. Some species.
Shinfield Grange, Shinfield. University of Reading Department of Agriculture gardens, including a rose garden.

BUCKINGHAMSHIRE
Cliveden, nr Maidenhead. National Trust. Roses old and new in a woodland setting and a fine display of tree-climbing Ramblers. Much else of interest in large garden.
Steart Hill, Mursley. Large collection of old and new roses.

CAMBRIDGESHIRE
Anglesey Abbey, Lode. National Trust. Beds of the finest modern Hybrid Teas.

CHESHIRE
Milnegate, Castle Hill, Prestbury. A collection of old and modern shrub roses.

CLEVELAND
Borough Park, Redcar. Display garden of RNRS award-winning varieties.

CUMBRIA
Holker Hall, Grange-over-Sands. A garden associated with Joseph Paxton, including a rose garden.

DERBYSHIRE
High Peak Garden Centre, Bamford. Exhibition garden with over 8,000 roses. Rose shows each weekend in summer.
210 Nottingham Road, Langley Mill. Col-

Roses in a cottage garden
Roses are not just for the gardens of large country houses and mansions. Here, at Jordans Cottage in Kent, a colourful mixture of bedding roses and Climbers shows what can be done on quite a small scale.

lections of both old and modern shrub roses and Climbers.

DEVON
Combe Head, Bampton. A collection of shrubs, trees, climbers and rose species.
Rosemoor Garden Charitable Trust, Torrington. Species and old roses.

DORSET
Kingston Russell House, Long Bredy. A large collection of shrub roses and a ¼-mile rose walk.

DOWN
Mount Stewart, Strangford Lough. National Trust. A mixture of roses old and new, blended with other plantings.
Rowallane Garden, Saintfield. National Trust. Old French roses in a walled garden and other shrub roses and Ramblers.

ESSEX
Evelyns, Little Easton. Floribundas, shrub roses and old Climbers and Ramblers.

GLAMORGAN, SOUTH
The Clock House, Llandaff. A collection of old shrub and species roses.
Roath Park, Cardiff. Display garden of the RNRS award-winning varieties and some old roses.

GLOUCESTERSHIRE
Hidcote Manor Gardens, Chipping Campden. National Trust. A fine collection of old French roses and examples of most other groups, together with various Climbers and Ramblers.
Kiftsgate Court, Chipping Campden. A fine display of old and some new roses, blended with other plants.

GRAMPIAN
Aberdeen. Not a rose garden as such, but the City of Roses, with bedding roses planted everywhere throughout the city.

GWYNEDD
Bodnant Garden, Conwy. National Trust. Terraced beds of Hybrid Teas and Floribundas, with some old roses and Climbers and Ramblers.
Brynhyfryd, Corris. Species and other shrub roses.

HAMPSHIRE
Hillier's Nursery and Arboretum, Winchester and Romsey. Large display gardens with old and new roses. A fine species collection.
Hurst Hill, Petersfield. Shrub and climbing roses.
Jenkyn Place, Bentley. A collection of old and species roses.

Mottisfont Abbey – see full description above.

HERTFORDSHIRE
Capel Manor Institute of Horticulture, Waltham Cross. A large collection of old and species roses.
R. Harkness and Co Ltd, Hitchin. Large nursery display garden of old and new varieties of all kinds.
The Royal National Rose Society Garden, St Albans – see full description above.

KENT
Goodnestone Park, Wingham. A collection of old roses.
Hush Heath Manor, Goudhurst. Old roses and Climbers growing up trees.
Sissinghurst Castle – see full description above.
The Old Rectory, Aldon. Principally old roses.

LANCASHIRE
Ravenhurst, Heaton. Italian-style garden with two rose gardens.
Windle Hall, nr St Helens. Rose garden of exhibition blooms.

LEICESTERSHIRE
Long Close, Woodhouse Eaves, south of Loughborough. A five-acre garden with many old shrub roses.
Prestwold Hall, Loughborough. Terraced lawns with large rose garden.

LINCOLNSHIRE
Gunby Hall, Burgh-le-Marsh. National Trust. Many old roses, Hybrid Musks, single Hybrid Teas, Climbers and Ramblers.
Springfields Gardens, Spalding. Large display gardens of the British Association of Rose Breeders.

LONDON
Queen Mary's Rose Garden, Regent's Park – see full description above.
Royal Botanic Gardens, Kew. Roses of every kind, bedding and in mixed plantings spread throughout the gardens.
Syon Park, Hounslow. A large display garden in conjunction with a garden centre, combining old and new rose plantings.

LOTHIAN
Saughton Park, Edinburgh. Display garden of RNRS award-winning varieties.

MANCHESTER
Edgewood, Blackrod. Display beds with many old scented varieties.

MERSEYSIDE
Rotten Row, Southport. Display garden of RNRS award-winning varieties.

NORFOLK

Alby Hall, Erpingham. Over 100 different varieties of shrub and species roses.

Heigham Park, Norwich. Display garden of RNRS award-winning varieties.

Holkham Hall, Wells-next-the-Sea. A large, formal 19th-century terraced garden with Polyantha roses.

NORTHUMBERLAND

Wallington, Morpeth. National Trust. Mixed plantings of roses, old and new, together with some species.

NOTTINGHAMSHIRE

R. Gregory and Sons Ltd, Nottingham. A large nursery display garden with many modern varieties.

The Arboretum, Nottingham. Display garden of RNRS award-winning varieties.

OXFORDSHIRE

Buscot Park, nr Lechlade. National Trust. Beds of Hybrid Teas and a collection of Hybrid Musks.

Greys Court, Rotherfield Greys, north-west of Henley. National Trust. A walled garden of old roses, with other shrub roses – ancient and modern – to be found elsewhere in the gardens.

Haseley Court and Coach House, Little Haseley. Roses of many kinds a special feature.

Kiddington Hall, Woodstock. A terraced rose garden designed by Sir Charles Barrie.

Langford Gardens, between Lechlade and Burford. Gardens of the village make a special feature of roses.

John Mattock and Co Ltd, Nuneham Courtney. A large nursery display garden of old and new roses.

Old Parsonage, Buscot. Walled gardens with old and rambling roses.

Pusey House, Faringdon. A large collection of mixed shrubs and roses.

The Old House, Wheatley. A Floribunda rose garden.

POWYS

Powys Castle, Welshpool. National Trust Terraced beds of Floribundas and Hybrid Musks. Some other shrub roses and old Climbers.

SHROPSHIRE

David Austin Roses, Albrighton. Nursery display garden with over 500 varieties. Extensive collection of old and species roses.

SOMERSET

Montacute House, Yeovil. National Trust. A fine border of various old shrub roses.

Tintinhull, Yeovil. National Trust. Old shrub roses, Climbers and Ramblers, blended into other plantings.

STAFFORDSHIRE

Moseley Old Hall, Fordhouses, nr Wolverhampton. National Trust. A fine display of old roses and species in a reconstruction of a 17th-century garden.

Shugborough, Milford. National Trust. Terraced beds of Floribundas and a rose garden in muted colours (bush roses and standards), with arches and pillars supporting Ramblers and Climbers.

STRATHCLYDE

Pollok Park, Glasgow. Display garden of RNRS award-winning varieties.

SUFFOLK

Ickworth, Horringer. National Trust. Displays of Floribundas, Climbers and Old Ramblers.

Lime Kiln, Claydon. The emphasis is on the roses of the Edwardian and Victorian periods, but there are other varieties as well.

SURREY

Polesden Lacey, Dorking. National Trust. Both old and new roses, Climbers and Ramblers in walled gardens with pergolas.

South Park Farm, South Godstone. A 17th-century farmhouse with a garden containing old roses.

Wisley Garden – see full description above.

SUSSEX, WEST

Charleston Manor, West Dean. A fine collection of old shrub and climbing roses on iron tripods in the French manner.

Nymans, Handcross. National Trust. A first-rate collection of all the old rose families, with Ramblers and Climbers up trees.

Tower House, Crawley Down. Mainly old roses and foliage plants.

WARWICKSHIRE

Alscot Park, Stratford-upon-Avon. Species and shrub roses.

WEST MIDLANDS

Wightwick Manor, Wolverhampton. National Trust. Mixed roses of all sorts.

WILTSHIRE

Kellaways, Chippenham. A large collection of old roses.

Sheldon Manor, Chippenham. Roses of all kinds.

YORKSHIRE, NORTH

Bewerley House, Bewerley. Old-fashioned and species roses.

Castle Howard, York. Two large walled gardens, one of old roses and one of the latest varieties, in extensive grounds.

Harlow Car, Harrogate. The gardens of the Northern Horticultural Society and display garden of RNRS award-winning varieties.

UNITED STATES

American Rose Center, Shreveport, Louisiana

The American Rose Center had its beginnings in 1969 when the American Rose Society decided to move its offices from Columbus, Ohio, to a new location where it would own its land and buildings and completely control its demonstration and research gardens. Shreveport was selected as the most desirable location, largely because it was in an area where all types of roses, tender and hardy, could be grown. In 1970 a 118-acre plot of land was given for the Center, and by 1974 the first phase of the building programme had been completed. The headquarters building was landscaped with roses and a cascading fountain, and the Windsounds Carillon Tower completed, to form the central feature of the entire development. Lakes, walks and parking areas were constructed, and to date some 36 individual rose gardens have been completed.

The plan for the Center has not been to show great masses of roses, but rather to present many different types of garden designs and arrangements, so that visitors, as they walk from one section to another, may get ideas which might be used on their own property. There are areas where masses of roses arranged for colour effects can be seen, but in most cases the emphasis is on the tasteful use of different kinds of roses in many different types of situation. Gradually a research programme is developing, and several companies are using the facilities for testing new fertilizers and pesticides, as well as carrying out experiments in general cultural improvement. A test garden for miniature roses is maintained and also a testing programme for roses originated by amateur hybridizers. Another feature is a memorial garden, and development of the 118 acres continues.

Elizabeth Park Rose Gardens, West Hartford, Connecticut

The first major public rose garden in the United States, this occupies 1¼ acres of the main public park, and is in the form of a large square with a mound in the centre surmounted by a large pavilion. Initially planted in 1904, the garden still contains a large number of the roses that were at the height of their popularity at that time, many of them long since vanished from commerce.

Around the perimeter and along paths elsewhere, festooning numerous arches, are a marvellous selection of early Climbers and Ramblers (including the Walsh introductions). Associating with them in the 200 or so beds, and on the mound of the pavilion itself, is a collection of Polyanthas and early Floribundas – which, at the time of their introduction, would have been known as Hybrid Polyanthas. When the garden was created, the Hybrid Teas had not yet completely ousted the old Hybrid Perpetuals, and quite a number of these, surviving from the original planting, can still be seen. However, this has always been a test garden for new introductions from all over the world, though now it relies largely on the new roses offered by American nurserymen and breeders.

The region is not especially favourable for roses because of the severe winters, and it is always necessary to provide good winter protection. Even so the plants are usually killed back to near ground level. For more than 75 years, however, this garden has provided much information on the care of roses in the north-eastern states.

Climbers on a New England house
It is not only ideas for garden design on the grand scale that travel long distances, as will be seen by a comparison of this view of climbing roses on the walls of a Cape Cod house, in Massachusetts, with the photograph on page 225.

Hershey Rose Garden and Arboretum, Hershey, Pennsylvania

Twenty-three acres of beauty well describes the Hershey gardens, for they are laid out with great imagination and with something to see in practically every month of the year. In addition to the roses, they contain collections of daffodils and other bulbs, magnolias, flowering cherries, and rhododendrons and azaleas for early colour, and chrysanthemums and Japanese maples and many other trees and shrubs for the time when the roses are past their best.

Strolling through the gardens from the picnic area, one first leaves the main path opposite Swan Lake to admire 6,000 or so bedding roses in the terraced rose garden with its double Italian colonnade. Opposite this, just beyond the lake, are Climbers and Ramblers in all their variety, and leading on from them along the path is the All-American Rose Avenue, where the latest selections are displayed. At the far end, turning right, one moves into the past, for here are planted some 400 different kinds of old roses. Hybrid Perpetuals, Moss roses, Albas, Damasks – all are there to be examined and admired. The rest of the gardens lie beyond, but at this point a rose fanatic would retrace his steps for a second look and to see what he had missed.

The construction of the present rose garden began in 1936, and it was intended that it should be a formal one of moderate size, but over the years it has expanded and developed. An area, surrounded by a picket fence and with box-edged rose beds, commemorates the original garden which the Hersheys planted around their home in 1908 and which was the nucleus from which the whole project grew (though it is not now in its original location). The gardens do contain, however, the crimson Hybrid Tea 'M. S. Hershey', raised in 1941 from a cross between a seedling and 'E. G. Hill'.

Huntingdon Botanical Gardens, San Marino, California

The special claim these gardens have for the rose lover is that they contain the largest collection of Tea roses in the United States, which means probably one of the largest collections of them anywhere. The San Marino climate does, of course, favour this far-from-hardy group, so that they thrive in the open, but there are many other rose groups represented as well.

However, the rose planting occupies only a comparatively small section of the grounds of what is basically an educational institution with a fine library and art gallery, with a number of specialized gardens as its setting. Apart from the roses, there is a Jungle Garden, a Shakespearian Garden, Australian and Japanese Gardens, a herb garden, a camellia collection, one of the most extensive collections of cacti and succulents in the world, and a number of others. Nevertheless, the rose is gaining ground, for a Rose History Walk is being developed, along which there will be over 1,000 species and varieties. Old rose symposiums are held at the gardens.

International Rose Test Garden, Washington Park, Portland, Oregon

Established in 1917 on a sloping site with a panoramic view over the city of Portland and Mount Hood, this is one of the finest – and one of the oldest – rose test gardens in the world. Each year, roses arrive from breeders in the United States and many other countries to be assessed, but such is the beauty of the setting and design that one can easily forget its true purpose.

The garden, of four acres, covers three wide terraces, divided from each other by long beds of Floribundas. Each terrace has distinct areas with its own speciality, and one might start, on the upper terrace, with the Royal Rosarium Gardens, a formal planting with many of the varieties going back forty years to the time when it was first laid out. In the Beach Memorial Fountain Gardens, mixed Hybrid Teas, Floribundas and Grandifloras surround a stainless steel fountain, and moving on from this the Upper Display Garden is reached, where there are 92 beds containing 18 bushes each, with Hybrid Teas predominating.

The Gold Medal Award Garden is on the central terrace, and here can be found those varieties that have exceeded all others in their performance in the Oregon climate over the years. Nearby is the McGredy Rose Garden – 17 beds of roses from this one breeder – with his latest varieties added yearly. Beyond this again is the extensive All-America Rose Selection Test Garden, with part of it set aside for sample plantings of former winners. Climbing roses form the framework in which these beds are set.

The Lower Display Garden contains 40 beds, each with a different variety, and in 1978 a new Miniature rose test garden was added to the trial area, the plants being grown in raised boxes so that they can be examined more easily.

Park of Roses, Whetstone Park, Columbus, Ohio

In these gardens, members of the Columbus Rose Club co-operate with the staff of the park in planting, growing and testing new roses in many different ways in what used to be the headquarters of the American Rose Society. In an area of 13½ acres, the rose gardens contain some 30,000 bushes in 200 varieties, and while the main plantings are of bedding roses – Floribundas, Hybrid Teas and the like – there is also a collection of old roses, so that all kinds are represented. A central feature is the Fountain of Roses, and there are many climbers growing on substantial wooden pergolas.

At the end of the garden farthest from the entrance, there is an AARS display garden. Planting, pruning and spraying demonstrations are carried out as part of the rose culture programme. A Rose Pavilion where concerts and other events are held, a collection of flowering crab apple trees, and a bird sanctuary are some of the other attractions for visitors.

Tyler Municipal Rose Garden, Tyler, Texas

More than half the roses produced in the United States come from east Texas, and most of Texas's 10 to 20 million plants are grown within a fifty-mile radius of Tyler. The story of the industry goes back to shortly after the Civil War, when nurserymen, in the first instance growers of fruit stocks, were attracted to Smith County by the suitability of the soil. Root diseases affecting the fruit trees caused a change in the pattern after a number of years, and gradually a switch was made to roses, which did not suffer in the same way. The new industry thrived until today Tyler roses are shipped to 48 states and to 25 foreign countries.

Visitors by the thousand flocked to Tyler to see the vast and colourful rose fields of the commercial growers, until one day the people of the town realized that they had a ready-made asset on their hands which needed only proper organization to become not only a local but a national attraction. Thus the yearly East Texas Rose Festival was born and the Tyler Rose Garden, one of the largest municipal rose gardens in America, came into being.

The garden itself is in a 22-acre park and contains some 30,000 rose bushes in about 500 different varieties. Some beds are set in spacious lawns, some terraced, and there are standard (tree) roses to give height where it is needed. Elsewhere, Climbers and Ramblers scramble over archways and pergolas, and pools and fountains complete the picture. Miniature roses are grown in special raised beds, and there is an AARS test garden, all these set against a background of pines, oaks and general shrub plantings. The garden centre building houses the four-day festival.

West Grove, Pennsylvania

Like the gardens at Tyler, those at West Grove are linked with the commercial production of roses, in this case with the Conard Pyle company, whose 40 acres of rose fields have something like 500,000 bush and 150,000 Miniature roses in bloom from July to early October each year, with garden centres for those who wish to buy. There is, in addition, one of the AARS test gardens, where the very latest examples of the rose breeders' art can be seen. For those who wish to see their roses in a garden rather than a nursery setting, wide grass walks lead through the beautifully laid out Robert Pyle Memorial Rose Garden, dedicated to the man who was president of the company for 45 years.

Part of the property was purchased in 1927, and it was discovered that it had at one time been leased to William Penn, grandson of the founder of Pennsylvania, for a rental of 'one red rose on the 24th day of June yearly if the same be demanded'. This old custom, reminiscent of similar ceremonies from the past in Europe, has been revived and is an important occasion in the garden's year. The payment is, however, now made in September rather than June, which is rather early in the year for the rose fields and gardens to be at their best for visitors. Then, on Red Rose Rent Day, a descendant of William Penn receives the red rose payment.

Among countless other American rose gardens, municipal gardens are in the majority, managed with great dedication by the parks departments of numerous cities. Most of the following are accredited All-America Rose Selections display gardens, which receive plants of the new AARS recommendations each year and are subject to inspection to ensure that they are well maintained. In general, unless otherwise stated, bedding roses – Hybrid Teas and Floribundas, together with Climbers in some cases – predominate.

ALABAMA
Battleship Memorial Park Rose Garden, Mobile. An attractive rose garden of modern varieties.

Bellingrath Gardens, Theodore. Many kinds of plants, especially camellias and azaleas, plus roses planted in a big Rotary International wheel.

Birmingham Botanical Gardens, Birmingham. A huge garden and arboretum with a special rose planting.

Springdale Plaza Park Rose Garden, Mobile. Wide range of contemporary roses at a large shopping centre.

ARIZONA
Reid Park Rose Garden, Tucson. Circular arrangement of beds covering about one acre.

CALIFORNIA
Berkeley Municipal Rose Garden. Some 4,000 roses and other shrubs and trees. Terraced planting with pergola above.

Capitol Park Rose Garden, Sacramento. In the grounds of the State Capitol.

City Rose Garden, Santa Barbara. Bedding roses, mostly modern.

Descanso Gardens, La Cañada. Old roses, showing their development from earliest times, are a special feature. In addition, new varieties – including all AARS recommendations – are displayed.

Exposition Park, Los Angeles. Contains a huge sunken rose garden with some 16,000 bushes and also AARS beds.

Fresno Municipal Rose Garden, Roeding Park, Fresno. Bedding roses.

Florida Cypress Gardens, United States
This general view of the Cypress Gardens at Winter Haven shows the small, classical pavilion. It is one of the many All-America Rose Selections test gardens, which act as proving grounds for new introductions – in this case in an area where frosts are virtually unknown and the period of winter dormancy very short.

Golden Gate Park Rose Garden, San Francisco. A small but effective garden in a ravine setting.
Huntington Botanical Gardens, San Marino – see full description above.
Inez Parker Memorial Rose Garden, Balboa Park, San Diego. Fine modern design and construction in a scenic location.
Los Angeles State and County Rose Garden, Arcadia. Peacocks roam through this garden and arboretum, which contains a special rose garden.
Morcom Amphitheater of Roses, Oakland. As the name suggests, a spectacular display.
Rose Hills Memorial Park Garden, Whittier. 7,000 roses in 750 varieties, set against a background of pines. Many large standards and weeping standards. Rose shows and cultural demonstrations.
San Jose Municipal Rose Garden. A popular garden with well-grown plants.
Visalia Public Rose Garden. A practical demonstration garden.

COLORADO
Denver Botanic Gardens. A general garden with fine rose plantings.
Memorial Rose Garden, Roosevelt Park, Longmont. Bedding roses.

DISTRICT OF COLUMBIA
Shoreham Hotel Gardens, Washington. A rose display and trial garden in a setting of azaleas and evergreens.

CONNECTICUT
Elizabeth Park Rose Gardens, West Hartford – see full description above.
Hamilton Park Rose Garden, Waterbury. Bedding roses.
Norwich Memorial Rose Garden, Mohegan Park, Norwich. Bedding and pillar roses in a terrace setting. Pergola.
Pardee Rose Gardens, East Rock Park, New Haven. A rose garden with bulb plantings for early colour and other shrubs and flowering trees.

FLORIDA
Cypress Gardens, Winter Haven. The cypress gardens, including the rose garden, are one of Florida's greatest tourist attractions. Picturesque landscaping and background plantings. AARS test garden.

GEORGIA
142 Bull Street, Savannah. Roses of the 19th century.
Greater Atlanta Rose Garden and Greenhouse, Piedmont Park, Atlanta. A formal garden of bedding roses.
Thomasville Rose Test Garden Many old roses, especially Teas, but also contemporary varieties.

HAWAII
Queen Kapiolani Rose Garden, Honolulu. A demonstration and experimental garden to develop cultural practices for the Honolulu climate. Modern roses; well landscaped.

IDAHO
Bois Municipal Rose Gardens, Julia David Park, Bois. Bedding roses in a setting of trees.
Memorial Bridge Rose Garden, Memorial Park, Lewiston. Rose test garden.
Rotary Rose Gardens, Ross Park, Pocatello. Some 2,000 Teas, Hybrid Teas, Floribundas and Climbers.

ILLINOIS
Cook Memorial Rose Garden, Libertyville. Bedding roses.
Glen Oak Park Conservatory and Rose Garden, Peoria. A formal rose garden set off by shrub plantings.
Merrick Rose Garden, Evanston. Delightful and well maintained.
Robert R. McCormick Memorial Gardens, Wheaton. Bedding roses are one of many features.

INDIANA
E. G. Hill Memorial Rose Garden, Glen Miller Park, Richmond. Small; well laid out.
Lakeside Rose Garden, Fort Wayne. Central formal sunken garden with Grecian columns and rectangular pools, plus informal area of beds containing 5,000 roses in over 200 varieties. Climbers at the perimeter.

IOWA
Davenport Municipal Rose Garden, Van der Veer Park, Davenport. Modern roses near the conservatory.
Greenwood Park Rose Garden, Des Moines. Mostly contemporary varieties.
Huston Park Rose Garden, Cedar Rapids. Floribundas and Hybrid Teas.
Iowa State Rose Society Garden, State Center. Test and demonstration garden.
Iowa State University Rose Garden, Ames. AARS test and display garden; rose breeding programme.
Mount Arbor Demonstration Garden, Shenandoah. Bedding roses.

KANSAS
E. F. A. Reinisch Rose Gardens, Gage Park, Topeka. 7,500 roses in 400 varieties. AARS test garden.
Kansas City Municipal Rose Garden, Huron Park. Bedding roses; test garden.
Manhattan Municipal Rose Garden and Kansas State University Rose Gardens, Manhattan. Bedding roses.

KENTUCKY
Kentucky Memorial Rose Garden, Louisville. Bedding roses.

The rose garden of the Florida Cypress Gardens is shown in the photograph overleaf.

LOUISIANA
American Rose Center, Shreveport – see full description above.
City Park and Worthington Memorial Rose Gardens, New Orleans. Roses, azaleas, gardenias and camellias.
Hodges Gardens, Many. A seven-acre rose planting with both old and new varieties. Fine collection of Teas.
Louisiana State University Gardens, Baton Rouge. Test gardens for roses and annuals in field-type planting.
Rip Van Winkle Gardens, Jefferson Island. 25-acre garden, including a fine rose garden.

MAINE
The Rose Circle, Derring Oaks Park, Portland. Hybrid Teas, Floribundas, Grandifloras and Hybrid Perpetuals in beds surrounded by circular hedges.

MARYLAND
Druid Hill Park Rose Garden, Baltimore. Bedding roses.

MASSACHUSETTS
Arnold Arboretum, Jamaica Plain. The most extensive collection of rose species, species hybrids and forms, and the largest herbarium of roses, in the United States. This was the repository for all specimens collected by E. H. Wilson and many other plant explorers.
The Stanley Park of Westfield. Formal rose garden.

MICHIGAN
Francis Park Memorial Rose Garden, Lansing. Bedding roses.
Matthaei Botanical Gardens, Ann Arbor. Contains a rose garden of bedding roses.
Michigan State University Horticultural Gardens, East Lansing. AARS bedding roses in the rose garden.

MINNESOTA
Garden Center and Rose Garden, Lake Harriet Park, Minneapolis. Shrub roses, Teas and a fine display of standards (tree roses).

MISSOURI
Blue Ridge Mall Rose Garden, Kansas City. Bedding roses.
Capaha Park Rose Display Garden, Cape Girardeau. A collection of old roses and AARS varieties.
Glendal Rose Gardens, Independence. Over 5,000 roses in a formal bedding scheme.
Laura Conyers Smith Municipal Rose Garden, Kansas City. An extensive public rose garden surrounded by Climbers. New and old varieties.
Missouri Botanical Garden, St Louis. A large general botanical garden with two rose gardens. AARS test garden.

MONTANA
Sunset Park Memorial Rose Garden, Missoula. 2,500 roses in test and display beds in the heart of the Rocky Mountains.

NEBRASKA
Antelope Park Rose Garden, Lincoln. Bedding roses.
Memorial Park Rose Garden, Omaha. Bedding roses.

NEVADA
Municipal Rose Garden, Idelwild Park, Reno. Many old and new roses.

NEW JERSEY
Brookdale Park Rose Gardens, Bloomfield. Bedding roses.
Colonial Park Rose Garden, East Millstone. Bedding roses.
Lamertus C. Bobbink Memorial Rose Garden, Thompson Park, Lincroft. Old and new roses. Honours a rose nurseryman.

NEW MEXICO
Community Rose Garden, Lea General Hospital, Hobbs. Bedding roses.
Prospect Park Rose Gardens, Albuquerque. Bedding roses and Miniatures.

NEW YORK
Central Park Rose Garden, Schenectady. Almost 5,000 bedding roses and Climbers.
Cornell Plantations, Everett A. Piester Memorial Garden, Ithaca. Collection of species and old garden roses.
Cranford Memorial Rose Garden, Brooklyn Botanical Garden, Brooklyn. Well designed and maintained, with 5,000 roses in 900 varieties.
Edwin De T. Bechtel Memorial Rose Garden, New York Botanical Garden, Bronx. A newly designed and constructed formal garden, beautifully landscaped. Mostly contemporary varieties, but with a good selection of old garden roses and shrubs.
Hildegarde Mercogliano Rose Garden, Queens Botanic Garden, Flushing. Bedding roses.
Humbolt Park, Buffalo. A planting of 3,000 roses in 250 varieties and including the Niagara Frontier Rose Trial Garden.
Maplewood Rose Gardens, Rochester. 7,500 bedding roses in a setting of flowering thorns and ornamental trees.
Sonnenberg Rose Garden, Canandaigua. Newly renovated formal rose garden of a large private estate now under municipal sponsorship. 5,000 roses.

NORTH CAROLINA
Biltmore House and Gardens, Asheville. A general garden but with 5,000 roses.
Raleigh Municipal Rose Garden. AARS and other roses.

Reynolds Rose Garden, Wake Forest University, Winston-Salem. An attractive garden of old and new roses.

OHIO
Charles Edwin Nail Memorial Rose Garden, Kingwood Center, Mansfield. Rose test and display garden.
Michael H. Hovath Garden of Legend and Romance, Wooster. A garden of heritage roses from past centuries.
Park of Roses, Whetstone Park, Columbus – see full description above.

OKLAHOMA
J. E. Conard Municipal Rose Garden, Honor Heights Park, Muskogee. Bedding roses.
Tulsa Municipal Rose Garden, Woodard Park. A magnificent large garden of some 10,000 bedding roses. AARS test garden.
Will Rogers Horticultural Park and Arboretum, Oklahoma City. A formal planting of about 5,000 roses, many old.

OREGON
Corvallis Municipal Rose Garden, Avery Park. Bedding roses.
George E. Owen Municipal Rose Garden, Eugene. 4,000 new and old roses.
International Rose Test Garden, Washington Park, Portland – see full description above.
Shore Acres State Park, Coos Bay. Small but well maintained.

PENNSYLVANIA
Hershey Rose Garden and Arboretum – see full description above.
Longwood Gardens, Kennett Square. A tremendous garden and botanical institution with large conservatories, indoor displays, water gardens and fountains. Modest-sized rose gardens with less hardy roses grown under glass.
Malcolm W. Gross Memorial Rose Garden, Allentown. Interesting garden with about 5,000 bedding roses.
Marion W. Revinus Rose Garden, Morris Arboretum, Philadelphia. A nice garden of contemporary varieties with species and old roses as background planting.
Mellon Park Rose Gardens, Pittsburgh. Bedding roses.
West Grove – see full description above.

SOUTH CAROLINA
Edisto Memorial Gardens, Orangeburg. A riverside site with nearly 10,000 roses of 350 varieties in informal beds.

TENNESSEE
Memphis Municipal Rose Garden, Audubon Park, Memphis. Roses (about 5,000 plants) one feature in a botanical garden.

Warner Park Rose Garden, Chattanooga. Bedding roses.

TEXAS
El Paso Municipal Rose Garden. Bedding roses and Climbers.
Fort Worth Botanical Garden. A large scenic park with a display of 3,500 roses.
Houston Municipal Rose Garden. Bedding roses in a well-designed garden associated with the Houston Garden Center.
Samuelle Grand Municipal Rose Garden, Dallas. 6,000 bedding roses.
Tyler Municipal Rose Garden – see full description above.

UTAH
Rose Gardens of the Territorial State House State Historic Monument, Fillmore. A display of bedding roses surrounding the State House.
Salt Lake City Municipal Rose Garden. AARS and other roses old and new.

VIRGINIA
Bicentennial Rose Garden, Norfolk Botanical Garden. A featured part of a large botanical garden with extensive plantings of azaleas, camellias, bulbs and many other plants mostly informally displayed to be viewed from land and from waterways through the garden.
Memorial Rose Garden, Arlington. Bedding roses.
Mountain View Garden, Roanoke. Bedding roses.

WASHINGTON
Fairhaven Park Rose Garden, Bellingham. Bedding roses.
Rose Hill, Manito Park, Spokane. Contains a sunken garden of mixed roses and lilacs.
Point Defiance Park Rose Garden, Tacoma. A huge wooded park with fine mixed rose gardens.
Woodlawn Park Rose Test Garden, Seattle. Large, with many Climbers and standards. 5,000 roses in all.

WEST VIRGINIA
Charleston Municipal Rose Garden, David Park, Charleston. A small but well-designed garden.
Huntington Municipal Rose Gardens, Ritter Park, Huntington. Bedding roses.

WISCONSIN
Alfred L. Boerner Botanic Gardens, Whitnall Park, Hales Corners. A beautiful, elaborate garden with an AARS test garden.
Horticultural Conservatory, Mitchell Park, Milwaukee. A grand avenue planting of 2,000 roses.
Olbrich Botanic Garden, Madison. Bedding roses and others.

CHAPTER FIVE

THE CULTIVATION OF THE ROSE

Anatomy of a rose bush
This composite drawing is stylized to show (a) the soil level; (b) a sucker; (c) a single flower; (d) pinnate foliage, with five leaflets making up one leaf; (e) hips; (f) a flower bud; (g) a footstalk or pedicel; (h) sepals; (i) a petal; (j) a solitary fully double bloom; (k) a cluster of semi-double blooms; (l) leaf stipules; (m) a node; (n) an axillary foliage bud; (o) a snag; (p) a breaking bud; (q) a dormant bud or eye; (r) the bud union; (s) the fibrous root system of the rootstock, or understock.

LOOKING AFTER ROSES – their cultivation and after-care – is really not at all complicated, though some of the individual operations, when put down in words rather than demonstrated in the garden by someone who knows what he is doing, may sound as if they were. This is a pity, because the object of growing roses is to enjoy them to the full and to enjoy looking after them, which is more difficult while worrying about doing the right thing or doing it in the right way.

Planting and most of the routine care are quite straightforward to describe, but if a writer, trying to cover all eventualities, were to give details of every insect that may possibly attack roses all over the world, and every disease that may weave its sinister web around them, a prospective rose grower might well go rapidly into reverse and opt for bedding plants. Again, the various operations which go to make up pruning can seem, when put into words, as complicated as a computer programme or as knitting instructions to a non-knitter. Yet many – or even the majority – of insects and diseases may never visit a particular garden at all, and once the reasons for pruning are understood, carrying it out is largely a matter of common sense. All this is not to say that the basic knowledge about rose care cannot be learned from a book. It can, but then experiment must take over to adapt it to the particular conditions of your garden, without which trial and error half the fun and fascination of growing things would be lost.

Every garden is different from all others in some way, and even the type of soil may vary dramatically between one part of a single garden and another, though this is probably exceptional in a small one. So positive statements about such things as soil composition or hardiness in relation to specific geographical areas are hard to make and they should be treated with caution. In a normally mild district the most vicious frost pockets can play havoc with new growth and conversely the skilful use of tree and hedge protection, whether natural or planted especially, can create small and much warmer micro-climates in an otherwise harsh environment. In hilly or mountainous areas, the conditions for growing roses on the upper slopes will be different from those in the valleys, though no more than a few hundred yards may separate them. Annual rainfall and the humidity, too, must play their parts, so only fairly detailed local knowledge will provide answers to particular problems – that and trying out a new approach if something does not work as expected. The rules laid down are only there for guidance and can and should be broken if need be, but not haphazardly. Have a reason for what you try next.

BUYING ROSES

If you have been wise and visited display gardens before choosing your roses, and know what varieties you want, there are still a number of things that are useful to know. You can, for instance, sometimes get a poor plant of a good variety, and for those who cannot for some reason make their choice other than from a nursery catalogue or from the pre-packed roses in stores and supermarkets, there are even more pitfalls. But these can easily be avoided if you know what they are.

Colour pictures of roses in catalogues are beguiling but not always accurate. This is not a deliberate attempt to deceive but because, in the first instance, something can be inadvertently lost from or added to the colour tones when the original photographs are taken, the exact colour of red roses being particularly difficult to capture on film. Something more may be lost (or added) in the printing of the catalogue, for to achieve absolute fidelity is a long and costly business involving many stages of proofing. The price of producing catalogues is growing so astronomically that some suppliers are already having to drop colour altogether and rely on verbal descriptions, which can never be very satisfactory. The subtle blends of colour in a rose need a poet to describe them, and poets do not figure largely on most nursery payrolls.

Floribundas are bought for their large trusses of comparatively small flowers, but the trusses will rarely be shown in catalogues because, if they are, the roses do not sell well. If, on the other hand, Floribundas are made to look as much like Hybrid Teas as possible by showing only one or two individual blooms, the orders for them come rolling in. So here the public is misled because it wants to be for some strange reason. It is odd, but the general lack of information about how healthy a rose is (about which I have often heard complaints) has a ready explanation. The reason for this is that the incidence of various diseases varies enormously in different parts of the country,

and no nurseryman in his right mind would want to scare a potential customer away from a 90 per cent marvellous rose by saying that it will want watching for a particular disease which may be non-existent where the customer lives. It may also, of course, be the healthiest rose in a nursery but behave poorly elsewhere in a way that the nurseryman is quite unaware of.

At the beginning of the section on rose gardens of the world, a brief mention was made of the different standards of judging for national awards, which some catalogues feature. Those awards made by the All-America Rose Selection, by the Royal National Rose Society, the British Association of Rose Breeders, and at the Belfast trials in Northern Ireland are among those based on a long enough trial period to be safely used as a guide – but with these and others, as a guide only within the country in which the trials have taken place. Many top-rated roses in the United States (though by no means all) have failed dismally in the British Isles and other parts of Europe, and the reverse applies.

Offers of collections of ten or twelve roses, varieties chosen by the grower, appear in many catalogues at a special cheap rate, which is possible because they are prepared in advance and there is no picking out of individual roses to a customer's order. From a good nursery, which is unlikely to be trying to get rid of unsold and possibly second-grade stock in this way, these offers can be helpful for a beginner, but even so it is wise to check each rose's description in the main part of the catalogue. I have seen the Floribunda 'Zambra' – 60 cm (2 ft) tall – in the same collection as 'Queen Elizabeth' and 'Yellow Queen Elizabeth'; any one expecting a bed of roses of more or less uniform height, which they would have every right to do, would have been in for a shock.

On the question of height, it should be remembered that the roses seen and ready for sale in the long lines of nursery beds during the summer before lifting are not fully-grown

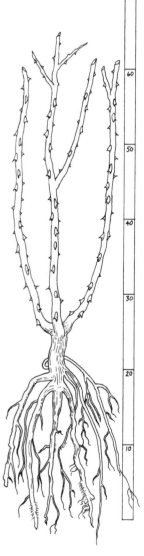

Buying roses
(above) A strong, First Grade Hybrid Tea rose, supplied bareroot. (opposite) A bareroot, First

plants. A good idea of the flowers can be gained, but not of the ultimate size of the bushes, which is particularly vital to know with the bigger shrub roses that take several years to reach their full stature.

I mentioned second-grade plants just now, but what is a second-grade rose? Roses, which have inspired the poets from time immemorial with their romance, have more recently inspired the British Standards Institution and the American Association of Nurserymen into producing quality standards. The British Standard Specification for rose plants bearing the description First Grade (BS 3936 – Part 2:1978, Nursery Stock) stipulates in essence that the root-stock where the bud is inserted should be at least 15 mm (⅝ in) thick, that the root system should be well developed and fibrous, and that there should be at least two firm canes no thinner than a pencil. Standard roses should be double-budded (two budding unions at the top of the stem, one either side), and climbers should have a minimum of two canes at least 75 cm (30 in) long.

The American system for grading bare-root roses is somewhat different and split into three grades. Again in outline, for No 1 Grade, Hybrid Teas and Grandifloras need three strong canes with at least two 45 cm (18 in) or more long, Floribundas the same though with a minimum length of 38 cm (15 in), and Polyanthas four or more canes of 30 cm (1 ft). The three canes of climbers must be 60 cm (2 ft) long. No 1½ Grade and No 2 Grade set progressively lower standards, coupled with a warning that, by the time No 2 Grade is reached, there is an element of gambling in what you buy. Good nurserymen in both countries will aim to better the highest official standards, but even when picking roses off the counter in a supermarket it is sensible to bear the ideal in mind. It is not difficult to assess the important dimensions by eye, but at the same time if you are going to pay less you cannot necessarily expect to get the best. With pre-packed roses the thickness and number (and health) of the canes is the thing to make sure of because the length may have been reduced for convenience in packing. For climbers, however, it should be more or less as specified, particularly with climbing sports. Too much cut away and they may revert to the bush form – though it is difficult to put forward a logical reason for this.

Incorrect – generally too warm – storage conditions can and often do play havoc with pre-packed supermarket roses. So, apart from assessing size, they must be carefully examined for dried-out, wrinkled canes and to make sure that the hot-house effect of a plastic wrapping has not induced disease or a premature growth of white, caterpillar-like shoots which waste the plants' strength and die off as soon as they are planted outside. A

Grade climber. Choose roses with thick, undamaged canes and a good, fibrous root system. The measuring scale shows centimetres.

guarantee to grow and bloom is open to many interpretations, and unless it is actually dead, a very low-grade rose will produce a few under-sized blooms – for a while. One cannot, without risking enormous unpopularity, unpack pre-packed roses to judge the root system, which is another serious disadvantage.

Do not hesitate when buying container-grown roses to ask if they really are container-grown. This is important because they can, regrettably, sometimes be made up from surplus stock (surplus perhaps because of inferior quality) with the roots chopped off no more than a few weeks previously to make them fit into the containers. There is a tendency in any case to use small plants for container growing because they are easier to handle, but this is not really an acceptable reason for container roses not being of the highest standard, which should be insisted upon. After all, they are generally rather more expensive when bought this way. When buying them in the summer it is all too easy to be led into temptation by an attractive show of flowers, which may draw the eye from a spindly plant underneath. Their great advantage is that they can be used at any time of year to fill in a gap if one of your other roses has died, but the range of varieties offered in containers is usually fairly limited and you may not always get what you want.

You may also be unlucky in this if you do not order your roses early. If a nursery is out of stock when your order for a particular variety arrives, a substitute will often be sent unless specific instructions not to do so have been given. This can be most annoying if you have set your heart on something special, but if you have said 'No substitutes' you are not obliged to take second-best. By going to a specialist grower you will almost always have a bigger range to choose from.

PREPARING THE SOIL

'Dwelling in the land of Roses, in a land where the woods and lanes and hedges are clothed in summer-time with Roses, they prefer the stolid conviction that the stars in their courses fight against them, that meteorology and geology are their bitter foes. Look over your garden wall with a beautiful Rose in your coat, and your neighbour, loitering with his hands in his pockets, knee-deep in groundsel, and his beds undrained, undug, will sigh from the depths of his divine despair, "What a soil yours is for the Rose!"'

So said Dean Hole, making the point about proper preparation of a rose bed far better than I, knee-deep in manure, could ever do. Roses will give at least twenty years of pleasure and enjoyment and this will be greatly increased if the ground is properly prepared to receive them. It may look all right, but you cannot tell simply by looking at it, and it may be far from ideal. Roses are very tough and will give results of a sort in the most unsuitable conditions, but it makes sense to give them something to grow in which will enable them to give of their best in return. There are very few soils that cannot be improved, though the amount of work needed on different ones will vary greatly.

Two or three months before the roses can be expected to arrive from the nursery is the time to begin. Early preparation gives the soil time to settle down to some extent after digging over, and for the manures and other fertilizers which have been added as required to begin the process of being absorbed into it so that their nutrients are ready for release to the fine feeding roots of the roses. Planting will disturb the soil again, certainly, but only to a limited extent in the immediate vicinity of each rose, and there you will be treading it firm again anyway.

As to the constitution of soils, let me first put another nail in the coffin of the myth that roses only thrive to perfection in clay. They do not. The ideal for them is a good, medium loam which retains a fair degree of moisture but at the same time drains well. Roses may surround a lily pond, but should not be in it.

The acidity (or otherwise) of soil is important, and small kits to enable you to test this can be bought cheaply from most garden shops or centres. Acidity is expressed in what is known as a pH number, and for roses this should be about 6.5, which is slightly on the acid side. The lower the number, the more acid it is, and it is tempting if your reading is low to give the whole bed a dressing of lime. Unfortunately – probably because lime is cheap in comparison with most garden chemicals – it is only too easy to overdo it, and then you will have chlorosis on your hands. This means, briefly, that the rose roots cannot get at the iron salts they need from the soil. These become, to use one of the quaintest of gardeners' terms, 'locked up', which means, quite simply, insoluble. Sequestered iron, sold in solution or powdered form under various brand names, will release its iron even in alkaline soils, but compare its price to that of lime!

And once there, lime is very difficult to get rid of, so avoid lime itself and also the spent mushroom manure which is often on offer at very low prices and is full of it. The addition of peat (peat moss) will help to increase acidity, and if you want to increase alkalinity a little the thing to use is nitro-chalk, which will provide nitrogen for the roses as well. Nitro-chalk is a fertilizer combining the advantages of sulphate of ammonia and nitrate of soda, and also contains lime. If unobtainable, you can use nitrate of soda itself.

Probably the most vital thing with all soils, and particularly so with light, sandy ones, is to add humus, which is basically well-decayed vegetable matter. It will help to break up heavy ground, will hold water and plant foods in light soils, will encourage the bacterial action necessary to plant life, and will also darken the colour of the earth so that it absorbs heat more readily and retains it afterwards. The ideal humus is well-rotted farmyard manure, for it contains ready-made plant foods – or does if it is not the lightly dyed straw which passes for manure in the hands of some suppliers. It is, however, less and less easy to get, and garden compost is a good second choice, provided that it is properly made. The bacterial action necessary to break down or decay vegetable matter (as distinct from that which takes place in the soil later) uses up nitrogen at a great rate, and this should not still be happening when the compost reaches the rose bed. The roses need all the nitrogen that is going.

The chief difficulty with compost is that few gardens produce enough of it for their own needs, and if your garden is a new one there is unlikely to be any there at all. Peat (peat moss) is then the answer as it forms good humus, but it has no food value for the roses so that a balanced fertilizer must always be used as well. It does, however, appear to contain certain compounds which tend to stimulate root growth, particularly with newly-planted stock. Make sure, though, that you use the specially-prepared horticultural peat. That dug straight from a peat-bog may be quite unsuitable.

An impatient owner of a new garden may be prepared to take a chance and plan to get rid later of those perennial weeds, the roots of which creep so sinisterly through the ground. If it is winter, they will probably be lurking below the surface of the ground, smirking to themselves with the thought that nobody knows they are there, and how in the spring they will embrace the roots of newly-planted roses like the tentacles of a sea anemone. The only sensible answer, if there is the slightest suspicion that you are harbouring them – which should be revealed by digging – is to wait a year if need be before beginning your planting to make sure that you really have got rid of them. Otherwise they will be with you for evermore.

During double digging on very heavy soils, manure, compost or coarse horticultural peat can be dug freely into the top spit, with bonemeal and hoof and horn meal added liberally – or some other type of fertilizer supplying phosphorus, such as superphosphate or basic slag. For light and medium soils, you need only bother about the top spit, for the old idea that deep digging is essential for roses on any type of soil has been proved a myth, for which we should all give thanks. Use a finer-textured peat, which will mix in more readily. Should you be unlucky enough to garden on solid chalk or limestone with only a thin layer

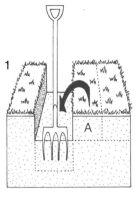

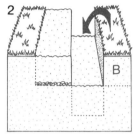

Soil preparation
Double digging is an excellent form of deep cultivation for very heavy ground. If your soil is waterlogged, precede the digging by laying land drains. This will prevent the double dug bed from becoming a sump for surrounding soil water.
(1) Take out a trench 45 cm (18 in) wide and one spit deep at one end of the proposed bed or border, using a spade. Mound this soil onto weed-free ground or sacking at the other end of the bed. Using a fork, break up the subsoil in the trench to a depth of one spit.
If there is turf or a covering of annual weeds on the surface of the bed, skim this off with a spade, lay it face-downwards in the trench and chop it up. Spread organic matter such as manure or peat along the trench and then turn the adjacent strip of soil A onto it.
(2) Fork over the subsoil left by the removal of A, add any chopped turf or weed, add organic matter and turn the next strip B into the trench. Continue this pattern across the bed, always removing the roots of any perennial weeds. Fill in the final trench with the soil from the first trench.

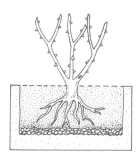

Replacing roses
To replace the odd rose in an existing bed, remove it and the soil in which it was growing. Make the hole at least 1m (3ft) across and 45cm (18in) deep. Add organic matter to the hole and plant the new rose in fresh planting mixture. Without this treatment the new plant will suffer from replant disease, failing to thrive in old soil which has become 'rose sick'.

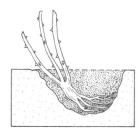

Heeling in
To heel in the plants prior to final planting, dig a shallow trench with a sloping side. Any convenient corner of the garden will do. Lay the roses in the trench against the sloping side and cover the roots with at least 15cm (6in) of soil. It does not matter if the soil is heaped over part of the canes as well.

of earth over it, dig out the chalk to a depth of at least 45 cm (18 in). Add plenty of peat to the soil you replace it with to help to increase the acidity and to prevent the yellowing of the rose leaves through chlorosis.

Do not plan to plant roses in a bed from which you have levered the half-dead stumps of a previous rose planting unless you are prepared to face up to replacing the soil entirely first. If the bed has grown roses for some time, new ones are unlikely to do well in it, even though any old ones which are left will continue to flourish. All anyone seems able to say in explanation of this is that the soil becomes 'rose sick', which is as good a term as any to cover bafflement. The old roses must either be foraging farther afield or else have become used to an unhealthy diet, which the tenderly nurtured new ones cannot take. If you do decide to put new soil in a big bed, remember that you will have to dig manure into it as well, and you may find yourself deciding that it is easier to pick another site. Leave the soil in the old rose bed to recover for a few years. It will be quite all right to grow other plants in it for the time being; they will not show signs of soil sickness.

PLANTING

The right time to plant roses depends on where you live. In a climate such as that of the British Isles, any time during the winter and early spring is quite satisfactory. The earlier you plant, wherever you are, the longer the rose roots have to establish themselves ready for the coming year. Where the winter temperatures go below −23°C (−10°F) for any length of time, as they will do in many parts of North America and northern Europe, wait until the spring. A good nursery will pack its roses well, and if you really cannot plant them at once they will be quite happy if left unpacked in a cool but frostproof shed. Never leave them in the house, for warmth is the last thing they want.

If the delay in planting is likely to be more than a week, it is best to heel them in. For this, or for immediate planting, provided that there is no frost about, unpack the roses and inspect them. Snip off any remaining leaves as these will give off moisture the roses can ill spare, and if any of the canes are damaged, cut them back to the first healthy bud below the damage. If you can recognize them, pull away any suckers you see, though this is something the supplier really ought to do before dispatch. Shorten long, thick roots by about one-third. This will encourage fine feeding roots to grow from them when the rose is planted. If the roses look dry, put them in a bucket of water for an hour or two before healing them in a sheltered spot or – if the weather is kind – proceeding to the permanent planting.

For actual planting, choose a mild, frost-free day, when the ground is nicely moist but not waterlogged after prolonged rain. For the best results, prepare a special planting mixture to put around the roots, made up in a bucket (or buckets) from soil and moist granulated peat (peat moss) in equal proportions, with a handful per plant of bonemeal or a proprietary slow-acting rose fertilizer mixed into it. The total amount of mixture you will need depends on the number of roses, but one good shovelful per plant should be about right. Before taking the roses to the planting site, particularly if it is a breezy or sunny day, wrap them in damp sacking or burlap to prevent them drying our after removal from the bucket of water.

The planting holes in the previously prepared bed should be dug wide enough for the roots to be spread out all round, but just how deep they should be is a matter of debate and can be influenced by climate and the type of understock on which the variety is budded. I have always had good results in a mild climate if the holes are deep enough for the budding union (the point at which the canes sprout from the roots) to be about 2.5 cm (1 in) below soil level. In very cold areas it is wiser to go deeper, with the budding union as much as 5–8 cm (2–3 in) down. This gives better protection, but may mean that fewer new canes will grow from the union, and not everyone agrees with this idea, provided other protection is given. Some, even in cold areas, have the union as much as 2.5 cm (1 in) above soil level on the theory that it is then easier to deal with suckers which may come from there. This is also the practice in sunny California.

It is often suggested that the soil in the centre of the hole should be mounded up. This would make excellent sense if rose roots always grew in a disciplined way so that they fitted snugly and evenly over the mound like the legs of a camera tripod – as is the case with roses budded on Multiflora cuttings or the 'Dr Huey' understock commonly used in the United States. It may well be, however, that all the roots will be pointing in one direction, and all you can do is to spread them out as evenly as possible. Their determination to go just where they wish is likely to be just as strong as yours is that they should not.

Firm planting is important to bring the soil in close contact with the roots and eliminate any large air spaces, but it does not mean that you have to jump up and down round the bushes turning the soil into concrete. Further firming after a week or so when things have settled down, and after a frosty spell which could loosen the soil, is a good idea. Roses planted in spring should be pruned at the time of planting. Water freely, and continue if the weather indicates that it is necessary.

In America it is common practice to mound soil up around the canes to keep them moist

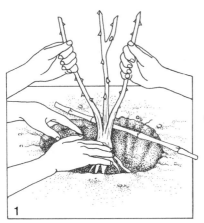
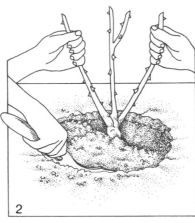
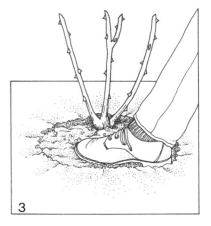

Planting bareroot roses
(1) Dig a hole wide and deep enough to accommodate the roots when well spread out. Place a cane across the hole to mark the soil level. Enlist help to hold the rose upright, so that the union is flush with the cane. Spread out the roots.

(2) Tip a shovelful of planting mixture over the roots and then draw in some of the soil which was initially dug from the hole. Shake the plant to settle the soil between the roots. Tread the soil lightly before again checking the planting depth. Adjust the depth when necessary at this stage.

(3) Finally, fill in the hole with more soil and tread firmly, more so on light soils, less so on heavy. The soil level should be at the budding union. If you live in a very cold area you can protect the plant by mounding soil over the union to a depth of 15 cm (6 in). Remove the soil when growth starts.

until the buds begin to break and new growth has begun, at which time the soil must be removed promptly. Other things can be used instead of soil and may be easier to remove. These include paper bags placed over the plants with the edges weighted down with soil, waxed-paper 'hot tents', or sods (turves) wrapped around the canes with the grass sides facing inwards.

CONTAINER-GROWN ROSES
For these it is not enough simply to dig a hole large enough for the root-ball to be inserted. In heavy soils especially, the roots may never spread out properly, or the hole may form a sump in which rain water collects, making it much too wet. The bed or beds should be properly prepared, with full-size planting holes.

Soak the roses in their containers before planting, as they may well be dried out. Put the first one complete into its planting hole, slit down the side of the container if it is one of the black plastic kind, and ease this from under the roots. Loosen the sides of the root-ball just a little, but do not break it up. Fill in the hole with planting mixture and then soil; water and tread firm. With metal containers, slide the root-ball out without breaking it up, place it in the hole and fill in as before.

Container-grown roses have the advantage that they can be planted when in full growth during the summer without doing them any harm, but it is important that the roots should have the minimum of disturbance or the rose will wilt and may take a long time to recover.

STANDARD (TREE) ROSES
These must always have strong stakes to support them, which should be driven firmly into the centre of the planting hole before putting in the rose. If put in afterwards they might damage the roots. If the latter are of Rugosa

stock they should not be planted too deeply, which would encourage suckers.

Ties should be left quite loose until the rose has had time to settle down in the soil. Then tighten them up, but not too much, for the stem will increase in diameter quite substantially over the years and must not be throttled. It is much easier to say that you will remember to loosen the ties a little each year than it is actually to do it, so make the necessary allowance at the beginning. Where it is available, vinyl plastic tape makes a good tying material because it is flat and will not cut into the stems. It stretches as the cane increases in size, but a buffer of some sort is always needed between stake and stem to prevent rubbing.

CLIMBING ROSES
Any flower-bed against the wall of a house will be dry, both because the wall itself will absorb water and because overhanging eaves will keep off rain. Watering at regular intervals after planting is especially important because of this, but at the same time the roses should not be in a direct line with water dripping non-stop off the eaves during long spells of wet weather. This would give them too much of a good thing.

ROSES FOR HEDGES
These roses can be planted in a single line, perhaps a little closer together than would be good practice for bedding as they will have plenty of air coming at them from both sides. The actual distance between the plants must, however, depend on their habit of growth. It could be as little as 45 cm (18 in) for an upright Floribunda, or as much as 1.25 m (4 ft) for one of the big, bushy shrub roses such as 'Roseraie de l'Hay'. Rugosas and Gallicas on their own roots will produce new growth from suckers which will thicken up a hedge considerably.

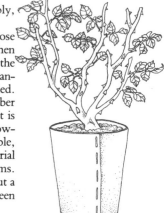

Planting container roses
Check the planting depth of container-grown roses by placing the container in the planting hole and checking that the bud union is level with the planting cane. (above) Remove the container before planting, taking care not to break up the root-ball.

FERTILIZERS

A well-prepared rose bed will be rich in food, but the roses will use it up fast, and many of the essential salts will, especially in light soils, be washed away out of reach of the roots by rain. They must therefore be replaced if the roses are to maintain their vigour and health. It is worth remembering that, the better a rose is nourished, the less prone it will be to disease.

The three most important rose foods are nitrogen, phosphates and potash. The former stimulates growth of the green parts, the leaves and the canes, and lack of it is shown by an even overall yellowing of the leaves, general debility and small, anaemic flowers. Phosphates (phosphorus) help the roots to grow well and speed up flower production. Not enough of them may mean dull green leaves (with the loss of some), weak stems and a reluctance of the flower buds to open. Potash (potassium) gives resistance to drought and disease, good growth generally and fine-quality blooms. A lack of it causes leaf margins to yellow and turn brown (though this can also be due to other causes), and once again a general lack of vigour.

Calcium and magnesium come next in order of importance (and of the quantity needed) and then a number of chemicals called trace elements, presumably because only a trace of them is needed. They include boron, chlorine, copper, iron, manganese, molybdenum and zinc. Unless your soil has a serious lack of one or more of these, all that will normally be needed is a proprietary rose fertilizer. This is made up to supply all the rose's needs and contains everything in the right proportions. Unless you are growing roses on an enormous scale, using one is certainly the easiest and probably the cheapest way of getting what is needed. If, however, you do wish to experiment and mix your own fertilizer, the proportions are given overleaf.

Having first watered the soil thoroughly if it is dry, sprinkle fertilizer on it at the rate of a small handful around each bush, keeping it clear of the stems. This should be done directly after pruning and again in late summer, before the second flush gets under way. Always use gloves when handling fertilizer. Hoe or rake it in lightly afterwards. Do not put general fertilizers on any later than this second application, or sappy autumn growth will be encouraged, only to be wasted when the winter frosts kill it off. However, a slightly later dressing of sulphate of potash at $75\,g/m^2$ (2 oz per sq yd) will help to ripen late shoots so that they will stand the cold better later on.

Foliar feeds, which are sprayed onto the leaves and absorbed straight into the plant's system, by-passing the roots, are not really needed in the average garden. They can, though, be an advantage on alkaline soils, where iron and other necessary salts are hard for the roots to take up. Use a commercially-prepared foliar feed, mixing it strictly according to the maker's instructions, and apply it preferably early in the morning, but at any rate not in the full heat of the sun. Rose leaves love it and will be remarkable for their size and quality. Many foliar feeds can be mixed with disease and insect sprays and so applied at the same time, which has obvious advantages. Some of them can also be used as liquid fertilizers for putting in the soil, and they can be useful if you want quick results. A slow-acting fertilizer of the kind discussed earlier is, however, much more satisfactory and, as its name implies, lasts a great deal longer.

Planting climbers
(below) Plant climbers at least 45 cm (18 in) away from a wall. Slant the canes towards the wall and fan out the roots towards the moister ground away from the wall.

Staking standards
Standard roses need maximum support.
(left) Choose a stake of sufficient length both to be firmly driven in and also to reach just into (but not above) the head of the tree.
(below) Provide two ties for the stem, one just above soil level and one just below the head. The ties should have a buffer between the stake and the stem to prevent chafing.

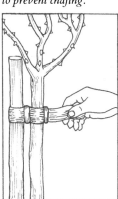

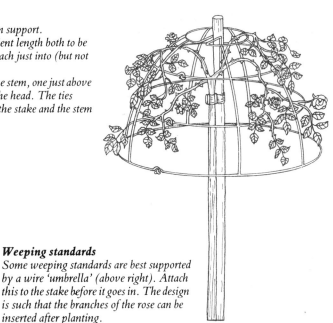

Weeping standards
Some weeping standards are best supported by a wire 'umbrella' (above right). Attach this to the stake before it goes in. The design is such that the branches of the rose can be inserted after planting.

FERTILIZERS FOR ROSES

FERTILIZERS SUPPLYING NITROGEN (N)

Organic	**Inorganic**
Dried blood (10–13% N)	†Ammonium nitrate (nitrate of ammonia; 35% N)
Fish meal (7–10% N)	†Ammonium sulphate (sulphate of ammonia; 21% N)
Hoof and horn meal (12–14% N)	Calcium nitrate (nitrate of lime; 16% N)
Meat and bone meal (6–12% N)	Chilean potash nitrate (12–14% N)
	Nitro-chalk (16% N)
	Potassium nitrate (nitrate of potash, saltpetre; 12–14% N)
	Sodium nitrate (nitrate of soda; 16% N)
	†Urea (45% N)

FERTILIZERS SUPPLYING PHOSPHORUS (phosphate; P or P_2O_5)

Organic	**Inorganic**
*Bonemeal (20–25% P)	*Basic slag (8–20% P)
Fish meal (4–10% P)	Superphosphate of lime (18–20% P)
Meal and bone meal (16% P)	

FERTILIZERS SUPPLYING POTASSIUM (potash; K or K_2O)

Organic	**Inorganic**
Blood, fish and bone meal (5% K)	Chilean potash nitrate (10% K)
Dry wood ash (4–15% K)	Potassium nitrate (nitrate of potash, saltpetre; 45% K)
	Potassium sulphate (sulphate of potash; 50% K)

FERTILIZERS SUPPLYING CALCIUM AND MAGNESIUM (Ca and Mg)

Organic	**Inorganic**
Bonemeal	*Basic slag
Fish meal	Calcium sulphate (gypsum)
Meat and bone meal	*Ground chalk or limestone
	*Magnesian limestone (Ca+Mg)
	Magnesium sulphate (Epsom salts; Mg)
	Nitro-chalk

*Alkaline fertilizers to be preferred on acid ('sour') soils
†Acid fertilizers to be preferred on alkaline ('sweet') soils

MULCHING AND WATERING

Mulching means the application of a 5–8 cm (2–3 in) layer, preferably of organic material, to the surface of a rose bed in late spring, as soon as the soil has begun to warm up. This will help to keep the soil moist by preventing evaporation, will smother the majority of annual weeds during the summer (though the tough, perennial ones are best removed before a mulch is put on), will break down into humus and will provide plant foods, particularly if the best mulch of all, farmyard manure, is used. A mulch will also keep the soil temperature more or less even, and with luck it will keep over-wintering black spot spores which may be in the soil firmly where they belong – underneath it.

Every conceivable kind of organic material has at one time or another been tried, from sawdust to newspaper, but from the point of view of appearance – which surely must be of importance in most gardens – compost, leafmould, shredded bark or peat (peat moss) come near the top. Manure does more actual good than any of these, and peat (which comes expensive for a large area) really must be kept moist or much of it may blow away.

Grass cuttings are an easily available mulch, but they can form a mat through which rain cannot penetrate if they are put on too thickly. And they should not be put on if the grass is seeding or if a weedkiller has recently been applied to it. In the parts of America where they are available, cacao hulls, ground corn cobs, buckwheat hulls, peanut shells or rice hulls may be used, but they each have certain drawbacks. Also, it must be remembered that

Shortage of nitrogen
Young leaves are small and pale green; leaf stalks and stems tinged light red. Stems weak and stunted; leaves fall early.

Shortage of phosphorus
Young leaves are small and dark green, though purplish underneath. Stems stunted and weak; leaves fall early.

Shortage of potassium
Leaves develop brown, brittle edges. Flowers small; buds may fail to open.

Shortage of magnesium
Oldest leaves become pale and yellowed between main veins; drop early.

Shortage of iron
Young leaves develop yellow areas; may become all yellow.

Shortage of maganese
Oldest leaves develop yellow bands between the veins.

Shortage of boron
Leaves become very dark green and can be misshapen.

Shortage of calcium
Young shoots die back. Brown spots around leaf edges, which fall eventually.

Remedies
For iron shortage, apply chelated (sequestered) iron and avoid liming. For manganese shortage, avoid liming and spray with 25 g (1 oz) manganese sulphate in 4.5 litres (1 gal) water. Treat all other deficiencies by applying a compound rose fertilizer. Buy this or make it up in the following proportions (parts by weight):

Magnesium sulphate	*1*
Iron sulphate	*1*
Ammonium sulphate	*2.5*
Potassium sulphate	*5*
Superphosphate of lime	*8*

Apply at a rate of about 140 g/m² (4 oz/sq yd), or a small handful per bush.

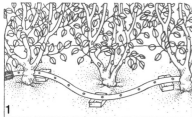

Permanent irrigation
(1) The trickle system directs the water into the soil and not onto the flowers, unlike the various methods of overhead watering. Buy a length of perforated tube to attach to a garden hose, or make it yourself by drilling holes in a straight line along each side of a length of hose. Make the holes no more than 1.5mm (¹/₁₆ in) in diameter and about 8 cm (3 in) apart. Seal the far end of the hose and then mount it on wooden blocks.
(2) In the 'spaghetti' system, tubing from the main pipe delivers water to each bush.
(3) Soil watering need not involve visible piping. Bury plastic pipe and arrange open-topped risers to project above the surface.

Dead-heading
Do not pull or snap off the dead flowers or hips. Cut the canes just above the third or fourth leaf below the dead flower, exactly as if you were pruning. The dormant bud in the leaf axil will then produce a worthwhile shoot.

when fresh or uncomposted organic materials are used, it is necessary to add extra nitrogen fertilizer. In autumn, the mulch can be lightly hoed in when the beds are being tidied up.

Since one of the functions of a mulch is to retain moisture in the soil, moisture must be there in the first place for it to retain, so put it on only after rain or a thorough watering. However, damp soil means worms, and birds seeking for these and also for insects under the mulch will, come what may, do their best to get it off again, scattering it over surrounding lawns as if they were giving it away to the poor. All you can do about this is sigh and get the rake out.

Whether or not watering your roses is a major part of routine care depends on both your type of soil and the climate. Light, sandy soil will absorb water rapidly but will not retain it. It runs more or less straight through, while with heavy clays it will penetrate much more slowly and be held for a longer period. The ideal soil, as I have said, retains moisture but not to the extent of robbing the roses' roots of oxygen by waterlogging. Adequate watering means penetrating to a depth of not less than 45 cm (18 in), which is about as far as most rose roots will go. A light watering, however often carried out, will not get down this far and will encourage feeding roots very near the surface, where they can be subject to damage from the hoe or from drying out in hot weather.

How much water is needed for proper penetration and how long the soil will retain it in a particular area can be discovered quite simply by watering two selected spots in dry weather for a given period, and then digging down into one of them after an hour or so to see how far the water has gone. If it has not reached the required level, a longer period of watering is, of course, needed. The other spot should be left for a day or two after it has been watered, and then dug into to see how moist the soil has remained below the surface. This should show how often watering is needed as opposed to how much. There are actually inexpensive instruments available to measure the amount of soil moisture, but considering the widely varying local climates and soil conditions where roses can be grown, perhaps the best advice on this subject is to ask local gardeners for their recommendations.

It is particularly important to keep newly-planted roses well watered and to remember

that a drought does not only occur at the height of the summer when the hot sun beats down. Long, dry spells can occur in spring and at other times, when they may not be so obvious if the skies are grey. Prolonged winds can dry the soil out rapidly, too.

DEAD-HEADING –
THE REMOVAL OF HIPS

The natural life-cycle of the rose each year is to produce flowers and after them hips, from which the seeds come in order to germinate in due course in the earth and perpetuate the race. Once hips begin to form, much of the growing energy of the rose is diverted into their development, rather than into the production of strong new growth and flowers. In more technical terms, the production of growth-regulating hormones by the developing hips inhibits the growth of the shoots, but if the hips are removed, roses which are recurrent flowerers will try again by producing a full new crop of blooms. The removal of the hips is known to British gardeners as dead-heading, a term that would have delighted the White Queen in *Alice in Wonderland*.

The easiest way to remove hips or the spent flowers which may conceal them, is just to pull or snap them off. You will then, with Hybrid Teas, be left with unsightly flower stems that will die back, and a not very vigorous new shoot may well grow from the first leaf-axil below it, to bear undersized flowers when it has developed enough. With a Floribunda which has produced a good-sized truss, you will have something left more nearly resembling a television aerial. The proper way to dead-head, or remove these spent shoots, is shown in the diagram.

Dead-heading performed regularly is very little trouble and can be carried out as you wander round admiring the roses. Watch particularly the varieties that do not shed their petals cleanly and those which become soggy after rain. Hips may be forming which you cannot see. Once-flowering roses do not need dead-heading – especially if you are growing them for the beauty of their hips – though if you follow the correct practice and spur back the side shoots of groups like the Albas and Damasks in late summer you will, in fact, be removing the hips as well.

DEALING WITH SUCKERS

Suckers are shoots coming from the rootstock – usually a species or near relative – onto which a cultivated variety has been budded. They must be removed as soon as they are seen or the root-stock, being more vigorous and being unrestricted by the bud-union, will divert most (and in time all) of its energy into them, and the weaker cultivated variety will be starved and eventually die from lack of nourishment. Some kinds of rootstock produce suckers more readily than others, but they can also be caused through accidentally nicking the roots when using a hoe.

Recognizing a sucker is something that many people find difficult at first. As the kinds of rootstock can vary, so their growth – canes, leaves and thorns – may also be different, though most of them will not differ markedly from each other. All, however, once you know what to look for, are so easily distinguishable that it will seem incredible that there was any problem. Generally speaking, in relation to the new shoots of a Hybrid Tea or a Floribunda, those of a sucker are likely to be very light green, with seven or more narrow leaflets to every leaf. There may also be different-shaped thorns, and more of them, but these are pointers only and must not be taken as an infallible guide, particularly if you suspect there are suckers on a shrub rose which much resembles a species itself. The diagram shows the only way to find out for certain which is a sucker.

Cutting a sucker off, especially at ground level, will be the equivalent of pruning it and will simply encourage new growth, but there may be problems in pulling it away if it comes from a root tangle right under the centre of a rose. Pulling could yank the whole rose out of the ground, so you may have no option other than to cut; but be sure to keep further signs of growth rigorously in check.

DISBUDDING

Disbudding is almost exclusively confined to Hybrid Teas. A minority of these grow naturally with only one flower per stem, and with them no disbudding is needed. The rest, however, have some blooms coming singly while other stems bear three, four or more, often very closely grouped at the top; this is particularly so with the second flush in late summer. Several flowers per stem means that each flower will be smaller, and in those varieties where they are closely grouped they may be so cramped as to prevent them opening properly.

For general garden display, this multiplicity of bloom may be welcomed, but if large,

high-quality blooms are wanted for house decoration or for exhibition, disbudding is necessary. British exhibitors sometimes leave at least one side bud as this will flower later than the terminal one, giving a better chance of there being a secondary bloom at the peak of its perfection on show day – though this would not be allowed under American show rules. In the garden the more buds you remove the shorter will be the flowering period of any one stem.

It might be useful to define at this point just what is meant by a bud, as there are two kinds and this can sometimes lead to confusion. The flower buds, which have been the ones discussed here, are those which, not surprisingly, open into flowers. The other kind, which feature in dead-heading, pruning and budding onto rootstocks, are to be found at the point where a leaf stalk joins a cane, and are sometimes known as leaf-axil or vegetative buds. These grow into new shoots.

Removing suckers
(above left) Trace a suspected sucker growing from a bush rose back to its point of origin by scraping away some soil from around the roots. If the shoot originates from below the budding union then it is a sucker. Pull it off firmly, thus removing the dormant buds where it joins the roots. Never cut suckers. This would only act like pruning, stimulating further growth. (above) The stem of a standard rose is part of the rootstock; any shoots which sprout below the head are suckers. Snap them off as soon as they appear, while they are still green.

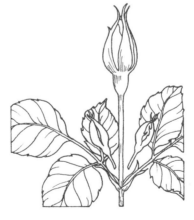

Disbudding
(above) Disbud Hybrid Tea roses to produce larger, specimen blooms. Pinch out all or some of the side flower buds with finger and thumb. Wait until they are large enough to be handled easily without risking damage to the main, terminal bud.

(above) Floribunda roses first produce a central flower in each truss, with the other buds opening after it. For exhibition or for a special occasion, remove the central flower one or two weeks before you want to cut the truss. This accelerates the opening of the other buds all at once.

PRUNING AND TRAINING

Some people when they hear the word pruning head for the hills saying that, if the good Lord had intended us to prune he would have given us leather hands. It is quite true that if your name is on a thorn you will get it, but the actual operation need hold no mysteries once the idea behind it is understood.

WHY PRUNE?

Consider in the first place how a wild rose grows. Each year it sends up from somewhere near the base long new shoots, which flower at their best the following summer. Over the next few years these gradually deteriorate, flowering less and less well until they die, having been replaced by others.

Cultivated roses grow in exactly the same way, though most of them if just left alone will send up fewer new shoots. Pruning simply gets rid of the old canes more rapidly so that the whole cycle is accelerated, there are strong new canes each year, and the weak, damaged or diseased ones are disposed of at the same time.

From this it would seem to follow that all roses should be pruned in exactly the same way, but they are not, and the reason is quite simple. With Hybrid Teas, for instance, the size and quality of each individual flower is all-important, and the strongest possible new wood is needed each year to achieve this end, so that they are pruned the hardest of all. With Floribundas and most other kinds of roses, as was mentioned when discussing their uses for hedging and bedding, the aim is to produce a mass of bloom and the size of the flowers does not matter so much. The pruning can therefore be lighter and the replacement of the main canes more gradual. Strong-growing shrub roses, particularly the species, come right at the other end of the scale from the Hybrid Teas, and with these it is only necessary to cut out wood that is dead or obviously dying, as and when it occurs.

There are two other reasons for pruning, unconnected with the growth sequence of the rose. One is to achieve a reasonably balanced bush, which will look better, and the other is to thin out the centre of tangled growth and so allow a good circulation of air, which is essential for health. This may mean sacrificing some good, strong canes, particularly if two are crossing and rubbing together, but it will pay in the long run to get rid of one of them.

SOME GENERAL POINTS

Many professionals use a knife for pruning, and there are special knives made for this purpose. Most other people, however, prefer to use secateurs (pruning shears), as they require less of a knack to handle efficiently. Buy a really good pair, even if it costs quite a lot more. They will be strong, properly designed and of the best-quality steel, and they will last a lifetime if well looked after. Some cheap and badly designed secateurs can bruise a stem badly below a pruning cut and set up die-back or disease. Always keep your secateurs clean and sharp. Pruning should never look as if it has been done with a blunt bread-knife. For cutting away old, gnarled rose stumps and very thick canes several years old (when renovating a neglected rose garden, for instance) a fine-toothed pruning saw or long-handled pruners or loppers may be needed.

If a cut cane reveals a brown, discoloured centre, this means that die-back is spreading down the shoot. Cut to the next bud down, and continue on until clean white wood is reached. For upright-growing varieties, cut to an outward-facing bud in the hope of increasing the rose's lateral spread – though your plans may well be frustrated when it is a bud lower down that decides to grow away more strongly and in quite the wrong direction! Growing roses demands a philosophic outlook on life, and one must just keep on trying. With lax, sprawling roses cut to an inward (or upward) facing bud in the hope that they will co-operate and grow upwards and inwards. Sixty per cent of the time it works.

There are certain areas of the world where it is advisable to dab pruning paint on the ends of the thicker canes after pruning to prevent the entry of disease spores, and of boring insects, particularly the pith borer. This is a small carpenter bee, which bores down into the pith of cut rose stems to lay its eggs, often causing the cane to die. Since it is difficult to define these areas precisely, advice from a local nursery should be sought if you are in doubt.

On poor, light soils pruning should be less severe than on good ones, as there is less goodness in them to build up the rose again. Prune newly-planted roses harder than established ones. The top-growth will not come so soon but will be stronger when it does, and meanwhile a lot of energy will be going into building up a good root system.

WHEN TO PRUNE

This is entirely dependent on climate, and in a mild one can be done at any time between the roses becoming dormant and the time when the buds are just beginning to break in the spring, though not in a frosty spell. Autumn pruning can, however, mean a second working over of the bushes early the following year if a harsh winter has killed off some of the canes already pruned.

Where winters are really severe, prune only in the spring, but again no later than the time when the buds are just beginning to show signs of life. Leaving it longer than this will waste all the energy that has gone into producing the first leaves and shoots, and may also

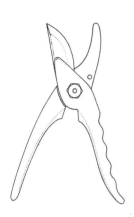

Pruning tools
Most pruning is best done by secateurs. These must be kept clean and sharp. (above) These scissor-type secateurs operate with a slicing movement and produce a very clean cut. (below) The anvil type of secateurs are less efficient and are more likely to bruise or crush the canes.

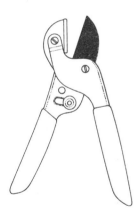

Pruning cuts
(below) Make all pruning cuts about 5mm (¼ in) above an outward-facing leaf and/or bud. The cut should slope downwards at an angle of about 45° away from the bud.

mean later flowering. In a climate where winter protection of the plants has been necessary, pruning can generally be done as soon as the protective materials have been removed.

Most of what has been said so far applies to a greater or lesser degree to all roses. Now we come more specifically to types and families and the variations (if any) from these basic principles that they demand.

HYBRID TEAS
Cut away completely all dead, diseased, weak and spindly shoots – anything, that is, that is less than pencil thickness. If this leaves you with nothing at all, your rose needs a plant doctor, but assuming that you do have something left, remove also stumps which have remained from previous prunings and may still be green, but from which no strong canes have sprouted in the last twelve months. If they have not done so already, they will not in the future. Open out the centre of the bush if it needs it and remove shoots that are throwing it out of balance.

Finally cut the remaining canes, each one just above a bud, leaving them for average garden display about 20–25 cm (8–10 in) long. This is the practice followed in the British Isles by the majority and it works very well, but elsewhere – in the milder parts of the United States, for instance – this would be considered hard pruning. There, the equivalent length would be nearer 45–60 cm (18–24 in). Exhibitors, wanting top-quality blooms if not so many of them per plant, would give much more drastic treatment, cutting down to one or two eyes if they are really after the top prizes. In this case, a great deal of extra feeding must follow to build them up again.

For those whose god is sophistication, the pruning of Hybrid Teas, and indeed some Floribundas, can be carried a stage further, for there are some varieties that need either harder or lighter pruning than others if they are to do well. 'Peace' and its more immediate descendants such as 'Rose Gaujard' are examples of roses that actively resent hard pruning, and if you have a rose which you are looking after well in all other ways but which is not living up to your expectations, it is worth while experimenting a little with your pruning. This may be the answer.

FLORIBUNDAS
Proceed through the first stages exactly as for Hybrid Teas, but leave the main canes longer by 10–12 cm (4–5 in). Very tall-growing Floribundas and Grandifloras should be reduced by about one-third of their height. Strong side shoots from the main canes of both types can be shortened by about one-third as well, rather than being removed altogether. In each case, cut to a bud as before.

If, with Floribundas or any other kind of rose, you cannot find a bud in what seems to

be the right place, choose the nearest one, either up or down the shoot. Pruning is not something that can be done with mathematical precision. Use your eye rather than a ruler to judge lengths, but keep within the limits set as far as possible.

STANDARD (TREE) ROSES
For those budded from Hybrid Tea and Floribunda varieties, follow the same sequence as for the bushes, taking the bud union as the point from which the canes are measured. A balanced head is especially important, as standards are likely to be seen from all sides.

CLIMBERS
Do not prune climbing roses in their first year. Most of them are slow to get away and may make very little new top growth in the first season, concentrating rather on developing their roots. They need what few leaves there may be to manufacture food, and if the canes are cut back there will be less of these. If the climbing sports of bush roses, such as 'Climbing Masquerade', are cut back there is a chance of reversion to the bush form.

Pruning a climber can be a formidable job, particularly if you do not like heights, and many of them flower perfectly well for many years with no pruning at all, other than for keeping them in bounds. It is worth trying this and seeing what happens, remembering however that when you do have to prune, you may have a much bigger job on your hands. If you decide to prune straight away, the permanent framework of main canes should not be touched, unless they have grown too long and are encroaching perhaps on a window. Even a rose-lover should not have to live like a troglodyte or have difficulty in getting in or out of the front door!

With a climber that has become bare at the base, one of the main canes can be cut back to about 30 cm (1 ft) or so in length, in the hope that new growth will come from it low down. There are some obstinate roses, however, such as 'Paul's Lemon Pillar', in which this will rarely happen and a bush rose or other plant must be used to cover up.

RAMBLERS
Ramblers of the small, cluster-flowered type – those in the main descended from *R. wichuraiana* – should have the old canes completely removed as soon as flowering is over in late summer. If you can face it, the best way to do this is to untie all the canes from their supports and let them rest on the ground. They are flexible enough to do this without breaking off – and flexible enough also to get in a fine tangle – but eventually you should be able to separate the old from the new. If the latter are rather scanty in some years, a few of the old canes may be kept, as they will produce some bloom. Shorten the side shoots.

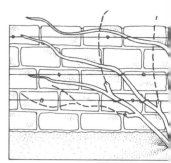

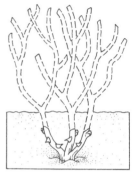

A Hybrid Tea bush before and after hard pruning.

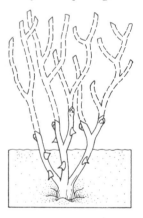

A Hybrid Tea bush before and after medium pruning.

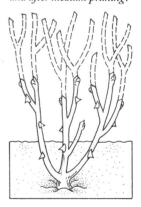

A Hybrid Tea bush before and after light pruning.

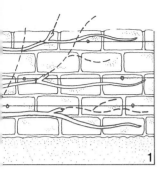

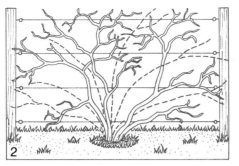

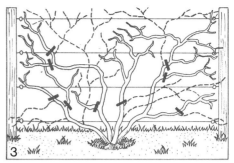

Pruning climbers and ramblers
(1) Prune climbing roses in winter by shortening the laterals which grow from the main stem. Cut these back to one or two leaf axil buds after flowering.
(2) Prune small-flowered ramblers immediately after they have flowered. Detach the canes from their supports, cut the old canes right to the ground and tie in those of the current year's growth in their place.
(3) Ramblers of the larger-flowered varieties such as 'Albertine' need less drastic pruning. Cut them back only to the point immediately above where a new cane has sprouted from the old. Shorten the side shoots.

WEEPING STANDARDS
If these are formed from small-flowered ramblers, remove the old canes; if from large-flowered ramblers, follow the procedure given in the diagram for 'Albertine'; if from climbers, cut back side shoots only to two or three eyes.

MINIATURE ROSES
A minimum of pruning is needed with these. Remove shoots that have died back and thin out occasionally those varieties which tend to produce a dense tangle of twigs. Trim back to the most convenient bud any of the extra-vigorous shoots that sometimes form and throw the whole thing out of balance.

SHRUB ROSES
These vary in their way of growing so enormously, even within a single group, that it is really only possible to generalize for each group, but one can give pointers that will suit the majority of them. There are some people who hold that the old roses (as opposed to the modern Floribunda-type shrubs) should never be pruned at all but allowed to ramble as they will. Certainly many of them will carry on quite happily for years with only the odd dead branch being removed, but in my experience pruning does (except with the species, which are better without it) greatly increase the number and quality of the flowers. And again, some bushes can become bare at the base after a while, when a drastic cutting back of one or two main canes in winter will encourage them to start again from low down. Prune once-blooming roses after flowering and they will form new shoots to bloom the following year. Those on which you expect decorative hips, leave until winter or spring.
Species Leave these alone except for the removal of dead or dying wood. A little trimming when the bushes are young may be needed to produce a balanced bush, but not afterwards. Do not buy species for which you know in your heart you really do not have room, for these are roses that really must be left to their own devices if they are to give of their best.
Gallicas The twiggy tangle of thin shoots of some of these should be thinned out. Otherwise only shorten the side shoots by about two-thirds. Clip over gently with shears if used for a hedge, but only to tidy them up and not to try to produce a regular, formal shape.
Damasks, Albas and Bourbons Remove about two-thirds of each side shoot and, if they are getting out of hand, main shoots can be reduced by about one-third of their length, cutting of course to a bud in each case. Prune Damasks and Albas after flowering; recurrent Bourbons in spring.
Hybrid Perpetuals For the more vigorous and well-branched growers, follow the pattern for Damasks, Albas and Bourbons. The rest can be pruned like Hybrid Teas – but with a light hand – or else pegged down. Autumn or spring, according to your climate.
Centifolias and Moss roses As they are lax in habit in most cases, the main shoots should be shortened by about one-third to encourage side buds to grow. Otherwise you may have long canes bending right over and trailing the exquisitely beautiful flowers in the mud.
Rugosas For most of these, only the removal of dead wood is needed, and with some varieties the occasional cutting back of one or two main canes to get rid of a possible bareness low down. Those hybrids more distantly removed from the species in habit, such as 'Conrad Ferdinand Meyer' and 'Sarah van Fleet', should be pruned like Bourbons.
Modern shrub roses, including Hybrid Musks The best, but I am afraid inescapably vague, advice for this completely haphazard group is to treat each one in the same way as one would a member of the family it most closely resembles. Thus modern shrubs of the Floribunda type should be pruned as Floribundas, and Hybrid Musks have their laterals and sometimes their main canes shortened – especially those enormous ones which sometimes come in late summer, shooting out at the most unexpected angles, often highly inconvenient if they are blocking a path.

TRAINING
Ramblers and climbers, and those shrub roses such as the more lusty Bourbons that are sometimes used as such, are the only roses that need regular training. For a wall or close-boarded fence, climbers should be tied in with plastic-covered garden wire or vinyl plastic tape to strong galvanized-iron wires running horizontally across the surface with about

45 cm (18 in) between each strand. The wires should be stretched taut between 10–12 cm (4–5 in) vine eyes or heavy-gauge rustproof nails driven into the brickwork or wood at about 1.2 m (4 ft) intervals. It is easier to penetrate brickwork if a hole of slightly smaller diameter than the nail or vine eye is drilled first with a masonry bit. The wires should be at least 8 cm (3 in) clear of the walls, as it is then easier to tie the rose canes to them and it also increases air circulation around them once they are in place.

Do not make the ties too tight, as many of the canes will increase their diameter several times over the years. Keep them outside the wires as far as possible, as this will make things much easier if you want to remove any of them later. New shoots will inevitably follow their own inclination and get in behind the wires, but there is nothing much you can do about this, especially if they are high up and hidden by leaves so that you do not know where they are straying.

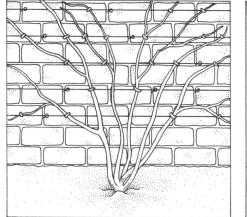
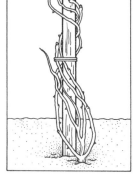

Training climbing roses
(above left) Train and tie in the canes of climbers more or less horizontally along their supporting wires. This encourages side shoots to break.

(right) Climbers or ramblers growing on pillars, pergola supports or tripods also need encouragement to break side shoots. Imitate horizontal training by tying them in a spiral.

WINTER PROTECTION

In a mild climate such as that of the British Isles, winter protection of roses is not usually necessary, though in a bad winter in the colder, more northerly parts, mounding soil over the crowns of the plants and weaving straw or dried bracken into the heads of standards can be a useful precaution. This applies to the average run of roses, but not to such kinds as Teas, which it would be chancy in any case to grow in the open in Britain. The more hardy of these can still be found in a few nursery lists, and might survive the worst the weather could do in the mild south-west, and there are also other kinds of roses which, while not quite so fragile, are still borderline cases. These are typified by the Banksian climbers, which should be given a warm wall or sheltered corner for them to survive and flourish. Elsewhere in the world things can, however, be very different.

Contrast, for instance, the climate in the south of Europe with that of the north; or of Florida, where roses scarcely have a dormant period, with many central and northern states of America and most of Canada, where they have to endure months on end when there is biting cold, way below zero. The work of the late German breeder Wilhelm Kordes has already been touched upon. He spent many years, largely using the chance species that bears his name, in breeding hardy roses for the north European winters. To a great extent he succeeded, as can be seen from the large numbers of his shrub roses and climbers that are such a feature of German public parks, where they not only survive but thrive.

Just the same, many of these have problems in the extreme and prolonged cold of the

Canadian winter (except for that of the western coastal belt) and in a number of states across the border southwards. There, if not killed outright, most roses will at the very least have to make completely new growth each year, using up a vast amount of energy and having very late and hence very short flowering seasons. Winter protection in these conditions is essential.

Hybrid Teas and Floribundas can usually get by in a temperature as low as −12 to −10°C (10 to 15°F) over a period of a week or more, provided that loose soil is mounded to a depth of 20–30 cm (8–12 in) over the crown. Remember, however, that the yellow and orange blends tend to be less hardy than the others, despite the fact that *R. foetida*, from which they are supposed to have inherited their lack of toughness, is certainly not the most tender rose in the chart.

Below −12°C (10°F), something more is needed, even for the hardier varieties, but a number of the old roses are considerably tougher. The table gives an indication as to how much, but it should be used with caution. It will be, I hope, a useful guide, but considerable variations occur with individual varieties, though these may sometimes be due to factors other than temperature alone. Apart from the species, all the old roses are hybrids, and some may have liberal helpings of the blood of less hardy hybrids in their make-up. The type plant may be as tough as old boots, but not one of the offspring.

One or two of these, such as *R. nitida* and *R. blanda*, are natives of very cold areas and their appearance so far down the list is not surprising. But that *R. rugosa*, coming as it does from Japan and China, should be so is as unexpected as *R. foetida* not far above it. However, this is a

Roses hardy to −20 to −23°C (−5 to −10°F)
Bourbons
Centifolias
China roses
R. californica
R. hugonis
R. moyesii
R. multiflora
R. pendulina
R. pomifera
R. primula
R. roxburghii
R. wichuraiana

Roses hardy to −23 to −30°C (−10 to −22°F)
Albas
Damasks
Gallicas
R. arkansana
R. carolina
R. foetida
R. palustris
R. rubiginosa
  (R. eglanteria)
R. setigera
R. spinosissima

Roses hardy to −30 to −37°C (−22 to −35°F)
R. canina
R. nitida
R. virginiana

Roses hardy to −37 to −45°C (−35 to −50°F)
R. blanda
R. rubrifolia
R. rugosa

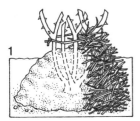
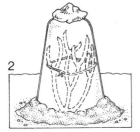
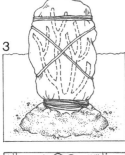

case where not all the hybrids are anything like as hardy as the species, as has been found during six years of investigations at the Ottawa Agricultural Research Station in Canada. Of those Rugosa varieties tried there, 'Belle Pointivine', 'Schneezwerg', 'Thérèse Bugnet' and 'Will Alderman' came out the best, with an average of less than 25 per cent of the plants succumbing.

The Canadians themselves have produced three new Rugosa hybrids, 'Jens Munk', 'Henry Hudson' and 'Martin Frobisher', the first two of which are quite outstandingly cold-resistant and the third only slightly less so. Elsewhere on the North American continent work is going on to produce hardier Hybrid Teas and Floribundas, but though some of these have already been put on sale and claims made for them, experience has unfortunately shown that so far they are very little, if at all, better than existing varieties. The considerably older Hybrid Perpetuals are hardier than any of them.

Much can be done with all roses to increase their resistance to harsh conditions by having healthy, well-grown plants and properly ripened wood as winter approaches, helped by avoiding the late application of nitrogenous fertilizers. The actual hours of sunshine for wood ripening are of prime importance, and carefully sited screens of trees, other shrubs and hedges can help in keeping away biting winds, which can often do great damage; they can also be used for blocking off the flow of cold air down a slope, which may cause a frost pocket at the bottom.

However, the winter protection needed on top of these general precautions may vary considerably from area to area, even within officially defined temperature belts, and some guidance should be obtained from a knowledgeable local rosarian or your local Agricultural Officer, Department or Board as to how far you need go. The height of your garden above sea level can, for instance, make quite a difference. Or a sheltered valley may be better than an exposed plain only a few miles away.

The reason for winter protection is not so much to shield the roses from the cold itself as to keep them at a reasonably uniform temperature that is consistent with dormancy. Frozen ground in itself is not a problem, but rapid changes in temperature – freezing the sap in the canes one moment and thawing them out the next – can destroy the plant's cell structure, and cold winds will dehydrate the top growth when it is impossible for the roots to take up moisture to replace what is lost. For this last reason, all remaining leaves should be removed before any sort of protection is applied, for it is through them that water evaporates most rapidly.

Other points to note, both before putting on protective covering and when it is removed in spring, include, first of all, not putting it on before you have to. At least two nights of hard, continuous frost with no sign of a thaw will be the sign to start operations. Make sure that all fallen leaves and mulches which could harbour disease are removed from around the plants. Soak the ground thoroughly with water and then carry on with your covering operations.

In the early part of the following year do not be in too much of a hurry to remove protection. Make sure that the cold has gone for good. The odd comparatively warm day or two can be most deceptive, and one night later frost crystals will be sparkling on the branches of the roses again, with disastrous results.

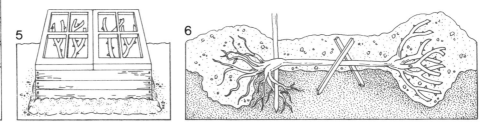

Winter protection
Winter protection may be necessary for roses in cold climates, particularly in northern Europe, the north-central states of America and Canada. The following are alternative methods of protecting bush, standard and climbing roses.
(1) Mound soil over the bud union to a depth of 30 cm (12 in) and leave it exposed until the soil freezes. Then cover the entire mound with straw to keep it frozen, and keep it all in place during wind or rain with wire mesh.
(2) Cover the bush with a purpose-made polystyrene cone held in place by a rock or brick. Mound soil around the base of the cone to keep it in place.
(3) Pack the bush with straw and wrap it with burlap. Tie the burlap securely in place and mound soil around the base. Alternatively, cover the bush with a tar-paper cylinder. Fill the cylinder with bark or peat moss and secure the top with a burlap cover. Mound soil around the base.
(4) Provided the winters are not too severe, climbing roses may be brought through by wrapping them. Untie and bunch the canes. Wrap them in straw and burlap, and mound soil around the base.
(5) If you have a portable cold frame you can place it over small bush roses. Mound soil around the base of the frame. Ventilate on warm days.
(6) Bush roses, standards and climbers can also be protected using no additional equipment. Dig a trench to one side of the rose. Dig up the roots on the other side and bend the plant over into the trench. Use crossed stakes to hold the stem, or stems, of standards or climbers in place. Cover the canes and roots with soil at least 10 cm (4 in) deep.

INSECT PESTS AND
ROSE DISEASES

Since much of the routine for dealing with both of these overlaps, a great deal of repetition can be saved by grouping them together until the point is reached where they really do diverge. The technique of spraying, for instance, is identical for each and can actually be carried out in one operation, and there are other general points about garden hygiene which apply equally to either.

While not wanting to minimize the trouble that insects and diseases cause in a rose garden, the majority can be controlled at least in part (and some completely) with the aid of modern chemicals. Quite a number of people do not like using these and so will have greater problems, but no one should spray at all unless they really have to. Sprays, if growing more and more effective, are also growing more and more costly, they can kill beneficial insects as well as the harmful ones, and nobody really knows what the long-term effect of them may be. It is not so long since DDT was the answer to all insect problems, but was eventually found to bring other much more serious ones in its wake.

At a more personal level, spraying roses, particularly if you have a lot of them, is one of the most boring occupations in the garden and should not be regarded as something which must be done, come what may. Greenfly (aphids) in some years seem to breed with the rapidity if not the panache of Greek gods, and one imagines that *Myths and Legends of the Ancient Aphids* would make stimulating reading. In other years they are hardly seen, and while some areas may be plagued by specific kinds of insects, these may be virtually unknown elsewhere.

Among diseases, mildew is quite unpredictable, coming and going as it pleases for no clearly discernible reason. Black spot has unfortunately spread into places that were once free of it, for which one must blame the anti-pollution campaigners. In the good old days when the air was rich with the smoke from factory chimneys, the sulphur in it kept black spot at bay, but those times have almost gone. Nevertheless, unless you know yourself or learn from friends and neighbours that black spot is a regular annual menace in your district and that preventive spraying must be carried out before it arrives, wait until you see the first signs of attack and then act. But then do so promptly or it will spread like a forest fire. In brief, find out what happens in your garden, what the minimum spraying programme is likely to be, and how *infrequently* – not how frequently – it needs to be done.

The effectiveness of sprays has advanced rapidly in recent times, but work on them is still going on, a particular aim being to find some-

thing that will really deal with black spot. At the moment triforine ('Nimrod-T') appears to be the best answer and may well replace the more established maneb and benomyl ('Benlate'). A list of sprays and their particular uses is given in the table on page 258, but one of the problems is that with a number of them both insects and diseases build up an immunity, so that the spray no longer works. This has certainly been the case with benomyl, and explains why there are such different reports about its efficiency. By far the best practice is to vary your spray chemicals from year to year, so that the immunity cannot build up.

The introduction of systemic sprays has made life a great deal easier. These penetrate the stems and leaves and enter the rose's system so that they are not washed off by rain and will be effective for a number of weeks. The theory is that they are carried to every part of the plant by the sap, but not all of them are equally mobile. They go in, but they may not move on, so when spraying it is safest to make sure that the whole bush is wetted, the undersides of the leaves as well as the tops, but at the same time do not absolutely drench the rose so that the liquid pours off. This is simply a waste of time and money. Never spray in the hot sunshine, or leaves may be scorched. The cool of the evening is best.

A number of sprays will kill the majority of harmful insects, so it is not necessary to have one for each. Insect and disease sprays can frequently be mixed (together also with a foliar feed if you want to use one) so that, as mentioned earlier, all the rose's enemies – or most of them – can be dealt with in one go. However, it is wise to make sure from your supplier that the particular sprays you are using can be so mixed or you may lose all the leaves from your plants.

In mixing and using all sprays, follow the makers' instructions to the letter. Making a stronger mixture than directed could do a lot of harm. Making a weaker one for the sake of economy will probably just waste what money you have spent. If mixing two different pesticides, make sure that you end up with the right final concentration for each. Do not dilute each separately in the correct amount of water and then mix the two solutions; the end result will be too weak.

Pest and disease remedies are also sold as powders to be puffed on to the plants from special packs. A cloud of powder settles in a thin film on the leaves. A calm day is essential or all the dust will blow away before it reaches them. It does help if the leaves are damp, though not if it is raining as the dust that does settle will simply be washed off again, which is one of the main disadvantages of this kind of treatment. Apart from that, dust is much more difficult to spread evenly all over the roses, particularly on the undersides of the

leaves, and if the applicator is not working perfectly – and they can be temperamental – the plants can end up looking as if they had come out of a flour mill. They are, then, only for very small rose plantings, where particular care can be taken over each bush.

Finally, before getting down to specifics, the best insurance against all rose health problems is to carry out good cultivation.

COMMON ROSE DISEASES

Mildew The signs to look for are greyish, powdery-looking spots on young leaves and on the foot-stalks under the flower buds. These can occur at almost any time and spread will be rapid, in a bad case covering the whole plant and distorting its growth. It will soon pass on to neighbouring roses as well, carried by airborne spores, and your whole bed will look a sorry sight in no time. Fortunately, modern fungicides do keep mildew under control, though nothing has been found that will stop it occurring in the first place.

Dryness at the roots has long been given as one of the causes, but my own experience does not bear this out. In the long and incredibly hot and dry summer of 1976 – incredibly hot and dry for England, that is – my roses had less mildew than ever before. It may be unsightly, but it is not fatal. The spores of mildew and other plant diseases, including black spot, may winter in crevices in the rose canes and in the surrounding soil. Clearing away all fallen leaves will remove some of this menace, and one or two winter sprays of the bushes with Bordeaux mixture will help, too.

Black spot This is a great deal more serious than mildew, as it can cause a rose to lose its leaves if it is allowed to spread. Loss of leaves will weaken the plant and can, over a period of years, kill it. There is so far no certain cure, though there are sprays which give some degree of control. Picking off and burning infected leaves – just about the most tedious job I know – will help to prevent it spreading. Round black spots with a fringed edge, generally appearing just after midsummer on the older, lower leaves of a rose, are the danger signs. These grow rapidly in size and spread over the whole surface of the leaves, which eventually yellow and drop.

Rust This shows first about the same time of year as black spot as orange pustules on the undersides of the leaves. If left, they will turn black about a month later and the shoots will shrivel. Until comparatively recently an attack of rust would spread from plant to plant with such lethal effect that it was recommended that roses which were infected should be dug up and burned. Now there is oxycarboxin ('Plantvax'), a spray which will control it completely, but it should be added that rust is not nearly so universal as mildew or black spot. Certain varieties seem unaffected by it and in many districts it is unknown.

These – mildew, black spot and rust – are the three most serious and widespread rose diseases. Other ones which can cause lesser problems are:

Canker Caused by a parasitic fungus entering a stem through a wound. It appears as a brown, sunken area on the stem with the edges swollen and rough, and this area will spread until the stem is encircled and dies. Cut away the cankered stem and disinfect your secateurs afterwards with alcohol or methylated spirit.

Crown gall Irregularly-shaped, rough-surfaced brownish swellings near the bud union (and sometimes higher up) or on the roots (where of course they cannot be seen) and caused by soil-borne bacteria. Cut out and burn the infected part and seal the cut with pruning paint. Crown gall is not really serious if it is confined to the canes and it is easily dealt with. If, however, perhaps when scraping away round a plant looking for the source of a sucker, you discover it on the roots, it is more so. Cut away the infected roots and disinfect the soil. Failure to do so will mean weak plants, distorted flowers and possibly the death of the rose. Crown gall is not, however, an everyday occurrence.

Rose anthracnose A fungus disease which causes white spots with red rims on the leaves, which are not as pretty as they sound. Sometimes there are brown raised pustules on the stems as well. The red turns yellow if left and the leaves will fall, but infected shoots should be cut away before this happens. The spores will over-winter and a fungicide should be applied to get rid of them.

Purple spotting This is not really a disease and can generally be got rid of by improving drainage and feeding with a balanced fertilizer, as a soil deficiency is the cause. Unfortunately it is very easy to confuse purple spotting with black spot, but the spots, which are actually a very dark purple and not black, are much smaller, less regular in shape and do not have fringed edges.

Die-back More common in some roses than others, the yellow and orange varieties being particularly prone, though it can happen with any of them if the wood is not properly ripened. The causes can be damage by frost, canker or some of the other rose diseases, or else a deficiency of potash and other chemicals in the soil. As the name implies, shoots gradually die back and become brown, beginning at the tips; unless they are cut at the first healthy bud below the trouble, they will be lost completely.

COMMON INSECT PESTS

Aphids (greenfly) The most common rose pest, but luckily very easily dealt with nowadays with systemic insecticides. Tiny, soft-bodied, green and sometimes brownish insects that cluster on the young shoots, sucking the sap, so that if they are left the growth will be stunted and distorted, and buds may fail to open. A sticky substance they produce, attractive to ants, is known as honeydew, and this will coat rose stems and leaves, soon becoming covered with a black fungus known as sooty mould. Greenfly, breeding as we know with an abandon which must be the envy of all, not only lay eggs but also give birth to live young. They can appear at any time from early summer onwards, and should be sprayed promptly.

Rose scale (scurfy scale) Dirty white or grey scales in clusters, mainly on old stems. These hide insects which suck the sap, weakening growth and causing the stems to wilt. If caught when the outbreak is confined to a small area, painting with methylated spirit or alcohol will prevent spreading. Otherwise, cut away and burn infected wood and spray the rest of the bush in case traces have been left which you have not spotted.

Shoot or pith borers Offspring of saw-flies, rose stem girdlers or carpenter bees, which lay eggs in the stems, the pith of which their maggots eat when they hatch. They can in some areas enter through the cut ends of pruned canes, though not if these have been treated with pruning paint, but none of the shoot borers common in the British Isles are likely to do this. Cut canes below wilting portions and burn. That old stand-by derris spray will prevent infestation in the first place.

Froghoppers (cuckoo-spit; spittle bugs) A small, greenish-yellow insect which hides itself in a blob of white foam, which can easily be seen on shoots and leaf-axils in early summer. Spraying will destroy them, but only if the froth or foam is washed away first with a strong jet of water. Small numbers can

be picked off by hand, but however you go about it, they should be got rid of or shoots can become distorted and wilt.

Ants These will not attack a rose directly, but they may build their nests among the roots and, if the soil is loosened, the plant may wilt. Most likely to happen in sandy soil. Apply an ant's-nest destroyer, but *not* (for the roots' sake) boiling water!

Chafers and Japanese beetles (Also, in some countries and having much the same effect, rose curculio and fuller beetles) These attack the rose in a number of ways, Japanese Beetles being quite devastating in their attacks in some parts of North America and chafers being the main culprits elsewhere. The petals and anthers of the blooms may be nibbled, irregular holes may be eaten in the leaves, and the grubs (in the case of the chafers very large, fat, white and straight out of a nightmare) will attack the roots and may kill or at least weaken the plants. When seen, beetles may be picked off by hand and destroyed. Otherwise, disinfecting the soil when planting and spraying later is the answer.

Leaf-miners White blisters on the leaves, often in irregular chain formation. Each blister contains a grub and the leaves should be picked off and burned.

Rose slugworms (bristly rose slugs) Greenish-yellow 12 mm (½ in) grubs which feed on the surface of the leaves early in spring, but they do not seem to be able to manage the veins, so the leaves are skeletonized in patches, infected areas turning brown. Some kinds do manage to devour the rest of the leaves later. Spray promptly or remove infected shoots.

Spider mites (red spider) In dry, hot weather, leaves that have brownish-bronze

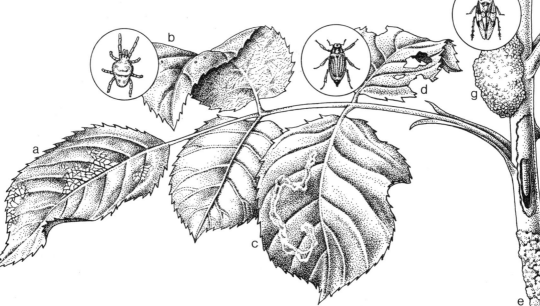

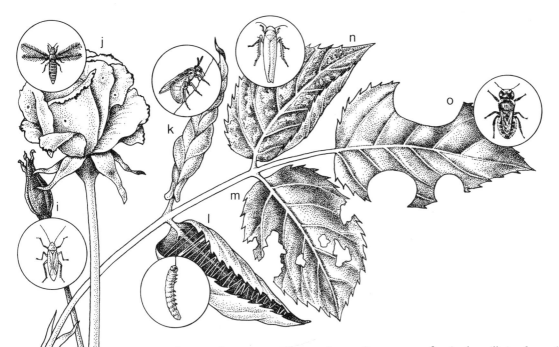

Rose pests

Shown on these pages are some of the common insect and other pests of roses and/ or their effects: (a) rose slugworm (bristly rose slug); (b) spider mite (red spider); (c) leaf-miner; (d) chafer; (e) rose scale (scurfy scale); (f) shoot or pith borer; (g) froghopper (cuckoo-spit or spittle bug); (h) aphid (greenfly); (i) capsid bug; (j) thrip; (k) leaf-rolling sawfly; (l) tortrix moth caterpillar and (m) damage caused by tortrix moth; (n) leafhopper; (o) leaf-cutter bee. The pests are not all drawn to the same scale.

patches on the upper surfaces and very fine webs just visible on the undersides mean that spider mites are sucking sap from them, but the pests are so small that the naked eye can hardly see them. The leaves will curl and may drop off eventually. Not strictly speaking an insect pest, but spray with a systemic insecticide such as dimethoate or a miticide like tetradifon (if you can get it).

Tortrix moths and other moth caterpillars and bud-worms The signs are holes eaten in the leaves, and the caterpillars can be picked off by hand if not too numerous, or else sprayed against. The tortrix moth among several others rolls the leaves, holding the edges together with silken threads while the caterpillars feed inside. They will also bore into rose buds and feed on them, as will those of the lackey moth, whose caterpillars, when not so engaged, can be found in tent-like silken structures draped about the plants. These should be destroyed.

Leafhoppers Very small, yellowish-green insects which jump like grasshoppers, and which feed on the undersides of the rose leaves, to which their discarded white skins can often be seen adhering. The leaves turn purple with mottled patches, and a bad attack can cause at least partial defoliation. Use a systemic insecticide.

Leaf-rolling sawflies The fly lays its eggs in the leaf margins, and the whole leaf then rolls up to protect the greyish-green grubs, leaving, in a bad attack, a very odd-looking rose bush. There is no effective remedy once this has happened, except to squeeze each leaf, dismiss from your mind what is happening inside it, and pull it off and burn it. If this is not done, the larvae can drop to lower leaves and spread all over the plant. An attack occurs

most often in the still air of a garden sheltered by trees, and can be held at bay by early preventive spraying.

Leaf-cutter bees A small bee which cuts completely circular pieces out of rose leaves and uses them most ingeniously to line its nest tunnels. Attacks are not usually serious, but there are some areas where they may turn the foliage to lace. As the leaves are not actually eaten, a systemic spray would be ineffective, but keeping the leaves heavily dusted will help to discourage them.

Thrips Tiny, brownish-yellow winged insects which thrive in hot weather, when an attack can be quite serious, particularly on pale pink and white roses, though none are immune. Thrips rasp the bud petal edges and the flowers become misshapen or fail to open at all. A spray or dust (which is not too difficult to use on buds) will give control and so, I believe, will metal foil spread on the beds beneath the bushes! This, for reasons which I feel do not need explaining, I have not tried; but, believe it or not, someone did and wrote about the results.

Capsid bugs Bright green insects which cause small brown spots on young leaves, and buds to become distorted and wither before opening. An insecticide will control them.

This catalogue of horrors has now thankfully come to an end, and I will finish it by saying once more what I said at the beginning. You will be most unlikely to have to fight off all of them at once, or even in one season. A mild attack of many will do very little harm, and a good general-purpose systemic insecticide and a rose fungicide will keep the majority of diseases and predators – except for flower-arrangers – comfortably at bay.

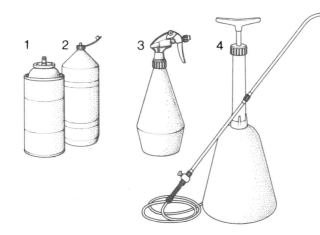

Applying pesticides
For spot treatments on only a few roses, some pesticides come in aerosols (1), while puffer packs of dry chemicals (2) are suitable in certain cases, as explained on pages 254–255. For most rose growers the best applicators are the small lever-action plastic type (3) for local treatment and the pump-up pressure type (4) for general spraying of rose beds. In the last case it is better, although more expensive, to choose a model with an on-off trigger control and a long spray lance.

FUNGICIDES FOR ROSES OUT OF DOORS

Active ingredient; trade and alternative names	Black spot	Powdery mildew	Rust
Benodanil ('Calirus')	−	−	+++
Benomyl★ ('Benlate')	+++	+++	−
Bupirimate+triforine★ ('Nimrod-T')	+++	+++	−
Captan ('Orthocide')	++	−	−
Dinocap ('Karathane')	−	++	−
Fenarimol ('Rubigan')	+++	+++	+
Folpet ('Phaltan')	++	+	+
Mancozeb ('Dithane', 'Dithane M-45', 'Karamate')	++	−	++
Maneb ('Dithane M-22', 'Manzate')	++	−	++
Oxycarboxin★ ('Plantvax')	−	−	+++
Thiophanate-methyl ('Mildothane')	+++	+++	−
Thiram ('Arasan', 'Tersan', 'Tripomol 80', 'ICI General Garden Fungicide')	++	−	++
Triadimefon ('Bayleton')	++	+++	−
Triforine★ ('Saprol')	+++	+++	−
Zineb ('Dithane', 'Dithane Z-78')	++	−	++

Note: most fungicides active against black spot will also control rose anthracnose and downy mildew.

Key: +++very active; ++moderately active; +slightly active; −inactive; ★systemic

INSECTICIDES FOR ROSES OUT OF DOORS

Active ingredient; alternative names	Aphids; leafhoppers	Caterpillars; chafers	Leaf-miners	Leaf-rolling sawflies	Rose scale	Thrips
Diazinon ('Basudin', 'Diazitol')	++	+	+	−	++	+
Dimethoate★ ('Cygon', 'Rogor')	+++	+	+	−	++	+
Fenitrothion★ ('Accothion', 'Cyfen', 'Cytel', 'Dicofen', 'Fenstan EC 50')	++	++	++	+	+	+
Formothion★ ('Anthio')	+++	+	+	−	++	+
Malathion ('Cythion', 'Malastan 60')	++	+	+	−	++	+
Menazon★ ('Saphos', 'Sayfos')	+++	−	−	−	−	−
Gamma-HCH (benzene hexachloride, gamma-BHC, 'Gamma-Col', 'Gammexane', 'Lindane')	+	+	++	*Aggravates attack*	−	+
Petroleum oil (white oil)	+	−	−	−	++	−
Pyrethrins	+	−	−	−	−	+
Trichlorphon ('Dipterex 80')	−	++	++	++	−	−

In North America, acephate ('Orthene') spray is used extensively for thrips control and it is also very effective against aphids, spider mite and other rose insects since it is systemic. Under glass, use either resmethrin plus pyrethrum, or bioresmethrin, except against red spider mite; for the latter, syringe with water or white oil.

Key: +++very active; ++moderately active; +slightly active; −inactive; ★systemic

CONTAINER-GROWN ROSES INDOORS AND OUT

ROSES UNDER GLASS

In a temperate climate it is possible, using only a cold greenhouse, to have roses in flower to cut for the house a full two months before they will be out in the garden. A little heat, with night temperatures varying progressively from 5°C (41°F) to 10°C (50°F) and 15°C (59°F) in the three months preceding flowering, and they can be brought into flower about another month earlier.

A lanky rose is difficult to handle in a pot and can look top-heavy, so select your varieties from among the compact and bushy Floribundas and Hybrid Teas, and if possible try to make sure that they are on a non-suckering stock. Traditional clay pots are the most attractive to look at and help to keep the potting mixture and roots cool by evaporation through their sides, but plastic ones are much easier to buy nowadays and are quite satisfactory from the practical point of view. They are much lighter to handle and less likely to get broken.

If clay pots are used, they should be well soaked in water before use so that they do not themselves absorb a lot of the water from the potting mixture. The latter should preferably be one of the commercial, ready-mixed brands, as it will then have just the right balance of firmness and water-retention, which is very important when the roots of the roses are confined into a comparatively small area. However, for those who wish to make their own potting mixture, this is best done a few weeks in advance of planting, keeping it in a cool, dry shed and turning it occasionally while it matures. A suitable recipe is good, turfy loam, well-moistened granulated peat (peat moss) and clean, sharp sand in the ratio of 4:2:1. For each 10-litre (two-gallon) bucket of this, add 30 g (1 oz) each of hoof and horn meal and superphosphate of lime, and 15 g (½ oz) each of meat and bone meal and potassium sulphate, all well mixed in.

The planting is done in early winter and afterwards the roses should be left for a full year out of doors in a sheltered but sunny spot so that they can establish themselves before being brought into the greenhouse. Water, spray and dead-head as necessary, but do not add any extra fertilizer.

When midwinter comes around again and if there is no frost about, prune the roses – Floribundas to 20–30 cm (8–12 in) and Hybrid Teas to 15–25 cm (6–10 in), and clean up the surface of the mixture in the pots. Bring them into the greenhouse two or three weeks later and add 30 g (1 oz) of a slow-acting fertilizer to a 25 cm (10 in) pot or 60 g (2 oz) to a 30 cm (12 in) pot. Top up with mixture if necessary to about 5 cm (2 in) below the rims in order to leave enough room for watering.

There is no hard and fast rule about how often water should be given, as this will depend on the temperature of your greenhouse and how much sun shines on it during the day, but the pots should never dry out completely. It is best to soak the pots thoroughly, preferably with rainwater, and to leave them until they are nearly dry before watering again. Some growers advocate the use of liquid fertilizers and even foliar feeding for greenhouse roses. Others find this quite unnecessary, and this has certainly been my own experience, but there is no harm in experimenting and seeing what suits your particular roses best. Good ventilation during mild spells, preferably from above so as to avoid draughts, is important to hold mildew in check. After the roses have flowered, they should be taken out of doors once more and kept in the same kind of spot as before until it is time to start the sequence again.

Roses raised and sold in containers will force quite well, and in this case there is no need to keep them a year in the open first. However, each winter after their first early blooming they should be transferred as their roots grow successively to 23 cm (9 in), 25 cm (10 in) and finally to 30 cm (12 in) pots.

Roses in containers
Choose containers of 25 or 30 cm (10 or 12 in) diameter for pot-grown roses.
(1) Bareroot roses may need their roots pruned to fit them in comfortably. Cut back some of the stronger roots. This will do them no harm provided that the cuts are made cleanly.
(2) Add a layer of crocks to each pot to help drainage. Add a layer of potting mixture, centre the rose at the correct depth and fill up with mixture.
(3) Ram the mixture firm with a trowel handle. Top up the pot, leaving a space for watering. Water the pot thoroughly after planting.

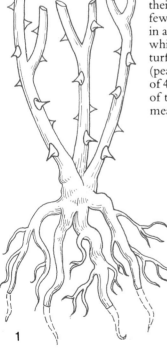

1

2

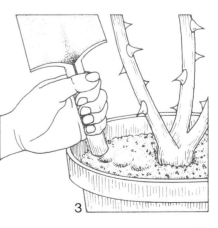

3

FOR THE PATIO

On a patio, roses will flower either at the normal time or a little earlier if it is well sheltered. The containers (and hence the roses) can be larger and more varied according to the space available, and there can be several bushes in one container to add variety, provided that it is large enough. In climates where winter protection is necessary, bear in mind, however, that the pots, tubs or troughs will have to be moved when the roses are dormant to a garage, shed or cellar where the temperature can be maintained at about −10 to −4°C (14 to 25°F), so they should not be too heavy and unmanageable. Buying commercially-prepared potting mixture would be quite an investment for large containers suitable for a patio and the home-made mix given above would be quite suitable.

Watering is most important, and the containers should never be allowed to dry out. However, water can in time leach the goodness from the soil, so that a liquid rose fertilizer (keeping strictly to the instructions on the bottle as to strength when mixing it) can be added to the water about every two weeks during the growing season. Or a slow-acting dry fertilizer can be worked gently into the surface soil with a hand fork early in the year, to be followed by a thorough watering.

MINIATURE ROSES

The fact that they are so readily available in shops and garden centres ready potted has led to the belief that these are house-plants. They are not, and special steps must be taken if they are to remain indoors for any length of time. The main problem in most houses will be that the atmosphere is much too dry, which will cause the leaves of the roses to yellow and eventually drop. A secondary difficulty may well be a lack of sufficient light, for if Miniatures are placed in a window through which the sun constantly pours it may be much too hot for them and can even scorch the leaves. About 21–24°C (70–75°F) is the ideal.

Despite all this, you can have Miniature roses flowering in the house, and there are two ways in which this can be achieved. The first and by far the simplest is to bring the pots into the house just as colour is showing in the flower buds. If the conditions shown in the drawings are kept to, the roses should flower well, but they should be taken outside again as soon as the last blooms have faded, in order to build up their strength.

If you want to be more ambitious and have Miniatures flowering in the house during the winter, they can be grown under fluorescent lights, switched on for twelve hours a day on average. Reflective surfaces above and a white-painted wall behind the gravel tray on which the pots should rest will give sufficient light, and the wall especially will direct a proportion of it on to the lower leaves.

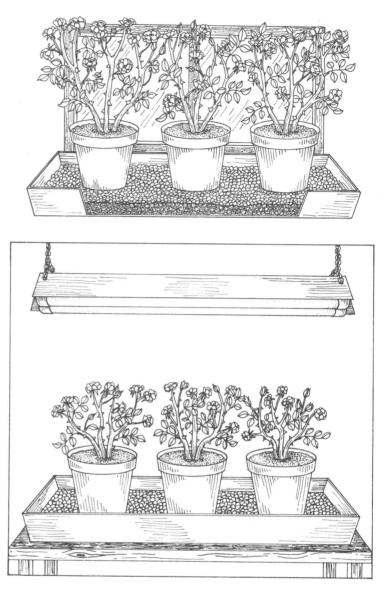

Miniatures in pots
Grow miniature roses on a tray of fine gravel with water to the level of the pot bases. The plants will take up the water and enjoy the humidity. Keep them on a sunny window sill. Do not let the plants touch the glass. (above) Miniature roses can be grown in light units purchased entire or made up yourself. Mount two 40-watt fluorescent tubes 25–30cm (10–12in) above the plants. Switch the light on for 12 hours a day. 'Gro-Lux' tubes are best. Prevent mildew by installing a small electric fan 1.5m (5ft) away.

ROSES AS CUT FLOWERS

Roses do not last as long as many other flowers when cut, but their beauty is such that it is worth giving consideration to what can be done to prolong their life. Some are much more suitable for cutting than others, and the length of time the flowers of each remain attractive in the garden is by no means a fool-proof guide. However, those with the fewest petals are generally the quickest to open and the soonest past their best. Those with high centres and many closely-packed petals, such as exhibitors favour, will hold their shape and last longer, provided that they have not been picked when wet. The above applies primarily to Hybrid Teas. Floribundas cut when the majority of the flowers in a truss are half-open will be found to have greater staying power.

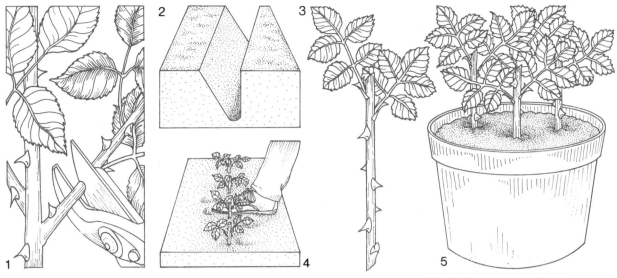

After a day of sunshine the plant sugars – the food materials – in a plant's tissues formed by photosynthesis are at their highest level, so late afternoon or early evening are the best times to cut. Early morning is second best. Do not cut a rose with a longer stem than you will need for your vases, for the more stem and food-manufacturing leaves you remove from the bush, the more you will inhibit its growth. Cut with a sharp knife or pruners at an angle just above a leaf-axil bud as if dead-heading.

There are many commercial preparations on the market for adding to the water to make cut flowers last longer. These provide a very small degree of nourishment and also help to prevent the formation of bacteria which can make it difficult for the roses to take up water. A small spoonful of glucose (which is what most commercial preservatives largely consist of) is an alternative, but most of the other ideas which have so long been current, such as adding an aspirin or a few drops of bleach to get rid of the bacteria, have been proved to be either valueless or even harmful.

Cut about 1cm (½in) from the end of each stem before putting roses in a vase, and if you have the time (and the energy) renew the water daily, removing the same amount from the stems each time. If you cannot do this, at least keep the vases well topped up. One of the greatest enemies of cut roses is dryness in the atmosphere, and if the vases are full there is a better chance of some moisture reaching them through evaporation.

Rather more trouble, but worth while if you have the facilities, is cutting the roses as suggested above, and then plunging them into tepid water so that about three-quarters of their stems are covered. The container is then put in a refrigerator for four to eight hours at 2–4°C (36–39°F). This will usually increase the life of the blooms by at least three days. Immersing the stems and leaves, even without refrigeration, also helps.

Hardwood cuttings
Take hardwood cuttings in early autumn. (1) Choose a shoot about as thick as a pencil and of the current year's growth – preferably one that has flowered at midsummer. Cut it away. (2) Choose a spot in the garden sheltered from the mid-day sun and dig a narrow, slit-like trench 18cm (7in) deep. On light soil this is best done by pushing a spade in vertically along a centreline and working it back and forth. Sprinkle 2.5cm (1in) of coarse sand along the trench. (3) Prepare two or three 23cm (9in) cuttings from each long shoot. Discard the soft tip growth. Remove the lower leaves from each cutting, leaving only two. Moisten the lower end of each cutting and dip it in a hormone rooting powder. (4) Insert the cuttings vertically about 15cm (6in) apart in the slit trench. Only one-third should project above the ground. Tread the cuttings in firmly and water well. In dry spells water again, and tread them in after frost which may loosen the soil, leading to failure. (5) Hardwood cuttings can also be rooted into light, sandy soil in pots. Keep the pots in a shady spot outdoors. Do not let them dry out. Protect from hard frost.

PROPAGATION

There are two main ways of increasing the stock of rose varieties you already have – apart, that is, from going to a nursery and buying them. The easiest, though it takes longer for the roses to grow to full size if it is employed, is taking cuttings. The faster but more troublesome – though it is the method most widely used by professional nurserymen – is budding or grafting.

TAKING CUTTINGS
Most roses, with one important exception, take or root easily from cuttings. The exception unfortunately, from the gardener's point of view if not from the nurseryman's, is the very popular Hybrid Tea group – though some gardeners have success even with these. It would appear that the more highly developed a rose is – and only a member of the European aristocracy could have a more complicated ancestry than a Hybrid Tea – the less inclined it is to take as a cutting. However, though they are likely to be temperamental, all are worth trying.

Floribundas have a much shorter line of descent from their wild origins, as have the old rose groups and the Climbers, Ramblers and Miniatures. I have taken cuttings without difficulty from all of them – species, Gallicas, Albas, Centifolias, Bourbons, Hybrid Perpetuals, Chinas and so on – though it should be added that some, especially the Floribundas, will not grow as vigorously as they would if grafted onto an understock. This can, with certain roses, be an advantage, as has been seen with the Miniatures.

It is likely to take a minimum of three years to produce a fully-grown plant from a cutting, for it has first of all to develop roots and can only then start on the top growth. On the plus side, you will never have suckers to deal with, as they cannot come from a rootstock which is not there. If flower buds should form on the infant plant during its first summer they should be pinched out, as the energy which would go into the production of blooms is better used elsewhere. Transplanting to permanent quarters can take place in the autumn that follows.

BUDDING OR BUD-GRAFTING

This means inserting a dormant leaf-axil bud from a cultivated variety under the bark just above the roots of a wild rose or one of its close relatives, which then becomes the rootstock or understock. In time, the bud sends out shoots, the top growth of the stock is cut away, and a new rose plant is born.

Roses on rootstocks of a nurseryman's choice are sent out, sometimes many hundreds of miles, to customers who may live in districts varying widely in their climate and type of soil, so clearly it is not too critical what type of rootstock is used. However, if you are doing your own budding, it is perhaps worth finding out what is best for your particular conditions, for there is no one species or variety of rose which is ideally suited for use as a rootstock in all soils and in all climates. Some are better for light soils, some for heavy; some give a more vigorous bush, but a shorter-lived one; some sucker more freely than others, but perhaps compensate in other ways.

In America, *R. multiflora* is widely used, particularly where the winters are cold, *R. canina* is popular in Canada, where it is both cold and the soil may be heavy, and the crimson-red climber 'Dr Huey' (bred by Captain Thomas and introduced in 1914, and at one time given, as a stock, the name of 'Shafter') takes over where the dormancy period is shorter. In Europe, *R. multiflora* (among its other virtues, good in poor soil and making a large bush), *R. laxa* (medium to light soils and relatively sucker-free) and *R. canina* or preferably one or other of its many variations – 'Brog's Thornless' (good on clay), 'Heinsohn's Record', 'Intermis', 'Pfanders', 'Pollmeriana' and 'Schmidt's Ideal' (frost-resistant) – are among the most common. *R. chinensis major* is one that suits a number of Mediterranean areas.

There are a number of commercial suppliers of rootstocks from whom you can order them, and they will be pleased to give advice as to the best sort for a particular soil or climate. They are, however, mainly wholesale houses, growing for the rose trade, and the minimum number that can be ordered may be much too high for the average gardener, who may well only want to bud half a dozen roses. In this case, a friendly local nursery may be prepared to give you the advice you need and let you buy a few stocks, though it must be remembered that the nursery will be doing you a favour. If they did not let you have them, they might instead be selling

Budding: obtaining buds

(1) Select strong shoots of your chosen rose variety which have recently finished flowering. A good shoot of budwood should give three or four plump growth buds.
(2) Snap off the thorns so that you can handle the shoot more easily. Do this with sideways pressure from your thumb.
(3) Snip off the leaves, but leave the leaf stalks which will be useful later in handling the buds lying in their axils. Place the budwood in a plastic bag to prevent it drying out while you are preparing the stock.

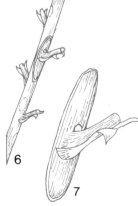

Budding: preparing the stock and scion

(4) Prepare the rootstock by clearing away soil from the neck. Wipe it clean with a damp rag.
(5) Using the sharp blade of a budding knife, make a T-shaped cut, just deep enough to penetrate the bark. The initial horizontal cut should be about 5mm (¼ in) long and the vertical cut 2cm (¾ in).
(6) Take a shoot of budwood from the plastic bag and use a scooping action to cut a bud. When removed from the budwood (7), the bud will be contained in a bark shield about 2.5cm (1 in) long. Hold it by the leaf-stalk handle and remove any coarse bark behind the bud, which will become visible as a small circular growth. Trim the bark to produce a bud shield as shown.

Budding: inserting buds

(8) Use the tapered end of the budding knife to open out the cut bark of the stock. Slide the bud shield downward under the flaps, until the bud is just below the cross-stroke of the T. Inserting two buds, one each side of the stock and staggered, will increase the chances of a good take.

(9) Bind the bud in place firmly, but not too tightly, with rafia, leaving the bud itself exposed, or use a rubber budding tie. Both types will rot away before they can inhibit growth.

(10) If the bud has 'taken', a shoot should have grown by late the following spring. Cut away the top-growth of the stock, leaving a stump about 1 cm (½ in) long. This will prevent canker spreading downwards. Trim it off later.

(11) Insert two, or even three, buds into standard rose stocks to ensure a balanced head. Insert them close to the stem in equally-spaced lateral growths on brier stocks, and into the main stem on Rugosas.

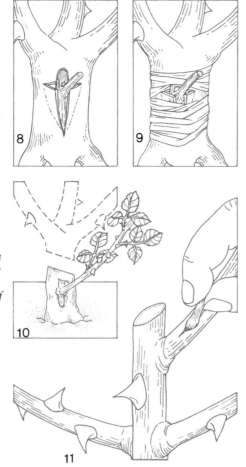

you, at a higher price, the cultivated roses that you wish to bud yourself.

The rose rootstocks used in nuseries have been generally grown from seed, as this is said to give longer-lived and more uniform results than if they were grown from cuttings. However, it is perfectly possible for someone whose ambitions are not too great to use cuttings, either taken from wild roses in the countryside hedgerows, from cultivated Wichuraiana ramblers, or even from suckers which have remained out of sight in your rose beds until they have reached several feet in length and have had time to ripen. Rub out all but the bottom bud of each cutting before putting them in the planting trench and you will have fewer suckers later on.

In late autumn, plant rootstocks in a nursery bed about 30 cm (1 ft) apart and with 75 cm (2½ ft) between rows if there is more than one. You will have to bud into the neck of the stock very close to the roots, so planting should not be too deep. Instead, earth them up afterwards to keep the bark moist and supple.

The two months following midsummer are the ones for budding, though not in the middle of a heat-wave. Cool, showery weather is ideal, for the air should not be too dry. It is easiest if you use a proper budding knife. This has a blade at one end, which should always be kept clean and razor-sharp, while the other end (which is tapered) is used for lifting the bark away from the stem before inserting the bud. The sharp blade would be likely to make cuts in the wrong places.

HYBRIDIZING

Breeding a new rose – a completely new variety that has never existed before – must to a rose lover be the second most exciting thing imaginable. Second because it surely cannot surpass – speaking as one who has never achieved it – the thrill of breeding one that is not only new but different from, or better than, any existing variety in its class. This hope is what keeps the dedicated amateur breeder going, even though he may know that the chances of success are so small as to be almost nil. He has to be a super-optimist.

Breeding or hybridizing consists of putting the pollen from the anthers of one rose variety on to the stigmas of another, with the idea that fertile seed containing the best qualities of both roses will be formed in the hips of the second one. But so mixed up is the ancestry of most varieties that only very rarely does this happen. Good varieties such as 'Wendy Cussons' have, on the breeder's own admission, been produced with no deep forethought as to the parentage, but even if you only try half a dozen crosses a year it does add point to what you are doing if the varieties are not chosen haphazardly.

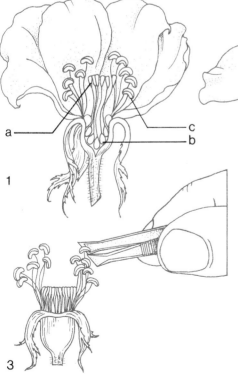

Hybridizing

(1) A cross-section of a rose shows (a) female stigmas; (b) unfertilized seeds; (c) male stamens.

(2) Remove the petals of the seed parent just as the flower is beginning to unfold and before pollination by insects. Do not leave any pieces of petal which may set up rot later in the swelling hip.

(3) Snip off the stamens.

Most people would agree that health in a rose is of prime importance, so choose as parents roses that are naturally more free from disease than others. Or try filling a gap in what is available from commercial growers, such as the complete and continuing absence of a healthy, rain-proof white Hybrid Tea; or a really robust and hardy, not too lanky, scented, unfading, bright yellow Hybrid Tea that does not become flushed with pink at some stage; or a dark, dusky red variety of good form that does not either mildew, 'blue' with age or lose its first bright sheen all too quickly. These are some worthwhile targets, but there are countless others, including the endless search for complete novelties.

Really serious breeders study the lineage of each rose they intend using, back through many generations, looking perhaps for a quality from the past which may re-emerge and blend with others to produce what they want. *Modern Roses 8*, due out at about the same time as this book's first publication, is the latest edition of the rose breeder's 'bible'. It is a monumental work and in it can be found descriptions and pedigrees of all the roses known to be in cultivation up to the date of publication. The cost and labour of updating it every so often must be astronomical, and one only hopes that it will continue for many more editions.

Valuable as this book is, there are factors in breeding other than heredity to be considered. For instance, some varieties make good pollen (male) parents (the roses that produce the pollen), but not good seed (female) parents (the ones that produce the seeds), and vice versa. Some roses – and I suppose that this is an inherited factor – are completely infertile, some almost so. Again, in a rose with a very large number of petals a proportion of these may have taken the place of the pollen-bearing anthers, so that little pollen is available; this is the case with the sterile Centifolias.

There have been interesting results in recent years from the introduction of species roses into the breeding lines of modern Hybrid Teas and Floribundas, and this is a possible area for the amateur to explore. There are many species that have never been used at all by hybridists, and for a professional using a species is not (at least in the short term) the most profitable line to follow while he has his living to earn from what he produces. Even with a comparatively straightforward cross between two Floribundas or Hybrid Teas, or a mixture of one with the other, it can take something like eight years from the time the cross was made to get a new rose onto the market.

The seeds must form and ripen, be harvested and stratified, be planted and then germinate, which can itself take two years. The seedlings have next to be grown on and the small proportion of hopeful ones budded onto rootstocks. Thorough trials of these are

likely to take several years, and even after a variety has been selected as being worth putting on the market, sufficient stocks have to be built up to meet the possible demand, which takes still more time.

Using a species cross in the first place would add considerably to this, for a first-generation cross between a once-flowering species and a recurrent rose will always produce a non-recurrent one, as has already been mentioned in connection with Joseph Pernet's work with the Persian yellow rose. It is not until the second generation that repeat-blooming may or may not come about, and even then it is by no means certain that something promising will result. More crosses with the best of the new seedlings will almost certainly have to be made, so it is only the more far-seeing and dedicated professional breeders such as Jack Harkness, Sam McGredy and the late Wilhelm Kordes who have considered it worthwhile, though the results they are getting now have proved them right.

To begin with, an amateur breeder should perhaps, just to get the feel of it, try the easiest cross of all, which is between two Floribundas. Getting a good Hybrid Tea is more difficult, but when the basic technique has been mastered with either of them, then is the time – at least if you have endless patience and if your eyes do not take on a special kind of gleam at the sight of gold – to try moving on to the species roses.

If you reach this stage, some account must be taken of the chromosome count of the varieties you intend using, because if you ignore it you are ignoring yet another factor that can lead to sterility. Chromosomes are the microscopic constituents of a plant cell that carry the genes which influence inheritance, but not all roses have the same number of them in their make-up, though the total number per cell in each case is a multiple of the basic seven. Most species have 14 (diploid), 28 (tetraploid), 42 (hexaploid) or 56 (octaploid) – all even-numbered multiples of 7.

When two roses are crossed, the chromosomes from each arrange themselves in pairs, each pair merging as it were into one in terms of the chromosome count of the resulting variety – which is just as well, as otherwise they would just increase each time and soon be sleeping in the corridors. Most garden roses are tetraploids (28), and two tetraploids brought together produce, through this merging, another tetraploid rose of 28 chromosomes. However, a diploid (14) crossed with a tetraploid (28), will result in 7+14 chromosomes, or a total of 21 (triploid) in the new rose. This is not an even number and there are seven chromosomes left, like wallflowers at a dance, without their opposite numbers to pair with. The result is likely to be problems when trying to breed with it.

This is an extreme simplification of what is

Hybridizing (continued)
(4) *Tie a small plastic bag over the emasculated flower so that no insect can reach it. Cut the flower which is to be the pollen parent and remove the petals.* (5) *Snip off the anthers into a small, clean container such as a plastic pill-box. Label the box with the name of the rose.*
The next day the anthers should have released the tiny orange pollen grains – while the stigmas of the seed parent will have exuded a sticky secretion ready to receive it. (6) *Remove the plastic bag and, using a fine watercolour brush, brush pollen from the box onto the stigmas of the seed parent.* (7) *Replace the plastic bag once more and tie onto the stem a dated label indicating the parents of the cross – eg, 'Peace' × 'Piccadilly'. Name the seed parent first. If more than one cross is planned with different roses, clean the brush thoroughly between each one, preferably with spirits.* (8) *Remove the plastic bag after about two weeks, when the hip begins to swell, showing that the cross has taken.* (9) *Unsuccessful crosses will shrivel.*
As an alternative to removing the anthers from the pollen parent and using a brush, transfer the pollen onto the stigmas of the seed parent using the whole flower minus its petals. Once the swollen hips have ripened, proceed as described in the main text.

4

5

6

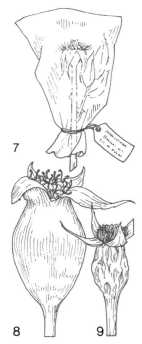

7

8　　**9**

a very complex subject, and anyone seriously interested in going further into it could not do better than read Jack Harkness on the subject in his book *Roses*. At the same time the thought of all this pairing off and chromosomal musical chairs should not discourage anyone with a non-scientific mind from defying the laws of nature and having a go. Luck plays a major role in all rose breeding.

Your luck is likely to be greater if, in anything other than a warm climate, you use pot-grown roses in a greenhouse, as this gives the seeds a better chance of ripening properly. And apart from temperature, keeping a check on humidity, insect pests and diseases, and so on – to say nothing of keeping track of what you have done, of what you have crossed with what – is a great deal easier if all your roses are in neat lines on the greenhouse shelves than if they are dotted about all over the garden. After crosses have been made, all the flower stems involved should be carefully labelled with the names of both parents, and these can easily come adrift in the wind and rain outside, or even through absentminded dead-heading.

The hips will swell and grow, smooth and green at first, taking about 2½ months to ripen, though this will depend on the climate and the amount of sunshine. When ripe, they will have changed colour to red, yellow, brownish-red, maroon or black if belonging to the Spinosissima group. Do not leave them on the bushes until they start to wrinkle.

After picking the hips, the seeds must go through a process known as stratification, also called after-ripening, as they would be unlikely to germinate if sown straight into the soil. There are three ways of stratifying, each one finding favour with different breeders, which almost certainly means that they are all equally good. The third is the one I have used myself, so I can say from actual experience that that one does work well. But whichever method you decide to follow, there is one thing that must never be forgotten. If you are not meticulous in the use of labels at every stage, marking just what is what and which is which, you will after a few weeks be in a state of complete confusion. Whatever you may think at the time, never trust to memory.

The first method of stratifying is to slice the hips so that the seeds can be removed, and to test these for viability (whether they are fertile) by putting them in a saucer of water. Those that sink ought to germinate, and should be put in small polythene bags (one labelled bag for each cross) filled with damp peat (peat moss) in the salad compartment of a refrigerator for about six weeks. The temperature should be around 5°C (41°F). In the second method put the whole hips in the bags without cutting them up, and once again put them in the fridge, while for the third, bury uncut hips in flower-pots of damp sand or peat and leave them out of doors in a place where

mice cannot reach them, but where frost can. This will help the stratification process.

Early in the new year the seeds should be ready for planting. If they are still in their hips, which will be black and rotten by this time, they should be removed. This is easiest under water, as the seeds will come free from soggy remains of the hips more easily and the viability test can be carried out at one and the same time. Roses vary enormously in the number of seeds per hip, which can be as few as one or well up into double figures.

You can sow the seeds in a seed tray (flat) at least 8 cm (3 in) deep, sowing them about 5 cm (2 in) apart and 1 cm (½ in) below the surface of a good, rather loose and sandy seed mixture. Or, if your climate is reasonably mild, you can sow them out of doors in a seed bed. They are quite large and easy to handle individually. If a seed tray is used, transplantation will be advisable as soon as the first pair of true leaves (the first two to appear will be oval and not a bit like those of a rose) have formed. Great care is needed in handling them, as the seedlings will be very fragile at this stage. Climate and to a lesser extent convenience are the factors in deciding whether to grow the seedlings in a greenhouse or out of doors, but if they are inside they should be taken out when the weather becomes mild, allowing a few days in a sheltered spot for them to acclimatize.

The seedlings are quite likely to flower in their first year – often within a few weeks of germination if in a greenhouse – but it is extremely difficult to judge them from this rather tentative initial blooming, and even an experienced hybridist may frequently be wrong. The whole business of deciding what is worth keeping is, at a guess, 50 per cent experience and 50 per cent luck, and there can be very little doubt that as many good roses have been discarded at some period in their early years as have ever been put on the market. Many will take a long time to show their true worth, and a professional breeder with thousands of seedlings each year cannot possibly keep and cosset every one of them. He picks out what experience tells him are the best for further development, and the amateur with only a few seed boxes must do the same, substituting judgement, instinct or even intuition for experience at first.

The second-year growth may give a much truer picture of what the rose will eventually be like. It may be freer of the mildew which frequently plagues seedlings, the flowers may be less washy and have a considerably greater number of petals, so, to start with at any rate, it will probably be better to wait a year before attempting to bud the seedlings onto rootstocks, though with Hybrid Teas and Floribundas especially this must eventually be done if the roses are really to show what they are capable of.

GLOSSARY

Anther: The tip of the stamen, the male sex organ that makes pollen.

Axil: The angle between the leaf stalk and stem; an axillary bud grows there.

Balled; balling: Terms used of a bloom when wet petals stick together and prevent it opening; may be due to rain or a constitutional weakness.

Bareroot rose: A rose dug from the nursery fields for sale without a container.

Basal shoot: A shoot coming from the crown of the plant or nearby; also known as a water shoot.

Bicolour: A flower with one side of the petals a colour distinctly different from that of the other.

Blind shoot: One that fails to produce a flower head.

Blown: Describes a fully open bloom.

Blueing: Flowers, generally red ones, turning purplish-blue with age.

Bract: A modified leaf at the base of a flower stalk, forming part of the flower head.

Break: The growing out of a bud. See also colour break.

Bud: A condensed shoot containing an immature flower (a flower bud), or a dormant or undeveloped bud that will grow on from a leaf axil (an axillary bud).

Budding: Propagation by grafting a leaf axil bud into the neck or shank of a rootstock.

Budding union: The point on the rootstock where the bud is inserted and from which new canes will sprout; also known as the union and in the US as the knuckle.

Budhead: The same as budding union.

Bullate: Puckered, as in the leaves of the Centifolia 'Bullata'.

Burning: The scorching of petals in hot sun.

Button eye: Found in the centre of some old roses, where the petals fold in to form a 'button'.

Callus: A protective growth forming over a wound in a plant stem or over the base of a cutting.

Calyx: The collective term for the five sepals.

Cambium: Thin layer of tissue between the bark and wood of a stem responsible for the growing together of stock and scion.

Cane: A rose shoot or stem.

Carpel: The female part of a flower, consisting of the stigma, style and ovary.

Chelated iron: A form of iron that is soluble and can be taken up by the roots of a plant even from limy soil; also called sequestered iron.

Chlorosis: Loss of chlorophyll, the green colouring matter of leaves, caused by lack of nutrients or disease.

Chromosomes: Microscopic rod-like bodies in the nuclei of plant cells, containing the genes which control plant development.

Climbing sport: A mutation in which a bush variety sends out long shoots and becomes a climber.

Cluster: A number of flowers on one stem.

Colour break: A mutant flower or sport that has developed an uncharacteristic colour.

Corymb: A flower cluster that is flat-topped, or nearly so.

Crocks: Broken pieces of flower pot used to improve drainage in the bottom of containers.

Crown: The point where the canes sprout from the rootstock.

Cruciform: Of flowers, having petals in a cross-like formation.

Cut-back: A rose bush from its second season after budding onwards, as distinct from an unpruned maiden.

Cultivar: A cultivated variety or hybrid, as opposed to a wild, or naturally-occurring, one.

Damask: Used as an adjective in Shakespeare's day to describe the colour of a Damask rose – ie, pink.

Dead-heading: The removal of dead or damaged blooms.

Die-back: Shoots which die back from the tip, caused by a fungus entering after damage or frost, or by a nutrient deficiency.

Disbudding: The thinning out of secondary flower buds to allow proper development of the remainder.

Dormancy: A period of rest during short days and low temperature when growth slows down or ceases.

Double: Strictly, describes any rose flower with more than five petals, but normally used for one with at least 25 (see also semi-double).

Emasculation: In hybridizing, the removal of anthers to prevent self-pollination.

Earthing-up: The drawing up of soil around the neck of a rose to protect it from cold; known in the US as hilling or mounding.

Eye: A dormant leaf axil bud, or the centre of a flower.

Flore pleno: A botanical term for the double form of a flower.

Flush: A short period of blooming.

Foliar feeding: Spraying the leaves and stems with liquid fertilizer.

Footstalk: The flower stalk or pedicel.

Full bloom: A double bloom with many petals.

Genus: A group of plants having common structural characteristics that are distinct from other groups – eg, *Rosa*. Consists of one or more species.

Habit: The overall form of growth of a plant.

Half-standard: A standard with the budding union on a stem of the root-stock 60cm (2ft) above soil level.

Hardiness: The capacity of a plant to withstand frost, or a stated degree of frost, outdoors.

Head: The canes of a standard rose growing from the budding union.

Heading back: The removal of the canes of a rootstock when the variety budded onto it has grown away.

Heel: The bark at the end of a shoot pulled away from a cane to make a cutting.

Heeling in: Planting roses temporarily in a trench.

Hep: The same as hip.

High-centred bloom: One in which long centre petals form a regular cone.

Hip: The fruit or seed pod of the rose.

Humus: Dark brown or black residue left when organic matter decays; it improves soil texture.

Hybrid: A rose resulting from crossing two different species or varieties.

Hybridizing: The pollination of one variety or species by another to create a new rose or hybrid.

Hybrid vigour: The vigour of a hybrid which is sometimes increased compared to that of its parents.

Imbricated: Of petals, closely overlapping.

Inflorescence: The flowering part of a plant.

Inorganic: A chemical compound – eg, a fertilizer – that does not contain carbon or is not derived from plants or animals.

Internode: The part of the stem between two leaf joints or nodes.

Lateral: A side-shoot growing from a main cane.

Leaching: The washing away of soluble nutrients from the soil by water.

Leader: The end shoot of a branch.

Leaf joint: The same as node.

Leggy: Having long, straggly growth with lengthy internodes.

Loam: An imprecise term, but basically a soil of medium weight and texture that is a mixture of clay, sand and humus.

Maiden: A rose in its first season after budding.

Moss: The dense resin-coated bristles found on certain roses.

Mulching: Top-dressing the soil with (preferably) humus-forming material to conserve moisture and suppress weeds.

Mutation: A spontaneous change in the characteristics of a plant (or part of it) due to a genetic change and not hybridizing. See also sport.

Neck: The part of a rootstock just above the roots, into which a bud is inserted in budding (also known as the shank). Of a flower, that part of the pedicel nearest the flower.

Node: The point where a branch or leaf grows or will grow from a stem.

Organic: Derived from living or once-living material.

Ovary: The female part of a flower that contains the seeds.

Own-root rose: A rose propagated by cuttings or seed rather than by grafting onto a rootstock.

Peat: A fibrous organic material used to improve soil condition and increase water retention and acidity.

Peat moss: The same as peat.

Panicle: A flower cluster in which several branches carry flowers.

Pedicel: The same as footstalk.

Pegging down: Bending down and pegging to the earth long main canes to encourage side-shoots to break into growth.

Pergola: An erection of wood or brick, usually along a path, and forming a support for climbing or pillar roses.

Petaloid: A small, partly-formed petal sometimes found in the centre of a bloom.

pH scale: A measurement of soil acidity and alkalinity. Below 7.0 the soil is progressively more acid, above it progressively more alkaline.

Pillar rose: A climbing rose with moderate vigour and spread, suitable for training up a pillar.

Pinnate: A compound leaf, having more than one leaflet, as in a rose.

Pistil: The female part of a flower, consisting of the stigma, style and ovary.

Pith: The white, fibrous centre of a rose cane.

Pointel: A small, shiny green growth at the centre of a few old roses (eg, 'Mme Hardy').

Pollen: Fine yellow grains produced by the anthers which carry the male cells that fertilize the ovules.

Pollen parent: In hybridizing, the rose that provides the pollen; the male parent. When stating a variety's parentage, it is given second.

Pollination: Applying the pollen of one rose to the stigma of another.

Pompon: A rounded bloom with regular short petals.

Pruning: Cutting back the canes of a rose to encourage new growth and remove dead and diseased wood.

Pruning shears: Small hand-shears for the above, also known as secateurs.

Quartered bloom: One (generally an old variety) in which the petals are folded into four distinct parts.

Recurrent: Blooming intermittently.

Remontant: Repeat-flowering.

Replant disease: A root-borne disease affecting plants placed in soil which has grown the same species for some years. See also Rose sick.

Reverse: The outer surface of a petal.

Reversion: When a hybrid reverts to the characteristics of one or more parents, or when a budded plant is overtaken by sucker growth.

Rootstock: The rose species or cultivar onto which a variety is budded; sometimes called the understock.

Rose sick: A term used of soil which has grown roses for some years and in which new roses are unlikely to thrive. See replant disease.

Rosette: A flattish, regular bloom with many short petals.

Rugose: Botanical term for a leaf with a wrinkled surface, as in Rugosas.

Scion: A shoot or bud used for grafting onto a rootstock.

Secateurs: The same as pruning shears.

Seed parent: In hybridizing, the rose that receives the pollen and forms the seeds; the female parent. When stating a variety's parentage, it is given first.

Seed tray: A shallow container for sowing seeds; in the US known as a flat.

Semi-double: A bloom with two or three rows of petals, making a total of between 6 and 24.

Sepals: The five triangular divisions of the calyx which protect the bloom before it opens.

Shears: See pruning shears.

Shield: In budding, the piece of bark containing the bud or eye.

Single bloom: Strictly, one having five petals only, but often applied to roses with up to seven or eight.

Snag: The stump of a cane left by pruning too far above a bud.

Species: The basic unit of botanical classification, consisting of individuals that have distinct, unique characteristics and that breed true in the wild; it is a division of a genus. Also, more generally, a term for a wild rose.

Spit: The depth of a spade's blade. Used as a measurement of the depth of soil moved in digging.

Split centre: Irregular or split formation of the petals at the centre of a flower.

Sport: A mutation in which a shoot bears flowers, or has a habit of growth, different from those of the other shoots of the same plant.

Spotting: The marking of petals by rain.

Stamen: The male organ of a flower, consisting of the stalk (filament) and head (anther); it produces pollen.

Standard: A rose budded on a 105cm (3½ft) stem of the rootstock; also known as a tree rose.

Stigma: The end of the pistil or female flower organ.

Stipule: Leafy growth at, or more often along, both sides of the base of a petiole, or leaf stalk.

Stock: The same as rootstock.

Stratification: The further ripening of rose hips after gathering, by temperature control or burying in damp sand or peat in the open. It aims to break dormancy, so allowing the seeds to germinate.

Style: The stem of the pistil which joins the stigma to the ovary.

Sub-lateral: A side-shoot from a lateral.

Sucker: A cane growing from the rootstock instead of from the budded variety.

Synstylae: Term applied to Ramblers in which the styles of the flowers are merged into a column above the oavaries; the scent comes from this column rather than the petals, and is released freely into the air.

Systemic: Describes an insecticide or fungicide that penetrates the plant system, making the plant toxic to attacking pests and diseases.

Trace elements: Essential chemicals needed by plants in small quantities.

Transpiration: The loss of water from leaf and stem surfaces.

Tree rose: The same as a standard.

Truss: A flower cluster, generally used to describe those of Floribundas or Polyanthas.

Type plant: A rose species, or earliest known member of a rose group (which may now be extinct), from which the first botanical description was made or whose existence is inferred, and from which other members of the group are supposed to have derived. (Eg, *R. gallica* is the presumed type plant of the Gallicas.)

Underplant: To surround and interplant roses with other, smaller plants.

Understock: The same as rootstock.

Union: The same as budding union.

Variegated: Of two or more colours.

Variety: Strictly, a naturally-occurring variation of a species, whether a sport or a hybrid; but the term is used more loosely for any distinct form of a species or hybrid, including a cultivar (which is produced in cultivation).

Viable: A term used for seeds that will germinate.

Weeping standard: Generally a Rambler variety budded 1.5m (5ft) or more high on the stem of a stock, so that the canes hang down or 'weep'.

Winterkill: The killing of a rose by extreme cold in winter.

SPECIALIST ROSE SUPPLIERS

While many of the large rose nurseries include in their catalogues a number of old or otherwise unusual roses, there are certain firms that do specialize in them and offer a much wider choice. Here are some of these, but while the list is up to date at the time of writing, things do change. Nurseries can go out of business or change their policies, reducing the range of what they sell, which is a pity but a fact of commercial life.

A regrettable result of the inclusion of a selection of old roses in the lists of many general rose nurseries has come about because in most cases only the most popular varieties and species have been chosen. This is fine for the buyer who is not too adventurous, but it does mean that the specialist firms are to some extent deprived of their bread-and-butter lines. Their sales of these did in the past help to finance the growing of other varieties, often of great historical interest and beauty, but for which, due to lack of public knowledge as to their worth, there was not a great demand. It can only be hoped that the ever-growing numbers of gardeners sampling old roses for the first time will reverse the trend as they decide to experiment further.

If you are ordering roses from overseas, find out first if there are special import or export regulations for plants. Remember, too, that not all nurseries undertake to send their products abroad.

David Austin Roses, Albrighton, Shropshire, England

Peter Beales Roses, Intwood Nurseries, Swardeston, Norwich, England

Dynarose, Brooklin, Ontario, Canada

Hillier & Sons, Winchester, Hampshire, England

George Longley & Sons, Berengrave Nurseries, Rainham, Kent, England

Moon Mountain Nursery, Saskatoon, Saskatchewan, Canada

Moose Range Rose Gardens, 407, 109th St, Saskatoon, Saskatchewan, Canada

V. Petersens Planteskole, Plantevej 3, Løve, 4270 Høng, Denmark

Pickering Nurseries, 670 Kingston Rd, Pickering, Ontario, Canada

Carl Pallek & Son, Box 137, Virgil, Ontario, Canada

Roses of Yesterday and Today, 802 Brown's Valley Rd, Watsonville, California 95076, USA

John Scott, The Royal Nurseries, Merriott, Somerset, England

Sunningdale Nurseries, Windlesham, Surrey, England

Thomasville Nurseries, PO Box 7, Thomasville, Georgia 31792, USA

Melvin E. Wynant, Johnny Cake Ridge, Mentor, Ohio 44060, USA

BIBLIOGRAPHY

The following books have been invaluable for the research carried out in preparing this book, and make fascinating further reading. The basic handbooks have been included mainly for historical reasons, their dates covering many years and thus revealing changes in rose growing. Publishers are in London unless otherwise stated.

R. C. Allen, *Roses for Every Garden* (Barrows, NY, 1948; rev ed 1956); practical rose culture for the various American climatic zones.

Bagatelle et ses Jardins (Librarie Horticole, Paris, 1910); an account of the famous French château and gardens.

W. J. Bean, *Trees and Shrubs Hardy in the British Isles* (Murray, 1914–1933; 8th ed edited by Sir George Taylor, 1973–1980); the 4th volume of the 8th edition, due in 1980, will have a most comprehensive survey of the genus *Rosa*.

E. Bois & A. M. Trechslin, *Roses* (Nelson, 1962; 2nd vol with untranslated text by A. Leroy, Silva, Zurich, 1967); each volume contains 60 very beautiful and accurate watercolour paintings.

Robert Buist, *The Rose Manual* (Lippincott, Grambo, Philadelphia, 1844; reissued as *The Culture of the Rose* 1854; facs ed, Heyden, Philadelphia & London, 1978); Buist, a Philadelphia nurseryman, wrote on every aspect of cultivation and hybridization, and described suitable varieties for the eastern states.

E. A. Bunyard, *Old Garden Roses* (Country Life, 1936; Scribner, NY, 1936; facs ed, Heyden, Philadelphia & London, 1978); a standard work by this scholarly Kentish nurseryman and pioneer of the movement to revive interest in old roses.

F. R. Burnside, O. G. Orpen & Page-Roberts, *Tea Roses* (Spottiswoode, 1904); one of the very few books on the Teas, written at the peak of their popularity.

P. Coats, *Flowers in History* Weidenfeld & Nicolson, 1970); not just about roses, but it does cover them both in the text and in attractive pictures.

P. H. M. Cochet & S. J. Mottet, *Les Rosiers* (Paris, 1896); French roses and rose growing during the transition from the Hybrid Perpetuals to the Hybrid Teas.

H. R. Darlington, *Roses* (J. C. & E. C. Jack, 1911; Stokes, NY, 1911); one of the best guides to the popular roses of the period, their cultivation and use.

Rev H. H. D'Ombrain, *Roses for Amateurs* (The Bazaar, 1887; last ed 1902); a practical handbook by a founder of the Royal National Rose Society.

Walter Easlea, *Hybridization of Roses* (R. & R. Clark, Edinburgh, 1896); a contemporary authority gives the early details of planned, commercial breeding.

H. Edland, *Pocket Encyclopedia of Roses* (Blandford, 1963; updated a number of times, latterly by L. G. Turner; latest ed 1969); a pocket reference book to over 400 varieties, mostly Hybrid Teas and Floribundas.

G. Edwards, *Wild and Old Garden Roses* (David & Charles, Newton Abbot, 1975; Hafner, NY, 1975); contains 31 really beautiful photographs of old roses.

R. G. Elliot, *The Australasian Rose Book* (Whitcombe & Tombs, Melbourne, 1920); a rarity, in that few books cover this part of the world and its needs.

H. B. Ellwanger, *The Rose* (Dodd-Mead, NY, 1882; last ed 1914); descriptions and the parentage of 965 old roses; interesting on the roses he considers unworthy and first-rate on rose growing.

C. H. Fitch, *The Complete Book of Miniature Roses* (Hawthorn, NY, 1964); one of the most comprehensive and well-illustrated books on Miniatures ever published; good coverage of growing them under lights indoors, little practised as yet outside the US.

H. L. V. Fletcher, *The Rose Anthology* (Newnes, 1963); snippets from a wide field of literature and legend.

Rev A. Foster-Melliar, *The Book of the Rose* (Macmillan, 1894; last ed 1910); much emphasis on the Hybrid Perpetuals as the show roses of the time.

S. M. Gault & P. M. Synge, *The Dictionary of Roses in Colour* (Ebury Press & Michael Joseph, 1971; Grosset & Dunlap, NY, 1971); a large-format book of colour photographs and descriptions of over 500 roses, from species through all the families.

John Gerard, *The Herball* (1597; selections pub by Spring Books, 1964); the most famous of the old herbals; includes a mention of 14 roses grown in the 16th century with their curative properties.

Michael Gibson, *Shrub Roses for Every Garden* (Collins, 1973; pub in German as *Strauchrosen*, Müller, Zurich, 1978); a basic guide to the history and choice of the best shrub roses and climbers; paintings in colour of 195 varieties.

C. F. Gore, *The Book of Roses, or The Rose Fancier's Manual* (Colburn, 1838; facs ed, Heyden, Philadelphia & London, 1978); descriptions of over 1,400 varieties available in France in the 1830s, and chapters on hybridization and culture.

Jules Gravereaux, *Les Roses* (Edition d'Art et de Literature, Paris, 1912); by the director of the famous Roseraie de l'Hay.

L. Günthart (ill), *The Glory of the Rose* (Harrap, 1965); a collection of 41 quite outstanding rose portraits from watercolours in large folio format.

Jack Harkness, *Roses* (Dent, 1978); one of Britain's leading nurserymen and hybridists conveys his deep knowledge and love of roses and their history with a rare lightness of touch.

N. P. Harvey, *The Rose in Britain* (Souvenir Press, 1951; last ed 1953; Van Nostrand, NY, 1950); rose history on a world scale as well as the British rose scene in the 50s.

F. S. Harvey-Cant, *Rose Selection and Cultivation* (MacGibbon & Kee, 1950); a small book but packed with information; a long chapter on exhibiting and many detailed rose descriptions.

Roy Hennessey, *On Roses* (West Coast Printing, Portland, Oregon, 1942; 3rd & last [?] ed 1954); a robustly irreverent and highly informative book by an eccentric grower from Oregon.

T. G. W. Henslow, *The Rose Encyclopedia* (Vickery, Kyrle, 1922; later rev ed, Pearson); includes a 92-page dictionary of rose varieties, over 30 to a page; also excellent on rose garden planning and culture, with good illustrations.

Shirley Hibberd, *The Rose Book* (Groombridge, 1864, retitled 1874 *The Amateurs' Rose Book*; last ed 1894); a first-rate guide to the roses of the 1890s and how to grow them if your garden is at least 2 to 3 acres in size.

Hillier & Sons, *Manual of Trees and Shrubs* (hard cover ed, David & Charles, Newton Abbot, 1972; latest ed 1974; paperback ed, Hillier & Sons, Winchester; latest ed 1979); produced by the world-famous Winchester nursery firm, its section on roses is particularly strong on the species.

Dean S. R. Hole, *A Book About Roses* (Blackwood, Edinburgh, 1874; many later eds); a classic of rose literature; discursive, sometimes opinionated, sometimes snobbish, but always with a nice touch of humour; indirectly informative.

L. Hollis, *Roses* (Collingridge, 1969; 2nd ed with new illusts 1974); probably the best guide on the British market to roses and how to grow them; descriptions of many varieties; less good on old roses.

Gertrude Jekyll & Edward Mawley, *Roses for English Gardens* (Newnes, 1902); concentrates on garden design and the best uses of roses, especially the Ramblers and early Climbers; good descriptions and photographs.

F. L. Keays, *Old Roses* (Macmillan, NY, 1935; facs ed, Heyden, Philadelphia & London, 1978); an indispensable book on the 19th-century roses, particularly strong on the Noisettes, Hybrid Perpetuals and the early Tea roses.

W. Keble Martin, *The Concise British Flora in Colour* (Ebury Press, 1965; latest ed 1978; paperback ed, Sphere, 1978); plate 30 shows in colour the 13 species roses native to the British Isles and their hips; the opposite page describes them, their habitat and range.

E. Kiaer & V. Hanke, *Methuen Handbook of Roses* (Methuen, 1966; translated from Danish); rose history and cultivation; several hundred roses shown in watercolour paintings.

Rose Kingsley, *Roses and Rose Growing* (Whittaker, 1908); contains lists of roses long out of cultivation, including many Teas; fully illustrated.

Wilhelm Kordes, *Roses* (Studio Vista, 1964; translated from German); rose history, cultivation and hybridizing.

Mary Lawrance, *A Collection of Roses from Nature* (1799); a flower painter, the author produced 90 plates from beautiful hand-coloured etchings which are of immense value as a contemporary record, despite some inaccuracies.

Edward Le Grice, *Rose Growing Complete* (Faber, 1965; rev paperback ed 1976); Norfolk nurseryman and hybridist, Le Grice wrote for amateurs with some original points on hybridizing.

John Lindley, *Rosarum Monographia* (Ridgeway, 1820; 2nd ed 1830); an early descriptive work written and illustrated by the man who was to become such a distinguished botanist.

H. B. Logan, *A Traveller's Guide to North American Gardens* (Scribners, NY, 1974); where the best American rose gardens can be found, with brief details.

J. H. McFarland, *Modern Roses 1* to *Modern Roses 7* (McFarland, Harrisburg, Pennsylvania, 1930–1969); an international checklist of roses, giving the raiser, parentage, date of introduction and a brief description of virtually every rose in cultivation at the time of publication; the long-awaited *Modern Roses 8* will be published by the

International Registration Authority for Roses at about the same time as this book. *Roses of the World in Colour* (Houghton Mifflin, Boston, 1937; 3rd ed 1947); useful for the hundreds of colour photographs.

S. McGredy & S. Jennett, *A Family of Roses* (Cassell, 1971; Dodd-Mead, NY, 1971); the story of this famous rose family and their varieties; interesting angles on hybridizing and marketing.

A. J. MacSelf, *The Rose Growers' Treasury* (Collingridge, 1934); contains colour plates and an 80-page register of roses.

T. C. Mansfield, *Roses in Colour and Cultivation* (Collins, 1943; last ed 1948; Dutton, NY, 1943); 80 full-page colour plates of varying quality; brief descriptions and cultural instructions.

R. S. Moore, *All About Miniature Roses* (Diversity Books, Kansas City, 1966); a practical book by a leading hybridizer.

Bertram Park, *Collins Guide to Roses* (Collins, 1956); now extremely out of date but valuable for its descriptions and colour photographs. *The World of Roses* (Harrap, 1963); 230 roses old and new depicted in colour and commented upon by Park, a leading professional photographer and rose authority.

John Parkinson, *Paradisi in Sole Paradisus Terrestris* (1629); Parkinson was an apothecary, herbalist and plantsman; here, in his first book, he covers 24 roses.

Francis Parkman, *The Book of Roses* (Tilton, Boston, 1866); one of the best books of its era; Parkman became the first professor of horticulture at Harvard University.

S. B. Parsons, *Parsons on the Rose* (Orange-Judd, NY, 1869; last ed 1917; first pub 1847 as *The Rose, It's History, poetry and Cultivation*); history, culture propagation and medicinal uses.

William Paul, *The Rose Garden* (Kent, 1848; last ed 1903; facs ed, Heyden, Philadelphia & London, 1978); a milestone in rose literature; the first section deals exhaustively with rose history and cultivation, the second with the roses available to the grower in 1848. The first editions had colour plates, omitted later because of cost. If you can afford only one old rose book, this is the one to buy. *Roses and Rose Culture* (Simpkin Marshall, 1874; last ed 1899); a shilling handbook for the rose grower which sold 10,000 copies. Paul's *Roses in Pots* went through six editions.

Rev J. H. Pemberton, *Roses, Their History, Development and Cultivation* (Longmans, Green, 1908; rev ed 1920); authoritative if a little solid; only the 1920 edition has full details of the Pemberton Hybrid Musks; most attractive illustrations.

Svend Poulsen, *Poulsen on the Rose* (MacGibbon & Kee, 1955; translated from the Danish ed of 1941); a small but interesting book by the Danish hybridist, with some history and a good chapter on indoor cultivation.

W. Prince, *Manual of Roses* (Clark, NY, 1846; reprinted 1848); written by an early American nurseryman, it contains descriptions of many old roses.

J. M. C. Prins (ill), *The Rose Today* (Ariel, undated but *c* mid-1960s); folio size, with 18 fine watercolour portraits of roses then popular.

Robert Pyle, *How to Grow Roses* (5th–17th eds, Conard & Jones Co, West Grove, Pennsylvania; 18th–23rd eds [with J. H.

McFarland], Macmillan, NY; last ed 1968); a rose primer important in its various editions for its progression from the early days of amateur rose growing in America to the modern era, by a nurseryman and hybridist who introduced many fine European varieties.

P. J. Redouté, *Les Roses* (Paris, 1817–1824; facs ed in 4 vols, Schutter, Belgium, 1978; selections pub as *Roses* and *Roses 2*, Ariel, 1954–1956); the original contains 170 of the roses in the Empress Josephine's garden at Malmaison depicted in colour with beauty and reasonable botanical accuracy.

A. Ridge, *For Love of a Rose* (Faber, 1965; paperback ed 1972); the story of the rose-growing Meillands of Antibes and of the creation of 'Peace'. *The Man Who Painted Roses* (Faber, 1974); the story of Redouté written in an irritatingly coy style but providing information not easily accessible elsewhere.

Thomas Rivers, *The Rose Amateur's Guide* (Longmans, Green, 1837; last ed 1877); by the Hertfordshire nurseryman.

William Robinson, *The English Flower Garden* (Murray, 1883; numerous eds, latterly rev by others); in the original, a classic compendium from the naturalistic school of gardening, with a section on roses.

F. F. Rockwell & E. C. Grayson, *The Rockwell's Complete Book of Roses* (Doubleday, NY, 1958; rev ed 1966); a comprehensive guide with 44 colour photographs.

Royal Horticultural Society Dictionary of Gardening (4 vols, Oxford University Press, 1956) and *Supplement* (1969); under 'R' is a comprehensive guide to species roses.

T. W. Sanders (ed), *Cultivated Roses* (Collingridge, 1899); a brief guide and checklist of varieties; led on to *Roses and Their Cultivation* (1904; last ed 1947).

Roy E. Shepherd, *History of the Rose* (Macmillan, NY, 1954; facs ed, Heyden Philadelphia & London, 1978); the standard and indispensable American reference work on the genus *Rosa*; comprehensive and very detailed on rose species and near derivatives, less so on desirable garden varieties.

Sacheverell Sitwell & James Russell, *Old Garden Roses Part 1* (Rainbird/Collins, 1955; *Part 2* by Wilfrid Blunt and Russell, Rainbird/Hutchinson, 1957); the only two volumes produced of what should have been a six-volume folio work; the first covers history and the main rose groups, part 2 rose literature and the Gallicas.

Nancy Steen, *The Charm of Old Roses* (Jenkins, 1967); how the author reclaimed many of the old roses brought by settlers to New Zealand but which had long reverted to the wild.

G. A. Stevens, *Climbing Roses* (Macmillan, NY, 1933); one of the few books devoted solely to the Climbers and Ramblers.

P. Svoboda, *Beautiful Roses* (Spring Books, 1965); contains illustrations and descriptions of roses grown in Czechoslovakia and rarely featured elsewhere.

Capt G. C. Thomas, *Roses for All American Climates* (Macmillan, NY, 1924); by the famous American breeder of Climbers.

Graham Stuart Thomas, *The Old Shrub Roses* (Phoenix House, 1955; latest ed,

Dent, 1979); *Manual of Shrub Roses* (Sunningdale Nurseries, 1957); *Shrub Roses of Today* (Phoenix House, 1963; latest ed, Dent, 1974); *Climbing Roses Old and New* (Phoenix House, 1965; latest ed, Dent, 1978). *The Old Shrub Roses* established Thomas as the outstanding authority in the field. *Shrub Roses of Today* followed, bringing in species and modern shrub roses. *Climbing Roses Old and New* completed the series. All of them are illustrated with the author's own delicate drawings and watercolours, plus some photographs. *Manual of Shrub Roses* is a descriptive list of varieties issued when the author was associated with Sunningdale Nurseries. *Gardens of the National Trust* (The National Trust/Weidenfeld & Nicolson, 1979); includes details of over 80 rose gardens.

H. H. Thomas, *Rose Growing for Amateurs* (Cassell, 1916); many Hybrid Teas of the time shown in colour and many old roses described; excellent on the aesthetics of rose growing.

R. Thompson, *Old Roses for Modern Gardens* (Van Nostrand, NY, 1959); first-hand descriptions up to the early Hybrid Teas.

Robert Tyas, *The Sentiment of Flowers* (Houlston & Stoneman, 1844); sentiment, whimsy and down-to-earth fact, with enchanting hand-coloured plates; mentions roses of the time.

Ellen Willmott, *The Genus Rosa* (Murray, issued in parts 1910–1914); a definitive but outdated treatise on wild roses of the world with fine plates.

Harry Wheatcroft, *My Life with Roses* (Odhams, 1959); the story of the famous Wheatcroft nurseries.

Lt Col A. H. Wolley-Dod, *Roses of Britain* (1924); by a leading rosarian of the time.

Norman Young, *The Complete Rosarian* (Hodder & Stoughton, 1971); a treasure-house of information based on extensive research. The author explodes some myths and draws some authoritative, if controversial, conclusions.

Journals, annuals, magazines, etc

American Rose Society Annuals (1916 on); articles, a register of all new roses accepted by the International Registration Authority for Roses and details of AARS award winners.

American Rose Magazine (monthly); pub by the American Rose Society.

Australian Rose Society Annuals; articles and recommendations of the most suitable new varieties for Australasia.

Canadian Rose Society Annuals; as above, for Canada.

Heritage Roses; a small American quarterly devoted to the old roses and their promotion.

Journal of the Royal Horticultural Society, retitled *The Garden* from June 1975; occasional articles on roses and rose gardens by leading authorities.

Royal National Rose Society Annuals (1907 on; under the title *The Rosarians' Year Book*, 1881–1907); articles, notices, details of award winners at the St Albans trial grounds. *Roses: A Selected List of Varieties*; brief descriptions of roses recommended by the society.

The Botanical Magazine (1786 on); a specialist publication sometimes containing learned articles on the rose.

The Rose; a small, illustrated quarterly published only from 1952 to 1969.

GENERAL INDEX

Page numbers in italics indicate an illustration.

INDEX OF PEOPLE AND PLACES

Mythological figures discussed in chapter 1 (mainly on pages 14 to 24) have been omitted from this index, as have the minor rose gardens listed alphabetically by country in chapter 4. The major rose gardens and the countries themselves are, however, listed here. For details of books, see the bibliography (p 268).

Page numbers in italics refer to illustrations.

INDEX OF ROSES

Here, as in the rest of this book except for captions to pictures, the international convention is followed of printing botanical species names in italic type (eg, *R. canina*, where *R.* stands for *Rosa*), common names in small roman (upright) type (eg, dog rose), groups or tribes in roman type with initial capital letters (eg, Hybrid Tea roses) and recognized cultivar or variety names in quotation marks (eg, 'Peace').

Page references printed in bold type indicate full descriptions of the species, variety or group concerned or of its development, while italics indicate an illustration.

279